1

THE MACMILLAN COMPANY
NEW YORK · BOSTON · CHICAGO · DALLAS
ATLANTA · SAN FRANCISCO

MACMILLAN & CO., Limited
LONDON · BOMBAY · CALCUTTA
MELBOURNE

THE MACMILLAN COMPANY
OF CANADA, Limited
TORONTO

# A HISTORY OF AMERICAN LIFE

IN

## TWELVE VOLUMES

### ARTHUR M. SCHLESINGER
### DIXON RYAN FOX

*Editors*

ASHLEY H. THORNDIKE            CARL BECKER

*Consulting Editors*

*A Scholar of Seventeenth-Century New Spain.*

*Sor Juana Inés de la Cruz in her library.*

A HISTORY OF AMERICAN LIFE
Volume I

# THE COMING OF THE WHITE MAN

## 1492-1848

BY

HERBERT INGRAM PRIESTLEY

PROFESSOR OF MEXICAN HISTORY, UNIVERSITY OF CALIFORNIA
and Librarian of the Bancroft Library

New York
THE MACMILLAN COMPANY
1929

*If, according to an opinion of Aristotle and of Cicero, only the finding or discovering of some art either liberal or mechanical, or of some stone, plant, or other thing which may be of service to men commands their praise, . . . of what glory are they not worthy who have discovered a World in which are found such innumerable grandeurs and riches? . . . Nor is the benefit of this same discovery of less, but of much greater value to that same New World itself; for, in addition to the light of the faith which we gave to its inhabitants, of which I shall speak later, we have also raised them up into social and political life, we have banished their barbarism, changed their wild customs into humane ones, and brought to them many useful and necessary things from our own land; we have taught them the real cultivation of the soil, how to build houses, to live in towns, to read, to write, and many other arts to which they were formerly totally alien.*

JUAN DE SOLÓRZANO PEREYRA, *Política Indiana*
(Madrid, 1776), I, cap. viii, par. 6-7.


*The French exceed in industry, economy, and the arts of conciliating the affections of mankind. . . . This people have a country where more is to be affected by managing [the Indians] than by cultivating the ground; where a pedling commerce, that requires constant motion, flourishes more than agriculture or a regular traffic; where they have difficulties which keep them alert by struggling with them and where their obedience to a wise government serves them for personal wisdom.*

EDMUND BURKE, *An Account of the European
Settlements in America* (London, 1767), II, 27, 56.

# CONTENTS

# ILLUSTRATIONS
(By the Editors)

ix

men in New Netherland. His elder son, Stephanus, founded the manor of Cortlandt. The artist arrived from Leyden before 1661 and painted a number of portraits in the province; of the four surviving, this is by far the best. Courtesy of the Pennsylvania Museum, Memorial Hall, Philadelphia. Other artists who painted in New Amsterdam were Evert Duyckinck I (arrived 1638), Jacobus G. Strycker (arrived 1651) and Gerrit Duyckinck (son of Evert I). At least two other artists came, but we have no evidence of their work.

On the text, "For I desired mercy, and not sacrifice," Hosea vi. 6. From a copper engraving, probably by Francisco Silverio, done between 1757 and 1761, of a kind issued in great numbers for the walls of humble homes in New Spain. Silverio was one of the most prolific of engravers especially in maps and in portraiture of the saints. The picture, which suggests a Mexican *Pilgrim's Progress*, indicates that it is good conduct alone which is pleasing to God, but that it is much harder to climb to Heaven than to slip into destruction.

# EDITORS' FOREWORD

In the broad view of the New World the history of
the United States, despite our fond appropriation of the
term "American," is only local history. This throws
no doubt upon its value, for as the history of a village
may exemplify the history of a nation, so that of a
nation may exemplify the history of mankind. Biology,
it may be observed, is mainly advanced by the scientist's
examination of a single new bit of tissue under the micro-
scope. But he can make this contribution largely because he knows the quality of other tissues and hence can
realize the significance of what he sees. He has standards
of comparison, and comparison is the key to understanding. All too often the student of local custom, and the
same is almost as true of the historian of a nation, misses
the meaning of what lies before him because he knows
so little of how other human groups have acted in more
or less similar circumstances. In this respect, probably,
his readers are under even deeper disadvantage. It is to
furnish some such standards of comparison that this
first volume of *A History of American Life* has been
designed.

To a certain extent the Spanish, French, and Dutch
settling within the middle zone of North America ultimately formed parts of the new nation and contributed
important threads to the fabric of its life. Professor
Priestley's chapters will give new meaning, it is believed, to the stately mission churches one now encoun-
ters in the Southwestern states, the galleried Creole man-

sions of New Orleans and the Dutch place-names and
farmsteads spread across the valleys of the Hudson and
the Mohawk.   But the more characteristic and permanent patterns of the transplanted Latin cultures are
found not in the history of the United States but rather
in that of New France and particularly that of New
Spain, where the white man first came to live.   To such
history, therefore, the author chiefly resorts in developing his pictures of these "other ways."   Such pictures
have a special interest as by similarity or contrast they
bring out the colors of that fuller view of the Anglo-
American settlements growing into the community of
the United States, offered in the next three volumes of
this series.   Much of this will be apparent without further comment, even to a hasty reader; much of it the
author is at pains specifically to indicate.

But these pictures, particularly that of society in New
Spain, are far more than border vignettes setting off the
main piece.   Indeed, the civilization between the Appa-
lachians and the sea for many decades seemed a puny
thing beside that of old Mexico, and this not only in
physical wealth but quite as much in intellectual effort
and achievement.   The account of seventeenth-century
artists, architects, poets, mathematicians, suggests how
New Spain had run through an entire cycle before its
northern neighbor had scarcely made a beginning.   The
reader may well be impressed with the elaborate variety
of life in New Spain.   Instead of a society of simple
farmers, with some recourse to the sea, and largely of the
same general race character, these chapters show a vast
and complicated edifice of racial castes developed in
sharply differing economic and military areas.   Thus in
addition to well-marked social classes there were pro-

duced contrasting types, miner, planter, ranchman, soldier, citizen, to say nothing of the similar modifications forced upon the clerical office by the circumstances of the capital, the countryside or the far frontier. Always, too, there is the sense of life by ordinance, specifying thought as well as action. All this the author accomplishes, as a glance at his citations will reveal, by laying under contribution a whole literature none too familiar to most readers.

Lastly, quite apart from philosophical analysis, the reader will be struck with the picturesqueness of the author's treatment. Through patient research and imaginative reconstruction the figures of the drama are made vividly alive again. One sees the ship's company at dinner aboard a Spanish caravel; the pageantry that solemnized a viceroy's induction; rebellious Apache circled in a fire-lit underground *estufa* plotting a massacre of their oppressors as the only means to save the precious mysteries of their ancient cult; the plumed and gaitered commandant and the brown-garbed friars leading the great march into California; the governor's cronies gayly playing *coq* in the palace at New Orleans, but at the same time chewing their quinine against the devastating plague of yellow fever; the Dutch *bosch-loper* tramping distant forests to reach fur-trading Indians before the French *coureur de bois*.

Such scenes enliven the record of American history in its largest aspect and have their value quite as much as the arguments and judgments by which the record is interpreted. Yet each serves the general purpose. Certainly, few if any other writers have brought into general and comparative survey the land systems of non-English colonies, their economic bases, their Indian rela-

tions, their population policies, their manifestations of
religious spirit, their literary cultures and their social
customs. If the outlines of the social history of the
United States will emerge more clearly by reason of the
background of this study, so, too, the Spanish, French,
and Dutch enterprises on this continent stand out as
well, each in its own character and color.

A. M. S.
D. R. F.

# THE COMING
# OF THE WHITE MAN
## 1492-1848

# THE COMING
# OF THE WHITE MAN

## CHAPTER I

### THE WESTWARD IMPULSE

IT is of prime significance for the life of America today that the first white men to settle on these western shores were Spaniards and Roman Catholics, representatives of a powerful nation that was the citadel of a united faith. If men from northern Europe had been the first to arrive in America during the Reformation and had discovered the wealth of Montezuma and Atahualpa, the direction of modern history would have been so different from what it has been that the imagination finds no halting place in its contemplation of the possibilities. Happily, it is not the task of the historian to speculate upon these. We shall do well if we seize upon a few of the significant phases of the great Spanish occupation. Almost within a half-century a motley group of men created an empire which strained the resources of the fatherland to organize and govern. Yet precarious as it seemed at first, the civilization which they planted has persisted in full vigor; nearly all the nations south of the United States still retain the language, the customs and the institutions transmitted from Catholic Spain.

It has often been said that the national development of Spain had brought her by 1492 to a state of preparedness for expansion. But at the moment of the discovery Spain lacked many of the traditional characteristics of nationality, such as a common tongue, a literature of commanding importance, a unified territory, a common religion or social ideal. She did not have a military or a naval establishment equal to the strain of overseas adventure. In fact, virtually all that she did have was the personal union of the two great kingdoms of Aragon and Castile and the newly revived spirit of conquest.

Among the many deficiencies was the absence of a general seafaring tradition. The Castilians had not been, before the voyages of Columbus, a maritime people. The Barcelonese, it is true, had for more than a century been prominent in the Mediterranean trade, and their code, the *Consulado del Mare,* was for hundreds of years the recognized maritime law of southern Europe; but the ascendency of agricultural Castile in the political unification of the Iberian Peninsula, as well as the Levantine interests of the Spaniards who lived along the coast within the Straits of Gibraltar, kept the Barcelonese from participating actively in the conquest of America. Once the wonders of the discoveries by Columbus became known, however, the inland folk forgot their ancient dislike for the sea and flocked to the coasts, sacrificing all they possessed on the chance of finding some new treasure such as those which actually did fall to Cortés and Pizarro.

Columbus, indeed, had by his contract the monopoly of westward discovery; but he had been so difficult to deal with while his first two voyages were being prepared, and his administrative troubles in the Caribbean were so numerous, that he raised up a host of enemies, chief among them Bishop Juan de Fonseca, who had had charge of outfitting the second voyage. The result was that, in spite of his monopoly, his maps were shown to other seamen, many of whom had been his voyaging companions, and they were given contracts to sail and trade in the seas he had opened to Christendom. The Catholic monarchs, Ferdinand and Isabella, forbade any-one to set forth on this business without royal license, but so great was the desire for the new seafaring that the burdensome contracts binding adventurers to share their gains with royalty were often evaded.

Nothing is more striking than the poverty of resources with which the conquest was undertaken. Vessels that had been used only in coastwise trade were fitted out to hazard the depths of the "Ocean Sea"; and many a lusty mariner set off without charts, instruments, or sufficient supplies, to follow the fortunes of those more favored ones who had a little knowledge and enjoyed the royal favor. Small wonder that too often they came to a stand somewhere in the open sea, with fuel and water all but exhausted, not knowing where they were. Greater indeed were the perils which they carried with them—perils of incompetence and ignorance—than any which they had to face upon the unknown western shores.[1]

The ships in which such voyagers essayed the Atlantic were tiny enough, but those used by respectable navigators were not so unseaworthy as has often been thought. The *Santa María*, flagship of Columbus, more than sixty feet over all, had a keel of over fifty feet, with an eighteen-foot beam, twelve-foot draft, and from one hundred and twenty to one hundred and thirty tons'

---

[1] C. Fernández Duro, *Disquisiciones Náuticas* (Madrid, 1876-1881), II, 165-166; J. Zaragoza, *La Historia del Descubrimiento de las Regiones Austriales* (Madrid, 1876-1882), I, pp. xxviii-xxxii, 25-29.

burden.[1] The *Pinta* was of fifty tons' burden and the *Niña* of forty. The caravel in which Cristóbal Guerra sailed to La Guayra was of fifty tons; those used by Solís were of sixty and thirty tons. Pinzón's caravel displaced forty-seven tons, and the famous *Victoria,* the first to circumnavigate the globe, but eighty-five. Tiny corks indeed, outrivaled by bay launches of a modern day! But they were long the vogue until replaced in the following century by larger and sturdier types. The caravels used by Columbus were three-masted, with square sails on two mainmasts, and foresail and lateen sails on the mizzenmast. They could achieve maximum speeds varying from eight to fifteen miles an hour, and made the voyage from the Canaries to the West Indies in thirty-six days.[2]

Vessels thenceforth employed on Atlantic voyages were of amazing variety in size, rigging and designation. The term "caravel" was not confined to a single type of construction, but was used to indicate the fact that a vessel was adapted to a specific kind of service; in the sixteenth and seventeenth centuries the caravel was simply a vessel appropriate for swift voyaging, quick evolutions and light draft. The larger *galeones* were developed because of the need for defense against pirates and national enemies and were employed in convoyed fleets. As vessels grew in size to several hundred tons' burden they often had more than one deck; but some of the small craft used as late as the last third of the eighteenth century on the Pacific Coast had no decks or sleeping

---

[1] Shipbuilding began early in America. Balboa and Cortés were among the first to construct them on the Pacific. *Cf.* A. de Altolaguirre y Duvale, *Vasco Núñez de Balboa* (Madrid, 1914), 156-157; M. Fernández de Navarrete, *Relación del Viage Hecho por las Goletas Sútil y Mexicana* (Madrid, 1802), pp. xxviii-cxxxiii.

[2] Fernández Duro, *Disquisiciones Náuticas,* I, 134-137.

accommodations for their crews.[1] High castles or towers in poop and prow were characteristic of the caravels and of the later galleons, whether Spanish or Portuguese, and they were found on merchant as well as fighting ships.[2]

The general aversion of the Spaniard for the sea was expressed in the popular refrán which the Reverend Father Antonio de Guevara, writing in the sixteenth century, used as a text for his El Arte del Marear, a proverb which might be freely rendered "Let God give a life on the galleys to him who knows no better." The Mediterranean galleys may have had special terrors of their own, but they could scarcely have been more formidable than those the rolling sea had in store for the transatlantic voyager. Conveniences there were none, the food was unspeakably bad; crews were of the lowest social type and their skill and devotion to duty seldom impressed the passenger. Eugenio del Salazar, who went from Tenerife to La Española in 1573 as judge of the audiencia, wrote letters to his friends vividly describing a sea voyage.

He, his wife and his children were crowded into a low-ceiled cabin five feet square, where in the midst of their suffering (for no one paid them the slightest attention during their days of seasickness) they could hear the ship's page outside doing official devotions: "Amen; God give us good day; a happy voyage; may the ship make a good passage, sir captain, master, and goodly

[1] "Primer Viaje de D. Francisco de Bodega y Quadra en una Goleta de 18 codos de quilla y 6 de manga," Dirección de Hidrografía, Anuario (Madrid, 1865), 279-336. The generic name for ship was navío, which was applied to all sorts of vessels until the eighteenth century. The famous "Manila galleon" was always known to the Spaniards as the "nao de China"—nao being the archaic form of navío.

[2] Fernández Duro, Disquisiciones Náuticas, I, 86-142.

company. Amen. May it make a good voyage, indeed. God give your lordships good day, my lords, from stern to prow." In the semidarkness inside they could feel swarms of cockroaches and could hear droves of rats ceaselessly active. When the good judge staggered to the deck he could see the "castle" at the prow and the *alcázar*, or quarter-deck, at the stern, so feebly supported that it seemed likely to be caught up by the next breeze. Between were the artillery, the tables for the attending garrison, and one or two pumps the water from which made little appeal to tongue or palate—"foaming like hell and stinking like the devil." Above the filthy deck stretched the shrouds endlessly intricate, so that the people below felt like fowls in a coop. When at evening the page sang out: *"Tabla puesta, vianda presta.* Long live the king of Castile on land and sea," the dirty sailors cried amen and scampered to their seats on the floor beside the evil-smelling food. The upper officers dined apart, and also the passengers, who prepared their meals at the same time as the others, else they found a cold stove.[1] It was a sharply graded little society: the pilot in charge of navigation, the captain of defense, the *maestre* of the treasure, the *contra-maestre* of stowing the cargo, the barber-leech, the guard whose honesty might be doubted, the caulker, the engineer, and then the sailors—the *chusma*, with its peculiar jargon—waited on by the cabin boys.

The sailors might be hired for a lump sum, by the month, the mile, for shares in the freight, or for the right to carry goods on their own account. They bound themselves by having their names entered upon the ship's

---

[1] "Cartas de Eugenio Salazar," Fernández Duro, *Disquisiciones Náuticas,* II, 178-200.

register or by shaking hands with the owner, in either case taking an oath of loyalty. Then the sailor could go nowhere except as the owner dictated, and must do anything he was told to do. He

> ought not to undress himself if he is not in a port for wintering. And if he does so, for each time he ought to be plunged into the sea with a rope from the yard arm three times; and after three times offending he ought to lose his salary and the goods which he has in the ship.[1]

The rations provided for the sailors on Magellan's voyage included wine, olive oil, vinegar, fish, pork, peas and beans, flour, garlic, cheese, honey, almonds, anchovies, raisins, prunes, figs, sugar, quince preserves, capers, mustard, beef and rice.[2] Such a variety would seem ample, but all the world knows how diligently Magellan's crew came to hunt the rats of the hold and gnaw the leathern parts of the ship's rigging for nourishment before they had gone far into the Pacific. Not only was provender uncertain, but not until the time of the voyages of James Cook were navigators able to cope with the dread disease, scurvy, which often proved fatal, leaving ships ill-manned and unable to withstand the stresses of bad weather. The Spaniards used the acid fruits of the Lower California Coast, including the *pitahaya*, to refresh the seamen returning from the Philippines. When Cook learned that acid fruits and fresh vegetables would

[1] Sir Travers Twiss, ed., *Monumenta Juridica; The Black Book of the Admiralty* (London, 1871-1876), esp. III, which contains the "Coustumes de la Ville de Barcelone concernant la Marine" (Consulado del Mare). Cf. Paul S. Taylor, "Spanish Seamen in the New World during the Colonial Period," *Hisp. Am. Hist. Rev.*, V, 631-661; Antonio Capmany y Montpalau, *Código de las Costumbres Marítimas de Barcelona* (Madrid, 1791), tit. iii, 35-84.

[2] Emma H. Blair and J. A. Robertson, eds., *The Philippine Islands* (Cleveland, 1903-1909), XXXIII, 278, n. 25.

bring recovery from scurvy, the terrors of the sea grew less and the day of the "lime-juicer" was not far away.

Spanish maritime officers were of as fine material and possessed as excellent *esprit* as those of any rival maritime establishment. In leadership and seamanship, captains like Pedro Fernández de Quirós in the South Seas or Estevan Martínez in the North Pacific have had few superiors in the annals of ocean discovery. The common sailors who went with Columbus were largely of the seafaring type, and not taken from the jails as Columbus had intended before the Pinzón brothers came to his aid.[1] Among the seventy-one names preserved of the ninety who went, one was that of an Irishman, one of an Englishman, one of a Jew, several were Basques, and at least one third were from the interior of Castile; the last were probably not of the seafaring proletariat. It was of course difficult for Spain to maintain the secrecy —heritage of medievalism—with which she tried to surround the discoveries, simply because this chusma was international in composition. In his complement of two hundred and sixty-five men Magellan carried, besides Spaniards, about thirty-seven Portuguese, over thirty Genoese and Italians, nineteen Frenchmen and a sprinkling of Flemings, Germans, Sicilians, English and six or seven other nationalities.[2] Despite prohibitions against Lutherans, Moors, Jews and "New Christians"—in fact, against foreigners in general—as the conquest advanced it was inevitable that some of these world wanderers

[1] Fernández Duro, *Disquisiciones Náuticas*, VI, 611.
[2] Andrea Ca da Mosto, *Il Primo Viaggio Intorno al Globo di Antonio Pigafetta* (Rome, 1894), 53, *n.* 2, cited in Blair and Robertson, *Philippine Islands*, XXXIII, 278; J. T. Medina, *El Descubrimiento del Océano Pacífico* (Chile, 1913-1920), chap. xvi, "Los Compañeros de Magallanes." Blair and Robertson (XXXIII, 278) say 268, others say as few as 235.

should find their way into the new Indies as settlers. One Scotchman, Tomás Blaque, for instance, was with Coronado in New Mexico, though whether he was Black or Blackie it is too late to determine.

But it would be far from the truth to think that all the Spanish settlers were sea rovers or the offscourings of society. In the beginning of the colonial enterprise on La Española, when Columbus was in Burgos in 1496, he asked for a number of salaried artisans and farmers and they were given to him. The colonial administration more than once made special arrangements to permit artisans of Catholic faith, even from other nations, to have a home and an opportunity in the New World kingdoms. In the first instance, that of Columbus, criminals not heretics were allowed to expiate their offenses by emigrating to Isabela in La Española. Murderers, smugglers of coin and those guilty of *lese majesté* were allowed to go at their own expense. The death penalty was to be commuted to two years in Isabela and lesser penalties to one year's service, after which the beneficiaries could return free to Castile.[1]

How numerous or how satisfactory these contingents proved we have little means of knowing; certainly the paid colonists proved unworthy of their hire, for they assisted the rebel *alcalde* Roldán in his mutinous disturbances against Columbus, and after a brief trial their use was discontinued. Troops of more highly born adventurers who belonged to the *entrepreneur* class—men of the nobility and warriors released from the Italian and other campaigns—helped to make the Spanish settlements heterogeneous, even fairly international in char-

[1] A. de Herrera, *Historia General de los Hechos de los Castellanos* (Madrid, 1601), I, 83-84.

acter; the "common man" as distinguished from the *conquistador,* of whom we shall hear more, came also, and a sprinkling of the lowest types.

The aims and objects of the Spanish conquest have been so persistently misconceived that English readers have come to regard them as essentially unlike those of the French, Dutch, and English. Color is lent to this tradition by the fact that the Spaniards actually found two great golden kingdoms, in Peru and Mexico, which set all the world, not alone Spain, agog with excitement and emulative zeal; for the great object of the times was to accumulate gold and more gold. But the Spaniards were not the only gold-thirsty men who labored under the misconceptions of the mercantilist theory of economics. Sir Walter Raleigh on the Orinoco was drawn, in 1595, to the wonder-city, Manoa, reputed to lie in the tropical interior; a little later John Smith in Virginia sought gold or copper mines and would be content with fur and fish only in their default. In 1576 Frobisher took home from his strait a cargo of iron pyrites, "fool's gold"; La Salle on the Mississippi thrilled to the hope of penetrating to the Nueva Vizcayan silver mines.

Finding gold in abundance, of course the Spaniards pursued it avariciously; but when it failed them, as it often did, they resorted to trade with as much acumen as their rivals. Indeed, their earliest voyages, including those of Columbus and Magellan, were monopolistic commercial adventures, their concessions being coupled with obligations to extend discovery and fortify and colonize the land as an encouragement to trade. They did not make use of charters, which in the case of the English were to serve as prototypes of colonial government, because the Spanish undertaking was royal, not under companies, and the leader of an expedition habitually followed the old Peninsular custom of erecting a city depending directly upon the king of Spain. The spread of the imperial eagles was everywhere under direct control of the crown through municipal organization before the establishment of viceroyalties and kingdoms.

When a leader went forth to add new domains to the crown he sought first the royal license. To obtain it, he had to show sufficient financial backing to insure probable success. His profits were to be taken from the area subdued. He was to have the right to exact labor from the Indians, to appoint municipal officers for the first year, to possess a tract of land in his own right, and to bestow lands upon his followers according to their merits or services. He might recruit companies of soldiers and of settlers, offering them inducements from the conquest and taking from them such pledges of loyalty as he himself gave the king or his representative. Sometimes royal funds were invested if the venture were of strategic importance. There were judiciously chosen missionaries, in large number usually, to effect a spiritual conquest. And there were never lacking the royal officials, or treasury representatives, who kept account of all treasure-trove, gold mines discovered, or any visible sources of wealth, of which the king and the leader were each to have one fifth. Never varying greatly in plan, all the expeditions of discovery and conquest closely followed this system.

According to his contract, a leader might become an *adelantado,* or lord of the marches, or a simple governor. Often he was made lieutenant general of the viceroy; sometimes he became a captain general and organized his kingdom under a more formal and important, because more completely developed, mechanism of government. Always he had to be a man of daring and resource, for he possessed potential enemies within the expedition in the missionaries, who sought the temporal as well as the spiritual advantage of the church, in the royal officials, who were intended as checks upon profits on behalf of the crown, and in his captains, who were all likely to have delusions of grandeur and watch eagerly for mistakes or missteps in his management.[1] Profuse and minute rules for conquest and settlement were codified under the *Ordenanzas de Pobladores* of 1563, providing for all the details of colonization, the bestowal of land, the election of administrative and judicial officers, the laying out of towns, utilization of Indian labor, and the like. Upon such a form, developed by experience from the earliest days in the West Indies and then on the mainland, grew up every local undertaking in the form of colonization, farming, mining or trade.

The former companions of Columbus were not slow to try the New World further. One of them, the dapper and intrepid young Alonso de Ojeda, after amusing Isabella by dancing a jig on a plank thrust from the upper window of the Alcázar at Seville, sailed away in 1499 to trade for pearls along the Venezuela Coast; he was accompanied by the distinguished geographers Juan de la Cosa and Americus Vespucius. Slave hunting and pearl trading helped build his success, as they did also for Alonso Niño, another who had sailed with Columbus and whose luck was so phenomenal that the monopoly

---

[1] H. I. Priestley, ed., *The Luna Papers* (Fla. State Hist. Soc., *Publs.*, VIII), I, 3-5; *Colección de Documentos . . . de Indias* (Madrid, 1864-1884), VIII, 484 ff. See also Zelia Nuttall, "Royal Ordinances concerning the Laying Out of New Towns," *Hisp. Am. Hist. Rev.*, IV, 743-755.

of the Genoese dreamer was effectively broken. In the same year Vicente Yáñez Pinzón, also of the Columbian company, under orders to advance the discovery of the strait that might penetrate to the Indian seas, sailed some two thousand miles along the Brazilian Coast, trading with the natives. Diego de Lepe, another pearl trader, simultaneously pushed the discovery southward below Cape San Agustín. While the Portuguese Álvarez Cabral was touching the Brazilian Coast on his way to India, discovering land in about 18° south latitude, Rodrigo de Bastidas and La Cosa continued Ojeda's north-shore discovery westward from Cabo de la Vela to Nombre de Dios on the Isthmus; they had licenses to trade and patents to hold territory.[1] Thus, before the fourth voyage of Columbus, his erstwhile companions, now competitors, had added three thousand miles of South American coast line to the sum of European knowledge, and had begun the spread from the islands to the mainland.

The final voyage of Columbus, in 1502, was animated, in emulation of Da Gama, by a determination to find the Spice Islands by westward sailing. The quest for the strait led to the Honduran Coast, where he encountered a canoeload of continental Indians bearing artifacts and produce which would have convinced him of the true character of his discoveries had he not been obsessed with the notion that he had reached the Far East. His attempts at trade and colonization were vain; but he advanced the discovery of an unbroken shore line to about sixteen degrees north latitude—his final geographical contribution. Continued search for the strait seemed imperative for Spain because of the success of the Portuguese and the exclusion, by the papal grants

[1] Herrera, *Historia General*, I, 135-138.

and the later treaties of Tordesillas (1494) and Vitoria (1524), of the Spaniards from enjoyment of the route around the Cape of Good Hope.[1]

But though, as it finally proved, no opening toward the Orient could be found, at least there was wealth to be had from exploiting the lands already theirs, where pearls and gold might yield a valuable return. Under this incentive Alonso de Ojeda and Diego Nicuesa undertook ill-fated colonial establishments on the north coast of South America. Ojeda failed at San Sebastián, west of his first settlement, and went back to Santo Domingo to die. Nicuesa's attempt at Nombre de Dios, near the modern Colón, ended also in failure and death. But to Darién, whither Ojeda's colonists had removed from San Sebastián, there came Vasco Núñez de Balboa, unauthorized leader and rebel, whose need for the king's approval spurred him to the effort which led to his discovery of the Pacific in 1513. This was achieved before the insular period of colonial occupation had ended and while the Atlantic Coast beyond Honduras was yet but hazily known.

This discovery of a South Sea so close at hand gave new impetus to the desire to find the connecting strait. On receipt of the news in Spain, Juan Díaz de Solís was sent in 1514 to explore beyond Castilla del Oro for seventeen hundred leagues to discover the elusive waterway. He followed the South American Coast to the La Plata, which for many years bore his name, and perished there in 1516 at the hand of cannibals.[2] His quest

[1] Frances G. Davenport, *European Treaties bearing on the History of the United States and its Dependencies to 1648* (Wash., 1917), 84-100, 118-130; M. de la Puente y Olea, *Los Trabajos Geográficos de la Casa de Contratación* (Seville, 1900), 67-69.

[2] Herrera, *Historia General*, II, 13.

was continued by the immortal Magellan, whose rounding of the continent in 1519 brought Spain at last within
reach of the Orient which Columbus had sought in vain.
In the short space of thirty years there were revealed to
mankind the main features of the globe on which it lived,
and all this by the skill, initiative and intrepidity of men
who bore the Iberian standards.

Meantime, the use of native forced labor had already
resulted in a serious decrease of the island aborigines.
La Española, upon which Columbus expended his first
efforts, was soon suffering from the fact that its natives
vanished under exploitation. Juan Ponce de León, who
had begun to trade with Porto Rico and had become
its first governor in 1509, had heard from slave raiders
among the Bahamas of the Island of Bimini. His quest
for it resulted in the discovery, or rediscovery, of Florida
and in his attempt at colonization at or near Tampa
Bay, after many vicissitudes, in 1521. Meantime Francisco de Garay had in 1519 sent Alonso de Pineda to
search for the strait, a quest in which he traced the entire Gulf Coast from Florida to Vera Cruz. The search
for slaves drove other Spaniards along the coast, though
they cherished, too, the strategic purpose of colonizing
and holding the approaches to the waterway if haply
it might be found. Lucas Vázquez de Ayllón of Santo
Domingo sent out Francisco Gordillo to explore north of
the Bahamas, thus revealing the present South Carolina
Coast in what was designated as 33° 30′ north latitude,
probably Georgetown Entrance. Following this examination, Ayllón, after again reconnoitering in 1525, set
out a year later and established a short-lived colony at
San Miguel Gualdape, probably at the mouth of the
Savannah River. The hunting of slaves on the mainland

led to neglect of the island and gave opportunity to Spain's rivals to seize some of them.

The most northern Spanish discovery, upon which claim to the upper latitudes was based, was that of Estevan Gómez, the Portuguese renegade from Magellan's circumnavigation. His voyage of 1524 from some point between Newfoundland and Maine down to the fortieth parallel left only a narrow gap, if any, between his own and Ayllón's explorations. This practical-minded man in his report discouraged further Spanish effort on the bleak northern shores, for he found trees, fruits and fish like those of Spain and reported the area of little value; "there was enough of such land and to spare" in Spain itself. Occupancy of the temperate zone was thus eschewed, leaving space for the later Virginia, and as a result there comes in the seventeenth century the long story of Spain's effort to win an outlet upon the scorned Atlantic shores as an offset to the colonization of the English. Nevertheless, these latter long shared Gómez's ideas concerning the uselessness of colonies other than those of the plantation or tropical-products type, enduring New England as a necessary evil.[1] It was not until the Industrial Revolution had placed new emphasis on markets that such colonies found welcome in the imperial economy.

The coast of North America had now been explored by Spanish ships from Labrador to Panama. Sebastián Cabot, in Spanish employ, was still willing to search for the Northwest Passage, but the death of his patron, Ferdinand the Catholic, prevented. The eastern coast of South America had also been run and progress on the

[1] T. J. Wertenbaker, *The First Americans* (*A History of American Life*, II), chap. i.

Pacific, begun by Hernán Cortés and carried on in the
north by Juan Rodríguez Cabrillo and Bartolomé
Ferrelo, and in the south by Alfonso de Camargo,
brought about by 1543 the discovery of the entire western littoral from the Strait of Magellan to the line of
modern Oregon. Practically all of this discovery was effected under the impulse to reach the Spice Islands, with
the added motives of pearl hunting and slave raiding.[1]

Before the shore lines had been marked out, the occupation of the continental areas attained a security which
no European rival could challenge. The exploits of
Cortés and Pizarro effected a momentous change in the
spirit of the Spanish adventure. The great treasure of
Montezuma and Atahualpa, with the existence of exploitable agricultural peoples on the two great continental plateaus, put the Oriental attraction into the
background. A more profitable opportunity than that
of Portugal in the East Indies had been found nearer at
hand. The Spanish enterprise would have vanished speedily enough had the Aztec and Inca been like the Carib
and Arawak; indeed, there would have been no inland
ventures had there not been reports of vast golden
kingdoms to conquer. From those days until the eighteenth century it was the dream of the Spanish conquistador to find such another treasure as those of the two
lucky rebels who gave the great Charles his fairest American kingdoms.

In 1527 all the mainland conquests were consolidated,
from Florida to Honduras, under the audiencia or
supreme court of New Spain. It was the cruel Nuño de

[1] See the account of the Spanish cartographic records of the discovery
of the Atlantic and Pacific coasts in Puente y Olea, *Los Trabajos
Geográficos de la Casa de Contratación*, 301-332.

Guzmán, enemy of Cortés and now governor of Pánuco, who first presided over this board of unified administration; but not even Guzmán's search for the Isle of the Amazons, or his addition of "Greater Spain" to the diadem of Charles, could save him. He was superseded in 1530 by a gentleman of a legal turn of mind, one whose blood was not aflame with the fires of fortune hunting. This first real administrator in North America was the beneficent and constructive-minded ecclesiastic, Sebastián Ramírez de Fuenleal, from Santo Domingo, whose insular experiences as a superior judge enabled him to lay, by wise legislation and administration, the bases of New Spain's stability. Shortly came the imperial decision to create here a viceroyalty, modeled upon those of Spain as adapted in her extrapeninsular possessions in Europe.[1]

Even the sober-minded Antonio de Mendoza, first viceroy, was sorely tempted by the glittering prospects of wider and richer kingdoms. Seven years before, it may be remembered, Pánfilo de Narváez had essayed to grasp in Florida the elusive fortune Ponce had missed. His ships gone and his supplies exhausted, improvised vessels rigged with sails of clothing carried him and most of his expedition to death at the mouth of the Mississippi. His great survivor Cabeza de Vaca, famous as the first European medicine man and romantic as the first transcontinental walker, brought back strange stories that sent Friar Marcos to find the turquoise-studded Cities of Cíbola. Mendoza, racing Cortés for the glory of so great a conquest, sent poor Coronado

---

[1] V. Riva Palacio, *México á través de los Siglos* (Mexico, 1888-1889), II, chap. xxvi; A. S. Aiton, *Antonio de Mendoza, First Viceroy of New Spain* (Durham, N. C., 1927), 30-33.

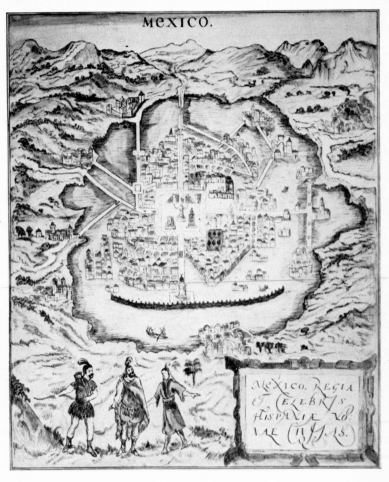

The Aztec capital, the island city of
Mexico, or Tenochtitlán, as the
white men first beheld it.

trailing away to New Mexico in their quest, where Indian lies about a mythical kingdom of Quivira led him to the tawdry reality of a group of Wichita tepees. Then Hernando de Soto in futile search for a realm of splendor was lured to his death and a secret burial in the Father of Waters. Without these dreams, this credulity urged on by itching ambition to solve the "secrets" of those lands, as the saying then ran, some of the dramatic episodes of early American history would have been lacking. Yet these men did little to change the current of human affairs. They represent a tragic disillusionment after heroic self-sacrifice and perverse refusal to accept the obvious limitations upon Spanish growth imposed by distance, wild Indians and inhospitable geographic conditions.

More substantial was the conquest of Nueva Galicia, west of Mexico City. In 1548 this farming and mining area, which had been overrun successively by the lieutenants of Cortés and of Guzmán, settled by miners and farmers, and saved by Mendoza from a perilous Indian revolt, was erected into a second audiencia district. By this time the frontier ran from Pánuco to Culiacán approximately along the line of the Tropic of Cancer. Soon raids against thieving Indians and prospecting parties brought about the occupation of the fabulously rich silver area of Zacatecas. Thence the way led along the silver lode during the early fifties into Durango.[1] Here the notable Ibarra family, related to the second great viceroy Velasco, developed the silver mines so exciting to the cupidity of the Hawkinses and Drake. Mining received further impetus from the discovery, at

[1] J. L. Mecham, *Francisco de Ibarra and Nueva Vizcaya* (Durham, N. C., 1927), chap. iii.

Pachuca in 1557 by Bartolomé Medina, of the amalgam process of silver extraction.

These first miners were not lone prospectors heading for the hills with pan and burro; they were large-scale operators with armies of men and caravans of animals at their backs. They found a vein, set up a great establishment, and when the ores were dug, spread them on the earthen floors of their *patios,* or courtyards, where droves of mules tramped in the quicksilver and salt which released the precious metal. The quicksilver was then smelted out and the bars of silver made. Once or twice a year they were loaded on pack trains to be carried to the great mint in Mexico City. By 1652 the new region, Nueva Vizcaya, was placed under a lieutenant general subordinate to the viceroy; it finally comprised the present northwest part of modern Mexico. In the vicinity of the mines were the great cattle ranges and estates whose inhabitants became self-sustaining.

After Zacatecas was founded the route to Mexico was guarded by fortified places. From one of these, Querétaro, advance was made into San Luis Potosí, and thence again northward the white metal led to Saltillo, founded in 1559. In the next decade advance moved west and northwest. In the eighties the Portuguese Jew, Luis de Carabajal, advancing from Pánuco, founded Cerralvo and in 1590, Monclova. From the line of the Tropic to very nearly the present bounds of Mexico the silver quest had led, by 1596, to practical occupation. New Mexico, comprising the immediate valley of the Rio Grande, was annexed between 1581 and 1609. There the natives led a sedentary life, unlike the wild nomads farther south. The old stories of the Seven Cities beckoned hither, and it became prized shortly, not for silver but as a trading area and outpost for wider conquests.[1]

In the meantime the latter fifties saw a revival of faith in the future of Florida. Soto was believed to have found a rich country, there was yet alive the thirst for new souls to save and, last of all, there was the desire to forestall rivals on the Atlantic. For now the French were suspected of designs in these parts—so near, they said, to Canada—and the pirates were capturing the plate fleets as they traversed the Bahama Channel homeward bound. After a period of hesitancy because of the inhospitable shores and the savage Indians, settlement was authorized, and Tristán de Luna led a promising company of one thousand five hundred people to Pensacola. Storms and quarrels prevented them from fixing a settlement, and an attempt under Ángel de Villafañe to fortify Ayllón's Santa Elena, on the Atlantic side, to defend the galleon route likewise failed. These enterprises engrossed viceroy Velasco's attention from 1557 to 1561.[2] Fancied security was shaken by Jean Ribault's efforts to plant strongholds at Fort Caroline and on the St. John's River. When this Huguenot venture was crushed by the fanatical efficiency of Menéndez de Avilés, that doughty ruler extended the Spanish occupation along the shores of Florida, Georgia and South Carolina. In 1570 a temporary hold was maintained as

---

[1] G. de Villagrá, *Historia de la Nueva México* (Alcalá, 1610; reprinted, Mexico, 1900); A. de Benavides, *Memorial* (Madrid, 1630, translated by Mrs. Edward E. Ayer, Chicago, 1916), *passim*.

[2] Priestley, *The Luna Papers*, I, pp. xxxii, 39, 165. The most recent synoptic survey of the Spanish overseas enterprises, to the close of the reign of Charles V, is R. B. Merriman, *The Rise of the Spanish Empire in the Old World and in the New* (N. Y., 1918-1925), III, bk. vi; see esp. chap. xxviii, "The Conquest of New Spain."

far north as Chesapeake Bay. La Florída flourished until about the end of the century.

It must be remembered that the driving force of Spain was at the same time going forward in South America and in the Philippines. The North American area used less than half the effort expended; yet even here it was surprisingly large in contrast with the French and English growth during the next cycle. This enormous expansion is explained by the wide distribution of silver mines, the aridity of many areas which made them useless for farming, and by the eagerness of the missionaries for souls to save. The man power was meager. The entire Spanish possessions in both Americas in the last quarter of the sixteenth century contained not more than one hundred and sixty thousand heads of families in some two hundred towns, and in many cases these heads of families (*vecinos*) were spouses of Indian women. Only about four thousand of them were *encomenderos* (feudal lords of estates worked by Indians in practical serfdom)—that is, men of *entrepreneur* type. The remainder were small settlers, miners, traders, clericals and soldiers. It is safe to say that the Spanish achievement in North America during the Great Century of the Conquest was brought about by an active group never numbering more than seventy-five or eighty thousand, less than two thousand of whom possessed qualities of leadership. It was a century of which Spain may well be proud.[1]

The sanity, sober judgment and idea of permanency with which this great occupation was effected are evi-

[1] J. López de Velasco, *Geografía y Descripción Universal de las Indias* (Madrid, 1894), 37, 91, 337. A hundred years later the total population of English America scarcely exceeded 160,000. *Cf.* also French and Dutch America treated later, chaps. ix-xii.

denced by the thoroughness with which the material elements of European life were introduced. These Spanish
conquerors are often pictured, blood-stained, sword in
hand, bent on looting the new country they had entered.
We overlook the tools, the plants and seeds, the livestock they carried, and their homelier achievement of
establishing the fundamental arts.[1] The important European plants first disseminated throughout Spanish America make a long list. They included wheat, barley, rice,
rye, beans (though there were American varieties of
these), chick-peas and lentils. The Spaniards also introduced almonds, mulberries, cherries, walnuts, chestnuts,
medlars, tulip trees, linen, flax, alfalfa, *alpiste* or canary
seed, quinces, apples, apricots and most of the other
pitted fruits (certain plums were already here), oranges,
limes, lemons, citron trees, cedars, pears, rosemary, wil-
lows, broom, roses, lilies and a multitude of the old-
fashioned flowers. From Africa they brought, by way
of the Azores or Andalusia, the sugar cane and certain
varieties of bananas, and from Asia the *cañafístula* or
*Cassia fistularis,* tamarinds, the huge orangelike *lukban*
or dry grapefruit of the Philippines and the delectable
mango. Virtually all of these transmissions occurred
during the sixteenth or Great Century of the Conquest.[2]

In the seventeen ships with which Columbus sailed
on his second voyage were many seeds and animals as
well as agricultural workers. At old Isabela in La
Española, Peter Martyr said, the truck gardens produced
vegetables in from sixteen to thirty-six days after plant-

---

[1] For an excellent article on this subject, see J. A. Robertson, "Some
Notes on the Transfer by Spain of Plants and Animals to Its Colonies
Overseas," *James Sprunt Hist. Studies,* XIX, 7-21.

[2] Puente y Olea, *Los Trabajos Geográficos de la Casa de Contratación,*
375. Much in the following pages is based on Puente, 374-446.

ing. Ojeda and Nicuesa took seeds to the mainland in 1509. Cortés reported to the emperor that Spanish plants were bearing well in New Spain and requested that no future ship come without plants and seeds. The most difficult transplantation was that of wheat. The elder Columbus brought some and Diego, when he came as governor, was ordered to try out two hundred bushels of wheat seed, but it spoiled on the voyage. "Three months' wheat" was tried in 1511, but probably failed; more was sent three years later, this time to Castilla del Oro in Central America, and again in 1520, with chick-peas, beans and flax. Several stories are told of the casual beginnings of successful wheat growing. One is that a Negro belonging to Cortés found three grains of wheat while cleaning some rice sacks; he planted them and got two to grow. One bore one hundred and eighty grains, from which the succeeding crops were sown.[1] Rice, which stood the ocean voyage better than wheat, was sent to La Española by Ferdinand the Catholic in 1512, though a native rice, *chenopodium quinoa,* was common in Peru and the Valley of Bogotá.

In 1514 Oviedo saw great groves of sweet and sour-orange trees in all the Christian towns of the islands and the mainland, and also lemons, limes and citrons as fine as those of Andalusia; he reported that the orange mar-malade was delicious. It is possible, but not probable, that some of the citrus varieties antedated the Spaniards, but none of the early voyagers saw such groves as did Oviedo. The grapevine did poorly in the Caribbean

[1] In Peru the first wheat is credited to Doña Inés Muñoz, who married Antonio de Rivera. Doña Inés also found her wheat in rice sacks. Prescott attributes the incident to one María Escobar. *Cf.* Bernabé Cobo, *Historia del Nuevo Mundo* (Seville, 1890-1893), II, 412; W. H. Prescott, *History of the Conquest of Peru* (Phila., 1879), I, 144-145, *n.*

islands, none being seen there in 1590 according to Acosta. It throve in Mexico, however, though wine could not be made at first because the summer rains spoiled the fruit, and viniculture on the northern continent did not equal that of Peru. The first cultivated bananas were taken from the Canaries to La Española in 1516 by Fray Tomás de Berlanga and known as *plátanos de Guinea*. From the island they went to Central America in 1519, and later to Peru. In La Española the trees were blamed for a pest of ants that threatened all the cultivated vegetation and in Lima in 1543 all those in the city were torn out for the same reason. Most of the fruit trees were sent first to the Antilles and later to the mainland, but in 1520 Dr. Sancho de Matienzo, associate of Bishop Fonseca in charge of the work of the transmission of plants and animals by the *Casa de Contratación* (or official board of trade), sent directly to Central America almonds, figs, cherries, pomegranates and quinces. The plants were kept on the decks of the Atlantic ships in half-barrels filled with earth, a custom long continued after the year 1531 when it was established by official decree. The olive tree got its start in 1531 in Mexico, later in Peru,[1] where the oil and the wood became notable resources of the Lima Valley. The "mission fig" and the "mission olive" of California came with the Franciscan fathers of 1769 and still constitute the staple varieties in California horticulture.

Sugar cane, as we have seen, was brought from Spain or her Atlantic islands where it had been established shortly before the discovery. Columbus tried to start it, but his plants did not thrive. No sugar was made in

[1] Cobo, *Historia del Nuevo Mundo*, II, 382-386. Antonio de Rivera succeeded in bringing three plants to Peru in 1560.

the Antilles before the beginning of the sixteenth century and in 1511 there was not enough made to supply local consumption. Six years later, however, the Geronymite friars sent home a precious casket bearing samples of field cotton, cañafístula and sugar, which they had been promoting. They encouraged sugar mills by a bounty of five hundred pesos on each one built, and the king in 1520 removed all duties on machinery needed for them. Experts were sent from the Canaries and the plantations throve amazingly. José Acosta said in 1590 that sugar was the greatest industry in the isles of the Indies—Santo Domingo could ship nearly two hundred thousand pounds of it—and there were large sugar concerns in Peru, Central America and New Spain, where it was *cosa loca lo que se consume*—"a marvel how much was eaten."[1]

Garden flowers were brought over in the same ways as the edible plants. Red carnations, and the white ones splotched with red, grew all over Peru by the middle of the seventeenth century but, like those of Mexico, they were not so fragrant as in Spain. Roses were plentiful; the first ones came by seed in 1552, and mass was said in Lima, with one of the seeds on the altar, to celebrate the event. But there were varieties native to the soil; the Franciscan fathers who pioneered the California Coast were cheered in their marches northward, just as the founder of their order might have been, when they spied in the forests the single pink blossoms which they named *rosas de Castilla*.[2]

[1] José de Acosta, *The Naturall and Morall Historie of the East and West Indies* (London, 1604), 295-298.
[2] Cobo, *Historia del Nuevo Mundo*, II, 406-407. The first geranium in Peru grew six feet tall. Rosemary was cherished in that region as a reminder of home.

In rehearsing the long story of this western' transit it must not be forgotten that the economic resources of Europe were enlarged by importations from the flora of the New World. Indian corn had been acclimated in Spain before 1530 and potatoes had been raised in Italy by the middle of the century. The tomato was in'general use in Southern Europe long before 1800. Most tropical plants were ill-adapted to the climate of the old country, but their products, previously rare or entirely unknown, like cacao and vanilla, became common articles of trade.

More spectacular was the revolution wrought by Spain in the transmission of European fauna. By 1525 they were shipping cowhides to Spain from the Antilles; cattle were so numerous that the people did not know what to do with them. Father Cobo declared that the spread of Spanish cattle had a great deal to do with ending the cannibalism of the Chiriguana of Los Charcas and of the Carib. Gómara said that the Indians of Mexico took very kindly to the cheese made from cow's milk, marveling that the liquid could be thickened to make it. As for horses and mules, "they blessed the beasts which relieved them from burden-bearing." [1] Horses and asses were taken to La Española by Columbus on his second and third voyages, later by Ovando. Vicente Yáñez Pinzón sent mares with his ships in 1507; Nicuesa and Ojeda took them to the mainland in 1509 and more went to Antigua in 1513. Probably the original stock, coming from Andalusia, was Arabic. How rapidly they spread over Spanish America is shown by the fact that horses were running wild, on the south-

[1] Francisco López de Gómara, *Historia de México* (Antwerp, 1554), 342; Puente y Olea, *Los Trabajos Geográficos de la Casa de Contratación*, 422.

ern plains of Paraguay and Tucumán, and in the hills
of New Mexico, by the middle of the seventeenth century.[1] They had become so cheap that they were hunted
instead of bred. Mexico got her supply of mules from
twelve jennies and three jacks sent in 1531. Bishop
Fuenleal asked for three hundred jennies to give to the
Indians.

Cattle for meat supply increased more slowly than
horses and mules.[2] Hogs showed remarkable reproduc-
tive power. By 1508 the people of La Española were
given royal permission to hunt for a pastime the droves
of wild descendants of the first hogs which had been
brought. Soto in Florida was accompanied by a herd of
several hundred hogs, and he left many behind; some
may have strayed, too, from those which Coronado took
with him for food in New Mexico. Sheep were the only
imported livestock that did not come to run wild; they
were brought to Mexico in 1531 and at a later date to
Peru. The good Bishop of Fuenleal, along with his other
benefactions, gave flocks to the Indians, who prized them
and raised them carefully. But for years the wool was
wasted, as there were no mills, but the manufacture of
woolen cloth became a leading industry of Peru in after

[1] The advent of the horse upon the continent would have had a greater
effect upon the social development of the sedentary Indians had it not
been for the legal prohibition against their use by the natives. On the
nomadic frontiers the ready adaptation of the native tribes to the new
mode of travel meant more effective resistance to the whites as well as a
more ample food supply. The white man also brought the wheel, greatest
of artifacts in the evolution of social economy, but it cannot be said that
the aborigines have yet risen to the capacity of using it as effectively as
those who introduced it.

[2] Pedro de Mendoza, abandoning Buenos Aires, where he settled in
1535, turned loose five mares and seven horses; by the end of the century their progeny overran the country down to the Straits of Magellan.
By 1600 uncounted droves of them had overrun the plains and made
their way into the mountains. See W. S. Barclay, *The Land of Magellan*
(London, 1926), 106.

years. The woolens of New Spain were, said Acosta, coarser than those of the home country.[1]

These first Christians brought with them the cross and the sword, it is true, but they also brought all they had of practical civilization. It was the judgment of Father Cobo that America in that early day received in plants and animals as much wealth as she returned in gold and silver; [2] the new land was just ripe for what the Spaniards had to offer. It was their misfortune that the papal bulls gave them broader domains than their strength sufficed for. But they were great in their conception of a New World to be won for Spain and for the faith, and they were notable in the simple practicality with which they undertook to make the wilderness blossom with a European culture by which the red man was to be elevated as a husbandman and Christian.

[1] Acosta, *The Naturall and Morall Historie of the East and West Indies*, 299.

[2] Cobo, *Historia del Nuevo Mundo*, II, 344. A. L. P. P. de Candolle says (in our opinion rather loosely) that of 247 plants cultivated in America, 199 originated in the Old World, forty-five in America, and one in Australia, while the native habitat of two cannot be determined. *Origine des Plantes cultivées* (Paris, 1883), cited by Robertson, "Some Notes," 20.

# CHAPTER II

## THE SPANISH ADVANCE

IN no region was the Spanish area of North America ever densely settled. Indeed, it may be said that frontier conditions began always just outside the bounds of the populous communities. Yet there was a distinctively pioneer area in which the conditions of life were especially precarious and inhospitable. To designate this region we may borrow an old colonial expression, *tierra de guerra*, the land of war, to distinguish the portion still overrun by wild Indians from that which was fairly well pacified, settled and established as *tierra de paz*, the land of peace. It is not possible to draw an exact line delimiting the two areas for any long stretch of years, but in general the territory in which frontier conditions prevailed, after the subjugation of the Chichimec Indians in the 1590's, lay north of the twenty-first degree of latitude. That is, the hardest and slowest conquest was in precisely that region to which the old Aztec Confederacy had reached but at whose border it had stopped before the coming of Cortés.[1] It is significant that the Spanish conquest found so strong a check at that line, and that beyond it modern industry, agriculture and commerce made but slow progress under the greater efficiency of the white man. The reasons lie in the character

[1] P. Beaumont, *Crónica de Michoacán* (Mexico, 1873-1874), IV, 559-560; V, 233, 552-557. *Cf.* H. H. Bancroft, *History of Mexico* (San Francisco, 1883-1888), II, 539-545, 760-764, and citations; C. W. Hackett, *Historical Documents Relating to New Mexico* (Wash., 1923-1926), I, intro. 14-19.

of the country and of the primitive inhabitants and in the lessened adaptability of the Spaniards to the new environment beyond the plateau and the sedentary tribes.

It needs to be remarked again that the motives for Spanish expansion were as varied as they were compelling and that they persisted, some of them even growing in intensity, as the power of Spain in Europe declined. Until the end of the eighteenth century men still hoped to find a water passage to the Pacific. In the early days this waterway was conceived as an inland sea separating America from Asia, the western lands supposedly being a fringe of insular masses appreciably close to the Oriental continent. In the later period, when the expanse of America had been in some measure appreciated, the search was still for a passage which should connect the oceans. The significance of such a find, and the need to control its approaches, formed the impelling idea behind all those dramatic but exhausting exploring expeditions preceding and accompanying the conquest of the silver country of northern Mexico throughout the sixteenth and seventeenth centuries. But the precious white metal itself proved a much stronger incentive to the practical-minded conquerors of later days whose lust for territorial expansion was not so boundless as that of Cortés.

The zeal of the great missionary orders for converting Indians must always be recognized as one of the most important forces of expansion,[1] and the use of the mission by the crown as an active but subsidiary

---

[1] H. E. Bolton, "The Mission as a Frontier Institution," *Am. Hist. Rev.*, XXIII, 42-61. For an unfavorable criticism see Z. S. Eldredge, *The Beginnings of San Francisco* (San Francisco, 1912), I, 163. Cunningham Graham, *A Vanished Arcadia* (London, 1901), 196-212, gives an estimate of the Paraguayan missions.

agent of subjugation is one of the outstanding features of the colonial system. Those scores of fathers of the church, like Eusebio Kino, the Jesuit, and Francisco Garcés, the Franciscan, who became notable frontiersmen, were also thoroughly imbued with the passion for empire. Their petitions for government aid to extend mission fields were invariably baited with alluring prospects of rich kingdoms to be won for the crown. Their aggressiveness usually found quick and warm response during the sixteenth century, when the mining region was being prospected; but as the seventeenth century waned, the monarchs of Spain lost the driving power of their predecessors. Appeals for expansion either for souls or territory went unnoticed save when foreign aggressions carried a threat that could not be ignored.

Unfortunately for Spain, defense of the border became the characteristic motive of seventeenth and eighteenth-century expansion along the whole frontier line from California to St. Augustine. To hold the wide stretches which could not be closely settled and exploited was therefore a definite feature of colonial policy. It overtaxed the expansive power of the nation and exhausted its resources, coming as a task close upon the heels of other difficulties and handicaps which retarded the growth of settlement.[1] The circumstances of the later advance show that Spain realized that the limit of her absorptive power had been reached. Had it not been for the aggressiveness of her rivals, she might have devoted her energies to the process of consolidation. But with her northern frontier presenting no secure natural barrier of mountains or water, the work of spreading thin lines

[1] See for instance the "Proposals for the Defense and Development of Nueva Vizcaya," Hackett, *Historical Documents*, II, 71-82. A score of illustrations might be easily cited.

of protection had to go on in spite of ever increasing burdens.

One great difficulty was distance. At each successive advance toward higher latitudes the frontier to be defended increased in width, and communication with the center at Mexico City became more costly and arduous. Indian wars were a constant threat for more than three hundred years, with only brief breathing spells of peace. Sixteenth-century Indian fighting had been against large forces of natives, but on the later border line it became a devastating guerrilla warfare. Nor was it always possible to keep the outposts of the several independent advances in defensive touch with each other.

Further baffling obstacles were presented by the character of the country.[1] In the broken and mountainous areas of the western and eastern Sierras progress was dependent upon the discovery of rich mineral deposits. As these ranges separate, one bearing to the northwest and the other to the northeast, the pursuit of silver mining tended to draw the eastern and western lines of advance farther apart as progress was made. Almost nowhere do the mountains line the edges of well-watered fertile valleys where an agricultural community might spring up in the wake of prospector or miner. The salient characteristic of the northern interior plateau of Mexico is its aridity; practically no native agriculture had developed there. Though there were seasons of copious rainfall in some parts of the north, even those which had occasional wet years were frequently denied enough precipitation for grazing, and the annals of the north are replete with tales of disastrous droughts. The average

[1] An ampler statement of geographic conditions in Northern Mexico is C. C. Colby, *Source Book of the Economic Geography of North America* (Chicago, 1922), chap. xiv.

precipitation today along the whole reach of the present
boundary between the United States and Mexico is eight
inches; on the Colorado and Yuma deserts it seldom
reaches more than two or three.[1] Scant rains on the interior plateau and the absence of mountain snows leave
the country with very few streams; in the seven hundred
miles between the Rio Grande and the Pacific the region
is crossed by only five streams of permanent character.
The seasons of rainfall differ from coast to coast, the
chief rains coming on the Pacific Slope in the fall and
winter, while in the northern interior east of the Colorado River the chief season is in summer. On the east
coast, as in the west, the rains are heavy, but the streams
are short and precipitous, offering obstacles, rather than
facilities, to a northerly line of march. They often over-
flow suddenly, rendering agriculture in their valleys precarious; the Conchos River in Chihuahua is almost
unique in offering assistance to the natural expansion of
settlement. On the west coast a number of streams like the
Yaqui, Mayo, Fuerte and Sinaloa rivers presented the
advantage of excellent tillable soil, but they lay athwart
the path of expansion.

Thus when advances were made they had to be undertaken with due respect to the accessible supplies of
water from small streams, waterholes and "tanks." Beyond the plateau country there are even now but fifteen towns of over ten thousand population; and most
of these, like Chihuahua, Saltillo, Monterey and Durango, owe their present size to twentieth-century mining interests vastly more valuable than those of colonial
days when ore could be extracted profitably only from

[1] G. B. Puga, "Consideraciones sobre la Distribución General de las
Lluvias y en Particular en la República Mexicana," Sociedad Científica
"Antonio Alzate," Memoria, XVI, 137-160.

very rich deposits and transportation was still in the wagon and pack-mule stage.[1] In those parts of the United States once included in this Mexican frontier the population has become relatively dense only in regions where agriculture under irrigation has been developed by modern methods not available to the colonial Spaniard.

Thus conditions of land and water conspired to limit the activity of the people to mining, grazing and a precarious agriculture. To these repressive influences was added another handicap, that of restricted markets for any surplus agricultural or stock production. The older settled area was approximately self-supporting except during drought, and there was no exterior market for anything but silver and "colonial products." Moreover, interminable distances precluded economical transportation. Thus the frontier, thinly peopled, drew its wealth from the mountains and the cattle ranges, sending scant exports southward and bringing its imports from Spain or the southern plateau region over the long, bad roads to the capital. There were no ocean ports north of Vera Cruz and Acapulco, but even if the coast had possessed suitable harbors they could not have become extensively used without modification of the strict monopoly preserved by commercial legislation. Through exclusive control of the import and export trade at the southern ports, and through central regulation by the government, the viceroyalty was held firmly in the grip of the mother country; but the centralization of commerce caused extremely high rates for overland freight, to which were added regional sales taxes increasing in amount in direct

[1] Anon., "The Frontier Region of Mexico," *Geographical Rev.*, III, 16-27. Chihuahua is supported by lumbering, agriculture and grazing as well as mining.

ratio with the distance, so that trade was always backward.

The spread of agriculture depended upon the location of streams having permanent water supply, for irrigation was widely necessary and no means of conserving water had been developed. Nor were there in the north, save at Querétaro, those immense aqueducts which marked the development of water supply farther to the south. Indeed, the variable character of the soil, much of it being alkaline, rocky or sandy, rendered many parts of the area unfit for irrigation.

An even greater difficulty was the lack of man power. There were not enough people, in Spain or in New Spain, to form a dense population under the most favorable conditions. This was in part due to the fact that the birth rate, while high under Spanish Catholic encouragement, was largely offset by high rates of mortality, especially among infants. In the rural population the lack of growth may be attributed to the general character of the lower levels of society. The great landlords who went out to take up vast stretches of land secured some labor for their estates by taking with them any available people of Spanish blood, but for the most part they had to depend upon forced labor by Indians held captive. This was the most unwilling, meagerly taught and, therefore, most expensive kind of labor, though there were better frontiersmen among the Aztec and Tlaxcaltec, who were used in many of the new settlements, even as far north as California.[1]

The dispossessed classes of the older cities, half-breeds and Indians, never displayed any marked tendency to

[1] Antonio Peñafiel, *Ciudades Coloniales* (Mexico, 1908-1909), III, 163, 165-172; Bancroft, *History of Mexico*, II, 764.

move to the north where free land might be had, though
they were sometimes forcibly invited. From an early
period criminals were often compelled to undertake
frontier life. While there was excuse for this reluctance,
both on account of the hostility of the Indians and the
dubious nature of crop raising, the lower class habitually
disliked responsibility and sacrifice. As the white and
Indian blood mixed in the lower strata, there grew up
about the cities a disproportionate number of social
riffraff designated *léperos,* who eked out a livelihood
from menial and seasonal service for white masters.
Many worked as muleteers in the immense mule trains
which connected the ports with the capital, while large
numbers resorted to highway robbery along the roads
of the interior. In the north there did indeed develop a
settler class which endured and preserved itself in spite
of all handicaps, but the conditions of rural life, the
nature of the frontier and the character of the lower
classes all joined to hamper the formation of a large
element of "hardy pioneers" bent upon hewing a fortune out of the wilderness.[1] It should be pointed out
with emphasis that the Spanish borderland, unlike the
Anglo-American frontier, was never a happy place for
the "common man."

Equally striking was the fact that the Spanish system
of disposing of public lands produced a class of great
landlords instead of a society of independent small farmers. The colonization laws provided that groups of from
ten to thirty heads of families might, if they wished,
move at least six leagues from an already established

[1] Arriaga to Gálvez, Madrid, March 26, 1765, (MS., Archivo General
de Indias, I, 88-5-20) ; *cf.* H. I. Priestley, *José de Gálvez* (Univ. of
Calif., *Publs. in Hist.,* V), 56.

town to free land, their new town being granted a total of four square leagues. There is no record of how many such towns were settled. Relatively, the number must have been small, for it was also provided that the leader of a certain number of families might obtain similar privileges, and, as a matter of fact, most of the enterprises were begun under the protection of well-to-do *entrepreneurs.*

Thus the seventeenth-century conquest of the north came to be a semiofficial, semiprivate enterprise, conducted by wealthy leaders, almost wholly of military training or experience, who usually went out licensed as governors by the viceroy or the king. The more primitive system of sending out an adelantado with semifeudal powers of granting lands to his followers disappeared with Juan de Oñate, the conqueror of New Mexico, but in parts of the north encomenderos were given holdings of land and dependent Indians, with the obligation to help defend the frontiers. Each leader, whatever his status, took with him a band of followers enlisted in military fashion, each member participating in the investment to the extent of his capacity.[1] Generally the most numerous contingent consisted of Christian Indian allies who were used both for defense and for their example in encouraging the barbarous tribes to become civilized. But such emigrants were hardly moving to the frontier in the hope of an independent existence. Subject to the personal government of their leaders, to the hazards of Indian warfare and the discomforts of back-country life, they had little prospect of greater prosperity or improved social position save by discovery of

[1] See the survey of this process of expansion in Carlos Pereyra, *Historia de la América Española* (Madrid, 1920-1925), III, pt. iii, chap. **v.**

mineral deposits; and from these they had little hope of profit unless they could obtain quicksilver. This essential commodity was a government monopoly and was kept quite out of reach of the small operator by high prices until the last third of the eighteenth century. With the families of soldier-settlers went numbers of Negro and Indian slaves to perform the hard manual tasks until the resident Indians could be subjugated.[1]

Each little colony was self-creating, self-protecting and self-exploiting. The leader always exercised his right to choose the best land or the best mine. Profit from this property and a practical, though unofficial, monopoly of communication with the capital or the nearest other market were his greatest incentives. In time the Indians would pay tribute unless they were made members of a mission organization. They would also bring him their tithes for bestowal upon the church. The Spanish people of lower rank, and those assimilated to them in social class, paid taxes on mineral or agricultural production for the support of government. The best of them acquired such positions as those of *alcalde mayor* or *corregidor,* in which they were the abetters of the governors in the scramble for wealth. They might also engage legally in trade on their own account if opportunity came. The heads of *alcaldías mayores* had in many cases the added title of *capitán a guerra;* that is, their chief duty was to maintain the defense of a small area under the general government of their leader.

[1] Detailed discussion of colonial agriculture appears in V. Riva Palacio, ed., *México á través de los Siglos* (Mexico, 1888-1889), II, 671-675; and Bancroft, *History of Mexico*, II, 603-619. There is no good comprehensive survey of the agriculture of New Spain; the study made by Alexander von Humboldt, *Political Essay on the Kingdom of New Spain* (London, 1814), remains the most important. See esp. III, chap. x.

Where *presidios,* or forts, were established for the protection of the frontier, the captains were also interested, quite as much as the governors and alcaldes, in developing a trade in which they personally engaged. Presidio officers brought to the frontier food and supplies which they sold to their men. The natural temptation was to keep their enlistment rolls padded and charge off to non-existent men supplies which they disposed of to others at a profit.[1] The ordinary settler was thus very much at the mercy of the official class. True, the governors and alcaldes were subject to official investigations, but these were apt to be performed by their successors, from whom leniency could often be secured for a consideration.

Where conflict existed between the official class and the ever present missionaries over control and exploitation of the natives, as it generally did, the strife was often a continuous deterrent to progress. The lay Spaniards wanted the Indians to work on their estates; the missionaries wanted them attached to the missions. In all cases where it was possible the missions became industrial as well as religious schools; they amassed notable economic resources, justifying their course by the inadequacy of the small yearly salaries of from one hundred and fifty to three hundred pesos paid by the royal government. The treatment meted out to the Indians was more humane than on the *haciendas;* but even in the missions corporal punishment and restraint were part of the amenities of civilization. The influence of the lower classes of frontiersmen and presidial soldiers upon

[1] Marqués de Rubi, Dictamen sobre la Mejor Colocación de los Presidios en las Provincias Internas de la Nueva España (MS., 1768, Archivo General de Indias, 104-6-13).

the natives was such that the missionaries preferred to have them at a safe distance or entirely absent. The mutual recriminations of laymen and churchmen were often the cause of terrible Indian revolts.

Theoretically the power of the viceroy reached to the farthest rim of settlement, but his voice was faint and distant. The provincial governor as his lieutenant general was fairly independent in matters of routine, and his prestige was enhanced in many unofficial ways. New movements of expansion or development on the frontier were subject to the recommendations of the viceroy's advisers, the *fiscal* of the treasury and the *auditor de guerra* or war counselor. To accomplish a result "without added expense to the royal fisc" was the ideal of every undertaking. The advice of the fiscal concerning expenditures was usually final, as he was the viceroy's agent for the protection of the king's treasury. The monarch and the audiencia, acting as an administrative council, also intervened in matters, important and unimportant, even to the promotion in rank of a frontier lieutenant. When enterprises of real moment were under contemplation the viceroy usually sought the advice of experts or persons of influence in occasional conferences called *Juntas de guerra y hacienda*. The opinion of these bodies, if he were forceful, he could usually shape to suit his own opinions and formalize his decisions. These were of course subject to interpretation on the border, where the actual situation had to be confronted. The pioneers possessed and exercised the right of redress of grievances through appeal to the viceroy and audiencia and often made their voices heard in the capital in this way. Very frequently those who fell out of favor with the governor had missionary backing. The fathers themselves had a strong organization through their provincial commissaries who were in charge of the mission provinces, and had no difficulty in obtaining a hearing by the central government. Nevertheless, central control was more perfect than on English frontiers.

Though the conquest of the settled area had not been without its bitter fighting and the recurrence of Indian rebellions or Negro uprisings, the Spaniards met a more critical problem when they entered the lands of the nomads. The northern tribes challenged every movement and served to hold progress on all fronts at a relatively slow and even pace.[1] The farther north the settlements went the fiercer was the native; indeed, the Apache and Comanche offered a resistance to the Spanish arms and religion which definitely checked the growth of the frontier. In the seventeenth and eighteenth centuries they fought with firearms furnished by French and English traders and used them with telling effect. The usual reaction of the Indians toward Spanish exploitation was one of chronic but ill-organized resistance alternating with periods of submission. This was as true of a new conquest as of a subsequent occupation. Such for instance was the condition throughout the northwestward movement in Sinaloa and Sonora. Begun about the middle of the sixteenth century, it was carried on as a side enterprise along with that in the central region of Nueva Vizcaya. Occupation advanced to the vicinity of the Rio Grande by the close of the seventeenth century, though presidios, or forts, did not command the actual frontier approaches until after determined governmental

[1] Baltasar de Obregón, *Historia de los Descubrimientos Antiguos y Modernos de la Nueva España* (Mexico, 1924), contains an illuminating picture of frontier conquests down to 1584, with able interpretation of the significance of the frontier advance.

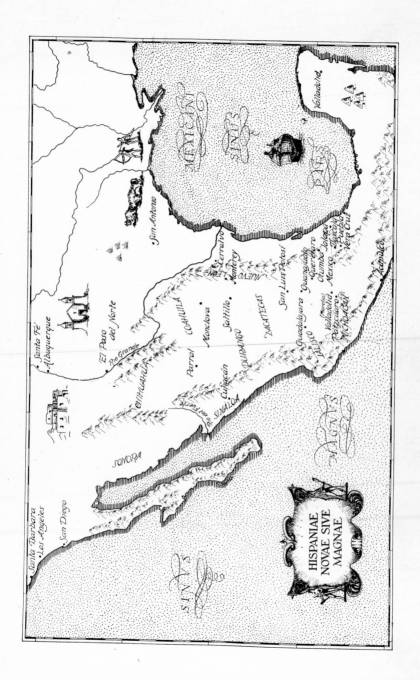

HISPANIAE
NOVAE SIVE
MAGNAE

MAIOR

SINVS

SINVS

MINVS

MAGNVS

SINVS

Valladolid

Santa Barbara
Los Angeles

San Diego

SONORA

Santa Fé
Ubiquerque

El Paso
del Norte

Rio Grande

San Antonio

CHIHUAHUA

Parral

Rio Fuerte

SINALOA

Culiacán

DURANGO

Monclova

Saltillo

ZACATECAS

COAHUILA

N° Cerralvo
Monterey

San Luis Potosí

MUEVO

Guadalajara

MEXICO

Querétaro

Guanajuato

Orumba Jalapa

Morelia

Valladolid

Patzcuaro

MICHOACAN

Mexico

Puebla

Otumba

Orizaba

Vera Cruz

Acapulco

effort, chiefly during the latter part of the eighteenth century.

The west coast was under the control of a military commander, the capital being at Durango in southern Nueva Vizcaya. In the southern coastal region, from Chiametla to Culiacán, the natives early became Christians under Franciscan ministrations. Here local affairs were under four alcaldes mayores, all appointed by the governor at Durango. In the north at Culiacán there was an alcalde mayor appointed by the audiencia of Guadalajara. He ruled over thirty or forty Spanish families and a few Aztec and Tlaxcaltec subsidiary settlers. Above was San Felipe where was kept a garrison of thirty or forty soldiers. Its captain was appointed by the viceroy, but since he also held from the governor of Nueva Vizcaya the title of alcalde mayor, he was usually called the governor of Sinaloa.

One of the most interesting tenants of this post was the burly old Indian fighter, Captain Diego Martínez de Hurdaide, who was in charge from 1600 to 1626. His cleverness as a frontier ruler was evidenced by his ability to retain the good will of the Jesuits and their converts while striking terror into the hearts of savages who resisted civilization. He conquered over twenty "nations" without letting a single soldier fall into the hands of the enemy. But he exhausted his own private fortune and died in debt, rather an unusual performance for a frontier officer in New Spain. Hurdaide, it may be noticed, "had a peculiar way of sending his orders, four seals of wax on a paper without writing forming the token borne by his messenger, who wore it in a reed stuck in the hair. It was understood that any interference with a messenger bearing this credential would be

promptly and terribly avenged, and before long the
seals were respected by even the most distant and hostile
tribes. A bloody knife was also occasionally sent as a
threat of punishment." [1]

In the proselyting labors carried on by the Jesuits with
this militant governor as ally the surrounding tribes
were reduced to Christianity vigorously, if not permanently. Missions were built among the Suaqui and
Tehueco on the Rio Fuerte in 1604. Now and then a
notable scamp of a chief would be admitted to salvation
as a preparation for hanging, in expiation of hostile
acts which not even conversion could render forgettable.
Hurdaide was one of the first to subdue the warlike
Yaqui. In 1610 the fort of Montesclaros was built on
the Fuerte, and campaigns against the Ocaroni, Suaqui
and Yaqui were brought to successful issue by the aid
of thousands of Mayo allies. The fierce Yaqui, enemies
of all subsequent white men, made a treaty of peace with
the Mayo and the Spaniards in the same year. But it was
an unusual thing for the Spaniards to admit natives to
the status of a treaty-making power. In the year 1611
the Tepehuane were also reduced. Missionary work, including military activity, advanced into modern Sonora
among the Mayo in 1613—conquest, revolt and repression alternating, as before, during the succeeding years
of the frontier advance. In 1636 the Jesuits had reached
Ures in the Sonora River Valley, and in 1650 Cucurpe
and Arispe. By 1679 thirty priests were teaching forty
thousand natives. There were six hundred Spanish families in Sinaloa, nearly as many in Sonora, with a still

[1] A. Pérez de Ribas, *Historia de los Triumphos de Nuestra Santa Fé*
(Madrid, 1645), 85-86; H. H. Bancroft, *North Mexican States and
Texas* (*History of the Pacific States*, San Francisco, 1882-1890, X-XI),
I, 209-210.

larger half-breed population at work in mines and on cattle ranges.[1]

Across the Gulf of California on the peninsula in which Cortés and Sebastián Vizcaíno had both failed to make permanent settlements, interest in pearl fishing was perennial. The government tried to found colonies, sending settlers and missionaries under numerous contractors who obtained pearl monopolies; but none of these attempts succeeded because the lucrative quest of pearls did not require actual occupation, the soil was barren and the natives unfriendly. In 1697, after some preliminary surveys, the Jesuits took over the territory as a mission field. They strove valiantly to keep settlers out for the sake of their neophytes, and to erect in isolation a "republic" similar in character to their more notable Paraguayan establishment. They succeeded in holding it with varying fortunes until their expulsion from Spanish America in 1767, on the eve of an expansion destined to be led by the Franciscans.

On the central plateau the new settlements spread up into Chihuahua along the Conchos River and the eastern slope of the Sierra. Jesuits in the west and Franciscans in the east dotted the country with missions. Without trying to follow the tedious thread of narrative history, a conspicuous example of the Indian problem may be given to show the character of frontier life during the first half of the seventeenth century. The Tepehuane of southern Nueva Vizcaya were the dominant group of natives living in Durango about the headwaters of the Rio Nazas. A number of Jesuits were working among them when, in 1616, there broke out, after sev-

[1] Juan Ortiz Zapata, "Relación de las Misiones . . . de la Nueva Vizcaya," *Documentos para la Historia de México* (Mexico, 1853-1857), III, 301 ff.

eral unheeded warnings, one of the most serious revolts against Jesuit control. It was directly due to hostility to the Christian religion. A medicine man who had been converted relapsed and was flogged for his sin. Hotly denouncing the missionaries, he proclaimed that his god demanded their destruction and the expulsion of all their countrymen. By threats of dire calamities against those who refused to follow him and promises of phenomenal rewards for those who did, the wily magician consolidated a following. The revolt was planned for a galaday celebration in the town of Zape, where all the Spaniards would be present. But some of the plotters becoming impatient, several Spanish traders were prematurely murdered. Two hundred men, women and children gathered in terror for self-defense at the hacienda of Atotonilco. Being forced to surrender, all but two of them were massacred. In other near-by places like horrors were perpetrated, ten Jesuits being murdered. The whole countryside was terrified.

Other tribes became disaffected, though some prudently remained loyal to their priestly advisers when the military preparations of the whites showed them the wisdom of this course. At the viceroy's behest troops hurried down from the north. There followed a punitive campaign in which it was discovered that many Negroes, mulattoes and half-breeds were serving with the rebels, a fact revealing discontent among the exploited groups of the district. Besides inflicting a loss of several hundred lives, the insurgents had destroyed enough mineral and agricultural property to set the country back half a century. But, Indian-like, they had not been able to construct or pursue any well-organized plan of campaign and were soon everywhere defeated. They lost one thousand men and many women and children, their fields were laid waste, and their hope in native religion had been dashed. The customary sequel of mutual losses and no gain attended this most serious revolt, which terrified the province for nearly two years. Gradually the Tepehuane were brought back to *pueblo* life and their bonds to their exploiters were sealed anew.[1] During the second half of the century this part of southern Nueva Vizcaya was considered a tierra de paz. The natives submitted to town life and accepted the necessity of exploitation at the hands of missionaries, settlers, miners and officials. It was an uneventful life of peace and subjugation not found on the farther and more exhilarating frontier.

In the Parras region to the eastward there occurred in 1645-1646 a typical instance of secularization of Jesuit missions for the benefit of the white settlers. The Spanish *villa*[2] of Parras laid claim to the irrigation water used by the mission Indians. Though the governor, Alvear, defended the Indian rights until his term expired, he then married into the proud Urdiñola family of first settlers and became himself interested in watering the lands of its estate. The mission Indians, appealing to the audiencia for protection, won their suit; but the Spaniards got the Jesuits expelled from the missions, put these into the hands of the secular clergy, and took the water through secularization of the mission. The secular clergy found itself unable to keep up the Indian

---

[1] Pérez de Ribas, *Historia de los Triumphos de Nuestra Santa Fé*, 302-303, 508-520, 597-628; F. X. Alegre, *Historia de la Compañia de Jesus* (Mexico, 1841-1842), II, 82-92; J. Arlegui, *Crónica de la Provincia de San Francisco de Zacatecas* (Mexico, 1737), 187-200; Bancroft, *North Mexican States,* I, 329.

[2] A *villa* was a municipality of less formal organization than a *ciudad,* but more than that of a *pueblo.*

property without a proper water supply, and the religious work as well as the agricultural fell into decay.[1] This episode was by no means an isolated or extreme illustration of the methods used by the white man to "come into his own" on the Spanish frontier.

In the eastern part of Nueva Vizcaya, where both Jesuits and Franciscans had missions, troubles were conspicuous in 1644 among the Conchos Indians. The missionaries were unable to check raids upon their establishments by the hostile neighboring Toboso, who used guerrilla warfare with all the acumen of the Apache. They were interrupted in their raids only by occasional Spanish flying squadrons and limited only by the small number of farms and tiny settlements which lay within their avenging reach. Throughout 1645 they kept up their fiendish enterprise, hardly checked by small skirmishes and by executions when taken captive. The miners, bent upon their own gain, looked on with indifference. They would neither help the missionaries recover runaways nor try to curb the immoral practices rife in heathendom and repugnant to civilized life, for, here as elsewhere, the same competition for Indian labor was going on. The mines were waiting for ignorant man power to exploit, often without wages for months on end; the lay Spaniards, jealous of church control over Indian labor, did not hesitate to quarrel with the fathers and impute to them the selfish purpose of monopolizing it.

The missionaries were habitually to be found upon the side of the natives whenever conflicts arose between the latter and the civil-military power of the settlers.

[1] Alegre, *Historia de la Compañia de Jesus, II,* 427, 436-437; cf. Bancroft, *North Mexican States,* I, 342.

Yet when savage wrath fell it included missionaries as well as laymen. Since practically all the historians' records are of missionary origin and disclose little of the attitude of the Indians, this fact suggests that the demands of the religious upon the natives were as irksome as those of the laymen. Sometimes, as in the case of the Tepehuane revolt already alluded to, and in the great New Mexican rebellion of 1680, resistance arose from the jealousy of native leaders of religion. Yet there can be little doubt, when the hundreds of cases of the flight of neophytes from the missions are borne in mind, that the Indians saw little distinction between selfish exploitation by lay Spaniards and the more altruistic compulsion of the missions.

The Indian was not prepared for the social transition to sedentary life. In mine, mission or hacienda he was obliged to perform labor which crushed his spirit. If he was faithful, the reward satisfied no deep necessity of his nature, but rather tore him from such spiritual foundations as experience had developed in him. The Spanish system of exploitation was, however, only at rare intervals varied for that of extermination, the method employed generally, though unofficially, by the English. For selfish motives the Spaniards caused the Indians to survive, in such numbers that the modern policy of the Mexican nation has pronounced at last for their moral and intellectual emancipation as the paramount feature of its political program.

Not always was the Spaniard capable of holding his own against savage vengeance. During a great Tarahumara revolt, two thousand rebels were able in 1650 to withstand all day the onslaught of three hundred Spaniards and their allies, and remained in possession of their hill fortress as the attackers withdrew discomfited. After the victory the savages grew in number to six thousand, and continued the warfare for more than a year until some of their own people joined the enemy. During the decade beginning in 1644 most of the Chihuahua missions were obliterated, only to be restored by the Franciscans and the Jesuits. By 1680 the frontier had been pushed northward to Cusihuiriáchic, Janos and Casas Grandes, nearly closing the gap between Nueva Vizcaya and New Mexico. Since 1620 the secular church had combined, in the diocese of Guadiana, the regions of Durango, Chihuahua and New Mexico. This move assumed, but in reality anticipated, the relative stabilization of the frontier.

# CHAPTER III

## PIONEERS OF NEW MEXICO AND FLORIDA

NEW MEXICO, meantime, projecting northward toward the heart of the continent, several hundred miles beyond the early Chihuahua settlements, lay at the utmost fringe of the white man's civilization.[1] Here a handful of Indians, half-breeds and mulattoes, led by a few civilians, missionaries and soldiers, were engaged in a highly dramatic episode in Spain's long effort to subdue and hold a continent. These leaders, too, dreamed of empire and of fabulous wealth, while fate mocked them with a stubborn meager country, peopled with a primitive race, dull and difficult pupils in the arts, though fierce and cunning foes in arms. Dreams and danger are the stuff of romance, but the long-drawn disappointment of New Mexico left little that was romantic in the end. Failing to conquer a continent from that direction, Spain turned to fairer valleys in the east, but, drained by the immense cost of new enterprises, faltered and finally resigned them to the English and the French.

The New Mexican effort was the last notable Spanish expansion before that eighteenth-century defensive thrust which added the northern Pacific Coast. There were

[1] When in 1665 the eight English proprietors received their grant to territory between the parallels thirty-one and thirty-six and "from sea to sea," the Spaniards already had within the area some twenty-five missions serving ninety villages, Santa Fé had a population of a thousand persons, and the province of New Mexico an effective military and civil government. See the map in H. E. Bolton and Mary A. Ross, *The Debatable Land* (Berkeley, 1925), opp. 32.

51

minor activities in the Texan and Gulf areas at the close
of the seventeenth century, and a continuous effort to
hold the Florida-Carolina frontier, but these were forced
reactions to foreign aggression and without the great
compelling lure which beckoned into New Mexico. They
were intended chiefly to hold, by adding new frontier
strips, that which had been already gained—defensive
operations instead of bold strokes for empire.

When the advance was made into New Mexico it was
by no means conceived of as the last step in the great
northward movement. The seventeenth-century governors and missionaries of New Mexico were quite as
willing, even as anxious, to press on in the path of expanding empire as were their swashbuckling predecessors
of the preceding cycle. They stopped where they did for
two cogent reasons: they had exhausted their man power,
and they had come upon a region in which the aspiration for sudden wealth could not be realized. No won-
derful silver mines appeared or fabled treasure stores;
the trade in hides and furs was precarious; the distance
to the real center of the life of the realm, Mexico City,
was not only cruelly long, but hazardous because of the
savage foe. Moreover, the pueblo Indian, as we have
seen, was a rebellious thrall of the Spanish exploitative
system. In the conflict with distance, aridity, poverty
and rebellion, this far-flung frontier presents all the elements of strength and weakness in the early conception
of colonial empire. It was, in that sense, a typical frontier; from its story, sordid or glorious, now presenting
meek men patient in Christian suffering, now vengeful,
contumacious rebels, may be gleaned an impression of
what the process of widening the borders of empire
really meant to its active participants.

During the sixteenth century New Mexico lay yet in the lands of northern mystery. It first dawned on the white man's consciousness during the romantic wanderings of Cabeza de Vaca, who learned of it by hearsay while on his pioneer transcontinental journey after the dismal undoing of the Narváez expedition along the shores of the Gulf of Mexico. Then, as we have seen, the overwrought imagination of the propagandist Friar Marcos of Nice, picturing the Cities of Cíbola with turquoise-studded doors, brought about the spectacular but unhappy quest of Coronado for a new kingdom that should excel in wealth and grandeur the lands conquered by Cortés.

After Coronado's expedition New Mexico was unvisited for a generation or more. Then, in 1581, an expedition explored the wide region between the Pecos River and the pueblos of Ácoma and Zuñi, and it was not long before efforts at occupation began. A host of would-be leaders competed for the opportunity, but not until 1597 was Juan de Oñate the successful contestant. In the next year he took possession and initiated several attempts at further expansion, after which the country settled down to the more prosaic pursuits of the missionaries and the exploitation of the pueblo tribes in the Rio Grande Valley.[1] Before the end of the year Oñate had won the general submission of the pueblos, and the Franciscans who went with him were assigned to missionary posts. The governor himself was chiefly inter-

[1] Authoritative and convenient outlines of the northward movements are in C. E. Chapman, *The Founding of Spanish California* (N. Y., 1916), chaps. ii-iii; C. W. Hackett, *Historical Documents relating to New Mexico* (Wash., 1923-1926), I, 10-19; II, 3-82; J. L. Mecham, *Francisco de Ibarra and Nueva Vizcaya* (Durham, N. C., 1927), *passim;* and L. F. Hill, *José de Escandón and the Founding of Nuevo Santander* (Ohio State Univ., *Studies,* no. 9), *passim.*

ested, as several of his successors continued to be, in plans
of wider empire—in the still-dreamed-of Quivira, the
eastern country sought by Coronado, which would yield
untold treasure, and in the equally mythical easy passage
to the great South Sea.

But there were practical achievements within New
Mexico. Shortly after Oñate's recall in 1608 the villa
of Santa Fé was founded by Governor Peralta, his successor, and the new frontier became one of the "kingdoms" of the viceroyalty. By 1617 the friars had eleven
churches built and professed to have converted fourteen
thousand Indians. The new province was headed by a
governor appointed by the viceroy. Under the viceroy
López Pacheco, duke of Escalona, it was ordered that
the defense of the province should be provided by the
creation of thirty-five encomiendas. The encomenderos
were to receive the tributes from the Indian towns under
their control as a stipend for furnishing men and horses
for military campaigns, all at the instant call of the
governor. Settlers of lower rank were also thus used as
they came in. The hard and almost endless duties of war
consumed much of the energy of the frontiersmen. In
the intervals of peace they engaged in cattle raising,
grain farming, and trading with the Indians of the
pueblos and with the unreduced Apache on their out-
skirts.

In 1621 the missions were organized into a *custodia*,
called San Pablo, of the Franciscan province of El Santo
Evangelio de México. At its head was the *custodio*, who
was presently made commissary of the Inquisition for
the region, the first incumbent being that notable friar
Alonso de Benavides, the earliest historian of the province. As chief of a well-knit organization of friars

with a territorial jurisdiction equal to that of the governor, his influence was really greater than that of the political executive, for he reached the entire converted Indian population through his friars, who were normally of a type superior to the alcaldes and settlers. Many of the latter were half-breeds and mulattoes of low intelligence whose departure from the older regions had been unmourned. When not held close to the friars by self-interest or religious zeal, they were usually of an unruly adventurous spirit, willing partisans of the governor in his traditional conflict with the missionaries.[1]

By 1620 a phase of the frontier situation had developed which was to characterize the whole century. The civil and ecclesiastical officers clashed with regard to the exercise of judicial authority. The governor asserted his right to appoint the petty Indian officials whom the missionaries used in reducing the natives to the Christian polity; the custodio refused to admit the governor's authority to do this and excommunicated him for his interference. The nub of the problem lay in the fact that the missions on the one hand, and the governor on the other, were competing for the opportunity to exploit the unpaid labor of the Indians. The conflict soon took the form of rivalry for the exercise of the full judicial authority. The custodio, under papal bulls and alleged permission by royal decrees, claimed free right to exercise ecclesiastical jurisdiction. This included all cases involving friars, and the usual affairs of life for everyone if they could be construed as arising out of the

[1] The most notable contemporary authorities on the contribution of the Franciscans to the northward movement were I. F. Espinosa, *Crónica Apostólica . . . de Todos los Colegios de Propaganda Fide* (Mexico, 1746), and J. D. Arricivita, *Crónica Seráfica . . . del Colegio de la Santa Cruz de Querétaro* (Mexico, 1792).

obligations created by the sacraments of the church.
Throughout the century the governors steadfastly con-
tested the pretension, and nearly all the troubles which
visited the province rose directly or indirectly from the
struggle.[1]

Lacking the local prestige to effect their will, the
custodios, as commissaries of the Inquisition, used the
powerful court of that institution to hold the governor
in subjection or to secure his removal and punishment.
The power of the commissaries forms a striking, though
incomplete, analogy to the powers and policies of the
French-Canadian bishops, whose corps of seminary
priests gave them great power over the settlers through
the confessional and excommunication,[2] as was generally
true throughout Spanish America. It is of more than
passing interest to find that the Spanish Inquisition,
against whose mystery and relentless severity so many
American writers of history have inveighed, was,
through its Franciscan commissaries, once the most potent
political influence in territory now a part of the American Union. We shall see, as we proceed, how it exerted
its power.[3]

Up to 1630 the province had but one Spanish settlement, the villa of Santa Fé, where lived two hundred
and fifty Spaniards with twice as many half-breeds and

[1] The situation in New Mexico was paralleled in the colonization of
Nuevo León, south of Texas, and roughly in the modern state called
Nuevo León.

[2] The Inquisition in Mexico may be studied in H. C. Lea, *The Inquisition in the Spanish Dependencies* (N. Y., 1908), chap. vi; *Documentos
Inéditos o muy Raros para la Historia de México* (Mexico, 1905-1911),
V and XXVIII; and J. T. Medina, *La Inquisición en México* (Santiago,
1905).

[3] Much in the following pages is drawn from manuscripts translated
by the writer of this volume for a forthcoming part of C. W. Hackett's
publication of the "Bandelier Papers" in *Historical Documents Relating to
New Mexico*, III.

Indian dependents.[1] Radiating from Santa Fé were friars in twenty-five missions serving ninety pueblos and claiming ninety thousand neophytes. But these alleged converts were resentful of the tributes levied on them, sullen toward their exploiters whether lay or clerical, and anxious to resume their old barbarous life. Churchmen and settlers alike kept alive the hope of finding Quivira and Texas, fabulous kingdoms of riches, through which they might open connections with the eastern inland country and the coast of the Gulf of Mexico. Gradually the western part of Texas, home of the Jumanos Indians, became an outlying goal for New Mexican trade. If only a little rich treasure could have been found, the pueblo region would have become at once a new focus of diffusion of Spanish power throughout the great interior region.

In the years 1640-1642 troubles over ecclesiastical jurisdiction caused a revolt which was blamed upon the friars. In its course the governor, Luis de Rosas, was stabbed to death by a half-breed. The tragedy increased the floods of bitterness; the king in Spain remonstrated

[1] Alonso de Benavides, in his *Memorial*, spoke in 1630 of the villa of Santa Fé as the head of the kingdom of New Mexico where the governor resided. The Spaniards numbered, according to his estimate, 250, only about fifty of whom had weapons with which to protect the settlement. Their arquebuses were, however, sufficient to keep the Indians in awe. All the Indians had to pay tribute of a *manta* (thirty-three inches) of cotton cloth and a *fanega* or bushel of corn each year. This meager support was required for the maintenance of the Spanish settlement. There were about 700 Indians in service to the Spaniards and the total population numbered about 1000. Up until the time of the good friar's writing no church existed in this early settlement within the present boundaries of the United States. There was a miserable shack in which religious services were celebrated, and Benavides began to build a church and monastery in 1662. The instruction conducted by the fathers was for the purpose of teaching the Spaniards and Indians to read and write, play musical instruments, sing, and learn the various usages of civilization. Alonso de Benavides, *The Memorial of Fray Alonso de Benavides* (Mrs. Edward E. Ayer, tr., Chicago, 1916), 22-23.

in 1653 against border conditions; and in the following year the viceroy gave the new governor strict, though unavailing, injunctions to preserve the peace. Attempts to get rid of the exploiters began as early as 1650, when the Teguas nation, near the southern part of the province, plotted with the Jemes and Cochití towns and some Apache confederates to exterminate them. This stroke for liberty was sternly repulsed by Governor Concha. Beginning in the 1660's and continuing to the great revolt of 1680, the non-Christian Apache added their hostility to that of the pueblos. On many occasions prior to the latter date, outbreaks were quelled or prevented by rigorous floggings and hangings of rebels. Even so, several of the isolated missions had to be deserted when the fierce Apache, now more formidable as cavalry fighters, raided and destroyed the little communities where they were located.[1]

The governors were likely to be men of little education who had seen service as alcaldes mayores, petty governors or the like. They had usually risen to the military rank of *sargento mayor;* many of them were frontiersmen of long experience, and had acquired small fortunes by barter among the Indian tribes for hides and furs, which they shipped south in the annual caravans known as "the king's wagons." These great freight trains traversed the two thousand miles of hazardous Indian country between Mexico and Santa Fé with nominal regularity after 1629 under command of a "general" with a military escort. One of the governors, Francisco de la Mora, took office in 1633 with the idea of gaining wealth by enlisting the friars to help him

[1] R. E. Twitchell, *The Leading Facts of New Mexican History* (Cedar Rapids, 1911), I, 343-350.

dispose of a large stock of knives which he brought out for barter, persecuting them if they did not consent to further his Indian trade. Soon he began to sow discord by seizing Indian orphans, "like calves and colts," to work on his own farms. He also encouraged the establishment of stock farms on the cornfields of the natives, and forced Spanish soldiers to leave their own small properties to work on his estates. As there seemed to be no curb on his ingenuity at the expense of the Indians, the friars appealed to the "fountain of law and justice" at Mexico City for relief.

In 1659 there came to the province as governor, Bernardo López de Mendizábal, a roistering frontier trader and soldier of wide experience who intended that his term of office should not be unprofitable to himself. He soon set the friars by the ears, not only by his own acts, but by those of his alcaldes mayores. Of these the most notorious was a half-breed, Nicolás de Aguilar, who, it was alleged, had murdered his uncle at Parral in Nueva Vizcaya and fled to the farther frontier to escape justice. He was in charge of the alcaldía which comprised Tajique, Chililí and Senecú, east and southeast of the later Albuquerque. It contained large salt deposits worked by the governor and a prosperous encomendero Diego de Guadalajara, deposits especially valuable since that mineral was indispensable to the patio extraction process used by the silver miners in the vicinity of Parral.

The sycophantic Aguilar—"Attila," the friars dubbed him—was the agent through whom Mendizábal delighted to pester the missionaries. The pair took puerile delight in encouraging the natives in their heathen rites, especially the dances known then and now as the

*Catzinas* [1]—ceremonies to invoke the benign interest of the gods of the crops. Led by medicine men in masks of horrifying aspect, the dances included flagellation and incestuous orgies; of course they were strictly forbidden by the missionaries as demoniacal and superstitious in character. The alcalde mayor, obeying with zest the commands of the governor, insisted that there was no harm here but mere barbarous diversion, and gave the Indians permission to continue the practice. Here was a challenge to be met by no hesitation. At Cuarac Friar Diego de Parraga tried to stop the rites by whipping the dancers. In Isleta Father Salvador Guerra went out to meet his disobedient neophytes with a cross upon his back, a crown of thorns upon his brow and a rope about his neck, lashing his naked flesh as he walked about the town. Thereupon his disciples gave up their celebration, tearfully assuring him that the governor had ordered them to dance. In the town of Chililí, it was averred, the alcalde threatened the natives with from fifty to one hundred lashes if they refused. One winter when the snow was deep they went up to the porch roof of the very church in Chililí, and while the scandalized friar looked on, the alcalde pretended to believe that his reverence had ordered them to do the dance there.

Nettled by the opposition of the friars, the alcalde forbade the Indians to assist them in the menial service of the convents, and threatened them with lashes if they should disobey. As a result, poor Father Juan Ramírez, eighty years old, had to totter out into the snow to gather fagots to keep from freezing at Christmas time. Father Perraga himself had to cook the meals at Chililí because

[1] J. W. Fewkes, "The Group of Tusayan Ceremonials Called Katcinas," Bureau of Am. Ethnology, *Fifteenth Ann. Rep.* [1893-1894], 251-313.

he could get no help. When the Indians of Cuarac went to Jumanos at the request of the friars to sing high mass on the patron saint's day, they were given fifty lashes each by Aguilar for going into enemy country. He prevented the use of an interpreter to translate the service of the mass at Abo, thus impeding the exercise of the sacred cult. For these sins, committed about 1660, Aguilar was arrested by the commissary and sent to the Inquisition in Mexico, though he claimed the status of a pious Christian. Among his literary or religious effects when he was incarcerated were a small catechism in two languages, a very small book of instructions for examining the conscience, a bag of reliquaries containing a memorandum of a restitution to be made, a copy of the four Gospels, a rosary with a little silver cross and a little worn book of "exercises and considerations." [1]

Aguilar's defense is of chief interest for its intimate picture of seventeenth-century life in New Mexico. He testified that he believed that false witness had been brought against him by his enemies, among them Father Parraga, whom he had accused of libertinage, and Father Freitas, who had once drawn a pistol on him in an altercation. Many of the friars, he said, were immoral and cruel to the Indians. In Moqui they had encouraged flagellations of Indian *penitentes*. They hindered him in his incessant effort to prevent Apache inroads, when these

---

[1] His personal appearance when placed in the dungeons is revealed by the court inventory of his effects. He wore a *faruadina* or short cloak of buff and black wool decorated with fine points of black, a white jacket dotted with blue wool, a scarf of cotton drawn work, and a raincloak of deerskin. In his box were several woolen jackets bedecked with colored spots, some fine shirts, some common ones of Rouen linen, a mixed assortment of socks, a pair of cordovan shoes, a cake of soap, and a little lavender wrapped in an old black rag, a leather cover for mustaches, herbs to cure mountain spotted fever and to heal wounds, an old black hat, and a quantity of bedding.

Indians, coming from Siete Rios to trade, stole into the woods near Tajique and carried off Christian captives. They would tie them to huge burning fagots and dance about them, cutting off slices of flesh which they cooked and ate while their victims were perishing. It was to prevent such acts that he had forbidden his charges to go to the woods for fuel. For this, Friar Fernando de Velasco had upbraided him, and in a quarrel tried to kill him with a knife. Though the glib alcalde never admitted an accusation nor retracted a charge, he was found guilty of scandalous language and lukewarmness in the faith, and was banished for ten years.

Mendizábal himself was also haled before the inquisitors, charged with practising such Jewish rites as putting on clean clothes on Fridays after having his feet bathed. He was a descendant of Juan Núñez de León, who had been convicted of Judaism, and his acts, it was alleged, showed that he despised the Christian religion, hated the friars, and said scandalous and heretical things about the privileges of the church. The evidence at his trial affords a luminous picture of the society he tried to rule. His hostility to the missionaries, it was testified, was manifest from the outset. When he arrived, the friar of one of the towns on his route to Santa Fé sallied forth to meet him with the formal manifestations of hospitality in vogue at the time; he went to the gate of the cemetery on the edge of the town with a tall cross, glad ringing of the church bells and gala music, only to be reproached by the object of these honors because he had not gone out to the more respectful distance of two leagues to render his homage. Reaching Santa Fé, the governor refused the request of several friars to allow them to use Indian singers for the mass, though the king's order permitted it. He also denied them the exercise of the ecclesiastical jurisdiction in spite of the king's declaration and the apostolic bulls. "There is no way," wrote Father Miguel Sanchristian at Isleta in 1660, "whereby to mitigate the aggressions of this governor. I cannot conquer him with patience. He does not investigate the Spaniards or Indians, but only the friars. . . ." This was apropos of the governor's general inspection of the province, during which he visited many of the towns, sitting himself down in the open plaza of each at a table with pen in hand, seeking information concerning the misdeeds of the friars. The effect on the Indian population was characterized by Father Francisco de Salazar of Senecú when he declared, "the Indians are totally lost, without faith and without devotion to the church or respect for its ministers, nor do they obey them." The friars threatened to abandon the province.

The governor required that no alcalde or other judge should punish the Indians for any misdeed whatsoever. This he especially enjoined in Las Salinas, even against the prevalent sin of adultery, in which the missionaries averred that many of the Indians habitually lived, rejecting the Christian marriage ceremony.[1] It gave the governor infinite delight when he found on his tour of inspection that many of the friars were guilty of moral lapses. Himself a notorious roué, his official appointees were of his own ilk. One of them, Diego Romero, first an alcalde and then an encomendero, was also tried by the Inquisition. He had created a scandal in the province by paying a trading visit to the Apache, where, like his father before him, he married an Apache maiden by the

---

[1] The Indians practised a form of polygamy, which, of course, the friars considered adultery.

heathen rites so that he might leave a son among them to be their chief; this flouting of ecclesiastical precepts endeared Romero to the governor. But the guilt, as has been hinted, was not all on one side. The governor's incriminations of the friars indicate that the atmosphere of the entire province was tainted with the offenses of people in every rank and calling.

Mendizábal justified his hostility to the friars on the ground that they controlled the settlers and frequently incited them to rebel against both the governor and the king. They had shot at Governor Argüello, they had arrested Governor Peralta, they killed Governor Rosas, "and they would have done the same with me but for the punishment meted out." Possessing no legal training, Mendizábal confessed that he was continually in trouble over points of law, for there was not a *letrado* or *asesor* in the entire province to advise him. Concerning the furor over the Catzinas dances, Mendizábal was frivolous if not contumacious. He declared that when the Indians came out to sing in this dance they said nothing but "Hoo, hoo, hoo; and these thieves of friars call that superstition!" As a matter of fact, the dance did embody the chief features of the indigenous cult; its celebration was a symptom of resistance to the Christian religion and the Spanish domination; and the governor, whatever his attitude toward the friars, should have been too intelligent to permit it.

Evidence of his somewhat more tangible culpability was brought forth to show that the governor caught Apache and sold them as slaves to the miners in Parral. Seventy such he sent down at one time. This traffic, forbidden under penalty of loss of office and estates, the friars justly characterized as the cause of the mortal hatred engendered against the Spaniards among these warlike people, and it explains their alliance later with the pueblo Indians to exterminate the odious exploiters. Slave-catching expeditions, indeed, menaced the safety of the New Mexican establishments, as when, in 1659, forty Spaniards and eight hundred Christian Indians went out at the behest of Mendizábal, leaving their homes and farms without proper protection, and inviting reprisals at a later time.

No less reprehensible was the governor's exploitation of the Christian Indians. When he began his term, he compelled native carpenters to make him nine wagons for his trading business; he made others knit for him six hundred pairs of socks, which he sold in the province. From convents and Spanish farms he seized two hundred head of cattle for his own freighting uses. To load his wagons he compelled the Indians to carry salt on their shoulders a distance of twenty-five leagues to the place of departure of the train, "with no recompense save violence and oppression"; and he forced many of them to follow his trains as teamsters and shepherds. When they reached Parral the freight, the cattle and wagons were all sold, the Indians being left to make their way home as best they could. To hold his monopoly Mendizábal prevented other traders from coming in, or detained them after they arrived, a course which injured the missions, for they needed to sell a few cattle in order to purchase ornaments and musical instruments. Mendizábal on his part claimed that the friars were trading in excess of their actual needs; that the missions each had some seventy servitors who were kept weaving cloth to sell in other provinces.

Indeed, far from humble before the inquisitors, Men-

dizábal belabored his enemies with lusty blows, laying
bare aspects of frontier life which the friars had dis-
creetly omitted in the statement of their case. A principal object of his spleen was his predecessor Juan Manso,
who had remained in the province for some time in the
capacity of *alguacil mayor* of the Inquisition. Manso, it
seems, had had a liaison with a married woman and had
induced Father Sanchristian to conceal his crime. When
the conscience-smitten ex-governor became the prey of
fears and bad dreams, the friar gave him a morsel of
the Holy Sacrament to wear as a talisman about his
neck. Just at the time Mendizábal first reached New
Mexico, Friar Sanchristian, rendered insane by fear and
remorse, hanged himself in the convent at Jemes with
the cord of his habit. It would seem that to some of
these remote adventurers the small voice of conscience
was still articulate, though most of those who were
brought to testify before the Inquisition maintained a
*sang froid* which betokened a waning of the power of
the Holy Office to terrorize.

The trial of the lusty and unrepentant Mendizábal
dragged on until March, 1664, by which time he had
fallen very ill. He died in the dungeons in the ensuing
September, but his wife was held in the prison until the
following year. The costs of the suit, over twelve hundred pesos, were paid out of his estate; but in 1671, six
years after his death, he was found innocent and his
bones were reinterred in consecrated soil. His old enemy,
the commissary Posadas, remained in New Mexico wag-
ing chronic warfare against the succeeding governor,
Diego de Peñalosa. This man, who had gone out to replace Mendizábal at the request of the friars, served in
office about two years when he was arrested in New

Mexico and sent to the capital under a guard paid from his own confiscated property.[1] He was possibly the most arrant rascal in the annals of New Mexico. His pretended discoveries, his banishment by the Inquisition and his subsequent attempts to enlist English or French aid in designs upon the Spanish silver provinces have been exposed by historians. He may serve us here as an interesting type of frontier governor.

In June, 1665, he was tried for having usurped the jurisdiction of the Holy Office, extorting testimony from witnesses who had appeared before it, and for swearing at that august court *con petulancia y soberbia*. He had earned the hatred of Mendizábal by trying to steal the effects of the latter after his arrest; hence Mendizábal's wife was very willing to testify that Peñalosa had professed to be superior to the Inquisition, the court of the Crusada and even the audiencia. He had gone so far as to arrest a criminal in a church, violating the right of asylum. When Posadas, the commissary, retaliated by placing an embargo on some goods which Peñalosa was shipping to Parral and excommunicated him, the governor clapped the commissary into prison. To the friars this was unendurable. They began to consume the Host in preparation for departure from the province; but after a secret conference with some of them, Peñalosa set the commissary free.

The governors of New Mexico, it appears from the testimony in this case, were habitually negligent in their

---

[1] Earlier accounts of his having gone to the south to solicit funds and permission to make the conquest of Quivira appear to be in error, though his interest in that fabulous region is unquestioned. The conflict between the Franciscans and Governors Mendizábal and Peñalosa is told in C. W. Hackett, "New Light on Don Diego de Peñalosa; Proof that he never made an Expedition from Santa Fé to Quivira," *Miss. Valley Hist. Rev.*, VI, 313-335.

respect for religion. One of them once seized the Holy
Sacrament, and taking it to his "palace," there celebrated
Holy Week with it. Another carried the Host about with
him in a silver snuffbox in his saddlebags. When Peñalosa made an expedition to Moqui, he entered the church
at Santa Fé with his hat on and partook of the Sacrament with clanking spurs at the very altar.

He was not only contumacious and sacrilegious, but
had also a highly developed acquisitive bump. After
trying to wheedle Mendizábal's property away from his
widow, he placed the encomiendas of two other men
arrested by the Inquisition under *escuderos* or government agents chosen from his own dependents, all this
causing the commissary the most jealous heartburnings.
Toward the settlers of lesser degree who respected the
church, the governor maintained an attitude of persecution. Those who did not have encomiendas were
conscripted for Indian campaigns oftener than those
who did; the less important persons were kept in recurrent service with respite so scant that they often could
not provide themselves horses and had to serve on foot.
Failure to obey a summons was punishable by banishment, confiscation of goods, or even loss of life. On the
other hand, many of the residents of Santa Fé, though
they had two, three, five or seven encomiendas, managed
to avoid service through influence with the governor.
Thus the lower stratum of colonists was exploited by
the upper, and there was no relief from oppression.

Peñalosa was finally sentenced in February, 1668,
after more than two years of trial. Besides being openly
reprimanded, he had to march in public as a penitent
with a candle in his hand, abjure his heresies and pay
a fine of five hundred pesos. More serious from his point

of view, he was denied the power to hold political or military office and was exiled forever from New Spain and the West Indies. Since he was already unwelcome in Peru, this sentence meant a change in his entire mode of life and method of seeking profit or adventure. It is hardly surprising that under the circumstances he should seek an outlet for ambition under the flags of the enemies of his country.[1]

Besides arraigning governors the Inquisition had plenty to do with the common folk. Take, for example, a case of unauthorized supernaturalism. A certain German trader, Bernardo Grüber by name, who went into New Mexico from Sonora with a pack train of merchandise in 1668, was arrested for sorcery. It appears that one day the alcalde mayor of Las Salinas was surprised to see his ten-year-old son demonstrating with a great sliver of wood that he was impervious to wounds. The good alcalde promptly reported this witchcraft to the friars, who set upon Grüber as an alien and a sorcerer. He had, it was found, gone into the choir in the church when mass was being sung and offered the boys some scraps of paper bearing cabalistic characters and crosses. He declared he did this in imitation of a custom he had learned in Germany; that he who ate such paper as the first mass of the Nativity was being sung became so potent that for twenty-four hours no weapon could harm him. Grüber was imprisoned, but managed to escape; the

[1] J. G. Shea, *The Expedition of Don Diego Dionisio de Peñalosa, Governor of New Mexico, from Santa Fé to the River Mischipi and Quivira in 1662* (N. Y., 1882); C. Fernández Duro, *Don Diego de Peñalosa y su Descubrimiento del Reino de Quivira: Informe presentado á la Real Academia de la Historia* (Madrid, 1882); Medina, *La Inquisición en México*; Hackett, "New Light on Don Diego de Peñalosa;" Pierre Margry, ed., *Découvertes et Établissements des Français dans l'Ouest et dans le Sud de l'Amerique Septentrionale* (Paris, 1879).

thrifty alcalde consoled himself by seizing over forty of the trader's mules and horses. There were numerous other trials for more worldly offenses, especially bigamy, for it was then, as now, a low-caste New Mexican practice to leave one's encumbering mate behind when faring forth to new fields. There was a considerable traffic in charms, albeit they did not always work.

It was not long before the great Indian revolt of 1680 began brewing. Probably the seizure and sale of Apache as slaves had a large part in rousing the nomadic tribes to coöperation with the rebellious pueblo Indians. By 1672 Apache raids on the towns and the murder of friars began. In stern reprisal for hostile acts in 1675 several natives were hanged, nearly fifty whipped and a large number imprisoned. The natives, however, had a numerical superiority too great for the faction-torn Spanish establishments. In 1676 the crisis was seen to be near and help was called for from Mexico; but the train left there tardily in 1679 and reached the frontier too late to be of aid.

The devastating revolt, led by Popé, a Tewa Indian who managed his campaign from Taos in the extreme north, was inspired by a long succession of abuses; but there can be little doubt that chief among them was the repression of native religious rites, such as the Catzinas dances. The uprising had been planned with great secrecy in the underground *estufas* or council chambers. There, dropping one by one down their rough ladders, the braves gathered around their council fires, which lit their sullen faces as they sat in a tawny circle plotting the resumption of their old cult and a bloody vengeance on their masters. Though the design was prematurely discovered, the blow fell on the Spaniards with blasting fury. Four hundred of them were killed and all the rest, numbering about two thousand, were driven out. The fugitives retired nearly to the southern limits of the present state of New Mexico to pass the winter near the site of the later town of Las Cruces.[1] El Paso del Norte (now Ciudad Juárez) was built by them in 1682; and from that point operations for rewinning the lost kingdom were carried on, more for the sake of Spanish pride than for any gain to be obtained. Once more the Indians, left to their own devices, were unable to maintain a cohesive society, and in 1696, after strenuous campaigns conducted by three successive governors, fell completely under the power of the frontiersmen and missionaries.

On the eastern side of the country expansion was undertaken as a measure against foreign aggression—foreign arms and, as far as the English were concerned, foreign heresy. The government at Mexico did not forget that Florida was Spanish, but it realized that it was so, as yet, only on the map. Ponce de León, Narváez, and Soto, as we have seen, had traversed its shore line, but in the middle of the sixteenth century throughout the peninsula and westward to the Mississippi no post or settlement flew a European flag. It was well realized that, if neglect continued, rival empires would not overlook their opportunities.

No servant of the crown excelled in imperialistic zeal the second viceroy, the first Luis de Velasco (1550-1564). His predecessor, Antonio de Mendoza, in the fifteen years of his incumbency had lost active interest

[1] Twitchell, *Leading Facts*, I, 354-366. The fighting began August 10, 1680.

in the region after Soto's failure and the king's orders to desist from its conquest; but Velasco in 1559-1561 made the occupation of Florida his most earnest undertaking, ill-starred though it turned out to be. When royal assent was given he chose for this enterprise his old friend Luna y Arellano, who had been with Coronado in New Mexico. While this leader was breasting through the eastern wilderness Velasco wrote him nineteen letters which have been preserved and which reveal the care for every detail and the capable and continuous foresight which the administration, at least in many cases, gave to such expeditions. After receiving news of the critical disaster—the loss of nearly all the ships and supplies in a hurricane at Polonza while the forces were ashore—the viceroy tried still to hearten his stricken friend: "You may be sure that the principal thing in which I shall busy myself will be in succoring you and your army in all that I can and with all I possess." [1]

Throughout this trying episode, which so unhappily resembled many others in the long expansive drive of Spain, Velasco gave good counsel concerning the treatment of the Indians and the management of the soldiers, suggesting adroitly that Luna might himself compose needless strife by suavity where rigor of discipline had not availed; but he backed the leader by admonitions to the friars and captains to do their duty. When mutinies came by reason of hardships and failure, he wrote for their benefit:

. . . As it is not a new thing with armies that there should occur shortage of provisions, misfortunes, and

[1] H. I. Priestley, ed., *The Luna Papers* (Fla. State Hist. Soc., *Publs.*, VIII), I, 67-69.

failures, so we need not marvel that such a thing has happened to your camp, nor need we despair because of it of achieving through the help of Our Lord the desired end, by which His Divine Majesty will be greatly served, as will also the king our lord; and you and all those captains and good and honorable soldiers will gain great honor by doing what good and faithful soldiers ought. . . . For after the rough and stormy weather usually come the mild and favoring winds.[1]

Yet when complete failure was evident Velasco, pressed by the Dominican and military enemies of Luna, felt obliged to order his removal. His letters, raising for a moment the curtain of oblivion, give us a glimpse of the grueling hardship which beset such expeditions, enterprises which we can now in comfortable libraries trace so easily on a map.

When at last the renowned Pedro Menéndez de Avilés planted the cross and the lions of Castile on the Floridian shore in 1565, his little post of San Agustín (the modern St. Augustine) brought to consummation a long series of endeavors, hitherto in vain, to fix the power of Spain on the area Estevan Gómez had spurned. Given a little more man power, a more inviting shore, a closer contact with the viceroyalty and a little more strength, the story of Spain's "window on the Atlantic" would have made North American history vastly different. Possibly the "oldest town within the United States" might not have become merely that; even as it was, this historic citadel of our southern peninsula stirs the imagination.

Always a citadel and little else, it possessed none of the glamour of the silver country. It interests us here as a little frontier community. We may say in the beginning that this most ancient city of our modern Black Belt

[1] Priestley, *The Luna Papers*, I, 185.

owed much to the labor of Negro slaves whom the Spaniards employed to establish their stronghold. Negro slaves
of the Spanish king were sent to Florida in 1581, and
a small party of them was engaged for two years in
making wooden platforms for the artillery of the fort
at old San Agustín. Black hands set up the first smith's
forge and there made needed repairs, while two of the
best Negroes were sent to Santa Elena to help the soldiers
saw out boards to be used for covering the fort there.
The soldiers, being free and white, received wages for
their work; but for the Negroes it was only needful to
see that they were provided with bread and meat and
wine. Nearly a dozen black slaves were used in these fortifications, in building the church at San Agustín, putting up dwellings and clearing away the forests for
planting crops. Some Negroes, possibly the earliest importations, remained in the province for forty years serving the white man's needs; at the end of that time they
were reported as having died, and a request was sent to
Spain for a dozen more men together with three or four
Negro women.

At the beginning of the seventeenth century the strong
presidio of San Agustín could boast two hundred and
fifty well-trained soldiers. A large number of them had
brought their families with them, so that they were hard
pressed for sustenance, even though they eked out their
scanty wages and rations with the grain they raised. But
their industry was reaping its reward; slowly the forest
gave way before their axes, the water holes were drained
and the mosquito pest, in consequence, was allayed. One
by one new homes were started, and on every side was
felt the breath of community life.

Yet life on the Spanish frontier was seldom smooth

and easy, and there was much here, as elsewhere, to discourage the pioneers. For example, there was the overbearing manner of the king's treasurers, whose traditional *hauteur*, added to the heavy burdens which the New World Spaniards everywhere bore, was especially irritating. "If you could devise some remedy for this," wrote the governor to the king, "all would be well." [1] Then in 1599 came the fire that partially destroyed the settlement; several homes were consumed and the church as well, causing Fray Blas de Montes, the missionary in charge, to take refuge in the king's hospital, which escaped the flames.

Periodically the near-by vassal Indian chiefs came in for a visit along with their retainers, sometimes as many as five hundred at once. The Spanish received them as best they could, tricked them out in the garb of civilization and sent them back to their people, as the record says of the spring powwow, "very happy and edified with the religious services and the processions of Holy Week." This cajolery was hardly sufficient, however, for there was an almost continuous state of warfare, punctuated by more presents to smug chiefs and imploring demands upon the king for more adequate means of defense against native treachery. As a matter of fact, this Atlantic colony had perhaps the fiercest Indian fighting of the whole frontier. The Franciscan missionaries quite generally failed to bring the savages within the fold of the true religion. In the northernmost province, Guale (a part of present Georgia), six of the friars who replaced the earlier Jesuits were done to death in 1597 as a reward for their ministrations, one of them, said their

[1] A. M. Brooks, *The Unwritten History of Old St. Augustine* (St. Augustine, 1909), 66.

assassins, "because he was artful and took away their enchantment or witchcraft, and would not allow them to have more than one wife." [1]

Indians, mosquitoes, fire and tax collectors were not the only plagues. Now and then there were pirates, though these did not much disturb the common folk. The governor dealt with them in accordance with the Menéndez tradition. In 1607 more than ten French and English pirates were captured, some of whom were baptized and all of whom were hanged. The whole city turned out to see them buried, but many saw the corpses lowered whose own conduct could not have borne a searching scrutiny. The governor wrote that the freebooters "are so many that they keep me in great anxiety . . . but the people shelter them and allow them to come and go at will." [2] This was, of course, only a popular counterbalance to the prying efficiency of the king's trade system. Throughout the seventeenth century there were frequent visits from these gentry, for this was the open century for Caribbean buccaneers, that pest of sea flies created, for the most part, by Spain's absurd colonial mercantile policy.[3]

The colonial government had problems in plenty, the morals of the settlers, among other things, requiring attention. In 1635 the monarch sent a new governor to San Agustín "to improve the conduct and manners of the people." Street processions were held for the expiation of the sins of the community, and the king threatened that, if need be, he would punish his vassals severely for their iniquities. Five years later the commissaries of

[1] Brooks, *Old St. Augustine*, 28-29, 41.
[2] Brooks, 74.
[3] Brooks, 102-106.

the Inquisition visited San Agustín, with what improvement of popular morals we do not know; apparently the most important fruit of their visitation was a decision as to the proper order to be observed in outdoor processions.

The truth is that there were never enough soldiers, settlers or missionaries, for the area Spain had seized was too great for her resources. San Agustín was an illustration of this weakness in all respects. Yet it had to bear attack as frequently as almost any of Spain's citadels. First of all came the Huguenot Dominique de Gourgues in 1568; then "El Draco," Drake the terrible, in 1586; later there were Governor Moore of South Carolina in 1702, Oglethorpe in 1732-1740, and, finally, all the incidents of the English seizure in 1763 and the retrocession two decades later. With all its weakness, San Agustín had justified its existence for more than two hundred years.

The town itself was three quarters of a mile long by half a mile wide, not counting the Indian villages outside its walls. It was built on a little bay at the foot of a wooded hill, with the four well-shaded streets placed at right angles in the traditional fashion legally prescribed for all Spanish-American towns. The well-built houses, three or four churches, fort, hospital and monastery, all gave indication of a definite plan of permanent occupation.[1] The best part was on the north side, in the immediate vicinity of the fort called by the English St. John's, around which was a ditch fringed with a *chevaux de frise* of "Spanish bayonets." The record pictures "a

[1] Outside the walls in some places were cultivated fields, but such agriculture was insufficient for the support of the garrison and many supplies had to be brought from Cuba.

square building of soft stone, with whole bastions, a rampart twenty feet high, with a parapet nine feet high, and it is casemated. The town is fortified with bastions and with cannon." [1]

The traditional *plaza mayor*, as characteristic of all Spanish towns as was the green of the New England villages, closely obeyed the laws made in the sixteenth century by being set facing the harbor. On one side of it was the spacious palace of the governor with its high windows, front balcony and galleries on the sides. At the back the watch tower commanded the harbor, with its lighthouse on Anastasia Island and its breeze-swept marshes. The houses were commonly built of "free stone," having two rooms on each of two stories and spacious balconies and windows. The entries were usually protected by porticoes with stone arches, and grapevines with excellent fruit grew on arbors before each door. The roofs were flat in conformity with universal Spanish style; the window-gratings projected into the streets sixteen or eighteen inches. On the west side of the houses the windows were quite small; the north sides had none, but here were placed galleries, with double walls from six to eight feet apart, within whose cool recesses were put the cellars and pantries. In their gardens the first inhabitants had planted the flowers and fruits of the homeland—fig trees, guavas, plantains, pomegranates, lemons, limes, citrons, shaddock, bergamot. The mandarin orange vied with that of Seville, while the familiar pot herbs were sturdy enough to survive cold weather. But the temperature rarely sank too low for comfort. There were no chimneys or fireplaces; for the

[1] G. R. Fairbanks, *The History and Antiquities of the City of St. Augustine, Florida* (N. Y., 1858), 160.

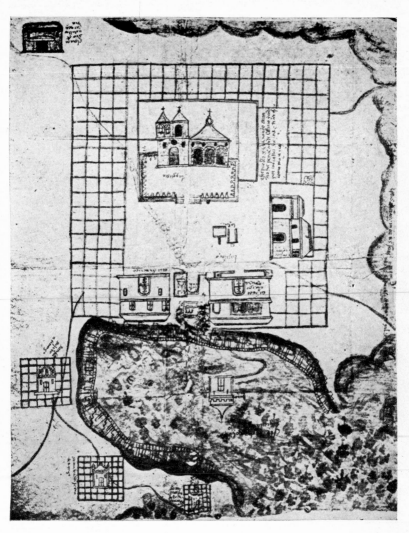

*A Specimen Town Plan in New Spain,
centering in the church gate.*

occasional cold days the people used stone braziers filled with charcoal.

When the English came in 1763 there were a number of centenarians among the departing dons, their many years being considered ample proof of the salubrity of the Florida climate, an advantage which has not gone unmentioned in our own day. The Spaniards, on departing, left as many as nine hundred houses, but those of the suburbs, being of wood, soon fell into ruins. The population, half of it comprising the military establishment, numbered about five thousand at the time of the evacuation. Those who remained were of all colors, white, black and mulatto, with a generous sprinkling of Indians.

When the fortunes of war brought Florida again under Spanish control, the English in turn generally left during 1784. For one generation the Spanish colors flew once more over the fortress; but the centuries-long strain of colonial competition had left no power to extend the province, or even to rehabilitate the ancient citadel.[1] To the north, meantime, the restless inhabitants of the newly established republic of the United States were beginning to push into the old Southeast as well as into the Ohio and Mississippi valleys. The political events, from 1812 on, which presaged American occupation of this ancient Spanish frontier, need not be retold here. In 1817, a year before the famous Florida exploits of Andrew Jackson, which demonstrated the sad decrepitude of the once important guardian fortress of the Bahama Channel, an English gentleman visited

---

[1] For a description of conditions along the northeastern border of Florida under the second Spanish occupation, see Caroline Mays Brevard, *A History of Florida* (Deland, 1924-1925), I, chap. i.

San Agustín and left a record of his impressions of the populace during playtime:

> I had arrived at the season of general relaxation, on the eve of the Carnival, which is celebrated with much gayety in all Catholic countries. Masks, dominoes, harlequins, punchinellos, and a great variety of grotesque disguises, on horseback, in cars, gigs, and on foot, paraded the streets with guitars, violins, and other instruments; and in the evenings, the houses were open to receive masks, and balls were given in every direction. . . .

The visitor found a variegated little community ready for this festive season. The governor, the judge, the treasurer and the notary, together with a detachment of the Royal Regiment of Cuba and some black troops, sustained the dignity of civil government, while a Franciscan friar acting as the *padre*, with the military chaplain and his assistant, wielded the authority of the church. At the other end of the scale were about thirty hunting warriors of the Seminole who had come with their greasy consorts to sell their furs to the traders and artisans of the town. "The whole of this society," gratefully wrote the traveler,

> is extremely courteous to strangers. . . . The women are deservedly celebrated for their charms; their lovely black eyes have a vast deal of expression; their complexions a clear brunette; much attention is paid to the arrangement of their hair; at most they are always well dressed in black silk *basquinas* (petticoats) with the little *mantilla* (black lace veil) over their heads; the men in their military costumes; good order and temperance are their characteristic virtues; but the vice of gambling too often profanes their social haunts, from which even the fair sex are not excluded.

Dancing formed one of their most common amuse-

ments. . . . The posey dance . . . was introduced in
the following manner. The females of the family erect
in a room of their house a neat little arbor dressed with
pots and garlands of flowers and lit up brightly with
candles. . . . The lady who has prepared it selects a
partner from among her visitors, and in token of her
preference honors him with a bouquet of flowers. The
gentleman who receives it becomes then, for the nonce,
King of the ball, and leads out the fair donor as queen
of the dance; the others take partners, and the ball is
thus inaugurated, and may continue several successive
evenings. . . . These assemblies were always informal,
and frequented by all classes, all meeting on a level;
but were conducted with the utmost polite decorum, for
which the Spanish character is so distinguished.[1]

This picture of social relaxation might have been
given, with variation in local color, for any time and
place under the Spanish flag during the colonial epoch.
It is especially interesting to the readers of this volume,
however, as an element in the prologue of "a history
of American life," a picture of a civilization largely supplanted by the followers of General Jackson.

There was comparatively little permanent expansion
from San Agustín. When the English began to work into
the lands of the Indians in those parts of West Florida
which finally became Georgia and Alabama, the Spanish,
in order to combat these efforts, undertook missions
among the Apalachee Indians and built a fort at San
Luis; and soon evangelization was carried to the Creeks
in Georgia. But the Apalachee missions had to be abandoned after an Indian revolt, in 1647, against the uniform system of tributes and personal service which the
Spaniards everywhere imposed.

Along the Atlantic seaboard missions and presidios

[1] Fairbanks, *City of St. Augustine*, 176-183.

had been strewn from St. Mary's River northward to Port Royal in present South Carolina, but in 1587 English aggressions had forced the line back to Santa Catalina, near the Savannah, where, after long occupation, the Spaniards held out until ten years after the Treaty of Madrid (1670) had acknowledged English sovereignty beyond the river. By 1686 Florida had been pressed back to the St. Mary's River, and in Queen Anne's War the retreat reached the St. John's, while, in the interior, Spanish missions in operation for seventy years in the Tallahassee region were destroyed by Carolina frontiersmen. In 1721 the English advanced to the mouth of the Altamaha on the Atlantic. Spanish protest merely provoked further expansion; in 1733 appeared Oglethorpe and his buffer colony of Georgia. Here developed a "neutral ground," like that of 1745 between the French and Spanish in Texas, and that between the French and English in Maine; but the aggressive English frontiersmen paid little respect to their king's command to observe the Altamaha line. Until the English cession after the Seven Years' War, however, San Agustín and, on the Gulf, Pensacola, founded in 1698, stood against the rivals along the northeastern frontier. The line at the St. Mary's River was reëstablished in 1783.[1]

We have surveyed the far-flung frontier of New Spain at its extremities, which fell within the present bounds of the United States; it is now necessary only to glance at the central border. The Monclova settlement in the eastern part of the present Coahuila had been abandoned about the end of the preceding cycle, and for nearly a hundred years Cerralvo was the post nearest the Rio

[1] H. E. Bolton, *Arredondo's Historical Proof of Spain's Title to Georgia* (Berkeley, 1925), 6-110.

Grande. After 1625 Nuevo León was held for the defense of the Gulf Coast against possible English and French intrusions in the Caribbean area, and attempts were made, though vainly, to consolidate the coast occupation with that of Florida, as a part of the policy to retrieve the Atlantic Coast. The defense of the territory against marauding bands led to the planting of missions in Coahuila, which was incorporated as an alcaldía mayor of the kingdom of Nueva Vizcaya. Monclova was at last permanently occupied in 1675, and here the Franciscans of La Cruz at Querétaro carried on evangelization. But slight progress, in the face of Indian enemies, was made toward the north in the Gulf area.

When the La Salle adventure,[1] combined with general hostility on the part of the maritime powers, threatened the West Indies and the Mississippi Valley, the Spaniards determined to oust the French from the Great River which their own enterprise had discovered. Movements overland led to a settlement on the Neches River in Texas in 1690, which had shortly to be abandoned. As a representative of a Spanish frontier town some years later, one might consider San Antonio, in Texas, at first a combination of the military and ecclesiastical types, and then a villa in 1731. In that same year five missions were established in the vicinity, beside that of San Xavier de Náxera already nine years old. The cathedral, built in 1734, was the center of the town not only socially but geographically, for by the city charter each boundary was to be three miles distant from its cupola. The city

[1] Robert Cavelier de la Salle in 1684, in an unsuccessful sea voyage in search of the mouth of the Mississippi, had landed on the shore of Matagorda Bay. This little company of disappointed Frenchmen stayed about three years when their leader was murdered and the enterprise came to an end.

stands today vibrantly American; yet in its plazas, missions, monuments and its characteristic architecture it evokes from the distant past memories of old New Spain.[1]

Subjects of His Catholic Majesty on this actual fringe of outposts were concerned with holding territory and preventing aggressions whenever possible, whether by Indians or by Europeans. Missions, farms, and mines absorbed the energies of the pioneers who were defended by detachments of soldiers from presidios when they could be spared; but, as elsewhere, chief place among the agencies for holding the Indians under Spanish influence must be conceded to the mission organization.

[1] I. J. Cox, "The Founding of the First Texan Municipality," Texas State Hist. Assoc., *Quar.*, II, 217-226.

/

# CHAPTER IV

## ECONOMIC LIFE IN NEW SPAIN

THE Anglo-Americans have met many of the problems that confronted their neighbors to the south, but in some cases only hundreds of years after the Spanish pioneers had passed into history. Not only is this true of such matters as the "race question," the organization of higher education and the efficient government of cities, but quite as much of the fundamental economic processes. Both peoples had to practise the elementary art of agriculture from the beginning, but the Americans of the upper Mississippi Valley did not come to herding cattle on the plains until the middle of the nineteenth century and to large-scale mining until much later. It is interesting, then, to turn back to the Spanish experience four hundred years ago, especially in mining and stock raising.

Mention has been made of the adventurous penetration of the unknown northern reaches of what was then Mexico by the mission organization. Meantime the back country over which the advance had been made was marked by the rise, one after another, of isolated towns whose life depended upon mines and grasslands. Durango, Parral, San Luis Potosí and Guanajuato were typical of the partial consolidation of the fairly pacified areas. Life in all these cities was very much alike, and a glance at the famous old mining town of Zacatecas will happily illustrate the characteristic civilization of the second century of the occupation. It was in the true hin-

terland of northern Nueva Galicia, the base upon which
rested the hope of wider conquests, at the expense of
Spain's rivals, within the present United States. It is to
be borne in mind that the later history of the Mexican
frontier areas was not connected with the development
of wide acres of farming land or the growth of diversified
industry, but with the clusters of population at such
mining centers as this, where the wealth of silver gave
the impulse to sudden and dramatic growth.

In 1576 Zacatecas had a population of about three
hundred; it rose in numbers, but by 1619 it was said
to have fallen to one thousand, the foot-free miners moving on to new workings as they had come to this. The
setback was temporary, however, and it so grew in dignity that an alcaldía mayor was organized about it. As a
rich mining center, it soon secured from the audiencia at
Guadalajara the privilege of the establishment of a
*Diputación de Minería*, a sort of mining operators' guild,
the forerunner of the eighteenth-century body organized
for the entire viceroyalty and known as the *Tribunal de
Minería*. The Diputación was composed of three influential mining men who did all in their power to develop
the business by securing reductions in the duty on silver,
increasing the supply of salt and quicksilver and building roads. It was in no wise concerned with the welfare
of the miners.

The industry grew rapidly. By 1562 there were
thirty-three mines extracting metal by the patio method.
They used the *arrastre*, or revolving-stone drag, drawn
by mules, to crush and spread the ore, mixing it with
salt and quicksilver for crude amalgamation. There were
also a number of primitive smelters in which fire was
used for handling ores "rebellious" to the patio process.

The supplies of salt were meager and during the early times, until a system of prorating was adopted, much trouble was experienced by those unfortunate enough not to control deposits of the coarse *sal tierra*. This and the lack of quicksilver—which could not be produced in America under imperial regulations lest the Spanish industry be injured—were the chief obstacles to development; there were also continual hazard, loss and delay in getting the silver ingots down to Mexico City. By 1736 the patio process was carried on in eighty-eight establishments, while some twenty "ovens" were employed for smelting ores that required that treatment. The product was sent to Mexico by wagon over difficult roads through the Chichimec country.[1]

In spite of all handicaps the Zacatecas area developed some of the largest fortunes of the colonial epoch. Cristóbal de Oñate, one of the founders, was a generous contributor to the public works and adornment of the city. Throughout his life he maintained a free dining table at his home, and a pealing bell invited the hungry to break bread with the lavish host. Baltazar Bañuelos de Treviño, another founder, was indefatigable in erecting chapels, churches and public buildings. Vicente de Saldívar made a small fortune of three million pesos and paid an annual tax of one hundred thousand in "fifths" to the king.[2] Bartolomé Bravo de Acuña amassed fifteen millions, Agustín de Zavala four millions. In one mine it was for a long time possible to make one thousand pesos daily over expenses; in another, in the eighteenth

[1] E. Amador, *Bosquejo Histórico de Zacatecas* (Zacatecas, 1892), 215-218. The Zacatecas-Mexico highway was said to have been begun by the industry of a friar, Sebastián de Aparicio, very soon after the discovery of the lode.

[2] The "fifth" was the royalty paid for the mining concession; as to its reduction, see later, p. 92.

century, six hundred thousand were reaped in one week; in still another a half-million in six months. The total annual revenue for the king averaged over two hundred and fifty thousand pesos while the owners obtained some two millions each year for two centuries. In the same period the monopoly of quicksilver produced for the king twenty-four million pesos. Such profits developed the legend of inexhaustible riches in New Spain.

The pueblo of Zacatecas obtained the status of a city in 1585 with the right to elect its own local authorities. Until 1581 the *regidores*, or town councilmen, of the pueblo had been elected annually, but by 1594 they had become proprietary, that is, the offices had been purchased and had become hereditary. Apparently no *ejidos*, or town lands, were granted, and the city corporation had only the most slender funds upon which to subsist, even in the midst of so much wealth. It is evident, however, that there was money to be made in the administration of public office, for in or about 1675 the post of alguacil mayor, or chief bailiff, was sold for thirty-two thousand pesos, and that of *alférez real*, or royal standard bearer, for ten thousand. What was paid for the town council-ships is not recorded.

The municipality observed during the year some twenty *días de tabla*, or public holidays, most of them religious, but rather fewer than were usually thought necessary in Catholic countries. There were frequent cele-brations on saints' days, when there were fireworks, jousts, tourneys, masquerades and other public rejoic-ings. In 1593 the first bullfight was presented. About the end of the century the Spaniards began to celebrate the conquest by the *Paseo del Pendón*, a colorful proces-sion in which the royal standard was carried. It was intended in part to impress the conquered with the puissance of Spain.

The chief idea of the Spaniards seemed to be to keep the plebeian population busy and in subjection, though measures for their protection were also taken.[1] In 1590 royal orders had to be sent out to prohibit traffic in Indian slaves; it was also necessary to issue a renewed command that they should not be branded on the face with irons. For the safety of society it was ordered, as elsewhere in New Spain, that no Indian might bear fire-arms or ride horseback, but the frequent reiteration of the order proves its nonobservance. An Indian debtor who could not pay was obliged to work for his creditor until his debt was extinguished, a means employed almost continuously since that day to keep a supply of labor on hand. No Negro or mulatto funeral cortège was allowed to consist of more than four of the race, all those present above that number being liable to a penalty of two hundred lashes. No Negro woman was permitted to wear jewels, linen of Castile or ornaments in her hair under penalty of one hundred lashes and the loss of her jewels. These rules suggest that the lower working class led a turbulent, vicious life, with little in which to invest wages except delights of the person, indulgences which led either to their own undoing or to a display which aroused the ire of their superiors.

The workers were ruthlessly exploited. In 1581 the king sent to the audiencia of Guadalajara a *cédula* in which he complained that the Indians were being destroyed, about one third of them having succumbed to mistreatment and those who survived being obliged to pay taxes for those who had died. They were bought

[1] Amador, *Bosquejo Histórico de Zacatecas*, 380-381, 399-401.

and sold among the encomenderos like cattle, and like cattle they slept in the fields where they worked. Some were beaten to death, and mothers killed their children that they might not inherit their parents' sufferings. The natives regarded the Spaniards as deceivers and quite naturally conceived a great hatred for the name of Christian. Those under crown administration suffered worse than those under the encomenderos; the corregidores and alcaldes mayores seized the women and the lands of the Indians, and inflicted all sorts of lesser ills upon the dispossessed unfortunates.

The king's cédula admonished the audiencia to remedy these abuses and insure the Indians proper indoctrination. In 1609 several tribes at Zacatecas petitioned the king for a visitor to stop the abuses. Complying, he ordered that the corregidor should have but one Indian servant, who should receive a daily wage of one *real* (five cents). Indians and Negroes should no longer be compelled to work without pay at making bull rings or other public works; they must be made to attend church on Sundays, and an Indian alcalde must be appointed to prevent them from indulging in gang fights and in drunken revels and riots. They must be unmolested on the properties which had been given them for homes. But these orders were none too well enforced and little but abuse and repression fell to the lot of those who did not have the good fortune to possess lucrative mining property.

Yet the age was interested in works of charity. A hospital was erected in Zacatecas in 1549, and others were added and placed under care of the friars. They maintained nurses and attendants, though there was no physician throughout the seventeenth century. The Jesuits also came in and ministered to the residents, for religion had as large a part in the minds of the people as one would expect. There were religious brotherhoods (cofradías) organized for the common people and having popular utility of many kinds. In 1601, during a drought, the cofradías met at the Hospital de la Vera Cruz, and bearing their respective standards, a crucifix and a Virgin, went through the streets sounding a little bell which was answered by those in the church towers while the priest intoned and the people prayed for rain. There was, of course, all through the century notable activity in religious matters. At Zacatecas was Guadalupe, one of the famous Franciscan colleges, from which missionaries went out into the north. The Inquisition here was in the hands of Dominican fathers; but it seems not to have been as active as in Nuevo León and New Mexico.

Outside of religion there was little self-expression either in literature, industry or the arts, though a few laborers of meager skill were to be found in the more common trades, as carpenters, tailors, masons, tinsmiths and the like. Most objects of common use or luxury came from the south. There were no painters, musicians or sculptors worthy of note, religious statues and paintings coming from Spain or from Mexico, Puebla or Tlaxcala. Music, at first limited to primitive Indian whistles and flutes, was later produced, somewhat less crudely, by trumpets, violins, oboes and kettledrums. At dances, ball games and elsewhere drunkenness was habitual; gambling was a universal vice. The earnings of working people were wasted in christenings, weddings and fandangos wherein extravagance and lust accompanied the active feet that danced to the clicking cas-

tanets.[1] The agriculture of the province was insufficient
to feed the people, and the grain supply was brought in
from the more favored regions of Jalisco, San Luis Potosí and Guanajuato. The rural estates, of immense extent, raised but small herds of cattle and horses. Yet a
sheep was reputed to have been worth only six reales
(thirty cents) and a bushel of corn but two reales.

In other words, in a typical town in an area not long
since passed by the frontier, there was little to engage
the interest of the population beyond the sole occupation
of mining. Zacatecas was somewhat less fortunate in this
respect than such towns as San Luis Potosí or Durango,
where the activity of the people was a little more
diversified. Even in more modern times Zacatecas has
suffered intensely from fluctuations of the price of silver;
its long hillsides, today filled with the roofless remains
of houses once the busy scenes of life, stand like robbed
honeycombs, monuments to the variable whims of mining luck and the progressive exhaustion of one of the
most fabulously wealthy of mineral sites.

Something remains to be said as to the methods of the
mining industry. At first it was heavily handicapped by
the exactions of the government, which demanded half
the profits. This was soon changed to one fifth and then
by stages to one tenth, though the name "fifth" was
continued to designate the levy. At the same time the
government increased its constructive interest; rewards
were offered for the discovery of gold and silver deposits,
and the exploiters enjoyed certain exemptions from at-

[1] Amador, *Bosquejo Histórico de Zacatecas*, 381-392, presents some of
the literary productions incident to church festivities. F. A. Navarrete,
*Relación Peregrina . . . de Santiago de Querétaro* (Mexico, 1739), 67,
85-92, 125-159, has lengthy descriptions of guild participation in civic
celebrations. See also, J. M. Zeláa e Hidalgo, *Glorias de Querétaro*
(Mexico, 1803), chaps. vii-viii.

The native workmen in the Spanish colonies gathered the ore from the deep
mines and the outcroppings on the surface;

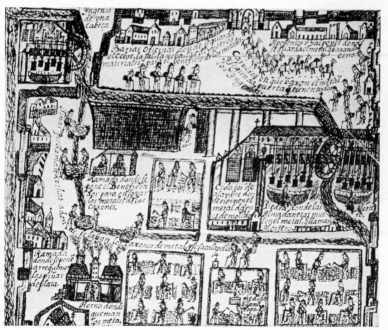

Delivered by pack-train, it was broken in the stamp-mills, duly washed
and smelted.

# Mining in the Spanish Colonies.

tachment for debt. Continuity of production was insured by the plan of tenure, for mining property was held under royal prescription, the operators enjoying a mere usufructuary right which lapsed if exploitation was stopped.

Patronage and governmental regulation might encourage the industry, but development had to come from the operators themselves. The primitive methods of extraction, in which the Spaniard was at first little superior to the Aztec, were left behind as the amalgam process was introduced and improved. This discovery, which, as we have noticed, employed quicksilver and salt to extract metal from ores, caused the crown to establish a monopoly of quicksilver, the metal usually being sent from the Almaden mines in Spain on war vessels. New World production was prohibited. It was sold at one hundred and eighty-seven pesos a hundredweight in 1590, but the price was gradually reduced until in 1777 Almaden quicksilver could be had for forty-one pesos and the German product for sixty-three. In 1800 the developed silver country covered about 12,225 square leagues with about three thousand mines in operation. Some of the veins, famous during the early centuries, are still profitably worked. In the more northern mines production was hampered by distance and Indian hostilities; the industry never rose to significance in any region now within the United States.

In spite of the absorbing interest in mining it was conducted for many years without a protective organization comparable to that perfected for the mercantile guild. But in 1777 the producers were organized into a *Cuerpo de Minería*, or mine operators' guild, with a court for their litigation and representation similar to that which was the kernel of the consulado organization which the merchants had long enjoyed. The Cuerpo established the mining college mentioned in an earlier chapter. It also maintained a fund for *avíos* or advances to operators for prospective developments, really an organized system of grubstaking. This financial feature, however, proved a failure because of favoritism in making loans and because, later, the government demanded a heavy contribution from it during the War of Independence. An important step was taken in 1779 in mining legislation and history with the compilation of the *Ordenanzas de Minería* of New Spain.[1] These ordinances, and the codification of Spanish mining law by Gamboa, helped to form the mining legislation of the United States, their influence being still observed.[2]

The course of the mining industry of New Spain eventually gave rise to a marked social and economic stratification unknown to New France or New England. The monopolistic control of quicksilver and its high price, the great expense of operation due to transportation costs and the deepness of mines, combined with social factors, kept mineral production in the hands of a small well-to-do class. The small prospector never became the feature of mining life that he was later to be in the United States.[3] Not only in Zacatecas but elsewhere

[1] *Reales Ordenanzas para la Dirección Régimen y Gobierno del Importante Cuerpo de la Minería de Nueva España* (Madrid, 1783). See also Joaquín Velázquez de León, Comentarios de las Ordenanzas de Minería (MS., Mexico, 1845).

[2] C. H. Shinn, *Mining Camps: a Study in American Frontier Government* (N. Y., 1885), 48-58; F. X. de Gamboa, *Commentaries on the Mining Ordinances of Spain* (Richard Heathfield, tr., London, 1830), I, p. vi; H. W. Halleck, tr., A Collection of Mining Laws of Spain and Mexico (San Francisco, 1859), p. iii.

[3] Allan Nevins, *The Emergence of Modern America* (A History of American Life, VIII), 133-141.

as well, producers of silver amassed great fortunes which lent glamour to colonial history. Famous for his lavish scale of living was the Conde de Regla, who paved the path for his daughter's wedding ceremony with silver tiles and who presented to Charles III a completely built and equipped battleship for his fleet.

At the other extreme was the mine laborer, who spent his days climbing up from the depths on notched log ladders, bearing two hundred pounds of ore at a trip, and living in squalor when his day's work was done. The mining ordinances strove, as a means of improvement of production, to ameliorate the condition of the workers, but it was very little improved during two centuries and a half. The most notable defect in the old mines was the absence of connecting galleries, which prevented ventilation and added to transportation costs. For drainage purposes water was carried out in leather bags and drawn up on windlasses moved by horsepower. German miners, sent out toward the close of the eighteenth century to make improvements, were met by such prejudices against innovations that much of their work was unavailing.

The total production of the mines of New Spain from 1690 to 1818, earlier figures being unavailable, has been estimated at one and a half-billion pesos, from which the total crown revenues were from sixteen to nineteen per cent. The annual average production at the close of the eighteenth century was about twenty-two million pesos; it has been thought that a million pesos annually were smuggled out. Small wonder that the silver country should have roused the cupidity of foreigners, men like the insatiable La Salle, led on by the solicitations of Diego de Peñalosa, whose story was given at length in an earlier chapter, or later wanderers like Louis St. Denis.[1]

It scarcely needs to be pointed out that it would have been difficult, if not impossible, to sustain a mining population if it had been dependent upon importations for its food supply. Agriculture was essential for a well-balanced community in any section, and in large areas it was overwhelmingly the major industry. A comprehensive idea of the status of the agricultural workers of New Spain is hard to convey. There never was any direct land tax in Spanish America; therefore the relative importance of agriculture can only be estimated by the figures for the tithe. After the liberalization of commerce, Humboldt estimated, agricultural production was greater by one fourth than the value of the gold and silver of the mines. At the beginning of the nineteenth century tithable products were valued at nearly thirty million pesos annually. New Spain was, in spite of its great mineral and commercial interests, very largely a patriarchal agricultural community.[2]

The farm towns which dotted the Mexican area were quite similar to the peninsular *municipios*; the roots of their organization may be traced in Roman precedent. Spanish towns, which must be distinguished from Indian towns, were legally established by groups of settlers numbering from ten to one hundred heads of families or vecinos. The grants to the towns were almost uniformly four square leagues (about eighteen thousand acres), the actual occupation, of course, being an approx-

[1] Instrucción from Arriaga to Amarillas in *Instrucciones que los Virreyes de Nueva España dejaron* (Mexico, 1867), 96; C. W. Hackett, "New Light on Don Diego de Peñalosa," *Miss. Valley Hist. Rev.*, VI, 313-314, and citations.

[2] Alexander von Humboldt, *Political Essay on the Kingdom of New Spain* (London, 1814), III, 96-97.

imation. As in the New England towns, the land was divided among the colonists in proportion to their merits, capacity or number of family dependents. The small husbandman received, inside the building area of the town, which was laid out four-square about a public plaza, a house lot measuring fifty by one hundred feet. Outside the building area he received enough land to sow one hundred quintals of wheat or barley and ten of corn. He also was given a measured plot of land for a garden and an orchard, besides pasture ground for ten sows, twenty cows, five mares, one hundred sheep and twenty goats, in return for which he must provide the beginning of these herds. This plot was the *peonía*, the free grant made to a head of family having the status of a common foot soldier. A pioneer who had the status of a mounted soldier might receive a *caballería*, which comprised a house lot one hundred by two hundred feet and cultivable pasture lands five times as extensive as a *peonía*. The town was established by a leader, or by the group acting as a unit; the officers were generally elected, though when a leader had taken the initiative he was permitted to appoint them for the first year. From this type of grant sprang the Spanish pueblo or town, so numerous and important throughout the country.[1]

All the cities of Spanish America, including those in the American Southwest, had such origin. Where the town did not develop into a city, there sprang up the class of small farmers known as *rancheros*, who, though not great in number, gradually developed a characteristic rural life oftentimes a target of ridicule as presented

[1] Antonio Rodríguez de León Pinelo, *Tratado de Confirmaciones Reales de Encomiendas* (Madrid, 1630), 168. In some cases it was possible for the small husbandman to receive as many as three peonías and the mounted soldier to receive five caballerías.

at the city theaters before smart and sophisticated audiences. On these little farms, ranging in size from five hectares up, according to the nature of the land—small self-sufficing empires remote from the markets of civilization—rose a half-breed and mulatto element tempering the taciturnity and melancholy of the Indian with the vivacity and pugnacity of the Spaniard. Their work not too strenuous, combined with untutored native intelligence, created a class of society comparable to the traditional rural population of other lands but without great social or political influence.

More significant both in social and in economic concerns was the society developed on the great estates or haciendas. There is, of course, no criterion by which the small landholder may be differentiated from the large one; but the point of departure has been ordinarily set at the possession of about two thousand five hundred acres.[1] In colonial days the large landholder was presumably a stockman; he received a grant of a square league (4440 acres), called a *sitio de ganado mayor,* or "site for larger cattle." This grant was a prevalent form of reward for service in conquest and of special favor to court dependents. On such estates grew up great manorial residences with stables and barns, often attached to the house, and the huts of Indian laborers near by. Here there blossomed a patriarchal society which, outside the cities, gave cast and character to colonial life. Grants might be perfected by titles after four years, when owners might sell, though not to the church. After 1630, however, this system was almost entirely superseded by that of direct sale.

[1] G. M. McBride, *The Land Systems of Mexico* (N. Y., 1923), 25; Elizabeth Kravchyk, A General Survey of the Mexican Land Question (M.A. thesis, Univ. of Calif., 1919).

The development of the *latifundia* in Mexico is an interesting phenomenon. The grantee was supposed to take great pains in establishing his metes and bounds. With a large cross in hand he or his surveyor was to go to the center of the plot asked for, place the cross with its arms on the cardinal points, and pace in each of the four directions half the dimension of his square league. Then the bounds were to be marked by clearings and a roadway was to be left open on all sides. Buildings were to be set back appropriately for this purpose, and encroachments upon Indian towns and lands were prohibited.[1] In the primitive conditions of land preëmptions of those days such provisions were thought nonsensical; as a matter of fact, bounds were established by sighting prominent landmarks, and the areas claimed were habitually in excess of the legal grant. By 1578 the crown discovered that squatting on untitled lands and the occupation of unwarranted extensions were so prevalent that orders were issued for return to the government of all unauthorized possessions. Throughout later years illegal preëmptions were regularized by the process of composition, whereby occupants were, after ten years' occupancy, given titular possession upon the payment of small sums. The most notable clearance of this kind occurred in 1754.

Before the last third of the eighteenth century all desirable arable land within reach of utilization had been taken up. Before Independence the great holdings, which began with the immense domain of the Cortés family in Oaxaca, included those of the noble families of Alba, Carpio, San Lucar, Montezuma, Tenebrón, Linares, Monteleón, Atrinca, Aguayo, Terrenova, Veragua and

[1] M. Galván, *Ordenanzas de Tierras y Aguas* (Paris, 1855), 181-197.

Berwick.[1] The constant tendency was toward the formation of large estates. The causes, beyond the mere will of
society as expressed in the *mayorazgo* or entail, lay in
the character of the soil, the aridity of certain sections,
and the dependent character, not only of the Indians but
of a large part of the mixed and white population. Just
as Independence was being won, a writer in 1821 thus
described them: "Either through error of understanding
or through malignity of heart, the hacendados are tigers
on two feet . . . the wasteful consumers of the state,
worse than usurers, the cause of misery, depopulation
and nearly all the ills of the kingdom." [2] In the northern
reaches of the frontier beyond the towns and presidios,
the desire for personal safety from the depredations of
hostile Indians tended also to the creation of the hacienda
type of holding rather than the small farm. The hacendado of old Mexico, transferred to the present area of
the United States, became the ranchero whose immense
holdings, expanded legally to eleven square leagues,
characterized the later rural tenure of the Mexican period
in California and New Mexico.

The colonial export crops were indigo, vanilla and
cacao. The widely used insect dye, cochineal, the production of which was an industry of the southern Indians,
also yielded important wealth. On the west coast between
Colima and Acapulco very fine cotton was grown. The
Parras district, where the grape was indigenous, had a
thriving wine culture at the close of the colonial period
in spite of the long and bitter war waged against colonial

[1] G. Desdevises du Desert, "Vice-rois et Capitaines Génèraux," *Revue
Historique,* CXXVI, 254.
[2] El Pensador Tapatío, 1-2, Papeles Varios (Bancroft Library), CLIX,
no. 3; Helen Phipps, "Some Aspects of the Agrarian Question in
Mexico," Univ. of Texas, *Bull.*, no. 2515, 21-39.

beverages by the Andalusian growers. Sugar, which had given early promise of immense export value, fell off in production until it barely met local needs; its culture was revived somewhat about the time of Independence. Cereals had a checkered career due to high export taxes and irregular seasonal production.

Cattle, both large and small, were a source of great wealth, especially along the northern frontier and the Gulf Coast. The hides of Guadalajara were in the eighteenth century worth four hundred thousand pesos annually. Great herds of horses and mules were used in transportation, mining and sugar manufacture, as well as in cultivation, where oxen were more numerously employed. A large business of supplying animals to farmers, Spanish and mulatto as well as Indian, was in the hands of the alcaldes mayores, who bought stock from breeders at low prices, from fifteen to twenty pesos for a mule, and sold it at a good gain, for from twenty-five to thirty pesos. The supply of animals, clothing, seeds and tools for Indian producers was also in their hands, under the same *repartimiento* abuse of forcing unnecessary purchases upon the natives which roused the wrath of Juan and Ulloa in their *Noticias secretas* of Peru.[1] To fend against this exploitation, which increased with the lapses of encomiendas, the Ordinance of the Intendants of 1786 provided that no intendant or his subordinates might make any sales or advances of supplies to Indians of over five pesos. The scheme was vehemently opposed by such a veteran alcalde mayor as Villaroel who predicted the ruin of the realm in the

---

[1] Jorge Juan and Antonio de Ulloa, *Secret Expedition to Peru, or the Practical Influence of the Spanish Colonial System upon the Character and Habits of the Colonists* (translated, Boston, 1851).

new method.[1] The probability is that the contemplated change was not abruptly or widely applied, for the alcaldes were but slowly replaced. The cessation of this legalized and official grubstaking inevitably forced large numbers of natives into debt peonage, long an accompanying evil of the hacienda system; one of the oft-repeated demands upon the present-day land subdivision program in Mexico has been that it should supply seeds, tools and animals to the Indian farmers.

Of the manufacturing interests it is difficult to give an adequate idea without abundance of detail. Inevitably little was made that would be sent out of the country, and yet manufacturing was a much more influential element in the life of the people of New Spain than of those of any other colonial area in America. The introduction of sheep had given woolen manufacture importance in Querétaro, Puebla and Valladolid, where sixteen thousand quintals of wool were used in making coarse cloth. Cotton, which had been woven and dyed in the old Aztec days, gave a flourishing weaving industry to New Spain in war times, but the activity languished during peace. Looms were located at Cholula, Puebla, Tlaxcala, Querétaro and Guadalajara. In the intendancy of Puebla the cotton product amounted to one and one half-million pesos per year during the late eighteenth century. Flax and hemp were experimented upon with a view to production though without success. Silk culture occupied a position of importance in the early days under encouragement from Cortés, but Andalusian jealousy killed it. In a similar way the cloth of Puebla, though coarse, was popular, and hence a cause of loud complaint

[1] Josephine Kravchyk, The Enfermedades Políticas of Hipólito Villaroel, I (M.A. thesis, Univ. of Calif., 1919) ; Justa Repulsa del Reglamento de Intendencias, IV, pt. iv, arts. 122, 144.

from Spain. Soap was made in large quantities in that city, and its ceramic products, as well as those of Cholula and Guadalajara, have long been famous and are frequently seen today in far-away markets. The crafts of the pre-Spanish period survived and made their impression on colonial society, so that New Spain preserved a native character distinguishing it from other parts of the colonial empire. Save in a very few articles, colonial manufacture was of simple character, adapted to the rough necessities of pioneer life; the artistic qualities of the Indians as of the Spaniards found their highest expression in building and painting. These latter were practically the only manual arts in use within the area now American.[1]

What with mining, agriculture, grazing and some diversified manufacturing, Spanish America even in the sixteenth century presented a fairly complex industrial society, though the production was that natural to a dependency; perhaps it were better said that the continued status of a dependency was appropriate because its people were almost exclusively concerned in getting out raw materials. Merchandising and its onerous supervision by the government may be left for later treatment;[2] we have here traced the fundamental processes of economic life. The material elements of wealth were found abundantly, but to convert them into use, in those days before machinery, required equally abundant human labor. This was also readily at hand; but if it supplied power, it was also human, and therefore, as we shall now see, a social as well as an economic factor.

[1] The survivals and development of the industrial arts of the Mexican Indians are happily portrayed in Gerardo Murillo ("Dr. Atl"), ed., *Los Artes Populares en México* (2 v, Mexico, 1922).

[2] See later, chap. vii.

# CHAPTER V

## The Wards of the Spaniards

Two basic considerations must be kept constantly in mind in arriving at an understanding of the historical significance of the Spanish neighbors of the English in North America. The first is that the social and political organization which Spain succeeded in planting within the present bounds of the United States was of a transitional frontier type, its spirit but feebly reflecting that greater Spain of which the conquistadores were vaguely conscious. To judge the influence of Spain in North America by the meager results of daring *entradas* or by the social development of Florida or Texas or California is to misinterpret an important phase of the subjection of the New World to European ideals. We must get back of the frontier to the type of life developed in old Mexico. The second consideration is the need to realize the significance of the survival of the Indian masses in Mexico, with all the social, political and economic implications of that unique factor in American history. Without the survival of Indian blood and tradition the growth of New Spain would have been quite unlike what it came to be; so, too, the life of the Mexican nation and its relations with the United States.

It requires a considerable effort of the imagination to appreciate the element of surprise experienced by both the Spaniards and the Indians when they first came face to face. Europeans had long been familiar with exploitable nonwhite peoples brought from Asia and Africa;

the slave ships of Portugal had been bringing home their cargoes of "black ivory" for many years before the voyages of Columbus began. But here was a new, strangely hued race with alien languages and customs, the tribes upon the mainland plateaus living in barbaric splendor with a highly developed social organization. The pugnacious character of the Spaniard, his belief in his divine mission acquired from his seven-century war on the Mohammedan invader, the freedom of action permitted by distance from Spain and by papal favor—all these, when brought in contact with the peculiar fatalistic stoicism of the American savage, were well adapted to create a unique situation, and necessitated some kind of a system for regulating the relations of two widely unlike types of culture. Thanks to his superior organization and his possession of firearms, the Spaniard could almost everywhere in the New World assume the rôle of conqueror and exploiter far more easily than could the Europeans in the Orient. There were minor variations in the methods of exploitation he adopted; from its worst forms, as we have seen, the Indians won temporary immunity by ferocious revolts, only sooner or later to become the subordinate element in the social group.

It seems not to have occurred to Columbus or to the royal pair who received him at Barcelona that the strange people he brought back could be anything but human beings with souls to be saved. That weighty problem was solemnly discussed a few years later and happily decided in the light of common sense. Accordingly the "Indians," so called in everlasting commemoration of the ignorance of the great discoverer and the conservative stubbornness of our race since then, were received into the bosom of society, to begin their centuries-long bondage to the worship of the white man's God. To the Spaniards this seemed the humane and, from the practical point of view, the advantageous thing to do. It was the direct command of the Holy Writ, made doubly obligatory upon the Spaniard by the fanatical proselyting zeal engendered in his secular strife with Islam.[1]

In the long run perhaps it would have been better for the world, as well as for the Indian, if the attempt to effect this spiritual change had been less peremptory and exigent. He might have been left to the enjoyments and consolations of the faith of his fathers until he could himself develop some volition in the matter of a more complete salvation. Such a policy commends itself today to the nations which control Islamic populations. If it is now expedient in the face of necessity, it would have been wise as well as generous four hundred years ago. As it was, the Indians never really assimilated the spirit and beauty of the Christian religion; there was something wrong with it from the Indians' point of view, which is the one that matters. The essential defect was that it did not, in its historical development or its philosophy, touch a responsive chord in their own tradition or experience. In moral precepts the faith of the Aztec touched a sublimity quite comparable with the teachings of Christ, but its social tradition and practice were utterly unlike that of the European.[2] Hastily imposed and imperfectly practised, Christianity could not amid

[1] *Cf.* R. Blanco Fombona, *El Conquistador Español del Siglo XVI* (Madrid, 1922), 20.
[2] See Alonso de Çorita, "Breve y Sumaria Relación," esp. chap. iii, in J. García Icazbalceta, ed., *Nueva Colección de Documentos para la Historia de México* (Mexico, 1886-1892), III, for a charming account of Aztec social philosophy and religion. *Cf.* Lucien Biart, *The Aztecs* (Chicago, 1887), 110, 213-225.

the social destruction of the conquest become a subjective development in the minds of the Indians. It could not, first, because it was alien; secondly, because they had a thoroughly accepted and well-tried-out set of gods of their own, to whom their spirits cried in the hour of anguish and to whom they addressed thanks or petition as occasion demanded.

Christianity unquestionably softened the asperities of the conquest, bringing the amenities of civilization in the wake of the Spanish swashbucklers. But its spirit was incomprehensible, and its indoctrination, given the practical social and economic code which in fact it protected, was the most refined persecution which could have befallen the red man. The imported religion would have proved more convincing, and its introduction better justified, had its exemplars followed the principles they professed with less lip service and more genuine spirituality.[1] But the world being for the Spaniard what his experiences had made it, such a theory of society was an impossibility. The strife with Islam had produced a consciousness of national aim before the New World was reached. Only unity of belief could be trusted to effect the national safety.

For the Indian, then, the process was a sharp crisis with a sequel of long-drawn-out tragedy, while for the Spaniards themselves the doctrine brought abundant trouble. Their great mistake in the colonial adventure was not so much in their harmful development of a rigid policy of commercial exclusion and governmental monopoly of all activity, or their scheme of social and

[1] For an excellent summary of Spanish Indian policy, see Lillian E. Fisher, *Viceregal Administration in the Spanish American Colonies* (Univ. of Calif., *Publs.*, XV), 312, 314-315, and citations.

political privilege; for in those respects Spain was by no means unique among the European colonizers. The chief error lay in the Spanish failure to grasp the fact that humanity was being liberated at last from the idea that social security lay in unity of religious thought.[1] By their policy of transplanting Europe to America under the theocratic formula, the conquerors set up an obscurantist ideal opposed to the current of ideas then newly gaining force, in much the same way as the New England Puritans "reverted to type" in the legal establishment of Calvinism.[2]

Yet the faith of the Spaniard was the best thing he brought with him; and in his own way, according to his own psychology, he bestowed it upon his new and unexpected charges. It was the most unselfish gift, the most beneficent agency at his command, for effecting the elevation of a dependent people to the standards of European culture. Ranking second among his settled ideals was his officially sanctioned program of encouraging the fusion of Spanish and Indian blood. To create in the Indies an entirely new society by amalgamating the races under a unified faith was the spiritual vision of the Catholic Monarchs, duly signalized by one of the earliest laws.[3] The faith was his most generous gift, the transfusion of his blood his most lavish compliment. Unity

[1] Cf. F. M. Stawell and F. S. Marvin, *The Making of the Western Mind* (London, 1923), 163-166; F. S. Marvin, *The Living Past* (Oxford, 1913), chap. vii.

[2] See T. J. Wertenbaker, *The First Americans* (*A History of American Life*, II), chap. iv.

[3] In 1514. *Colección de Documentos . . . de Ultramar* (Madrid, 1885-1926), IX, 22. Cf. E. G. Bourne, *Spain in America* (A. B. Hart, ed., *The American Nation: a History*, N. Y., 1904-1918, III), 265. The "Catholic Monarchs" were Ferdinand and Isabella and no others. They alone had this title, obtained from the pope. Later Spanish rulers have been called "Catholic Majesties."

of spirit and identity of body, these were the basic con-
cepts out of which grew the institutions upon which
society rested.

A corollary of these two ideas was that of the physical preservation of the red man for the double purpose of evangelizing and exploiting him. Indian social
and political organization rapidly went the way of
Indian religious practice. In one feature only was it
preserved, the utilization of the tribal or village organization for providing pressed labor gangs. In this preservation of the natives Spain's policy was comparable to
that of the French in Canada, but in sharp and happy
contrast with the English and Dutch policy of expulsion
and annihilation. The Anglo-Saxon method was to
treat the Indian as an alien and independent political
entity with whom treaties of mutual exclusion could be
solemnized so one-sided in application that white viola-
tion was the normal course of action. This left the ab-
origine entirely out of reach of the protective influences
of the white social structure. On the contrary, while the
Spaniard did occasionally recognize the treaty-making
power of the Indians—as with the chieftain Enrique in
La Española and the Chichimec of New Spain—the
customary practice denied them such status and contemplated complete absorption in race, religion and
exploitation.[1]

Sixteenth-century colonization, being in the hands
of Latin peoples, was free from the racial antipathies
which cloud the contacts of dominant and subject peoples of the more modern world. The idea of interracial

[1] José de Gálvez, Informe de el Visitador (MS. in Bancroft Library),
34-50: "Rather should they submit their throats to the knife," wrote the
bellicose visitor to the local officers of San Luis Potosí, than submit to
humiliating capitulations with rebellious Indians.

marriage was not repugnant to the throng of adventurers who overran Middle America, and unions, even of legal status, were normal and frequent. Of still greater influence in the amalgamation of the races were the illicit unions which have placed their stamp upon the Spanish-American peoples. Though the fusion has never been completed, the half-breed element has long been predominant, and there are probably very few Mexican families, relatively speaking, in which some strain of Indian blood may not be found.

The preservation and Christianization of the Indian, and his fusion with the Spaniard even though on the exploitative basis, made the Spanish colonial system inherently different from those of the rival nations. Portugal tried it with dismal failure in the Orient, with somewhat better success in Brazil; France tried it in Canada with the same ideal, but with less favorable outcome because of economic environment and social organization. The path of English expansion was strewn with treaties violated immediately they were signed, but with no set of laws governing interracial relations comparable to that of Spain in the Laws of the Indies. One seeks vainly in English or French-colonial literature for such a treatise as Solórzano's *Política Indiana,* the one thousand and more pages of which are devoted to laws and commentaries expounding the status of the bondsmen.

Of course this process of unification had a bad effect upon the white man. While the government encouraged legal unions, concubinage, common enough in Spain under various legal and extralegal devices, was widely promoted by the reckless living of the conquistadores and the complacency of the natives, male and female alike. Even as early as the arrival of Nicolás de Ovando in La Española as governor, no less than three hundred Spaniards were living, in spite of Franciscan protests, with the daughters and wives of chiefs and principal men; he ordered them to marry or leave their dusky consorts.

King Ferdinand wanted to send out white Christian slaves for wives, but Diego Columbus objected that by so doing the chances of matrimony of numerous "New Christian" women (that is, converts from other faiths) already come from Spain would be lessened.[1] It was probably due to the already established practice that Ferdinand issued the ordinance of 1514, though the idea had been contained in Isabella's earlier legislation. For the most part, Spanish officials were required to bring their wives with them; license to sail was granted by the king alone, and only on consent of the wife if she remained at home. On the mainland illicit unions marked the path of the conquering expeditions. By 1553 foundling half-breeds numbered thousands in New Spain and for them the viceroy Mendoza established the orphan school of San Juan Letrán.

The prevalent Spanish attitude may be illustrated, at least for the early period, by the testamentary instructions to his sons left by one of the ordinary run of first settlers, Diego de Ocaña. After suitably disposing of his estates and making numerous other bequests, he stated as to the woman servant, Antonica:

Item: I say that I once had relations with the said Antonica my servant, who bore a child named Alosico. But she was ill-watched, for she also had relations with

[1] A. de Herrera, *Historia General* (Madrid, 1601), I, bk. vi, chap. xviii; J. de Solórzano, *Politica Indiana* (Madrid, 1776), I, 200; Bourne, *Spain in America*, 265.

an Indian of my household. However, judging by the color of the child, everyone declares that he seems to be the son of a Christian. It seems so to me, for it may be that he is my son; and since in case of doubt it is better to acknowledge him than to ignore him, I command my sons to bring him up, have him indoctrinated, and do something good for him, for I believe that he is a son of mine, and not of an Indian.[1]

The acknowledgment depicts the moral atmosphere of the 1530's and illuminates the mental and spiritual character of the Spanish settler; but it also sets the half-breed offspring at the level of social inferiority above which not even the benignant regard of his well-to-do parent could raise him.

The dearth of women among the colonists, and the fact that Peninsular officials usually returned with their families to Spain after their terms of service, made it inevitable that pure-blooded Spanish women should be negligible in number. In the absence of other data we must rely upon Humboldt's statement, made about the end of the eighteenth century, that not one tenth of the European-born Spaniards in Mexico City were women. Of course the ratio would have been even smaller in the provincial towns, though the general female population exceeded the male.[2]

In a theocratic scheme of things it was logical that the process of evangelization should be one of the prime functions of the supreme government. It is doubtful whether any other western nation so completely fused church in state and state in church as did the Spanish.

[1] *La Vida Colonial* (Mexico, Archivo General, *Publicaciones*, VII), 5.
[2] Cf. H. H. Bancroft, *History of Mexico* (San Francisco, 1883-1887), III, 752; Bourne, *Spain in America*, 266; Alexander von Humboldt, *Political Essay on the Kingdom of New Spain* (London, 1814), I, 254.

*A Spaniard, his Indian wife and their child, a* mestizo.

*A Spaniard, his wife, an* octoroon *or* albina, *and their child, by chance a*
torna atrás.

*Castes in New Spain.*

The kings all insisted that conquest should be softened by being designated "pacification," and that surrender to the political power should be followed by prompt incorporation into the church. Far from offering any essential obstacle to his complete exploitation, the evangelization of the Indian materially aided it. The church definitely avowed and participated in it and built itself up thereby. Churches, monasteries, convents, hospitals, schools, as well as government palaces and other public works, were built by taxation of Indians and their unrecompensed labor. A regulation put into effect under the second viceroy, Velasco, provided that erection of churches should be paid for, one third by the king, one third by the Spaniards and one third by the Indians! It would have made no material difference if the king had paid the whole cost, for in any case it all fell ultimately upon the Indians, who paid with continual labor for the perpetual salvation of their souls.[1]

As time went on, the institutions through which race contacts were made took form. On the high plateau the church, the monastery, the school and the encomienda were the chief agencies. As the conquest progressed into the nomadic areas of the mines and the missions, the haciendas and the mines themselves became focal points of interracial fusion. Along with these local agencies went the conception of wardship promulgated by the royal government, out of which, as we shall see, sprang the régime adopted for the government of Indian towns, the recognition of native land rights, and the policy of manual and intellectual education. All contributed to the sum of the social forces designed to make the Indian one physically, morally and spiritually with the Spaniard.

[1] Solórzano, *Política Indiana*, II, 192-193.

It was a basic conception that the direction of all this should be in the hands of the crown. The royal monopoly was based upon the sovereign rights plus the property rights, both bestowed by the papal grants. The combination of these two rights, the one adverse to the pretensions of rival nations and the other exclusive of the vassals of Spain, was an extension of the royal prerogative beyond its scope in the Peninsula. The kings of Spain possessed legally and actually more power in America, whose soil they never trod, than in their European dominions. It was the pervasive and universal application of this principle that helped give the Spanish colonial institution its unique character. It exerted practical, if not theoretical, power over the lives and property of all the vassals. Monopoly of land, of industry through license and control, of commerce through exclusion and localization, of religion in that the church was national with the king as its head, monopoly even in thought and feeling through the intrusive attention of the Inquisition—these were the ingrained principles of the first great modern colonial enterprise. Individual enterprise was subordinated and controlled.

It was an undertaking by and for the crown, not the Spanish nation. In no other case save that of Portugal was the system placed so immediately and thoroughly under the care of officers appointed by the crown and responsible directly to it. The absence from the Spanish plan of the joint-stock-company device, the attempted monopoly of all trade as well as of all territory, the almost continual use of a single Spanish port for trade, and the appointment of crown employees not only to supervise but to conduct actual business operations—all these made the king the official head of the greatest business organization in the world.[1] From the day of the conquerors and first settlers there grew up a society of great rigidity, dominated by an official class in both the civil and the spiritual fields. Private individuals performing no administrative duties were few in number among the upper classes; in this aspect society in the colonies became a variant from that of Spain. And however unhappily this system worked in the long run, it possessed marked advantages at the beginning. It was fortunate for the immediate purpose that this rigidly formal officialdom could be organized, though it proved disastrous in the end when it became crystallized and had to meet fierce outside competition.

Once the Columbian contracts were voided in practice, the crown took upon itself some of the responsibility for failure and a large prospect for gain. But not at the hazard of everything. Financial responsibility was shifted by enlisting private capital; thus, losses from shipwreck, uncompleted voyages, and unsuccessful establishments were largely borne by the unhappy victims of misadventure. The leaders of all enterprises for conquest and settlement invested their own fortunes in them in the hope of fabulous wealth from discovered treasure or spoliation of the Indians. Always the king's share was at least one tenth of the wealth acquired; sometimes it was very much larger, up to the half of treasure-trove. Usually the entire cost was met by the leaders, who an-

---

[1] If the treasures of Montezuma and Atahualpa had not made the American adventure remunerative beyond expectation, joint-stock-company exploitation might have been undertaken. The possibility had been discussed even in the time of Columbus. Charles V did himself try one such venture, that of the Augsburg Welzers in Venezuela; but neither before nor after their bootless undertaking was the colonizing type of company employed, though in the eighteenth century at least three semiprivate commercial organizations were utilized for both trade and colonial defense.

ticipated immense gains in the outcome, and their followers, who hoped to share as well. Yet occasionally,
under stress of necessity, the king contributed a significant portion. Thus, when Luna was sent to occupy the
lands of Florida, Philip II gave nearly three hundred
thousand pesos for supplies, ships and arms; the members of the expedition contributed as much more from
their private fortunes; and all was lost.[1]

Those who assert that the English colonizers were
more successful than the Spanish often attempt to explain the alleged fact by crediting the former with
greater personal initiative and a more adventurous spirit.
The facts belie such a conclusion. The conquistadores
habitually risked their lives and their entire fortunes,
with no recourse in case of failure, and often with tardy
royal acknowledgment of their deeds and poignant suffering in case of success. The rival nations which grew
by use and development of the chartered joint-stock
company protected their early adventurers by special
licenses, and thus by the exclusion of all others among
their nationals. The Spaniards, on the other hand, had
often to meet the most grueling competition and rivalry
from their own compatriots. It was not until the competing nations were able to challenge successfully the
Spanish monopoly, when Spain's system had begun to
decline, that rival operations loomed portentously. She
endured the buffetings of competition, setting the pattern
which other powers strove to adapt to their own uses
while destroying the Spanish strength. For a century the
boldness, daring and initiative exhibited by her sons
demonstrated a vigor of personal initiative not surpassed

[1] H. I. Priestley, ed., *The Luna Papers* (Fla. State Hist. Soc., *Publs.*,
VIII), II, 143, 223, 327-329.

by her rivals in their epic seventeenth-century transplantations.

The Spanish colonial empire, monopolistic, exclusive,
endowed by virtue of priority with a vast income from
the exploitation of native peoples and great silver-bear-
ing regions, formed the example, the norm, and at the
same time the obstacle against which strove the emulative spirit of the rivals. The all-pervasive Spanish institution, which unified the Tagalog, the Argentinian, the
Sonoranian and the Madrileño into a single civilization,
was blended in the minds of the Raleighs, the Hudsons,
the Cartiers and their ambitious successors into one great
impediment. It was counted in with the hazards of angry
seas, strange shores, savage Indians and an inhospitable
climate, to be overcome before the lavish bounty of the
New World could be gained. Within a century after the
discovery, Spain's loss of sea power relegated her to a
minor rôle in history; the drain of her colonies told on
her population and her national life; but always while
the Old Régime persisted she was an important American power, if not the most important. Her human spirit
and social influence persist, with their strength and weak-
nesses, as the controlling forces in the lives of some fifty
million Spanish Americans today.

Without a very thorough knowledge of the difficulties involved, the Catholic Monarchs adopted in La
Española the policy of considering the natives as free
vassals. The Castilians were not to molest their properties nor subject them to forced labor, and were to pay
them wages. It presently developed, however, that there
could be no progress upon this basis, for the Indian had
to be compelled to labor. When discontent among the
settlers taken out by Columbus caused lands to be allotted

to them, groups of Indians were told off to work these under the species of serfdom called the encomienda. The Indians of the Caribbean islands were rapidly destroyed by the system. Before the continental areas were entered, the island population had to be recruited by slave-catching expeditions to till the farms and work the mines. This quest, as we have seen, initiated the series of voyages which led Cortés to the conquest of Mexico.[1] There the emperor Charles V, recognizing the presence of a higher type of culture than the insular one, recommended the adoption of the system of Indian wage-labor which Isabella had vainly tried to establish.[2] But the practical-minded conquerors foresaw no reward for their campaigns in the wage system, and so, in the logic of events, the encomienda spread to New Spain and each of the successive conquests. Only in Venezuela, California and Texas did it fail to become fixed.

This interesting rural institution took best root among the higher Indian cultures. The formula was in general as follows. A leader of an expedition pacified an area and obtained the right to govern it. He then granted in the king's name to his followers, according to their merits of service and social position, tracts of land contiguous to Indian villages whose inhabitants were required to work for their overlord with but nominal pay. He was also paid the tithe and the tribute, keeping most of the latter for himself. He was to see that his tributaries were taught the Christian religion, but this obligation was little observed.

Such grants were made to Spanish vassals in the

[1] See earlier, chap. i.
[2] Hernán Cortés, "Carta Inédita," October 15, 1524, *Escritos Sueltos* (Biblioteca Histórica de la Iberia, XII), 56-61.

smaller towns, while the chief regional seats, or *cabeceras*, and the seaports were reserved under the king's direct control.[1] In such areas the Indians were no better off than those in encomienda, for the corregidor or alcalde mayor in charge of them bore the same relation to them as did the encomendero to his serfs. Thus the natives were held in a tutelage initiated by custom and sanctioned by law. They became the base of the social pyramid, the foundation of the colonial structure, upon which the upper parts pressed with relentless force. The system had the advantage of preserving the race, but the disadvantage of preserving it in habitual abjection and misery. The lot of the Indian was mitigated, however, by softening influences as the conquest gave up frenzied expeditions and turned to agriculture, commerce and mining, and by the refinements of art, literature and science, which modified society into a semblance of its European prototype.

The spirit of rapine, greed and cruelty which imbued the encomienda system was bitterly censured by Bartolomé de Las Casas before the conquest had passed to the continental stage. His propaganda for the amelioration of the condition of the natives is the best-known incident of the Spanish conquest. In 1542, when the colonial experiment was nearly half a century old, it led to an attempt to remodel its entire economic basis. His "New Laws of the Indies" are always characterized as regulations for the better treatment of the Indians; but the gist of the reform lay in their prohibition of the permanent encomienda. It had indeed been the purpose of the original grants that they should endure only

[1] A report of 1560 showed one hundred such towns and districts reserved for the king at that time. G. Latorre, ed., *Relaciones Geográficas de Indias* (Seville, 1920), 116-119.

through the lifetime of the grantee, the Indians then to become free vassals under the administration of an alcalde mayor or corregidor with the right to receive wages for labor and pay tribute to the king. The hostility of the monarch to the encomienda was based on its feudal character, which was inimical to the autocratic centralist form of government; he was also anxious to collect the tributes, the chief source of revenue from the Indians. As might be expected, the New Laws brought a storm of protest from the encomenderos. In Guatemala the new program evoked expressions of deep discontent and in Peru a desperate rebellion; in New Spain the practical-minded viceroy Mendoza deferred promulgating the laws and succeeded in having their more objectionable features revoked. They never became a working part of the legislation for the Indies, as Charles V repealed the prohibition against the inheritable encomienda in 1545.[1]

Encomiendas flourished best among the sedentary Indians of the high plateau, where the native nobility was speedily impoverished or destroyed and the common herd set to work for their new masters. Once beyond the area of the sedentary tribes, the system worked less advantageously. The reduction of the nomad to town life, to mission tutelage or mine working, was all one in the savage mind, and the frontier was for three hundred years the scene of guerrilla warfare in protest against exploitation, or "reduction" as it was then called. The right of inheritance in encomiendas was gradually, though not uniformly, extended to four or even five generations, and sometimes in perpetuity. The practice of commuting the perpetual encomiendas for annuities

[1] J. García Icazbalceta, *Obras* (Mexico, 1896-1905), V, 301-302.

began as early as 1577; down to 1791 the heirs of Cortés and Montezuma were receiving government annuities in lieu of tribute from encomiendas which they had lost.[1] If encomiendas lapsed by reason of lack of heirs they might be regranted, but it was made law in 1602 and 1612 that such lapsed grants should revert to the crown. Even after this, thirty-five encomiendas were granted in New Mexico for the purpose of border defense, though this seems to have been the latest instance of numerous grants.

It was hoped gradually to bring about the elimination of the institution. A general decree for its abolition was issued in 1720; in 1765 José de Gálvez was instructed to concern himself, in his general visitation of New Spain, with the condition of Indians who were being exploited by the governors and alcaldes who apportioned merchandise to them. Hence it is to be inferred that most of the encomiendas had by that time lapsed. Until the promulgation of the ordinance of the intendants in 1786, reorganizing the government of New Spain, the privilege of supplying the Indians with food, supplies, seeds and animals as advances upon their crops had been in the hands of the alcaldes mayores. This aid was then withdrawn; as a result the Indians fell under the system of debt peonage which only ended with the revolutions beginning in the time of Porfirio Díaz.[2]

[1] F. Fonseca and C. de Urrutia, *Historia General de Real Hacienda* (Mexico, 1845-1853), I, 426, 455-474. The persistence of the burden of the discovery is curiously illustrated by the fact that, when the Spanish War ended, Spain tried to induce the United States to assume payment of the annual pension to the Duke of Veragua, Columbus's heir, of $7400 per annum. Irene Newton, The Treaty of Paris, 1898 (Ph.D. thesis, Univ. of Calif., 1927).

[2] The literature on the encomienda is extensive. For a comprehensive treatment see Solórzano, *Política Indiana*, I, 244-433. Bourne, *Spain in*

The theory of legal wardship for the natives was exemplified by legislation giving them certain immunities, but at the same time placing them under restrictions which have, because of subsequent developments, seemed to warrant the assumption that the status of legal incapacity was intended to be made permanent. While it did turn out to be so, there is abundant evidence that the social institution was planned to be modified as soon as the native should become morally capable of profiting thereby. The mission system, with its contemplated process of secularization after a ten-year period, and the gradual abolition of the encomienda system just described are evidences of the desire to assist the evolutionary process where possible.

The mission system was an example of the quick modification of the machinery of the church to fit the needs of the progressive spiritual conquest. The mission most closely fitted the Indian situation because it embodied the altruistic and beneficent ideals of the conquering nation, and through it the blander side of the Spanish character was exhibited. All those paternalistic solicitudes which today characterize the civil state were then displayed by the church. Regrettable as it came to be

America, 254, cites a brief note in E. Armstrong, Charles V (N. Y., 1902), II, 100, to the effect that the Cortés and the communes, taking part in the controversy raised by Las Casas over the encomiendas, petitioned for the freedom of the Indians. For lapse of the institution, see the Recopilación de Indias (3d edn., Madrid, 1774), II, 231, laws xiv and xv, and Humboldt, Political Essay, I, 183. Icazbalceta, Obras, chaps. xv and xvi, has a disquisition on the early phases of the institution. See also F. de Azara, Viajes por la América del Sur (Montevideo, 1850), chap. xii. The Jesuit method is described in chap. xiii. Bourne calls the attention of Americans to the parallel between the nonenforcement of the encomienda legislation and the history of the Fifteenth Amendment to the Constitution. For a modern evaluation of the Spanish policy in the Indies, see Jerónimo Becker, La Política Española en las Indias (Madrid, 1920), esp. pt. i, chap. v, and for the abolition of the encomiendas in Chile, pt. iii, chap. xv.

in later years when the spirit of the state had developed, the very absorption by the church of the gentler duties of governmental activity served amiably the cause of humanity in the early period.

The mission was the most effective and widespread of of the social agencies.[1] It was developed by the regular clergy, notably by the Jesuits and the several branches of the Dominicans, Augustinians and Franciscans. Each mission was initiated on a frontier, of course, by one or more fathers imbued with apostolic zeal. The beginning depended upon the consent of the Indians, usually obtained by gifts or argument, and the permission of the government. The chief practical essentials were good farm land, irrigating water and building materials. Each mission became an agricultural school, for self-support was indispensable. After stability in crop production was attained came instruction in building, weaving, sewing, leather work, pottery making and other practical arts and crafts. These became the surest means through which growth was maintained.

Not much appeal was made to the neophyte's pride in the possession of property or the fruit of his handiwork. This unconscious weakness is easily explained. The fathers observed the rule of individual poverty, though their order might acquire unlimited collective wealth; hence the collectivity was the sole object of solicitude. The friar's pittance from the king was spent for such normal necessities of life as had to be imported to the frontier; the thousand pesos similarly bestowed for robes and vessels made no provision for upkeep and repairs. As a result the missions tried to produce more than they

[1] Fr. Z. Engelhardt, *The Missions and Missionaries of California* (San Francisco, 1908), II, chaps. xv and xvi.

could consume, and disposed of the surplus to pay for costs of maintenance or expansion. In sharp contrast with the history of the secular church little or no evidence remains of the accumulation of ostentatious wealth or the indulgence of physical luxury in the missions, though the Jesuits of Puebla in the early days undoubtedly made large profits in the sugar industry, and by research perhaps such instances might be multiplied. It was a common accusation during the entire colonial period that the religious engaged in smuggling oil, wine, chocolate and other articles primarily used by them for the support of the cult, and put their merchandise in the avenues of trade, reaping the advantages of their immunity from taxation and duties on such articles. This is vehemently but unconvincingly denied by many stout defenders of the religious orders.

The routine of the Indian in the mission included frequent religious exercises, sacred music, and crude but practical manual training.[1] The actual toil of the estate was shared by the fathers, two of whom were usually attached to each institution. Baptism, at first promiscuous and political in character, was early made contingent upon acceptance by the neophyte of the tenets of Christianity to the best of his understanding. Morality was guarded by insistence upon monogamy under Christian rites. Unmarried neophytes were locked up in separate buildings at night, as were the families, for the added reason of preventing flight. Recently reduced nomadic groups were permitted seasonal excursions to their traditional food-gathering resorts, both for economic

[1] Cf. H. E. Bolton, *The Spanish Borderlands* (Allen Johnson, ed., *The Chronicles of America Series*, New Haven, 1918-1921, XXIII), for characteristics of the frontier missions; their place in the scheme of conquest, 188-191, secularization, 282-285.

and sentimental reasons. Fugitives were persuaded to come back by gentle means, if possible; but in many instances their return required the use of the small escort-guard of soldiers which was usually stationed near enough for protection, usually too near to avoid corruption of Indian morals. Moral lapses by friars were occasionally scandalous, but the mission as an institution was characterized by the integrity of most of the missionaries. The punishment of offenders fell to the ecclesiastical jurisdiction, and was not, it must be confessed, remarkable for its frequency or severity. Indians who transgressed were whipped for offenses ranging from absence from mass to adultery. There are no cases on record of executions of mission Indians, though when rebellious they often met death at the hands of punitive expeditions. As in the case of all Indians, the Inquisition was prohibited from interfering in their lapses from the faith.

Theoretically the neophytes were the owners of the lands and buildings they occupied; but none of them seem to have comprehended this, and they had little conception of the idea of private ownership. When missions were secularized—that is, when the Indians were considered civilized and their religious care taken from the missionaries and given to parish priests—the lands belonging to the missions were apportioned to the natives collectively as needed; but almost inevitably the best lands were sooner or later seized by Spaniards. Secularization was the ideal goal of missionary effort, the theory being that the neophytes would be ready to be made free vassals in ten years. The result was seldom realized, principally because the Indians were incapable of the required progress, but also because the missionaries developed a natural proprietary attitude toward the institution that they had created. They never failed to resist secularization to the utmost of their ability. The religious history of New Spain is replete with accounts of their clashes with the secular clergy and the state officials over the issue.

The government of the missions, actually in the hands of the priests, was given a fictitious political organization for the sake of civil instruction. The principal Indians were given annual positions as governors and alcaldes, and taught to carry with true Castilian pride the gold or silver-topped canes, which were the insignia of their proud consequentiality, as they were of Spanish official positions. But it is not to be supposed that the Indians, official or nonofficial, ever attained anything like a proper conception of town or city government from such a tutelage.

Much has been written about the futility of the mission system by those who are either hostile to the church or skeptical of the capacity of the Indian. The missions did fail to bring him to the cultural stature of the whites; but, on the other hand, they furnished him a refuge from the more selfish exploitation of the lay conquerors. They were the schools in which the native learned more, and enjoyed greater peace and security, than in any other institution devised for his improvement. They measurably advanced his status, and probably would have worked greater permanent benefit had their opportunity been of longer duration, and had the ideal included the development of the notion of personal chattel property and then of individual ownership of land. As a social institution the mission compares favorably indeed with the modern reservation or Indian school. Its disappearance

*Christian Doctrine for the Indians.*

was as much due to the cupidity of its competitors, the lay Spaniards, as to any weakness inherent in its conception. Its accomplishment challenges the result of any other system of control of dependent peoples developed in the field of modern colonization.[1]

The wardship of the Indian was further manifested in numerous protective laws and in certain repressive ones. For protection Spaniards were forbidden to plant their towns where they would injure or restrict Indian villages. Possession of lands by Indian towns was often confirmed to them by the king, and many which had not sufficient area had grants made to them. No Indian land could be alienated except by action of the audiencia, and no transfer made unless it be shown that the native would be the gainer by the transaction. The Spanish grazier and farmer was obliged to observe the integrity of Indian holdings, keeping his activities separated from theirs by a strip of neutral ground about a thousand yards wide. If Indians ran away from their encomendero, deserting their lands, as they frequently did, such lands reverted to the crown and not the encomendero. In taxation the natives had certain immunities. They paid tribute and tithes, but were exempt from licenses on their small business enterprises, such as the refinement and sale of salt; indeed this industry was by law specifically reserved to them. If a number of Indians were gathered together upon an agricultural estate, when they reached a sufficient number they must receive a square league of land within which to have their town and communal lands.

The repressive legislation, however, shows that in

[1] For a judicious estimate of the mission system, see F. W. Blackmar, *Spanish Institutions of the Southwest* (Johns Hopkins Univ., *Studies*, extra vol. x), chaps. vi-vii.

spite of the avowed intention to make Christianity universal the attitude of the Spaniard was not unreservedly benignant. No Indian might possess a firearm or ride on horseback, the order being reiterated throughout the official documents. No Indian was admitted to any of the hundred or more trade guilds which flourished during the seventeenth and eighteenth centuries. None of them ascended to the priesthood during colonial days or to any other position of trust or public confidence, save that some of their nobility served as leaders to build defensive towns along the frontier.[1]

The evidence is conclusive that the Indians were ruthlessly and promiscuously deprived of their lands by the conquistadores and their heirs. The pre-Spanish towns had definitely allotted plots of ground for each family, with certain areas left untilled for rotation or expansion. These untilled lands were the special objects of Spanish cupidity. Alonzo de Zurita averred in 1582 that there was "no farm nor land which has been given to Spaniards which has not injured the Indians. . . . In some of the towns they are so surrounded by the fields of the Spaniards that they have no place left to sow in." [2]

Though the first onslaught of conquering bands was destructive of the Indian land rights, it was the early and continuous policy of the crown to safeguard native tenure. As most of the new lands conquered were given municipal status, so the Indian towns were protected by a similar form of grant for the benefit of free natives not held in encomienda. This was done by royal recog-

[1] M. Galván, *Ordenanzas de Tierras y Aguas* (Paris, 1855), 188-206; the laws included here form the legal basis of the agrarian reforms of 1915-1927.

[2] Çorita, "Breve y Sumaria Relación," Icazbalceta, *Nueva Colección de Documentos para la Historia de México*, III, 95-96.

nition of the towns or villages in which they lived as communal owners. This practical recognition of the native communal tenure was effected by decrees of Charles V on March 21, 1551.

Under very early laws the Indian towns acquired legal possession of a *fundo legal,* or square of land measuring six hundred yards in each of the cardinal directions from the door of their church. This plot was the "shell of the town" for residence and garden plots. Beyond this limit the natives were to have "as much more as they needed," and Spaniards were not to intrude within one thousand one hundred yards. The outside allotment, known as the ejido, was for grazing purposes. Sometimes it was much restricted; its metes and bounds were probably never very accurately determined. The natives, through natural propensity and well-founded apprehension of the self-interest moving their legal protectors, were traditionally jealous of their boundaries, and adept in slyly extending their limits at the expense of abutting Spanish haciendas. But in this contest with the white landowner the Indians were handicapped by their indigence and lack of thrift, by the fact that their crops often failed, and by the iniquitous but apparently indispensable debt-labor system. The social and economic result of the land and labor systems was that most of the "reduced" Indians were driven into debt peonage.

Aside from their communal lands Indian individuals as well as towns received grants from the king. Sometimes they even made purchases. The wise provision that Indian lands should not be alienable protected a primitive people from selling lands at ridiculous prices during food scarcity or for any transitory need or whim. The process of sale was rendered as difficult as possible, in the rare cases when it was permitted, by the regulation that it must be sanctioned by the audiencia.[1]

Indian towns were more numerous than Spanish ones, though individually they were, of course, of very much less importance. Protected from Spanish greed by royal legislation, they were an important agency, possibly not even second to the church, in preserving the native population even though at a low level of culture. The agencies for cultural growth in such groups of huts were of course few. To the benefits of the sedentary life were added the ministrations of the parish priest, either a resident or a visiting minister. His usefulness was limited by his training and interest and by the size of his parish; often it extended little beyond the formal demands of the sacraments. Sometimes the priests were mere tyros in the use of native languages. Parochial schools were limited in number and scope, their purpose being chiefly to train acolytes for the dignified observance of the liturgy. No medical aid was available other than that afforded by native *curanderos;* in large Spanish towns there was usually hospital accommodation where nuns served as nurses but patients did without medical attendance. There was little interest in intellectual matters, and more tragic still was the absence of general markets to stimulate local industries beyond supplying the needs of the community. The Indian towns had their annual elections of officers under the observation of the priest, much as did the missions under the friars. The *governa-*

[1] Martín de Mayorga, *Instrucción*, February 23, 1781, quoted in S. Moreno Cora, "Reseña Histórica de la Propiedad Territorial en la República Mexicana," *Las Leyes Federales Vigentes sobre Tierras* (Mexico, 1910), 20; José Díaz de las Vegas, Memorias piadosas de la nación Indiana (MS. in Bancroft Library), chap. xiii, par. iii, "Indios que por su nobleza y lealtad fueron honrados con títulos de encomiendas."

*dorcillo,* or head man, was the native *cacique,* his position being hereditary. He was allowed to try minor cases at law, but not to inflict the death penalty.

It is the opinion of some scholars that the condition of these serfs, for such they were, was superior to that of the English peasantry of their day, and that the exactions upon them were not more oppressive than the French *corvée.* Thomas Gage found in Guatemala artisans, such as smiths, tailors, carpenters, masons and shoemakers, but as we have seen, they were not members of the corresponding Spanish guilds. Hipólito Villaroel, a sharp critic of Spanish civilization in New Spain, declared in 1786 that the protective laws issued for the Indians had outlasted their utility. He believed that the officers of the audiencia were injuring the natives as well as society in general by insisting on the observance of legislation which pauperized the Indians and reduced agricultural production. Abad y Queipo, Bishop of Michoacan, shared this opinion nearer the end of the century, and recommended that the paternalistic regulations should be relaxed so as to give freer opportunity to the natives to make the most of themselves.[1]

Miserable as were the Indian towns in general, some of them stand out conspicuously on account of the special favor accorded them or because of their virile character. The well-known case of Tlaxcala, which had special privileges because it had aided Cortés, is an example of the higher standards. The Tlaxcalan were widely used for colonization throughout the northern frontier. The

[1] Thomas Gage, *A New Survey* (London, 1677), chap. xix, cited by Bourne, *Spain in America,* 262; Hipólito Villaroel, Enfermedades Políticas (MS. in Bancroft Library, 1785-1787), I, 12, 43; M. Abad y Queipo, "Estado Moral y Político . . . de Nueva España en 1799," Luis Mora, *Obras Sueltas* (Paris, 1837), I, 60-61.

city rapidly diminished in population during the colonial epoch, and never approached the importance of its pre-Cortesian days, probably because the better standards of life in Spanish towns drew the inhabitants away. Warfare for the Spaniards and disease must also have played their part.

A less well-known Indian town, whose origin throws light on the life of the people as well as on certain features of colonial administration, was the city of Tehuacan, somewhat to the southeast. In 1654 Philip IV found that the exigencies of his treasury demanded increased revenues to meet the expense of maintaining armies on his frontiers. After many conferences of his officers in Peru, New Spain and Spain, an acceptable plan of replenishment was evolved. It was decided, in the first place, to extend municipal organization by urgent suggestion, in order that initial gifts to the king for this favor would be forthcoming, and, secondly, to provide a great number of salable municipal offices, the purchase of which would yield goodly sums. Wherever practicable, villas and pueblos were to be raised to the status of ciudades.

In the pueblo of Tehuacan which, though inhabited by Indians, was surrounded by Spanish farmers, this measure aroused an interesting competition between the two constituencies. On March 15, 1660, the Spaniards, urged by a viceroyal commissioner sent out for the purpose, organized a town government as a first step toward converting the Indian town into a Spanish villa. They offered in return for the expected grace the sum of one thousand pesos, to be paid in three installments. The Indians, through their native officers, immediately sought to protect their prior rights as a pueblo. They urged that the old laws of Philip II, providing that no Spanish families or houses should be united with them, be properly observed,[1] and sweetened their demand by duplicating the bid of the Spaniards and, in addition, offering to pay a bonus of three thousand pesos. This they could do because the town had received that sum as a legacy from a deceased resident. In return they asked that Tehuacan be raised from the status of pueblo to that of an Indian city with all the privileges and exemptions enjoyed by Tlaxcala. The Spanish commissioner the next day held several conferences with the Spanish farmers in which he informed them that their offer had been too low. By close figuring they managed to raise it five hundred pesos and promised to pay for the required municipal offices the sums for which these might be auctioned. This was not enough; and when the Indians renewed their offer, the commissioner in the spirit of an auctioneer gave the Spaniards one hour's grace to make a new proposal.

Not getting any response, he then tried to get the Indians to increase their bid. This they could not do, though they agreed to pay half their gift in cash and the balance during the coming May. At once the commissioner ordered the money received and accepted the bonus of three thousand pesos pending the viceroy's final decision. In this manner Tehuacan was granted title as a *ciudad de Indios* with the same privileges as Tlaxcala. The Indians secured the right to elect their own council and other officers annually, a coat of arms, all the privi-

---

[1] The laws prohibiting Spaniards from living in Indian towns were honored in the breach, not the observance. A census report of 1560, listing the towns of Spaniards, adds: "There are many Indian towns in which there are many Spaniards, but they are not set down here, lest they bulk too large." Latorre, *Relaciones Geográficas de Indias*, 112.

leges of Indian cities—these being chiefly nominal exemption from certain taxes—and proper documents setting forth their new municipal status, lest the alcaldes mayores should encroach upon their rights as though they were still a mere pueblo.

They then proceeded to a chamber on the public plaza opposite the king's house, which they had designated as the meeting place for their council, accompanied by General Don Antonio Monroy Figueroa the alcalde mayor, the Indian officers and the local head of the Inquisition. The commissioner installed the council with much good advice, receiving their assurance that they would be loyal vassals. The public now withdrawing, he confirmed the officers of the city by turn—the governor, three ordinary justices, a bailiff, a standard bearer, six councilmen and a clerk. For procurator he named one of the councilmen, "so that he might petition for all that seemed suitable for the welfare of the city." Taking their seats in order of seniority, they then "all swore together by God Our Lord and the sign of the cross, which they made with the fingers of their right hands, to govern well and keep secret the affairs of government." Thereupon the session closed; the commissioner went to his quarters; and the proceedings were set down in the Book of the Council, and all signed them who knew how to do so.[1] Tehuacan and Tlaxcala were the outstanding examples of Indian cities of first importance.

The results of Indian policy, after the lapse of nearly three hundred years, were anything but consoling to the intelligent officers of the viceroyalty. The expectation of a speedy and general conversion to Christianity and a

[1] A. Peñafiel, *Ciudades Coloniales* (Mexico, 1908-1909), III, 102.

genuine absorption of the civilization of Spain had been realized in far less degree than had been anticipated. The condition of the Indian towns about the close of the eighteenth century was drawn in somber colors by Villaroel, who, viewing the body politic through jaundiced eyes, found it diseased in all its members. Many of the towns, he said, did not really merit the name, being mere aggregations of families scattered about at random on the plains, in dark ravines or on river banks, connected by trails leading from one miserable hut to another. Often not even a barber was to be found to render the services of leech, while a surplus of physicians resided in the capital. Many priests also refused to leave the capital, pleading that the towns were not able to support them. As to education in the Indian towns, it was of very indifferent quality since the priests were often college graduates without experience. Naturally the Indians felt little respect for such pastors, and made scant progress as compared with that of the early days of finer apostolic zeal. The agricultural education, dispensed informally by the alcaldes mayores in the pursuit of their official vocation, was little better, for these officers were bent only upon gain, those who showed real interest in their work receiving small encouragement from the central government.

The only remedy, thought Villaroel, lay in overcoming native idleness and developing real internal commerce through production and manufacture. Lacking correction, the Indian lived in idolatry, drunkenness, thievery and other vices, but one priest with only two vicars in a large parish could not be present everywhere.[1]

[1] Josephine Cuneo, The Enfermedades Políticas of Hipólito Villaroel, III (M.A. thesis, Univ. of Calif., 1919), 48-59.

Some towns were fifteen or twenty leagues distant from the priest's residence, and the Indians scarcely saw the father once a month. Since the regulars of the orders made better pastors and more of them were available, Villaroel advocated turning the parishes back to them. The regulars did not oppose the establishment of schools and the teaching of Spanish, nor would they suffer the hostile litigation over school establishment which often arose under the seculars.

The specific reforms which Villaroel suggested throw interesting light on the social life at the base of the pyramid. It is true that he was a bitter cynic who contemplated the defects of the colony through prejudice, but he had been an alcalde mayor for twenty-five years and thoroughly understood his subject. First of all, he would abolish the law which prevented Spaniards and other castes from living among the Indians, for the isolation of the natives was the greatest hindrance to their development. He would compel them to move their villages out of the mountains and forests, where, hidden away on their little corn patches, they felt free to indulge their customary vices. He would see that all should receive ample land since many towns had been deprived of their holdings by the aggressions of the Spanish farmers. Moreover, the towns, instead of being limited to the customary twelve hundred yards square, should have enough land so that half of it might be left fallow in alternate years. He would also do away with the prevalent vagabondage, preventing the natives from wandering from place to place to escape the penalties of their crimes or to avoid payment of the tribute. Enforcement of regulations like these should be intrusted to the priests and alcaldes.

Much was made of the idea that the Indians ought
to be subjected to the Inquisition because of their widespread and persistent idolatry. He also warmly recommended that a new code of legislation should be drawn
up to fit the actual state of affairs and the well-recog-
nized selfish astuteness of the Indians.

> The old legislation was thought necessary when the
> Indians were tender plants, irrigated by the healthful
> waters of the doctrine of Jesus Christ. But now, when
> for lack of a systematic method they have become ro-
> bust trees in every manner of vice and evil . . . it is
> necessary to give thought to their conversion, and sub-
> ject them by punishment to acknowledgment of their
> social obligations; otherwise they will be lost both to
> God and to the State. . . . For experience teaches that
> the more gently and suavely these people are dealt with,
> the more insolent do they become, the more insubordi-
> nate, and the more deeply are they rooted in their abom-
> inations, vices, and evil habits.[1]

Happily the modern age has learned, in a small degree
at least, that this attitude of self-righteous impatience
with backward races is not an aid to happy relations.
The path upward does not lie through sudden compulsion by the stronger nation, but rather through a patient understanding of the desire of the dependent people
to direct its own development. In the case of the half-
civilized natives of the central plateau the Spanish system raised up a moderately successful society. In the
farther northern reaches, now within the bounds of the
United States, the savage nomads were less amenable.
That the mission and the encomienda, with a social
structure based on the legal wardship of the red man,

[1] Villaroel, Enfermedades Políticas, I, 55-70; see Loretta Wilson
(M.A. thesis, Univ. of Calif., 1918).

did not become the foundation of the life of Florida, Texas and California, is due to the combination of human geography and the inflexibility of the Spanish colonial ideal.

# CHAPTER VI

## Spanish Colonial Life and Letters

THE Anglo-Saxon idea that the Spanish occupation of America brought few of the amenities of civilization is the result of ignorance and national prejudice. The belief arose during the beginnings of commercial competition between the English and the Spanish; it grew to great bitterness of feeling in the Elizabethan period and scarcely lessened throughout the seventeenth and eighteenth centuries. When England sought to aid the Spanish-American colonies in their struggle for emancipation from Spain in the early nineteenth century, the evils of popery and the stagnation resulting from colonial monopolies were invoked as justification, whereas the historian finds the more important springs to action in the generous self-appreciation and commercial instinct of the English, who hoped to open Spain's American dominions to the benefits of political liberty, Protestantism and free trade. The Americans have nourished the English tradition, reënforced by many unpleasant memories of their political and military contacts with the Mexicans and the traditional instability of a number of the southern republics. The trend of nationalistic aspiration with its scant respect for vested interests, demonstrated in the recent Mexican revolution, has given further occasion for a misunderstanding really based on racial antipathy.

In the perspective of the colonial epoch it is easier

to see how far from true are these harsh judgments of our neighbors' culture. Even in her self-imposed isolation Spain was for three hundred years a potent agent in transmitting European institutions to the New World, and the area and the population which she affected were greater than those of her rivals combined. Civilized life in Spanish America was inferior to that of no other colonial area; it even closely approximated in many ways the culture of Europe itself. The amenities were manifest in the fields of education, literature, painting, sculpture, music and the drama and in those little social graces, once regional in character, which are today a rich heritage from Spanish days cherished over wide reaches of the United States.

It is a popular misconception of history, repeated by no less a person than Blanco Fombona, that the Spanish "struggle with the Saracens fortified faith, but diminished intelligence." Of the Spaniards in America, he says "they lacked intellectual curiosity in the face of the unique civilizations they were about to destroy"; the religiosity of the Spaniard he deemed "the fruit of his worst defect, a lack of the critical spirit." [1] If the learned critic meant that the men who fought under Cortés, Pizarro and Pedrarias were not scientific in their outlook upon the New World, we may answer that even in this modern age the ruck and run of society exhibit little intellectual curiosity, even about those everyday applications of scientific principles which make life easy for us. But Señor Fombona would have modified his judgment had he paused a moment to recall distinguished writers like Oviedo, Mendieta, Sahagun, Clavigero,

[1] R. Blanco Fombona, *El Conquistador Español del Siglo XVI* (Madrid, 1922), 15, 18.

Medina and Hernández, who came to the New World and wrote their observations so effectively that Humboldt, to whom all Latin Americans bow, sprinkled his *Cosmos* with the record of Spanish contributions in the Occident to modern science. That great savant said, to cite one instance:

> The groundwork of what we at present term physical geography, independently of mathematical considerations, is contained in the Jesuit Joseph Acosta's work entitled *Historia natural y moral de las Indias,* and in the work of Gonzalo Hernández de Oviedo, the *Historia general y natural,* which appeared hardly twenty years after the death of Columbus. At no other period since the origin of society has the sphere of ideas been so suddenly and wonderfully enlarged in reference to the external world and geographical relations.[1]

Neither teachings of the church nor the eyes of the Inquisition could keep the mind of New Spain in the narrow path of complete orthodoxy. Intellectually as well as politically the colonist was an individualist. This intellectual independence was not confined to the eighteenth century, nor was the smuggling of books characteristic only of the age of the philosophical revolt led by the Encyclopedists. Indeed, the upper stratum of society in New Spain of the sixteenth century exhibited keen enthusiasm for the European literature of that day. The importation of books went on with little hindrance until 1571, when the court of the Inquisition was given

[1] Alexander von Humboldt, *Cosmos* (London, 1864), II, 635. This work is so full of the recognition of Spanish scientific achievement that Latin American publicists may confidently turn to it for confirmation of the patriotic claims of writers like Puente y Olea, who delight to amass evidence of the scientific reaction of the Spaniards to the New World as shown in their contributions to geography, cartography and the embryonic physical sciences of their day. M. de la Puente y Olea, *Trabajos Geográficos de la Casa de Contratación* (Seville, 1900), *passim.*

permanent organization for the entire viceroyalty. It was
inaugurated under the control of the versatile, sancti-
monious and meddlesome Pedro de Moya y Contreras,
visitor general, inquisitor, bishop and, later, viceroy.

In that year he issued an edict governing the importation, sale and reading of books. Constant inspection of the mental pabulum of the country was to be
performed at Vera Cruz, it being "the port of all
nations," where books were "creating public wells of
poison and deep roots of venom," especially works by
followers of "the accursed heresiarch Luther." But
Lutheranism was not the only well of heresy in which
the pious subjects of New Spain might find spiritual
death. The growth of Judaism was extensive, even if we
may not quite believe the statement of one of its ad-
herents, a rabbi of Mexico, who averred that there were
more followers of that faith than Catholics among the
Spaniards of the colony.[1] It was believed that the policy
of the enemies of Philip II was to seek the destruction of
Spain by breaking down her chief defensive and offensive
weapon, religion. Hostile propaganda was to be fought
with an instrument adapted to her hand.

Hence Moya ordered a round-up of all works mentioned in the general censure published at Valladolid in
1554, and of all books listed in the Catalogue of 1559.
Also, as other books of false doctrine had been printed
since those lists were published, a general visitation of
all the bookshops was ordered, the inhabitants were forbidden to read any works in the lists and dealers prohibited from importing or selling them, under pain of

---

[1] F. Fernández del Castillo, ed., *Libros y Libreros del Siglo XVI*
(Mexico, Archivo General, *Publicaciones*, VI), 584.

The city and fortress of Vera Cruz in the seventeenth century.

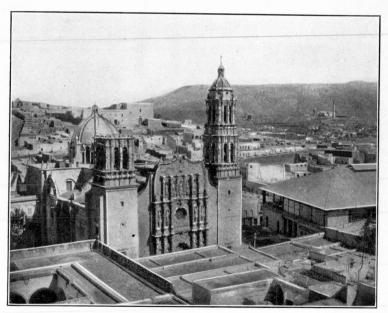

The roofs of Zacatecas, a mining town for nearly four centuries.

## Old Towns of New Spain.

excommunication.[1] All churches, monasteries, schools and book dealers, as well as private persons, were required to send to the inquisitor's agent the titles of all books in their possession, with the names and addresses of the owners. Every dealer, before opening his boxes of importations, must report his bill of lading. Treasury inspectors, loaned to the Holy Office, examined the boxes at the ports, not daring to read any books, but merely reporting titles. This inspection, however, was to be conducted under the dictates of good judgment and common sense and must neither impede business, it was said, nor annoy importers. Books containing scattered errors in theological teaching, but not entirely depraved, were to be emended and returned to their owners. Images and religious prints containing any other letter or couplet than the name of the maker and place of manufacture were also contraband, as subtle devices for the introduction of heresies. The edict was generally obeyed.

Moya was quite right in asserting that the regular convoyed fleets, as well as the single registered ships, had brought hundreds of books from Spain and foreign countries. The printed lists of the vessels inspected by the Inquisition from 1572 to 1600 show that over five hundred boxes of books were examined, besides hundreds of separate items mentioned by title as among the personal effects of passengers and marine officers.[2] One consignment of forty boxes in 1585 contained as many as sixty items in each. Thus it may be estimated that thirty thousand volumes were imported into New Spain during the last quarter of the sixteenth century, not to mention those smuggled. Among the interesting importations

[1] Fernández del Castillo, *Libros y Libreros*, 459-463.
[2] Fernández del Castillo, 351-446.

were certain prohibited versions of the Bible. A consignment mentioned contained nearly two hundred copies of the *Biblia de Vatablo,* so named after Francisco Vatable, a Picard professor of Hebrew in the Royal College of France.[1] In 1583 a confiscation on a grand scale took place; two years later owners whose books had been collected for inspection complained that they had not been returned. On many occasions books were secretly burned on suspicion, or because the proper censoring would entail too much labor.

The book census taken by Moya's orders gives a fair idea of the colonial literary tastes of the time. The list covered twenty-five printed pages and included the names and addresses of all owners of books. A similar list, made for Puebla in 1588, named over three hundred residents of that provincial town as the possessors of one or more volumes. In the list for Mexico City in 1573 there were six hundred and more owners, including convents. Favorite subjects, of course, were: *The Ascent of Mount Zion, The Soul's Awakener, The Soul's Retirement, The Light of the Soul, The Rule of Christian Life* and *Instruction and Refuge of the Soul.* The inspection revealed possession of one hundred and twenty-five copies of the Bible, together with a much greater distribution of the parts of it separately printed, such as Psalms, Proverbs, Ecclesiasticus, the Apocalypse, the New Testament, the Gospels in romance and numerous Epistles.

---

[1] Fernández del Castillo, *Libros y Libreros,* 254-371. In 1545 Robert Etienne published the Latin Bible of León de Judá with certain notes, to which he put the name of Vatable, although they were not by the latter but taken from certain reformers; they had been condemned by the Sorbonne. This Bible contained the Hebrew text, the version of the Vulgate, and that of León de Judá, which Etienne had printed. It was reprinted at Seville. Upon the importation in 1585 to New Spain, all copies were required to be censored before they could be read.

All were to be closely examined to see if they had been properly corrected by the Inquisition. "Alonso Caballero," wrote the inspector, "has a Bible which states that it has been emended by me; it will be necessary to look at it, for at that time there were many things which I did not delete that are now ordered stricken out by this Holy Office." The first volume of St. Augustine and the fifth of Chrysostom required deletion before the faithful might be trusted with them.

Cicero's *De Officiis* and *Epistolae* mustered a number of copies each, though the former, when annotated by Melancthon, was prohibited by the Catalogue. The works of Erasmus, particularly the *Scholia* and the *Chiliades*, were numbered by the score or more; there was a sprinkling of the *Epitome* and the *Adages*. Not only the works of this famous pensioner of Charles V, but those of suspected commentators like Fero, and heterodox Bibles of numerous imprints dating between 1531 and 1551, were commonly found. But books of piety by no means made up the whole list. Works on chivalry, headed by *Amadis de Gaula,* included *El Caballero de Febo, Oliveros de Castilla, Palmerín, Celidón, El Determinado, Don Olivante de Laura, Don Belianis, Roncesvalles, Roldán, Orlando el Furioso* and many others. They were extremely popular and no doubt had their effect in heartening adventurous enterprise for the territorial conquests of the day. One Pedro and one Sebastián de la Pacarán, naughty residents of the lower quarter, had copies of Boccaccio, which was in the Catalogue.

It is an agreeable surprise to note that the ancient classics circulated freely. The works of Homer, Virgil, Cicero, Ovid, Lucan, Terence, Plutarch, Marcus Aurelius and Ariosto were popular. The verses of Petrarch and Camoens were very commonly found. The Spanish classics were abundant; poets, dramatists, novelists and mystics, such as Jorge de Manrique, Juan de Mena, Herrera, Garcilazo, Ercilla, Lope de Vega, Francisco de Rojas, Diego de San Pedro, Mateo Alemán, Espinel, Cervantes, Luis de Granada and Luis de León, were often read on board transatlantic vessels by passengers and officers and sold on land to those of literary thirst. This would seem to disprove the statement by Medina, followed by Bancroft, that the writings of the followers of St. Francis, who were taught "not to profess sciences and books, but to study humility," stamped the literary taste to a great extent in all directions.[1]

Some fifty persons were engaged in the business of bookselling during the first century in Mexico City alone. They carried books with other merchandise, or were only occasional venders. Printers sold their own wares and also speculated in paper, which was at times so scarce that old books were torn up to remake it. Printing began in 1535 or 1536, no less than seven or eight master printers operating establishments in succession during the century. The business seems to have been a good one, protected as it was by practical monopoly. Some nine thousand sets of playing cards were printed every year, testifying to sociability if not to a general habit of gambling. The print shops employed Indians to some extent in the lower grades of work, though a few printers and some other artisans refused to teach them anything of their trade lest they themselves be deprived of a livelihood.

[1] H. H. Bancroft, *Essays and Miscellany* (*History of the Pacific States,* San Francisco, 1882-1890, XXXIII), 486.

Most of the products of the early presses have disappeared because of the ravages of climate and insect pests, storage in damp cellars and the destructive wear on books printed for use as mere texts. Thirty-six books of this century, now known only by reference, were listed by Francisco Fernández del Castillo in the *Libros y Libreros*.[1] All were books of devotion, grammars or calendars save one, the *Suma y Recopilación de Cirugía* (1578, expanded in 1595) by Alonzo López de Hinojoso. Works of which one or two copies only are extant number eighty, among them a *Graduale Dominicale* of 1575, it being the first music book with an American imprint. Among the eighty those lying outside the fields of religion, law or grammar include a *Relación* of the terrifying earthquake of 1540 in Guatemala, a *Tratado breve de Medicina* (1579, amplified in 1592) by Fray Agustín de Farfán, and *Diálogos Militares* (1583) and an *Instrucción Náutica* (1579).

All these books, including the religious ones, were practical rather than literary. The large number in native languages is proof of the active propagation of Christianity and a notable testimonial to the linguistics of the day. Practically the only writings of the first century which still command the attention of modern readers are the famous *Letters* of Cortés and the inimitable *True History* of Bernal Díaz. Father Toribio Benavente's *Historia de los Indios de Nueva España,* Father Juan Mendieta's *Historia Eclesiástica Indiana* and Father Torquemada's *Monarchia Indiana* are readable and authoritative monuments of early historical writing. Agustín Vetancurt, Antonio Tello, Mota Padílla, Baltazar Medina, Dávila Padilla and Francisco de Florencia,

[1] Fernández del Castillo, *Libros y Libreros*, 564-577.

chroniclers of religious orders, yield a valuable grist to
historical investigators. Suárez Peralta and Cervantes de
Salazar wrote on the conquest. The historical writings
of the eighteenth century by the American-born Jesuits
Alegre, Clavigero, Cavo and Veytia show by their improved style, point of view and philosophical interpretation that the Spanish American authors could
make contributions equal to the best of Jesuit scholarship.

The development of scientific thinking in Mexico
followed the same trend upward. It is not surprising
that the beginnings should have been made among the
medical profession, by such men as Farfán and Juan de
Cárdenas. The latter undertook a book of universal
knowledge, of special interest to the student of intellectual history, displaying as it does the crudities of the
author's reasoning, the lack of scientific observation
then common, and aspects of the life of the times not
touched upon by historical or religious writers.[1] The
author was only twenty-six years old when he wrote,
but had traveled extensively in Peru and Mexico. He
was a professor in the University of Mexico and practised medicine in Campostela and Guadalajara as well as
at the capital.

Writing for *curiosos romancistas* rather than men of
science, he preserved a mass of old lore of little scientific value, but brimming with human interest. The
inquiry of the first part was into the phenomena of
the physical world. Why were there in New Spain so
many earthquakes, volcanoes and hot springs? Why did
it rain in summer and not in winter? Why did hot and

[1] *Primera Parte de los Problemas y Secretos Maravillosos de las Indias*
(Mexico, 1591; reprinted, 1913), *passim.*

cold lands alternate so closely? The second part dealt with the extraction of ores, explaining why salt was mixed with them and why the quicksilver disappeared in the process. There are also discussions of cacao, maize, chocolate, the common gruels, and the beneficent qualities of tobacco smoke, of which "if one but swallow a few mouthfuls, even though he should eat a whole sheep, he would feel no sense of fullness whatever." The third part dealt with the qualities of men and animals born in the Indies. Why were Spaniards born there of light and delicate mental faculties; why did their hair early turn gray; why were there so many stomach ailments; why did the Indians have no beards but seldom become bald?

In that day the basis of philosophy and medicine lay in the existence of heat or cold, dryness or moisture; hence the first object of inquiry was why the torrid zone in the Indies was warm and wet. The warmth, said the young doctor, was due to the fact that in the tropics the sun's rays are direct. Humidity, he explained, came from the fact that in New Spain the earth is full of great caverns; these naturally fill with water from the vapors that fall and condense in the caverns because of their great coldness. Then the sun draws up the moisture and humidifies the air. The sun does not warm the air but the earth, and the latter warms the air. Iron heats in the sun faster than earth; that is, the denser the material the more heat does it receive. Thus the many caverns occur because the sun's rays penetrate into the abyss of the earth and consume the solid substances through their exhalation into gases, leaving the surface hard but below it many caves and grottoes. In more temperate zones the less direct rays of the sun have not drawn up the solids as they have in the tropics. The winds of the torrid regions are caused by the heat of the sun falling upon the earth, creating exhalations which blow away with great force. Deposits of great masses of minerals were thus created beneath the surface, a condition assisted by the fact that New Spain lay directly under the signs of the zodiac, so that the heavenly bodies which affect the earth caused an influx of minerals to compensate for the exhalations caused by the sun's heat.[1]

His comments on the people present the salient characteristics of society. Eliminating those who died with their boots on, Cárdenas believed that if longevity depended on good constitutions Spanish Americans lived much longer than Spaniards, for the latter were too choleric. But humidity and heat, the light nourishing values of American foods and the pursuit of idle and vicious habits tended to make Americans shorter lived by about ten per cent of the normal span. The prevalent stomach disorders, due to bad habits of eating, tended to ripen men for old age prematurely. This process was hastened by the softness of the flesh of the Americans, caused by the excessive humidity of the climate which made their bodies unable to conserve their "natural heat."

People born in the Indies were generally of sanguine disposition; that is, following the ideas of Galen, they were of "hot and humid constitution." This was due to the hot sun and humid climate and to the fact that Spaniards are by nature choleric. At the same time they were frank, liberal and animated. These "light and delicate humors" caused the people to lack perseverance in their affairs—the standard Spanish opinion of the cre-

[1] The reader will find many of these ideas preserved in the explanation of natural phenomena offered by Descartes.

oles, as colonial-born Spaniards were called. They wanted also the counter quality of melancholy, compensating for it by kindly and delicate traits. Yet the author was convinced that there were people in the Indies whose sensitive understanding, balanced by constancy and perseverance, made them superior to other nationalities. Not only were there many families illustrious in the history of the New World, but among its scholars were many who, if better known, would rank among the wisest of the earth. If two rustics, one colonial-born and the other Spanish, should come together, the former would use a language so full of rhetorical turns as to make it appear he had been raised at court; in comparison the *chapetón* would sound brusque and rough.

His compatriots of the Indies, the author observed, were wont to turn gray prematurely, even those in the best circumstances. This, he thought, was due to loss of bodily heat, which caused the blood to diminish and be replaced by a phlegmatic humor that, being white, produced white hair. That the Indian, who was most phlegmatic of all, rarely turned gray, Cárdenas accounted for by reasoning that with the savage phlegm was natural while that of the Spaniard was accidental, being caused by lack of exercise, overeating and drinking and sexual indulgence. Indians had no beards, Cárdenas argued, because their progenitors had long lived exposed to the weather and the sun had dried their skins. This did not affect the hair on the head, which grows with more force than that on the chin; for the hair and the beard grow from the humors cast off by the brain, and it is natural for these humors to rise as the fissures of the skull encourage their escape.

Among the Spaniards, he averred, the ravages of syphilis were so extensive that hardly a man failed to show some trace of it by a swollen temple, a black velvet patch covering a lesion on the face, a scar denoting a bone lost from the head or some similar defect. To cure it they employed great quantities of mercury, guaiacum, China-root, sarsaparilla, henna, dodder, polyposium and hermadactyl. The disease was spoken of commonly as one of the "products of the country," and was widespread among Negroes and Indians. The origin of it, Cárdenas thought, was in America, from which the Spaniards had communicated it to Europe.

Virtually no one was exempt from maladies of the digestive tract. This he thought was due to injudicious eating, resulting in a coldness of the stomach which prevented that organ from "cooking" the food; it was also superinduced by study and prayer. The very prevalent blindness, painfully noticeable during Holy Week when swarms of sightless mendicants gathered to beg alms, was the result of the incessant smoke in which the lower class steeped themselves about their domestic fires and of the wines they drank. He did not note that the blindness was syphilitic, though he did consider it a sequel to smallpox.

From Cárdenas we catch a glimpse of the beginnings of Western science before the day of differentiation and specialization, and are able to appreciate the great distance which the mind of man had to travel before reaching the enlightenment of modern times. The medical profession in New Spain was never widely practiced or highly advanced. The cure of bodies was much less efficiently attended to than that of souls, and, as we have seen, the number of practitioners was relatively small

—even of those with as much medical experience and knowledge as Dr. Cárdenas. Empirical and superstitious methods long held sway, while medicine men and quacks had wide influence. Yet there were a few men of great industry and of creditable skill.

Spanish writers on medicine worthy of notice, besides Hinojoso and Farfán who have already been mentioned, were Cristóbal Méndez, who discoursed on exercise and its benefits (1553); Pedrarias de Benavides, the author of *Los Secretos de Cirugía* (1567); Dr. Bravo, who wrote *Opera Medicinalia* (1570); and Francisco Hernández, whose *Natural History of New Spain* (1651), written in compliance with royal orders, remains an authoritative work on the fauna and flora of the region. Juan de la Fuente, the teacher of Cárdenas, was a sturdy investigator of disease. During the widespread epidemic of 1576 he sought to discover the origin and seat of the pestilence by studying the cadavers of its victims in the Hospital Real.[1] Many years later Charles IV made effective efforts against the baleful effects of smallpox upon the American colonists by introducing vaccine virus and encouraging a wide application of it to his subjects at a time when the controversies aroused against Jenner were almost as virulent as the disease itself.[2]

The early pursuit of the mathematical sciences in America led to useful observations in astronomy, mathematics and physics by transplanted scholars from France, Spain and Portugal. Clever use was made of the astro-

---

[1] H. H. Bancroft, *History of Mexico* (San Francisco, 1883-1887), II, 658-659, speaks of this epidemic.

[2] Bancroft, *History of Mexico*, III, 757-760; Edna Fisher, Medical Knowledge and Practice in New Spain during the Sixteenth Century (M.A. thesis, Univ. of Calif., 1921); F. A. Flores, *Historia de la Medicina en México desde la Epoca de los Indios hasta la Presente* (Mexico, 1886-1888).

nomical ring, a modification of the astrolabe, by such missionary fathers as Eusebio Kino, Nadal, Juan Díaz and Pedro Font. Antonio de Mendoza, first viceroy of New Spain, obtained a fairly accurate longitude for Mexico City in 1541 by observing two lunar eclipses and so computing the difference in time from that of Toledo. This yielded a longitude slightly in excess of the true value, 25° 42′ 42″, but it was accepted as correct during the remainder of the century. In 1577 the eclipse of the moon on September 23, observed by scientists in several parts of the world, made it possible to fix the latitude of Mexico City at less than 4° in excess of its true value.[1] An eclipse of the moon observed by Enrico Martínez [2] at Huehuetoca, on the same meridian as Mexico, was compared with concurrent European ones by Fray Diego Rodríguez of the University of Mexico, whereby the longitude was corrected to 101° 27′ 30″ west of Paris, a result more accurate than Humboldt obtained a century and a half later and only twelve seconds different from the modern reading of 101° 27′ 18″ obtained by Francisco Díaz Covarrubias. Unfortunately this computation did not become known in Europe, where eighteenth-century geographers persisted in the old errors. Among the best eighteenth-century determinations was that of Antonio León y Gama, a native of Mexico, who, like many of his contemporaries, was a highly successful generalist in science.

The scientific study of comets was begun fairly early in Mexico. In 1653 Gabriel López de Bonilla published

[1] Florian Cajori, "The Mathematical Sciences in the Latin Colonies of America," *Scientific Mo.*, XVI (1923), 196.

[2] Beside being the builder of the Huehuetoca drainage canal, this notable Dutchman gave evidence of his versatility by serving as a type founder and as an interpreter of Flemish and German before the court of the Inquisition in 1598. Fernández del Castillo, *Libros y Libreros*, 531-532.

a discourse on the comet of December of that year. The comet of 1680 aroused both scientific and theological debate at Mexico City. Carlos de Sigüenza y Góngora, mathematician, philosopher, historian and antiquarian, a professor in the University of Mexico, issued a manifesto in 1681 reassuring the Mexicans that comets, contrary to popular belief, had nothing to do with the wrath of Providence. When his notions were opposed by a Flemish nobleman, Martín de la Torre, who defended the superstitious attitude toward them, Sigüenza replied with a pamphlet entitled *Mathematical Bellerophonte against Astrological Chimeras.* This rejoinder drew the criticism of Kino the Jesuit, who arrogantly attacked Sigüenza's theories and led the latter to answer with a *Libra Astronómica y Philosóphica,* the same title as that used by P. Orozio Grossi in replying to Galileo on the comet of 1618. In this work such technical questions were discussed as those of parallax, astronomical refraction, and the rectilinear paths of comets advocated by Kepler in contrast with the idea of helixes based on Descartes's theory of vortices. "Sigüenza challenged the reliability of Kino's observations on the ground that the comet of the year 1680 could not be observed with accuracy in Europe because of its great declination and its appearance in twilight." This was the first clash on a scientific subject to occur on American soil.[1]

While the scientific work in Spanish America was

---

[1] Cajori, "Mathematical Sciences," 200. A work on an astronomical subject, printed in Mexico in 1727, was on the solar eclipse of March 27 of that year: Juan Antonio de Mendoza y González, *Sperographía de la Obscuracion de la Tierra, en el Eclypse del Sol del 22 de Marzo de 1727. Methodo de observarlo, y de corregir los Reloxes;* listed by J. T. Medina, *La Imprenta en México* (Santiago, 1907-1912), IV, no. 2941. See also Florian Cajori, *The Early Mathematical Sciences in North and South America* (Boston, 1928).

mainly observational and its best value was obtained from comparisons made in Europe, yet it was a source of satisfaction that some of it represented the achievement of men born and educated in America. Even before the nineteenth century, Americans, distant though they were, had to be reckoned with by the scholar who sought to keep abreast of scientific thought.[1]

In *belles-lettres* the colonial epoch produced a few works which brought their authors established reputations, but literary activity of lesser quality was immense. Among those worthy of mention were Fernán González Eslave, whose religious poetry exhibited a purity of diction and grace of style in happy contrast with the heavy productions of his time; he died before 1610. Rafael Landívar, Jesuit creole of Guatemala, in his *Rusticatio mexicana* gave an example of New World *Georgics* which entitled his work to remembrance and republication in 1925. The one feminine prodigy of Mexican letters, Sor Juana Inés de la Cruz, driven by her creole inferiority complex into the profession of religion, was world-renowned even in her own time for her lyrics and sonnets. Among her dramatic compositions *Los empeños de una casa* is a portraiture of Mexican daily life, in which a number of love scenes are delicately depicted. Sor Juana has today greater vogue in Spain than in her own land during her life; in very recent times a renewed enthusiasm for her work has grown in America.[2] Possibly ranking with her was Juan Ruiz de Alarcón y Mendoza, a creole hunchback born at Mexico City

[1] Cajori, "Mathematical Sciences," 204. *Cf.* Alexander von Humboldt, *Political Essay on the Kingdom of New Spain* (London, 1814), I, 211-225.

[2] Dorothy Schons, *Bibliografía de Sor Juana Inés de la Cruz* (Mexico, 1927).

about 1580. His dramatic comedies made him famous in Spain. The most noted of his works, *Verdad sospechosa,* was generously acknowledged by Corneille as having inspired his *Menteur.* Alarcón lent his energies to portraying nobility of character and exposing the viciousness of low living. In Mexico he is considered the creator of the national dramatic literature.[1]

In the eighteenth century were written numerous poems of occasional character, biographies, and other versifications, among them *La Hernandia* by Ruiz de León. Father Anaya and others added to the voluminous compositions in honor of the Virgin of Guadalupe. Soria's comedy, *La Mágica Mexicana,* and his description of Tehuacan de las Granadas deserve mention, as does Ruiz de León's *La Conquista de México.* Father Castro wrote another *Conquista,* and a description of Antequera de Oaxaca and the ruins of Mitla.[2]

In a land of innumerable public processions the literary *certamen,* in high favor among the intellectuals of the age, is illustrated by the record contained in *Amorosa contienda de Francia, Italia, y España sobre la augusta persona del Señor Carlos III* (Mexico, 1761). For the announcement of such a contest it was customary to hold a sparkling procession on the main streets amid the pealing of church bells. Kettledrummers led the van, followed by students on horseback; the leading gentlemen of the city, doctors, prelates, public employees in profusion, and the religious communities were followed by some person of distinction who bore an immense banner announcing the competition. Soldiers marched with

---

[1] Bancroft, *Essays and Miscellany,* 524-530.
[2] Francisco Pimentel, *Historia Crítica de la Literatura y de las Ciencias en México desde la Conquista* (Mexico, 1885), 709; Luis Urbina, *La Vida Literaria de México* (Madrid, 1917), 17-135.

them to keep order. The procession ended at the university, where the rules of the contest were read in the *aula mayor*.

The delight of the Mexicans in poetry is shown by the existence of numerous "academies" named for saints, in which metrical compositions were written and read. The bibliographer Beristain listed some hundred versifiers, of whom Pimentel accepted twenty as demonstrating respectable capacity. Over three hundred contestants competed for various prizes at a literary contest in 1585, and more than two hundred at the time of the erection of Manuel Tolsa's equestrian statue of Charles IV in 1797.[1]

Fostered by the religious orders, the schools of New Spain were among the earliest establishments. Schools ripened rapidly into colleges and universities. The University of Mexico, established in 1551, was the prototype in the New World, after the tradition of Paris and Salamanca, of seven Spanish American universities founded before the close of the seventeenth century. The Franciscan college of Santa Cruz de Tlaltelolco for Indian boys in Mexico City, Father Gante's primary school of a thousand singing boys, the foundling college of San Juan Letrán, another school for foundling girls and the Augustinian school begun at Tiripitío in 1543, were institutions in which labored many learned teachers of European training.

As time went on, these institutions spread throughout the older provinces, but none of note were established in

[1] Pimentel, *Historia Crítica de la Literatura y de las Ciencias en México desde la Conquista*, 361. Bernardo de Balbuena, *Grandeza Mexicana* (Mexico, 1604; reproduced in facsimile by the Sociedad de Bibliófilos Mexicanos, Mexico, 1927), is a gem of seventeenth-century poetry in praise of the City of Mexico, from the famous press of Pedro Ocharte.

the remote frontiers now in United States territory. Most of them were conducted for Spanish boys; their courses led to the practice of law or to church positions. Some, but not many, half-breeds were admitted to this highly practical training. The instruction of the Indians was not entirely neglected, however, for they were clever in adapting their natural manual skill to the arts and crafts brought by the Spaniards. Manual education as well as the spiritual was encouraged by the building of churches and monasteries, and in the trade guilds Indians sometimes found opportunity if not generous welcome.

Students from all ranks of society received instruction from priests and friars in reading, writing and music. There was some instruction in Latin, drawing, painting and, now and then, in the mechanical arts. During the later colonial days the education of the lower classes by the church was not favored enthusiastically; even white children came to receive training in private schools, often conducted by laymen. It was habitual to the end for many families to send their sons to Spain for university work.

Just about the end of the eighteenth century the teaching of the sciences and the industrial and fine arts received great impetus. At that time New Spain enjoyed a high place among the cultured communities of the world. In 1783 the school of mines at Mexico City gave practical courses in mineralogy, and José Fausto Elhuyar and Andrés del Rio of its faculty were more than locally known authorities in that science. About the same time Antonio de Alzate began publishing his encyclopedic articles covering scientific interests in his *Gacetas de Literatura;* he has a place, especially as an astronomer, among the founders of the modern sciences. Cárdenas de

León and León y Gama were likewise distinguished in many fields of scientific research.

The Royal Academy of Beaux Arts, founded in 1773, gave free instruction in architecture, sculpture and painting. It is still open to the public on the same terms and is actively patronized. Its initial work had been preceded by the activities of a respectable group of Spanish painters in New Spain as early as the sixteenth century, among whom were Rodrigo de Cifuentes and Alonso Vásques. Among twenty-six artists of praiseworthy accomplishments during the seventeenth century were Baltazar Chávez and several other followers of the Seville school. In the last century of colonial rule over one hundred painters were added to the roll of notable producers, of whom five or six, including Miguel Cabrera, Juan Rodríguez Xuáres, José Alcíbar and Francisco Tresguerras, attained undisputed reputations.

The quaint architecture of the sixteenth century survives in Mexico in numerous buildings whose plain façades are covered with elaborate stucco relief work and border ornamentation. In the seventeenth century the old simplicity of decoration was followed by the baroque style, and in the eighteenth by the churrigueresque.[1] The buildings of the later days were often the work of native architects without European masters, and the old churches of the capital and the provincial towns stand

[1] Both are forms of the Free Renaissance style, characterized by interruption of straight lines, varied curvature of arches and lintels and ornamentation of panels. In the baroque the column is retained, though panels may remain undecorated and profiles regular. The distribution is conventional. Churrigueresque, named from Churriguera the architect, is florid with decoration, the sculpture becoming an integral part of the structure. Its luxuriance fell into disrepute about the middle of the eighteenth century. Sylvester Baxter, *Spanish Colonial Architecture in Mexico* (Boston, 1901), I, 23-42; A. C. Bossom, *An Architectural Pilgrimage in Old Mexico* (N. Y., 1924), p. x; W. H. Kilham, *Mexican Architecture of the Viceregal Period* (N. Y., 1927), *passim.*

*"Los Desposorios de la Virgen," painted by Sebastián Arteaga.*

*Sixteenth-Century Art in Mexico.*

as monuments not only to the faith of the fathers and their skill in construction but also to their ability to exact continuous work from the Indians. Standing in the presence of some of these ancient shrines of culture, even the most enthusiastic modern must acknowledge that the colonial epoch, with all its unloveliness, possessed a spirit of craftsmanship and devotion that has now largely vanished. The churches are found in all three styles of ornamentation mentioned. Among them is the most dignified structure in the republic, the cathedral of Mexico City. Begun in 1573 and completed in 1813, it is a masterpiece of colonial construction and still the grandest as well as the oldest church edifice in North America. The simpler style of the frontier missions and churches has a continually widening influence in our modern domestic architecture.

But letters, painting, sculpture, music, drama, architecture and the like, however great their range and richness, are not the only arts by which the human mind can interpret and adorn the common life. There are, for example, the arts of courtesy and ceremony, which may lay all others under contribution, but which have a spirit and technique of their own. In such arts no people have surpassed the Spaniards as represented in the cities of the Indies not less than in their prototypes across the sea. An account of civilization in New Spain could be scarcely called complete which did not portray a public celebration, for in such all these tastes and instincts had their play and the general social character was strikingly revealed. No example perhaps could serve our purpose better than the demonstration on the coming of a viceroy. Sixty times during three hundred years the ceremonious reception of a new administrator roused the people to a vivid pageant of all New Spain in outbursts of hospitality and enthusiasm comparable with the welcome accorded in 1640 to Don Diego López Pacheco, duke of Escalona, seventeenth viceroy. It may aid us in feeling once again the atmosphere of that picturesque age if first we trace his journey from the Old World.[1]

The young duke was a direct descendant of the great Braganza of Portugal, King Manuel of the Golden Age. He was the first grandee of Spain to become viceroy, and a Knight of the Golden Fleece. He was a young and gallant courtier, proud, elegant, blasé, with white forehead, rosy cheeks and soft silky beard. On receiving his appointment he set out for the port of Santa María in company with three friars—whom he always kept by him—many members of his family and a retinue of servants. Before him were driven a hundred packhorses laden with equipage and a hundred saddle mules, while he and his most distinguished companions rode in eight coaches. The cavalcade cost him no less than six hundred ducats daily. Escalona was met at Santa María by Juan de Palafox, who was to sail with him as visitor general, and in that capacity to prove his undoing and become his successor in two short years. Apparently his Excellency embarked in good appetite, for his own vessel carried live stores consisting of two thousand hens, a dozen calves and two hundred lambs; there were also six huge chests of sweetmeats, innumerable kegs of fruit pastes and an enormous quantity of biscuit, hams, rice, macaroni, lentils, chestnuts, chick-peas, wines and raisins. The supplies were sufficient to have victualed another ship, but all the others were amply provisioned.

[1] The following account is drawn largely from the biography of *Don Juan de Palafox y Mendoza* (Mexico, 1918) by Genaro García in the final contribution of this gifted author to American history.

His Excellency was a pious youth and his quarters on the poop deck were more like a monastery cell than a palace chamber. In order to conjure the perils of the sea all on board were confessed and received the sacrament. The Canaries were passed on April 28; five days later he ordered the observance of the feast of the Holy Cross. An improvised altar and cross were set up beside the mainmast and mass was said to the accompaniment of oboes, lutes, bassoons and cornets. Merry ballads were recited and a procession was held amid salvos of cannon and musketry. For the rest of the day there was gala dancing before the cross, followed by burlesque bull-fights. At the Lesser Antilles the fleet anchored off San Martín, and the small-boat went ashore to inquire for enemy sail, for this was the heyday of the filibusters. The governor sent word that there were none, with a present of muskmelons, watermelons and fowl. At Porto Rico similar attentions were exchanged, and the feast of Corpus Christi was celebrated here by music, dancing, comedies and a poetical contest.

Off Cape San Antón at the west end of Cuba a terrific tempest broke which sent all hands to prayers for salvation from shipwreck. As powerful aids to such petitions Escalona had brought some of the milk of the Virgin, a thorn from the crown of Christ, a finger of St. Andrew, a bit of lace that had belonged to Our Lady and her image done by St. Luke, but all proved inefficacious. At high noon, however, the good Franciscan Matías Cencerrado died, and his body, cast into the depths, floated miraculously and calmed the waves at once. This danger past, three of the vessels were presently attacked by pirates, who, however, fled when the viceroy overhauled them. Soon the voyagers could descry the towering peak of Orizaba, the Cofre de Perote and then, with tears of joy, the welcome hills of Vera Cruz. They had been seventy-eight days at sea.

The ships were moored to stout bronze rings in the wall under the guns of the fort. On the morrow everyone disembarked. Arriving unannounced, the duke lodged for a week in the fort of San Juan de Ulúa to give time for his proper reception. Then, midst the roar of a royal salute, he set forth for Vera Cruz in a felluca canopied with carmine damask, clad in a suit of white silk embroidered with silver. Two trumpeters in green satin livery, with carmine damask pennants on their clarinets, accompanied him, along with a troupe of dependents and militia.

At the sea wall in Vera Cruz the honorable town council with all the local nobility were drawn up in solemn welcome; on the near-by strand were two companies of horse and two of foot. Dispensing with the proffered royal ceremony of reception under the pall, the viceroy set forth toward the city on a mount led by red streamers in the hands of the corregidor and one of the captains; the trumpeters preceded him, a page between them bearing the guidon of the Escalonas. Hastening to the church, the youth knelt in thanks to God for his safe arrival, and then repaired to the "king's house," in which the council held its meetings, and was there lodged. Now began the formal welcome. For a week there were illuminations and bullfights. From thirty leagues roundabout came the Indian chiefs to kiss his hand and present their garlands of flowers, which the duke accepted with embraces and promises of favor.

On the road toward Old Vera Cruz he was met by a litter and liveried servants offered him as an attention from Cadereita, the retiring viceroy. Shortly he was greeted by a delegation of the town council of Mexico City, sent down by the royal audiencia. Resting a week amid the natural beauties of cool Jalapa, the viceroy received the dignitaries of all the religious orders and most of the nobility of the realm. At the Venta de Perote he was tendered a banquet of twenty-four courses, the viands representing the products of every part of the viceroyalty. All classes received him with attentions commensurate with their resources. There were unending gifts, music, triumphal arches, religious festivals, sports, mystery plays, sham battles and bullfights in every town traversed. The Indians gave their characteristic performances, adorned with gaudy plumed headgear, singing and dancing day upon day. Everyone was in love with the charming young nobleman; even the women forgot their native restraint to call to him, "Your face says you are the child of a seraph," or, "You have a goodly face, promise of good deeds."

Just outside Otumba, in August, the new ruler met the departing viceroy on his way to the coast. With ceremonious punctilio both viceroys descended from their coaches at the same instant. Escalona received Cadereita in his own carriage and side by side they rode back into Otumba. Such an encounter was traditional; it afforded opportunity for a conference on affairs of state as well as for the ceremonies so dear to the Spanish heart. On August 12 Escalona reached Chapultepec, "the royal hospice and recreation of the viceroys," only two miles from his journey's end. The City of Mexico, which had voted to expend "up to forty thousand pesos" on the reception, prepared at Chapultepec a welcome with "all ostentation." But when Escalona saw the luxuries designed for his use he ordered them all put away, "for he had not come to receive but to give; not to seek his own increase, but that of the realm." For sixteen days at Chapultepec there were *mitotes* (dances) by four hundred Indians in long *tilmas* (cloaks) and feathered crests, illuminations as grand as the burning of Rome, castles and towers from which sallied mailed warriors to fight a mammoth serpent—all at the duke's expense, that everyone might be entertained.

Entry into the capital was set for August 28. The largest and richest city in North America throughout the colonial era, Mexico rested upon the placid waters of Lake Tezcuco, suggesting something of Venice with its shining waters and diaphanous skies. Laid out in a square, it was surrounded by four canals, three others crossing it from east to west. Upon them myriad canoes plied incessantly with passengers and cargoes. The main streets, crossing at right angles, most of them fourteen yards wide, were paved, and many had limestone bridges over the canals. Sumptuous churches dotted the scene. Nearly all the houses were of two stories, with balconies and windows barred with cleverly wrought iron gratings. Four great gates stood at the cardinal points. There were two playhouses where Spanish and Mexican comedies were given, a colosseum, and many inns and hospitals "for gentlemen and plebeians." Around the city were gardens, fields and olive orchards, and here and there country homes of the rich built with fine scorn for expense.

On the day set, Escalona departed from Chapultepec amidst general acclaim. On all sides rose cries beseeching him to "do away with the rigors of former times," warm the chill of their spirits and "heal the system of the republic ere all go to ruin." The viceroy passed through the jammed masses of humanity to a floral arch where a delegation of the town council presented him with two superb steeds. One, a jet black with bright trappings, had cost the city eight hundred pesos and was the best in the land; the other was a dun bedecked with silver mountings. Two European lackeys guided the black, a third carried an ornate parasol, another the mounting stool, another the golden spurs, and a sixth led the dun. Then came two councilmen, resplendent in gold chains and diamonds; between them a page, wearing a costume defying description, bore the municipal guidon. But Escalona would accept the horses only for the ceremony!

Meantime a cavalcade had sallied forth from the capital city to meet him, consisting of twenty-four mounted musicians, a swarm of bailiffs, and caballeros richly attired. They were followed by the imperial and pontifical university headed by its mace bearers, the students in satin and black plush caps and embroidered gowns—white for the theologians, green for the canonists, red for the lawyers, yellow for the doctors and blue for the masters. Next came "the very noble and loyal city," also with mace bearers, and the ordinary justices; then the mace bearers of the royal audiencia, the royal collector of the *alcabala* duty, the *alcaldes de corte*, or criminal judges, and finally the *oidores* of the audiencia their very selves, the ranking judges closing the procession. The courtesies of greeting ended, the cavalcade with its brilliant colorings and pirouetting steeds, headed by the viceroyal coach, reëntered the city.

Arrived at the corner of the Church of Santo Domingo, the young duke beheld a royal portal—ninety feet high and seventy wide—erected for his reception.

On the façade appeared in a generous democracy Venus, Saturn, Mars, Phoebus, the Olympian eagle, America as Diana, Prudence, Temperance, Justice, Pity, the kings and emperors among the duke's forebears and the legendary eagle of Tenochtitlán; Mercury, oft-repeated, represented his Excellency. The very noble city now received the viceroy's oath to respect the municipality's privileges and guard the kingdom for his Majesty. The portals were then flung open, and with grand acclaim the viceroy entered the city. Turbulent throngs on the roofs, balconies and streets had to be beaten back by the guards to clear the way to the cathedral, where, before another great arch, the clergy chanted the *Te Deum*. Inside the basilica the duke listened to ballads, a dialogue and a *loa* in his praise consisting of one hundred and fifty quatrains. In the Zócalo the swarms awaited while he passed across the plaza just as the sun was setting and myriad candles gleamed in all the windows of the town.

Two months had elapsed since the celebrations began at the coast; they were to last still another two before the cares of administration could receive undivided attention. These were augmented by an angry dispute over episcopal preaching licenses between Palafox and the Jesuits of Puebla, in which Escalona sided with the latter and was worsted by the doughty bishop. He was too nearly a Portuguese to be left in so high a position when Portugal was struggling to recover her autonomy, and the masterful visitor general superseded him in 1642.[1]

The induction of a viceroy was only rivaled by the splendor of the ceremonies if he chanced to die in office. The death of the marquis of Casafuerte, a Peruvian

[1] García, *Don Juan de Palafox*, chap. iv.

creole, in 1734 illustrates the possibilities of the occasion. On March 16, when the public first learned that he was dangerously ill, they began general prayers for his preservation which were kept up until nightfall when his physicians ordered the sacraments. The *viaticum* was administered by the archbishop and extreme unction by the bishop of Durango. In the presence of favorite Franciscans the viceroy expired shortly after midnight at the age of seventy-six. Immediately the churches began tolling the one hundred strokes of the passing bell; and four hundred and seventy-seven salvos of artillery at fifteen-minute intervals gave public notice of the dolorous event. On the succeeding morning, at five o'clock, the royal audiencia, convened in the room nearest that in which lay the remains, sent two notaries officially to verify the demise. In the secrecy of the chamber they then opened the royal provision for the succession in such an exigency. As was customary, the choice fell upon the archbishop, a fact "which calmed with consolation this sad day."

Meantime the most skillful surgeons opened, examined and embalmed the body with unguents, aromas, powders and varnishes. Then, clad in the capitular mantle of Santiago and the decorations of a captain general and *comendador,* it was laid in state upon a bed of carmine under a crimson canopy, guidon at the foot and lighted tapers about it. There it was viewed by respectful throngs, while four hundred masses were said in especially erected booths. The following Sunday the funeral procession, nearly a mile long, moved solemnly from the palace at seven in the morning along Calle San Francisco of historic memories to the Recollect Cemetery. Stout palisades six feet high at each cross street held back the concourse of spectators who since before dawn had crowded every point of vantage.

It was a colorful and imposing array; practically all the officialdom of New Spain, resident in the capital or represented, had a jealously prized place, in set order of precedence, in the solemn obsequies. First marched eighty lay confraternities and congregations, with guidons and insignia, each brother bearing a scepter and taper. Next were Indian delegations from the native precincts of Santiago and San Juan, their governors and justices bearing long staves of office and dressed in baize mourning. Behind them marched the *archicofradía* of the Holy Trinity, wearing red tunics and carrying tapers and bells; next, the numerous membership of the third orders of the Augustinians and Franciscans. Then came the colleges, each group in gowns of some dark color surmounted by vivid-colored *becas* (bands) of white, red or green and headed by its rector with a banner. After the colleges followed the religious orders, with crosses and candles—Bethlehemites, St. Hypolites, the order of San Juan de Dios, barefoot Carmelites, Augustinians, Franciscans of the Observance, barefoot Franciscans and Dominicans. Behind them was borne the miraculous crucifix which had belonged to Pius V. Next came the archicofradía of the Holy Sacrament of the metropolitan church, the clergy, the Congregation of San Pedro in stoles, the Infantes, the Seises with crimson mantles and blue becas, the acolytes, and the venerable Cabildo and Dean of the Cathedral; after them the catafalque, with guidon and tapers, borne through the first station by the audiencia, and by each of the lesser courts in turn. The members of the viceroyal household were followed by two unshod horses bearing the dead grandee's heraldic

*The Cathedral in the City of Mexico, as it appeared in 1725.*

symbols. Then came the lesser courts of the *protomedi-cato* and the *consulado*. The university preceded the very noble and loyal city in full regalia, the chamber of accounts, the royal treasury and his illustrious excellency the archbishop in appropriate robes. Behind him several aides alternated in the distinction of bearing the ornate lid of the sarcophagus. Then followed a guard of infantry and cavalry with reversed arms. Finally came coaches festooned with black, that of the dead marquis leading in somber elegance.

After three hours and a half the majestic cortège reached the chapel, the guardian and community coming out to meet it at the Puente de Alvarado. The dean sang the mass; the body was lowered at the right of the high altar; the clerks of the chamber certified the official act. Then all the corporations, mounting their coaches, returned with the archbishop to the palace. The viceroy is dead; long live the viceroy! [1]

The pageant of New Spain—its institutions, its elaborate caste system, its many-sided artistry—has thus passed before our eyes, but it reflected a culture found in full development in the great towns alone and only faintly shadowed on the frontier. Yet it was upon the wide borders of the realm, the far northwest and the almost equally remote northeast, that New Spain showed the most energetic resurgence of life during the closing days of Spain's continental empire. Among the pioneers of the borderlands the hard task of taming the soil to the plow, dealing with the intractable northern Indians, fur trading, and the building of forts, missions and towns—these were the concerns which were substituted

[1] *La Vida Colonial* (Mexico, Antino General, *Publicaciones*, VII), 53-58.

for the affluence and circumstance of life in the great capital.[1]

[1] A useful survey of literary activity on the northern frontier, during the closing days of the colonial period, though chiefly concerned with the years of Independence, is Rafael Garza Cantú, *Algunos Apuntes acerca de las Letras y la Cultura de Nuevo León en la Centuria de 1810 a 1910* (Monterey, 1910). For the spread of Spanish and Mexican art and architecture over wide portions of the United States the literature is wide. See Mary G. Holway, *Art of the Old World in New Spain and the Mission Days of Alta California* (San Francisco, 1922). Rexford Newcomb's books, *The Old Mission Churches and Historic Houses of California* (Phila., 1925), and *The Spanish House for America* (Phila., 1927), record and help account for the dominant trend in architecture within the borders of the United States.

# CHAPTER VII

## THE LAST CYCLE OF NEW SPAIN

NEW SPAIN under the Hapsburgs had not been well governed, the monarchs being little inquisitive so long as their revenues were steadily received. The viceroys had sold their favor in the administration of justice, in grants of lands and titles and in appointments; some made a profit by maintaining gaming tables in the palace chambers. What present-day Americans know as "graft" was general and customary. For example, when one viceroy [1] found that an epidemic had been traced to the filthy vats kept by the lard makers he ordered the vats destroyed; but when the owners submitted an exculpatory argument in the shape of a bribe of six thousand pesos, the order was rescinded. In such an atmosphere efficiency and *esprit* were scarcely to be found. It is true that a magnificent area had been brought under control and a great organization devised, but in the last years of the seventeenth century and the beginning of the next the old energy had abated and complacency and routine had taken its place. It was to require the statesmanship of Charles III, aided by an able staff of modern-minded ministers, to initiate those generous reforms which were to set Spain and her possessions marching once again on the highroad of empire.

[1] The Count of Fuenclara (1742-1746), the last grandee to be made viceroy. Though he served under Philip V he illustrated very well the type of administrator in the days of the decline. Sister M. Francesca, The Viceregal Administration of Pedro Cebrian y Agustín, Conde de Fuenclara (M.A. thesis, Univ. of Calif., 1924).

The advent of the Bourbons upon the throne of Spain marked the beginning of a cycle of imperial reform that brought her near the forefront of European powers after a century of threatened disintegration. Bitterly opposed by the conservative Spaniards, the new program made her again a power to be reckoned with during the closing decades of the Old Régime. Though the Seven Years' War (1754-1763) brought disaster, the rivalry with England was not given up; Spain set herself resolutely to the task of recouping her losses in an amazingly comprehensive plan of resuscitation, which might have yielded enduring results if her expansionist power had not been checked by the opening of the Revolutionary epoch in the 1770's.

In America the most visible effects of this rejuvenation appeared in a new policy of territorial expansion with imperial defense as its underlying motive. England had been a continuously successful aggressor in the War of Jenkins' Ear, merged in that of the Austrian Succession, and in the Seven Years' War. As a result of the last conflict Spain lost all her territory in North America east of the Mississippi, her fishing rights off Newfoundland, the exclusive usufruct of the Honduras logwood cuttings, and the right to decide admiralty suits for previous British seizure of her vessels. France relinquished all her hold on the American continent as well as her dominion in India. When she turned Louisiana over to Spain the latter found herself in unwelcome proximity to the English along the Mississippi River, bound to withstand the coming shock of Anglo-American overland expansion. Thus Spain, by considerations of self-defense, felt obliged to keep up an interest in the alliance with France, or Family Compact, which since its formation in 1761 had effected nothing but disaster.

To balance these losses and handicaps she sought control of the Pacific Ocean approaches as a safeguard to her extended colonial shore lines. In 1770 she drove the English out of the Falkland Islands which they had seized. The French Pact failing Spain in this crisis, she was forced to the humiliation of returning the islands to England, though she subsequently regained them. In 1772-1776 an attempt was made to anticipate England in the seizure of Tahiti.[1] The establishment of the viceroyalty of La Plata in 1776 was a defensive measure against England and Portugal, as the formation of the viceroyalty of Nueva Granada in 1718 and 1739 had been against the Dutch. By *rapprochement* with Portugal in 1777 and the dismissal of the unfriendly minister Pombal, danger from England in the dispute over the boundary along the Rio de la Plata was dissipated. The loss of Florida was retrieved in the American Revolution when Spain, entering that conflict reluctantly in 1779, was able to use French soldiers under the gallant young governor Bernardo Gálvez of Louisiana to retake her coastal holdings there. In the 1780's exploration of the southern Argentine was followed by settlement to secure that strip of coast.

In 1772 the presidial line along the northern frontier of New Spain was readjusted and strengthened, including the far-away presidios of Northern California, the new area which had been occupied in 1769. The new Louisiana domain was pushed northward and westward by well-planned Indian policies. The occupation of the

[1] B. G. Corney, ed., *The Quest and Occupation of Tahiti by Emissaries of Spain during the Years 1772-1776* (London, 1913-1919).

far northwest with California missions and presidios was motivated by fear of Russian aggression down the coast from Alaska and of British advances from the heart of the continent. In 1776 the Comandancia of the upper frontier, comprising the northern tier of provinces, was detached from the viceroyalty for the sake of military efficiency; here was waged a systematic warfare to repel the hostile Indians, who were supplied with English firearms. The colonization of Lower California and the northwest was also begun although it had scant success. Progress up the northwest coast resulted in the occupation of Nootka in 1789 as a means of stopping Russian and English advances and controlling activities of foreign vessels, but defeat came here in 1790 when the French government repudiated the Pact. Communications with the northwest were sought by sea from west-coast ports and by land routes from New Mexico and northern Sonora. The wide borders of empire now had their first systematic attention from the statesmen of Spain.

Care of the periphery was matched by constructive colonial reforms intended to pay the costs of the new defensive institution. The suggestions of economic writers like Bernardo Ward and José Campillo y Cosío, who advocated a general visitation and inventory of the American possessions, were adopted and set in motion.[1] A long-drawn-out but finally successful liberation of the governmental trade monopoly was begun in 1765, finding its counterpart in the destruction of the exclusive features of practically all economic activities. The Bourbons sent to America as viceroys vigorous men of military training who had been successful in administrative

[1] J. Campillo y Cosío, *Nuevo Sistema de Gobierno* (Madrid, 1789); Bernard Ward, *Proyecto Económico* (Madrid, 1789). The manuscripts of these books lay in government offices before the accession of Charles III.

posts in Spain, doing away with men of the old grandee or the ecclesiastical type and the interregna of unwieldy audiencias. The general visitation of the American empire, initiated by the two scientists Jorge Juan and Antonio Ulloa in the 1740's, was taken up with energy by Charles III when he succeeded to the throne. In accordance with his plan José de Gálvez reached Mexico in 1765, destined to affect the Spanish possessions by the most numerous and thoroughgoing reforms.[1]

Gálvez was at the beginning merely the agent for Choiseul's program of uniting the economic and political interests of France and Spain under the *Pacte de Famille;* but in the end his measures looked toward the complete independence of Spain from the influence of the French, and the dominance of Spanish over British colonial enterprise. Through his tireless energy Spanish force was asserted in the Californias, the frontier was reconquered from the Indians, and the transcontinental line of presidios—as great in conception as the Roman defenses against the Gauls—was readjusted. His reformation of administration and of the treasury of New Spain was followed, when he became minister of the Indies, by the liberation of Spanish commerce from the old monopolistic trammels and by the inception of the intendancy system of centralized administration of the

[1] The visitor general of Nueva Granada, Juan Francisco Gutiérrez Pineres, was sent to Santa Fé in 1781 to increase the government monopolies, tributes, brandy and tobacco revenues and other revenues, and to raise troops. This errand, identical in character with that of Gálvez in New Spain, and of Areche in Peru, caused a rebellion led by Antonio Galán and Isidro Molina. The archbishop espoused the cause of the old system, and the Council of the Indies, opposing the reforms, suspended a forced loan and the inauguration of the bills of lading and vouchers similar to those which Gálvez had initiated at Vera Cruz. Much the same conflict ensued in Peru. G. Desdevises du Dezert, "Vice-rois et Capitaines Généraux des Indes Espagnoles à la fin du XVIIIe siècle," *Revue Historique,* CXXVI, 17 ff.

New World possessions. No Jules Grévy or Cecil Rhodes ever "thought in terms of continents" with more insistent and consuming zeal than did José de Gálvez.

The revival of executive efficiency was accompanied by a changed attitude of government toward religion, which had its origins in the quarrels of Philip V with the papacy. Under the Hapsburgs the religious institution had been supreme; the state existed for the support and propagation of the faith. With the Bourbons the church became an agency of the state. Where the institutions of the church stood in the way of the complete assertion of the power of the state, they had to go. Such was the fate of the Society of Jesus, whose form of organization, assimilated to that of the old military orders, had made it an international competitor of "benevolent despotism." Following the expulsion of the Society from Spain, it was in 1767 driven almost simultaneously from all her colonies.[1]

The expulsion entailed the most far-reaching social change made in New Spain during the colonial régime. The actual exile was effected under the supervision of the visitor Gálvez and his subservient though capable coadjutor, the viceroy Francisco de Croix. Managed by even such masterful agents, it was feared the event might disturb the public peace. The Society had begun its labors in New Spain in 1572, and from the very first had maintained a most influential position. It had entered the educational field, receiving lavish private gifts and government support for its colleges, such as that of San

[1] Bernard Moses, *Papers on the Southern Spanish Colonies of America* (Berkeley, 1911), 103-126; C. E. Chapman, *A History of Spain* (N. Y., 1918), 448-452; Pablo Hernández, S. J., *El Extrañamiento de los Jesuitas del Río de la Plata y de las Misiones del Paraguay* (Madrid, 1908), *passim.*

Pedro y San Pablo in Mexico City, and at Tepotzotlan forty miles north; its colleges at Pátzcuaro and Valladolid were also important. The college at the capital was even able to force its way into the University system and compel recognition of its degrees by that royal and pontifical institution. Its *Casa Profesa* in Mexico City trained its novitiates and exercised a highly prized social and political influence.

Moreover, the Society had borne an active part in the pacification of the natives, from Florida on the east coast to Nayarit, Sonora and Lower California on the west. In pursuit of its aims it had not stopped at the destruction of viceroys, as instance Gelves in 1624, or at the confusion of archbishops, as in the notable quarrel with Palafox when it prevented him from collecting licenses from Jesuits serving as preachers. It had resisted payment of the tithes, and felt very little concern over the requirement that its priests exercise parish duties only under episcopal license. It had with fair success kept its Lower California holdings free both from the intrusion of lay Spaniards who sought pearls and from absorptive governmental agencies. Its wealth was the envy of the crown.[1] Hence any mischance in the execution of the decree of expulsion would have resulted, as José de Gálvez declared, in "the gravest tragedies, for there was in fact no other authority recognized than that of the regulars of the Company."[2] This great order was just on the eve of expanding its activities from Lower into Upper California when its elimination was effected. What difference would have ensued had the Pacific Slope

[1] Manuel Rivera, *Historia Antigua y Moderna de Jalapa* (Mexico, 1869-1871), I, 137-140.

[2] José de Gálvez, Informe de el Visitador de este Reyno al Exmo. Sor. Virrey Marques de Croix (MS. in Bancroft Library), 3.

been served by Jesuits instead of Franciscans may be left to conjecture.

The expulsion from the important Jesuit centers in Mexico City and Puebla was effected with little disorder, but in the provinces the expectation of trouble was partly realized. There were riots at Valladolid and Pátzcuaro. In the mining centers of San Luis Potosí and Guanajuato, where the people were often turbulent, the move increased the discontent created by measures taken at the same time to stop the forbidden use of firearms and to collect excises on the regional drinks. The protracted riots caused the visitor general to go in person to the provinces, armed with the full powers of the viceroy, and he succeeded in carrying out the order against but little resistance.

The condition of affairs disclosed by his tour of the great bishopric of Michoacan was far from creditable to the Spanish domination. Gálvez apparently apprehended widespread revolt unless the sternest measures were taken. After riots at San Luis de la Paz, he executed four leaders of the Jesuits' partisans and exiled two others. At Guanajuato repeated disturbances arising partly out of resistance to taxation necessitated throwing a cordon of eight thousand militia about the city for three months to keep the miners at work and prevent escape of opponents of the expulsion. At San Luis Potosí the government had likewise to set up a heavy guard and march the Jesuits away from their college under military escort.

Here, as elsewhere, the expulsion was made the excuse of any sort of violence that discontent might suggest, especially among the Indian population. In the near-by San Pedro mines recent republication of the laws against the natives carrying firearms and wandering about brought riots involving a jail delivery, a desecration of the national flag and a plot to seize the city, massacre the Spaniards and set up the old Indian rule. Defying the troops, the natives seized the Jesuits and took them away to another convent for protection, though not without loss of life. When the visitor arrived, therefore, the whole region was in turmoil and it required all his force to recapture the Jesuits, dispatch them to Mexico City and reëstablish peace. Twenty-six leaders were put to death and many more imprisoned for life or banished. Ruined homes and grisly heads displayed on pikes were left as warnings.[1] At El Venado, La Hedionda, San Francisco and elsewhere there were similar scenes. All compromise with Indian dissent was roundly condemned; the visitor alleged that local administration had been nerveless and vacillating.[2]

To the southwest, in Valladolid (Morelia), the decay of government had been worse, though the region was the most populous of New Spain outside the capital. In the vicinity of Pátzcuaro and Uruápan more than one hundred villages were enlisted under the banner of the half-breed Pedro de Soria Villaroel, who aimed to throw off the Spanish yoke and establish an independent government. When the government recruited the militia at Uruápan, conscripts were dragged away from the officers, Spaniards were hauled out of bed and threatened with death, and other disorders occurred. In retribution thirteen of the rebels were hanged and scores whipped or banished, though no Spanish life had been lost. Within a period of four months the plebeian element in these

[1] Gálvez, Informe de el Visitador, 65-68.
[2] Gálvez, 48.

regions was completely cowed; some ninety persons were executed, scores whipped and hundreds imprisoned or banished. Such rigorous measures received bitter comment from the secretary of the viceroyalty, who had been commissioned by the jealous minister of the Indies, Julián de Arriaga, to make confidential reports on the visitor's activities.[1]

The general fears of an uprising were probably exaggerated; yet it is clear that governmental control in the interior was in an enfeebled state and that energetic reforms aroused violent discontent a full generation before the wars of independence began. It was more than bare coincidence that these troubles occurred in the very town where the first significant outbreaks of the war of separation were to take place. It is also worthy of note that such severe penalties could be safely inflicted on the half-breeds of New Spain at the very moment when the English colonies of the seaboard were uniting to resist the relatively mild tyranny of the Townshend acts. The concessions and surrenders in London were in sharp contrast to the speedy quelling of riots in the bishopric of Michoacan. In the latter case we have a subject people rising for the basic liberties of men and summarily put down by organized military government—a short servile war; in the former, citizens joining as equals in constitutional debate with a ministry which had not sufficiently respected their views in drawing up its measures—citizens who could express themselves with telling effect in state papers or in economic pressure.

The Jesuit expulsion has often been characterized as

[1] Charles François Crois, *Corréspondance du Marquis de Croix* (Nantes, 1891), 212; Pedro de Rada to Arriaga, Mexico, September 26, October 14, 17, November 18, December 21, 1767 (MS., Archivo General de Indias, Estado, Aud. de Mex., leg. 1, doc. 99).

a direct cause of the movement for independence in 1810 under Father Hidalgo. The influence of the Society had certainly been profound, and while not always conducive to respect for royal institutions, it was certainly a support for religion and the privileged classes. The hold of religion upon the Mexican mind was weakened by the event, since the other religious orders were not in such close touch with the upper element and lacked the intellectual capacity or political acumen of the Jesuits. Nor were the lower ranks of the secular church equal to them in influence; such seculars as possessed superior intelligence became imbued shortly with Jansenist ideas, and, having been long discriminated against by the upper clergy, were influential actors in the War of Independence.

The viceroyalty profited heavily from the sequestration of Jesuit missions and church estates; the properties of twenty colleges, one hundred and twenty-three haciendas and the missions of the Northwest were confiscated. The seizure included the famous California Pious Fund, which was used for national expansion along the northwest coast and for other governmental purposes, though it had been intended by the donors for religious work.[1] That the Jesuits were admired by many Mexicans is made evident from the fact that eleven petitions for their restoration because of their services to science and to the propagation of the faith were presented before 1810. They were indeed restored for a moment under the reactionary government of Ferdinand VII in 1819, only to be expelled again in 1820.

[1] *Comisión Mixta de Reclamaciones de México y los Estados Unidos. Tadeus Amat . . . y Joseph S. Alemany . . . contra México* (Mexico, 1876), *passim*; J. Maniau y Torquemada, *Compendio de la Historia de la Real Hacienda* (A. Carreño, ed., Mexico, 1914), 59-60, 130.

The general attitude of the House of Bourbon toward the church was also demonstrated in 1749 by the program of secularizing those curacies still held by the regulars. It was expected that the process of assimilation would be encouraged by placing the Indians more thoroughly upon their own resources; but even such an enthusiast for this means of increasing efficiency in taxation as the second Revillagigedo, writing in 1793, had to acknowledge failure. The change to the secular clergy proved one of the potent reasons for the decline of civilization among the Indians during the last years of Spanish control.

The comprehensive reforms undertaken by Charles III required that the viceroys bend every energy toward the increase of revenues. By consistent and pertinacious effort the royal income—in contrast to the course of history in the English colonies—was more than quadrupled during the period from 1765 to 1789 without diminishing the prosperity of the realm or disturbing the well-being of .many of the inhabitants. Some of them, however, were materially injured by changes like the establishment of the tobacco monopoly. Reform had to contend with the inherent conservatism and hatred of change manifested by the beneficiaries of ancient church privileges and the old looseness of administration in the realm of commerce.[1]

The most striking example of this was in the case of the revenue reforms at Vera Cruz, the only port suited for the entry of European merchandise. Until the period of the reforms imports were carried in "annual" fleets, though down to 1776, when the last one arrived, there

[1] Juan Vicente Revillagigedo, *Instrucción Reservada* (Mexico, 1831), arts. 218-224; H. I. Priestley, *José de Gálvez* (Univ. of Calif., *Publs. in Hist.*, V), 383.

had been only one hundred and one of these. After 1720 great fairs were held to dispose of the merchandise at Jalapa in the cool zone, the climate at Vera Cruz being too unhealthful for such an immense concourse of buyers and sellers. The fair was both a social and economic event, closely supervised by the government. The large fleet, coming under convoy, was announced in advance by a single messenger ship with dispatches to the viceroy, who in conference with the merchant guild, or consulado, fixed a date for the fair. The roads were presently declared open for the transport of goods, and at Jalapa gathered the merchants of the viceroyalty, most of them from Mexico City.[1] There they bid for merchandise in order to maintain their stocks until the next fleet.

Before the middle of the eighteenth century a surprising amount of crookedness had entered into the reckoning in the shape of smuggling, avoidance of duties and the simulated sale of goods not sent direct to the capital. Methods of introducing goods at Vera Cruz were traditionally lax; there was no special customhouse, duties being collected, or ignored, in the offices of the royal treasury. Marks of identification, prescribed to prevent smuggling, were either omitted or overlooked (for considerations), the customs officers having developed a system of conniving with importers to admit goods without duty. In 1759 over five thousand barrels of brandy escaped duties that should have produced twenty thousand pesos revenue. Peculations in three years on this one import reached nearly eighty thousand pesos. Between 1745 and 1765, it was estimated, brandy

[1] Cf. Edmund Burke, *An Account of the European Settlements in America* (London, 1808), 176-179.

frauds at Vera Cruz lost the crown over three hundred thousand pesos. The public was equally injured, for the importers refilled barrels with the local brandy, called *chinguirito*, which was libeled as a very injurious beverage perhaps in order to favor the Andalusian growers, and sold it in the interior as imported brandy. Other revenues showed similar mishandling; the customs officers employed many subordinates for whom there was no salary provision, depending upon irregular practices for money with which to pay them. The corruption fund, for which all comers were levied upon, was dubbed the "Vera Cruz Pig."

Every ship from Caracas and Maracaibo had to make a present of one hundred pounds of cacao to each of three officials and two hundred to the governor. Every ship from Spain gave each official a barrel of wine and copious *douceurs* of raisins, almonds and other products. Collections of duties were often deferred or ignored entirely. The Vera Cruz subtreasury had developed a practice of its own whereby many old cumbersome methods were ignored to the advantage of officials and merchants, not to that of the crown. The final confirmation of the reforms of Gálvez, described below, by the fiscals of Castile was responsible for a large part of the increase in revenue which distinguished the closing years of the Bourbon period.[1] The pity was that the government spent so much thought on administrative ills that the neglect really constituted an injury to society the needs of which demanded attention.

To stop the frauds it was necessary to adopt a very

[1] Informe de los Señores Campomanes y Moñino sobre el Nuevo Método para la Administración de Real Hacienda y Otros Juntos que Estableció el Visitador Don José de Gálvez (MS., Archivo General de Indias, 88-5-25 art. 144).

disagreeable set of precautions. Under these reforms of 1767 all imports had to be marked and listed, and bills of lading made out to accompany every mule load sent up to Mexico. The ignorant Indian muleteers were obliged to obtain receipts upon the delivery of goods and carry them for checking back to Jalapa or Vera Cruz, as the case might be. To prevent dishonesty it was provided that the always odious sales tax should be paid at Vera Cruz. Since it had previously been the practice not to collect the tax on goods consumed at the port but only on those which went inland, the result had been that merchandise was ostensibly sold for consumption in Vera Cruz and then smuggled into the interior, where payment of duty was again evaded by ignoring the customhouse or by arriving upon a holiday. As there were customs officers in every town and hamlet of moderate importance as well as in the cities, a disproportionate number of employees was engaged in collecting revenues, and consignees and shippers had many opportunities to connive with officials to avoid payment.[1] Irregularities were encouraged by the fact that all visible sources of profit were directly taxed under cumbersome regulations; indeed, if they proved unusually profitable, they were taken over and administered as crown monopolies. The utmost vigilance was required to make collections, and the mere inconvenience of honesty helped excite the speculative instinct, which found its easiest outlet in evading the rules. It was a potent influence in undermining the morals of the community.

The conflict aroused by the Gálvez reforms at Vera

[1] José de Gálvez, "Instrucción Provisional para el Arreglo en la Administración y Manejo de las Rentas y Derechos de su Majestad en la Nueva Ciudad de Vera Cruz," *Informe General* (Mexico, 1867), 359-411.

Cruz illustrates in characteristic fashion how the mercantile organism actually worked, and affords a shining example of the resistance to change which imbued Spanish American society quite as much as Spanish. The merchants of Vera Cruz took up the gauge of battle with the visitor, asking the consulado of Mexico City to protest the new rule for collecting the sales tax on the ground that it meant a doubling of the burden as it would still be levied at the place of actual sale. The consulado espoused their cause, petitioning the viceroy and visitor to revert to the old system, and finally carrying its plea to Arriaga, minister of the Indies, in Madrid. That minister quite properly referred the protest to the Council of the Indies, which, being dominated by merchants, sustained it, and the question after three years of further bickering was referred for decision to the fiscals of the Council of Castile.[1] But these officials defended the Gálvez reforms in every detail, attacking with lusty blows the conservatism intrenched in the Council of the Indies, and as a result the new measures stood.

On the Pacific side Acapulco enjoyed the monopoly of commerce, then carried on only between Manila and Mexico City. The smuggling was relatively as great as that which attended the Atlantic trade, though there was but a single annual galleon. Frauds were effected by the incoming galleon making landings at small way ports near Acapulco, by misrepresenting the contents of packages and by carrying cargo in excess of the legal amount. The chief reform—actual examination of all packages—resulted in increased revenues of five hundred thousand pesos in three years' time.[2]

[1] Campomanes y Moñino Informe (A. G. de I., 88-5-25).
[2] Croix, Corréspondance, 201, 207.

The Acapulco investigation of 1766 resulted in the arrest of the customs officers, who were left to languish in jail two years before their cases were heard; and even then hearings were reluctantly granted. Three of the accused men were not exonerated until 1771, and the remaining four a year later. For four years they had remained uncertain of their fate, without recourse whereby to recover the sums they had paid for their offices and, of course, without opportunity for other government income. Concerning the merits of their cases there is not sufficient evidence to determine. The exoneration granted by the Council of the Indies may have been as full of political animus as their arrest was full of administrative zeal.[1] Their experiences demonstrate the risk incurred by officials in assuming public responsibility, and the terrible slowness of justice, especially when invoked by officials against each other. The reform of justice was not seriously undertaken during the Bourbon régime. Indeed the appetite of the Spaniards for litigation was continuously fed by administrative activity. Reform bred countless suits, and it was a rare instance in which justice was promptly and impartially administered.

A good example of quick administrative decision was that of the viceroy Croix regarding a protest against the establishment of the tobacco monopoly. This project involved closing out all private interest in the manufacture, sale or production of tobacco save in certain favored districts where the government bought the entire crop. Long a governmental aspiration, the step had been repeatedly deferred for fear of popular disorders. Production was limited to the region of Orizaba, Córdova

---

[1] Council of the Indies, Acuerdo, December 11, 1772 (MS., Archivo General de Indias, 88-5-23).

and Teziutlán, prices were fixed, and nonproduction elsewhere was enforced by military aid in pulling up the plants. When producers in the areas discriminated against remonstrated, Croix made them the memorable reply that they must accept the decision as final and cease to present petitions, "for it is the duty of the vassal to obey and be silent"—an expression of Bourbon ideas of the rights of man often quoted as typical of the colonial régime.[1] The establishment of the monopoly was one of the notable Bourbon successes; from 1765 to 1809 it produced one hundred and twenty million pesos revenue. When observed by Humboldt, production was restricted to an area of four or five leagues square, the industry having been destroyed in many parts of Nueva Galicia, with a consequent dwindling of population there. He argued that freedom of production in this, as in other monopolized industries, would have produced greater natural wealth, from which higher returns to the state could have been obtained.

The intervention of the royal treasury in every phase of the life of the individual was incessant.[2] It made the old colonial régime so odious that law breaking became the usual practice, with the result that the moral stamina of the community was weakened. The burden was not that taxes were unbearably high—for they were not as great in proportion to wealth as our modern impositions —but that they were so multifarious and so visible and that their collection meant the removal of resources to far-away Europe for expenditure. The mere statement

[1] Justo Sierra, ed., *Mexico, its Social Evolution* (Mexico, 1900-1904), I, 129; Gálvez, *Informe General*, 39-43.
[2] Revillagigedo, *Instrucción Reservada*, arts. 1104-1156, 1366-1380; Alexander von Humboldt, *Political Essay on the Kingdom of New Spain* (London, 1814), III, 39-40.

that the people of New Spain paid forty-odd varieties of taxes, many of them involving complete monopolization of the source of production in the most lucrative avenues of industry, brings this consideration into sharp relief. The late-eighteenth-century reforms, although they did away with the execrable system of tax farming, served rather to increase than lessen irritation and confusion. Although the annual contribution to the income of the empire grew in a generation after 1765 from five million to twenty million pesos—at which time New Spain contributed two thirds of the whole revenue of the empire—the enormous army of collectors ever present at the citizen's elbow made avoidance of public responsibility seem a private virtue. Even the honest vassal, said Revillagigedo, could not be sure that he had paid all that the government demanded of him— a comment which ought to comfort the modern income-tax payer with the realization that, in one concern at least, society has not grown perceptibly worse in the last one hundred and fifty years.[1]

Perhaps nothing more clearly demonstrates the tendency of absolutism, the consciousness of self-perfection in benevolent despotism, than the trend of municipal government already noticed. It contrasts sharply with the experience of local administration in the English colonies, and reveals a difference in the make-up of the two peoples. In New Spain the movement was toward atrophy and decay; it was one of the conspicuous results of the attempt to graft European civilization upon a great mass of Indians whose absorptive capacity was equal to the externals but not the essentials.

The towns of New Spain began promisingly enough.

[1] Revillagigedo, *Instrucción Reservada*, art. 1367.

All Spanish America was colonized and administered, from the first new settlement to the last, upon the framework of municipal organization and regulation, even to the utmost frontier.[1] In the beginning the Spanish towns chose procurators whose duty it was to represent them in the Spanish Cortes. Upon one occasion they actually sent them, but they were rebuffed by Charles V, whose victory over the *comuneros* at Villalar eliminated the element of popular representation from Spanish political life. In New Spain the Indian towns retained procurators to represent them before the superior government of the viceroyalty, but they never served for any united representation, being merely petitioners in incessant land litigation with the Spaniards.

The retrogressive tendency of municipal expression was due to the fact that control, originally in the hands of prominent citizens elected as councilmen, came to be hereditary in the hands of descendants of the first tenants, who had bought the offices as inheritances for their sons. Decay of the municipalities was thus a direct effect of the widely used policy of the sale of offices, and it was necessary, when reform was sought, for the crown to repurchase such rights or effect composition thereof in the shape of pensions. These became inordinately heavy charges upon the public treasury, absorbing funds for private advantage which should have been applied to the public benefit.[2]

[1] Lucas Alamán, *Disertaciones sobre la Historia de la República Mexicana* (Mexico, 1844-1849), 197-323, has an interesting portrayal of the early municipal development as manifested in Mexico City. See also J. L. Mecham, "The Real de Minas as a Political Institution," *Hisp. Am. Hist. Rev.*, VII, 45-83.

[2] J. A. García, *La Ciudad Indiana* (Buenos Aires, 1911), 161, 293; Bernard Moses, *The Spanish Dependencies in South America* (N. Y., 1914), II, chap. xviii. For a notable instance of the persistent burden of the pension system, see earlier chap. v.

The condition of towns of such great mineral importance as San Luis Potosí and Guanajuato in 1767 illustrated the general decline. In the former, with a population of perhaps eight thousand, the town council had so decayed that it had only two of the prescribed eight councilmen, and these were only substitutes. The presence and energy of a royal officer like Gálvez were needed to effect a reorganization of the council and a renewal of provisions for financial solvency. In Guanajuato a similar revamping of the local organization was necessary, even to reviving the use of the ancient strong-box with its three huge keys and locks for the preservation of funds. The real reason for such conditions was the continual intervention of the governor or the alcalde mayor in municipal affairs, the regional one-man power of the viceroyal system serving to strangle any attempt at municipal independence.

The final blow to municipal responsibility in New Spain was effected by the visitation of Gálvez. Many towns kept no records of those small funds devoted to local sanitation and holiday observances; as a remedy a central accounting house was established at Mexico City for all the cities in the viceroyalty, each contributing toward the salaries of the accounting officers, and municipal expenditures had to be authorized in advance by the central authority. This meant greater economy but not necessarily greater efficiency. Its effect upon self-reliance and self-respect cannot have been salutary; but where a sense of responsibility was lacking, probably no other method would have been so efficacious.

In the capital itself the tendency toward a reduction of autonomy was equally marked. The corregidor of Mexico City, who was in all his glitter of formality an officer of consequence, and should have been so in administrative responsibility, maintained a most obsequious attitude toward the viceroy. The fifteen councilmen, who grew presumptuous because, though creoles, they now had offices, were placed under check by the appointment of six honorary councilmen by the viceroy. This measure so piqued creole pride that the council succeeded in 1794 in absorbing the power to name the honorary councilmen. This virtually destroyed the intended check and was a unique instance of the effective assertion of municipal vigor before the bursting of the storm of Independence.[1]

The organization of the colonial militia was a recourse to which Spain was driven by stress of military competition with England. To defend her colonies her man power was otherwise inadequate. The policy of arming the natives was adopted with utmost reluctance as the lesser of two evils. The troops were not given the status of regulars of Spain; officered in part by colonials, they were of course intended to oppose whatever troops, white or otherwise, might be sent against them, for no outcry was raised in that day because of the color line. They were not intended for operations on European fields. When the organization of colonial militia was undertaken, at least a dozen towns were scenes of rioting by the inhabitants against the conscription and levy of supporting taxes. In the case of so important a city as Puebla the municipal council showed its opposition to the militia by voting to dispose of fifteen thousand pesos, then in its treasury, in such a way as to prevent the fund from being used to provide uniforms, as had been ordered by the viceroy. Since, however, a visitor

[1] Revillagigedo, *Instrucción Reservada*, art. 158.

general was in the country expressly charged with the inspection and regulation of municipal treasuries, he ordered the council not to divert the funds as had been voted, but reserve them for the uniforms, lest their constituency incur a new tax for that purchase. Instances of such intervention might be multiplied. The viceroyal comment that the militia organization, by utilization of local funds, had "cost the treasury nothing," indicates the philosophy of the central power toward regional political authority.[1]

The social effect of the militia system in New Spain was shown in the hostility of the lower classes. Yet it was welcomed by many members of the creole class, who obtained military commissions and utilized the troops levied in their own neighborhood for defensive war against hostile Indians or for their own economic advantage. The social demand for militia commissions superseded the old purchase of titles of nobility which had under the Hapsburgs served as an outlet for creole aristocratic ambitions. The need of the militia was the underlying motive of the general reorganization of the royal treasury which absorbed so much administrative zeal during the reign of Charles III. Pursued as a measure of grave necessity for imperial defense, the policy was viewed by the Spanish residents with an apprehension well warranted ever since the days of Mendoza. Even the viceroys charged with its enforcement looked upon the idea with suspicion. One objection was that military service would free too many Indians and mulattoes from the tribute, though as the

[1] J. Fernando de Palacios to J. de Gálvez, Puebla, October 17, 1765 (MS., Archivo General de Indias, 88-4-20) ; H. I. Priestley, "Spanish Colonial Municipalities," *Calif. Law Rev.*, VII, 410-411.

whole establishment consisted of less than fifty thousand men, the loss to this revenue was not remarkable.

The social phenomenon of keeping the colony dependent by using its own inhabitants to enforce control did have at least two untoward consequences. For one thing, it created a class of strutting creole officers numerically disproportionate to the enlisted men. Their natural self-esteem was thus unfortunately fed until military trappings and titles became objects of gibes more deserved, possibly, than those directed against the once famous Kentucky colonel. More seriously, the development of a colonial army, soon to become intoxicated by the Napoleonic tradition, served to give the provincials a confidence in their own prowess which was to be borne out on the battlefields of the wars for Spanish American Independence.[1]

The commercial reforms at Vera Cruz were part and parcel of the later and great ones embodied in the Grand Pragmatic of Free Commerce promulgated in 1778. This fundamental change has not been adequately appreciated by historians because it had such gradual inception and such scant trial before the revolutions burst that its importance has been obscured. The movement has been credited to the inspiration given by the English occupation of Havana in 1762; but this is explaining a great policy by a single incident of one war. The liberality of the French policy in Santo Domingo, made increasingly effective after 1724, could not have failed to be impressive, and the influence of Choiseul in Spanish commercial policy was just then at its height. Indeed,

[1] Von Humboldt, *Political Essay*, IV, 248-258; D. E. Smith, *The Viceroy of New Spain* (Univ. of Calif., *Publs.*, I), 199-228; H. H. Bancroft, *History of Mexico* (San Francisco, 1883-1887), III, 401-425.

the French assumed credit for the whole reform of Spanish administration.[1] The Spaniards had had many scores of years in which to observe the British policy, and had suffered from it and envied it; it was rather by a coincidence of dates than an historical sequence of ideas that the liberalization took effect just after the Seven Years' War. The liberalism of the Spanish regulation was an approximation of the restrictive legislation of the English.

The first step in the reduction of duties on commerce came in 1720 with the *Proyecto de Comercio* of that year. The use of four annual mail ships began in 1718, these vessels carrying merchandise as well. In 1735 the merchant fleets began to be superseded by single ships. After the War of Jenkins' Ear the liberal movement was accelerated, small concessions being made, such as allowing the Tabasco Coast to receive European exports from Vera Cruz instead of from Spain only. There was also some shipping between Vera Cruz and Cartagena and Maracaibo before 1766. In that year long-urged reductions were made on exports of wheat and flour to Havana. This move had already been preceded in 1765 by a decree removing the Cadiz monopoly by opening five Spanish Caribbean islands to the trade of ten Spanish ports. At the same time customs duties were reduced and put on an ad-valorem basis. Further liberalization for Campeche and Yucatan, followed in 1774 by measures opening the colonial trade still more, were crowned by the promulgation on October 12, 1778, of the Grand Pragmatic.

This notable document abolished the convoyed fleets

[1] Sister Mary Austin, The Reforms of Charles III in the Light of the Pacte de Famille (Ph.D. thesis, Univ. of Calif., 1927).

and permitted individual sailings under the national flag, gradually opened a still greater number of ports, made generous reductions in duties on Spanish goods and gave certain important colonial products free entry into Spain. It also provided special consideration for Spanish-built ships, though allowing purchased ships concessions if manned by a crew mainly Spanish. New Spain and Venezuela were not at first affected by the measure, but on February 28, 1789, the complete reform was made effective for New Spain.[1] In 1794 the trade between Peru and New Spain was opened after a long period of prohibition; in 1799, during the war with England, even neutral vessels were temporarily allowed to trade directly between the Peninsula and the American ports. This privilege was again granted from 1805 to 1809, and when it was withdrawn certain merchants were permitted to import goods directly from foreign ports. In 1820 Vera Cruz lost its mercantile predominance when, as a final commercial measure, several ports on the Atlantic and Pacific were opened to foreign trade.[2]

The social and economic effects of this liberal policy were far-reaching. The old monopolists, who had grown rich by controlling prices during the intervals between fleets, were, of course, loud in protest. In fact the period after 1780 was marked by numerous bankruptcies because merchants could not adapt themselves to the more frequent supply of wares; foresight and acumen were required to adjust imports to a natural instead of a controlled demand. As a result, there sprang up a new class of merchants, with less capital but greater sagacity and

[1] Pablo Macedo, "La Evolución Mercantil," *Tres Monografías* (Mexico, 1905), 23-24.

[2] M. Lerdo de Tejada, *Comercio Exterior de la República Mexicana* (Mexico, 1853), 20-21.

spirit of adventure, and they crowded out the old monopolists who had lorded it over commerce. The latter,
discouraged at the change, withdrew their capital to
invest it in mining and agriculture; a more general distribution of wealth was secured while attendant benefit was felt by the industries thus favored. The greater
collection of tithes, which soon amounted to nearly five
million pesos, was in part a reflection of the diversion
of capital to new activities. Similar increases in mining
revenues were accompanied by the development of commerce itself, the sales tax showing an increase. There
is no doubt, however, that a considerable part of the
additions to the revenues was due to greater efficiency
in collection and honesty in accounting.[1]

This efficiency was aided by another important administrative reform, long recommended by imperial
officials and opposed by local vested interests, the introduction of the *intendant* system whereby, between
1764 and 1786, the entire colonial government assumed
the same type of organization as old Spain itself. The
intendants administered justice also, their subdelegates
superseding in many respects the numerous alcaldes mayores who though unpaid had, through peculation and
inefficiency, wasted five hundred thousand pesos annually. The provincial governor, of course, was largely
a military commander.[2]

From a social point of view the most important work
of the intendant was with that branch of the service
known as *policía,* which included rather more than the

[1] *El Viagero Universal* (Madrid, 1799), XXVII, 6-16.
[2] Julián de Arriaga, Instrucción Reservada to José de Gálvez, March 14,
1765 (MS., Archivo General de Indias, 136-5-3) ; *Ordenanza de Intendentes* (Madrid, 1786) ; Informe y Plan de Intendencias (MS., 1768,
Ayer Collection, copy in Bancroft Library) ; Priestley, *José de Gálvez,*
289-293.

modern police work of governing. Unfortunately for the full development of this service the emphasis was placed upon increase of revenue. A glance at the regulations concerning policía, however, demonstrates at once the need and the desire for a more perfect social organization and the amelioration of the condition of the people. In the rules governing both justice and police the moral uplift of the inhabitants was to be sought. The criminal and idle population, unfortunately large, was to be constrained and kept at work. Special attention was to be given to encouragement of agriculture and mining. Crops not yet suitably developed were to be encouraged by financial aid. Increased water supply, improvement of cattle breeding, conservation of forests, subdivision and sale of lands, construction of roads—in short practically all the economic aspirations voiced by the revolutionists of the period of 1911-1929—were provided for in the royal legislation of 1786.[1]

There was strikingly little demand on the part of the people for the right to do these things for themselves. Three years earlier, with indirect Spanish aid, the people of the United States had secured such rights by their independence; three years later the plebeians of France, much to the distress of Spain, were to begin their epochal struggle for the same freedom from the exploitative benevolence of the Old Régime. Thus curiously did Spain find herself facing both ways amid the complexities of the Revolutionary epoch.

The extension of New Spain into Alta California was the last great Spanish territorial effort in North America, contemporary with the attempts to occupy

[1] *Ordenanza de Intendentes*, arts. 57-63; Lillian E. Fisher, Ph.D., *The Intendant System in Spanish America* (Berkeley, 1929).

*Santa Barbara, established 1786.*

*San Luis Rey, established 1798.*

*San Francisco de Asis, at Dolores, established 1776.*

*Three Franciscan Missions of Alta California.*

western Louisiana. The story of the quest for empire on the western shores of America is too long to detail here; it may be said to date from the advent of Hernán Cortés in Pacific waters. Ever inspired by fear of competition from the Drakes, the Cavendishes, the Spilbergens and the Behrings, the Spanish enjoyed the advantage (lost too early on the Atlantic side) of anticipating all rivals and getting a foothold in spite of long odds of distance and attenuated man power. The climax of the quest came under Charles III, and its success was largely due to the vision and energy of José de Gálvez, whose ambitions for Spanish empire have already been amply illustrated. A prime purpose was to draw the Indians into their proper place in the grand defensive-offensive which should anticipate Russia or England, then approaching these northern reaches, the one by sea from the north, the other by land from the east.[1] The agents of Gálvez were skillfully chosen for the California adventure. Father Junípero Serra, spiritual father of the enterprise, was a Majorcan; Gaspar de Portolá, the commandant, and Pedro Fages, his second in command and his successor, were Catalans. The "New Establishments" of California owed their birth in 1769 to such "Yankees" of Spain.

One is struck by the meager physical resources which entered into such imperial projects. The great coast line of California was taken for Spain by a joint sea and land expedition from Lower California. The land forces were in two detachments totaling eighty-six men; the sea forces in two tiny packet boats numbered ninety. So

[1] Francisco Palóu, *Historia de la Vida del . . . Fray Junípero Serra* (Mexico, 1787), *passim*; same author, *Historical Memoirs of New California* (H. E. Bolton, ed., Berkeley, 1926), *passim*.

ill equipped were the vessels that, when they were blown far out of their course on the voyage, the food and medicines became exhausted long before the arrival at San Diego, and shortly after their landing two thirds of the expeditionaries were dead. The land parties, on the other hand, succeeded in crossing the two hundred miles of desert from Santa María to San Diego without incident or loss of life. From San Diego a land force of sixty-four promptly traversed the one hundred and fifty-odd leagues to occupy Vizcaíno's famous port of Monterey. Of the forty people left behind, half were dead when Portolá returned from the north in January, 1770.

This first white man's march up the coast must have provided thrilling entertainment for the red men. In advance went a sergeant with six or eight *exploradores* to select the route and fix the next camp site. The main force followed, headed by the plumed and gaitered commandant, his second in command and his engineer. Beside them jogged the two brown-garbed Franciscans, spiritual conquerors, with an escort of Catalans. Then came the Christian Indians of Lower California, with adzes, mattocks and other tools to cast up the highway; next, the troops in four squads, each guarding a part of the hundred pack animals. A rear guard convoyed the extra beasts. These *soldados de cuera* were experienced frontier fighters, able to make daily advances of from two to four leagues through unknown country. Clad in leather jackets thick enough to stop an Indian arrow not driven at too close a range, they wore bull-hide shields on their arms to protect themselves and their mount's flank. On their pommels were leather aprons, or *armas*, hung to the stirrups to shield the legs in brush riding. As arms they carried lances, muskets and broad-swords.[1]

The route was in large part over what came soon to be known as the *Camino Real*, a name usually thought by modern language-fanciers to mean the "King's Highway," but which meant to the actual pioneers merely the "main road." Scattered along it for official convenience and hospitality's sake there quickly appeared, at intervals of a day's march, the twenty-one missions—inviting structures with red tiles and cool *adobe* walls, shady *portales*, surrounding gardens, Indian quarters, and fields of grain and fruit, with pasture lands farther out. Along the sun-swept reaches of this old road, today smelling perpetually of burned gasoline, trudged or rode the cloaked and sandaled sons of St. Francis on their errand of love and empire. For their protection against possible annoyance by the natives four presidios were erected—San Diego in 1769, Monterey the following year, San Francisco in 1776 and Santa Barbara in 1782. The commander at Monterey was governor.

In the presidios the tedium of garrison life was broken by occasional escort service, now and then a rounding up of renegade neophytes and a little gardening. As elsewhere on the fringes of civilization, the influence of the troops tended to debase the lives of the none too Edenic savages. In time villages grew up about the presidios. Only two other towns were founded in the Spanish period—San José in 1776 and Los Angeles in 1781. Their populations consisted mainly of a mixed assortment of pioneers, often retired presidial soldiers with Indian wives, though members of the ancient sedentary

[1] Z. S. Eldredge, *The March of Portolá and the Log of the San Carlos* (San Francisco, 1909), 27-32.

tribes and the mulatto-Indian half-castes of New Spain were by no means missing.

In the presidios and missions, and on the few ranchos —which were set as far as possible away from the missions since the good fathers had keen eyes for the most desirable lands—the Spanish population never exceeded three thousand persons. In the Mexican period, when outside ships came to the ports more freely and the advance agents of American pioneering, the fur traders, began to slip over the mountain passes, not more than ten thousand white people awaited the day of annexation to the United States.[1] In these later days life continued in the pastoral and agricultural stage undisturbed by the separation from Spain or the far-away control of Mexico City.

The missions, as the paternalistic agencies of civilization, were naturally the chief directors of economic life. The holy fathers had brought the wheat and barley, the fig, olive, pomegranate, orange, lemon and vine, in a long plant-migration from the Moroccan shore, the hills of Andalusia and the slopes of the Canaries. In the busy mission centers were produced the crops, and also the herds of horses, mules and cattle, from which were derived the chief articles of commerce, hides and tallow, in the days of the hide droghers. As everywhere in New Spain the Indian was at the base of society. Though the law knew neither encomiendas nor chattel slavery, the savage was a virtual serf unless he were clever enough to stay in the foothills out of contact with the white man's culture.

California Indians did not inspire the whites with any

---

[1] Alexander Forbes, *California, a History of Upper and Lower California* (London, 1839), chap. v.

great respect; there was no Montezuma among them, still less a Philip or a Tecumseh. Their greatest sins were reversion to sexual laxity, desertion of the missions and a liking for the flavor of stolen horse meat. They drove off the stock in great numbers and received frequent attention from the *juez de campo,* the civil officer whose business it was to harry the redskins from their retreats with such refinements of cruelty as were familiar to the whites everywhere in America in dealing with the natives. Most of the expeditions sent out in the later days to find mission sites were prompted by the desire of the civil arm to occupy strategic positions from which the marauding bands could be better restrained.[1]

The mission neophytes were trained in morning prayers, sent to work with their spiritual fathers in the fields, nurtured again with physical and spiritual pabulum, and locked up at night by sexes safe from the lusts of the flesh and the call of the wild. They learned the rude craftsmanship of the farm, mingling with it some of their native skill. They pined and died, or, escaping, sought again their old haunts whence they sallied forth to forage off the mission cattle unless haled back by the mission guard. The remnant of their progeny forms a negligible part of Californian society.

Among the townsmen and rancheros outside the missions and presidios life flowed an uneventful course. Men spent their lives in the saddle, and the horses were good. Women stayed at home; they were often beautiful and almost invariably domestic, religious and chaste. Social intercourse was an unending round of simple amenities, punctuated with outdoor amusements, such as the hunt

[1] T. H. Hittell, *History of California* (San Francisco, 1885), I, chaps. xii, xiii, xiv.

and the *rodeo,* and with church festivals. The gaming table was by no means neglected. California hospitality became proverbial among the traders and voyagers from other parts. Since there were no inns, travelers were everywhere welcome at the table and in the guest chamber, with generous provision in the form of food and mount for their departure.[1]

There were no schools to go to and little to read.[2] The first press, set up at Monterey in 1834, was used to issue governors' orders and little else. When the Hijar colony arrived in the same year, it brought a teacher for the proposed normal school at Monterey and eight others for the primary schools, but education did not prosper. The Californians objected to some of the masters on moral grounds and others returned to Mexico because they did not find conditions in the colony to be as represented to them. Richard Henry Dana's description of the people of Monterey in 1835 would do for many a Spanish-American town of those days and later:

> The officers were dressed in the costume which we found prevailed through the country,—broadbrimmed hat, usually of a black or dark brown color, with a gilt or figured band round the crown . . . a short jacket of silk, or figured calico . . . the shirt open in the neck; rich waistcoat, if any; pantaloons open at the sides below the knee, laced with gilt, usually of velveteen or broadcloth; or else short breeches with white stockings. . . . They have no suspenders, but always wear a sash round the waist, which is generally red. . . . Add to this the never-failing poncho, or serape, and you

[1] Alfred Robinson, *Life in California before the Conquest* (New York, 1846), 103-107, 143.

[2] Hittell, *History of California,* II, 236-237; H. H. Bancroft, *California Pastoral* (San Francisco, 1888), chap. xvi.

have the dress of the Californian. . . . The *gente de razon*, or better sort of people, wear cloaks of black or dark blue broadcloth, with as much velvet and trimmings as may be; and from this they go down to the blanket of the Indian, the middle classes wearing a poncho, something like a large square cloth, with a hole in the middle for the head to go through. . . . Among the Mexicans there is no working class (the Indians being practically serfs, and doing all the hard work); and every rich man looks like a grandee, and every poor scamp like a broken-down gentleman.[1]

About the time of Dana's memorable voyage to California there were thirty thousand Indians in the missions. Four hundred thousand horned cattle, sixty thousand horses and three hundred thousand sheep, goats and hogs attested the growth of pastoral interests in sixty short years. Cereals amounted to one hundred and twenty thousand bushels a year, and there was also a considerable production of wine, brandy, soap, leather, oil, cotton, hemp, and tobacco. Two hundred thousand cattle were killed annually for their hides at ten dollars each, the missions supplying half. The annual wealth of the missions alone was as high as two millions, even after the initial steps were taken in "secularization," which was carried out to gratify the white man's cupidity under the zealous Mexican plan of putting the Indians into full status as "citizens." With its wealth, its indolent inhabitants, its incomparable climate and its favorable position for the fur trade, it was small wonder that the path of American empire should shortly include it.[2]

[1] R. H. Dana, jr., *Two Years Before the Mast* (Boston, 1868), 84-85.
[2] *Cf.* T. F. Cronise, *The Natural Wealth of California* (San Francisco, 1868), 59-63.

In summing up the merits and demerits of the Spanish occupation of America, it may be said that, given the defects of the society and the handicaps of the field of operation, the result was better than might have been expected. A constant difficulty throughout the three hundred years was the political necessity for territorial expansion beyond the strength of the available man power, a deterrent influence which the English escaped through their advantage of concentration behind the Alleghanies. For the Spaniards the need was to defend their holdings by interposing great distances, in a scantily cultivable area, between rich treasure mines and the enemy. This policy involved a further necessity for holding territory against the hazard of hostile Indians where the benefits were not commensurate with the outlay of energy. Long seacoasts and a futile attempt at restriction of trade added to the useless expenditure of resources. A century of indolent kings without insight or policy led to the stagnation of the old system, which not even the energy of Charles I or Philip II could make work successfully. The great reformative period of the Bourbons was full of the promise of recuperation until dynastic decay set in again. The principal weakness, after all the notable reforms of Charles III, was his failure to raise up a worthy successor in his son. The growth at the same time of the English system, sharply competitive and everywhere intrusive, roused Bourbon Spain to an energy that would have effected permanent results had society continued on its old basis of the organization of the plunder of dependent peoples.

The worst handicap during the whole period was the immobile character of the colonial population. The Spanish policy of restricted immigration and the liberal importation of Negro slaves resulted during the sixteenth century in a greater influx of black men than of whites into New Spain. The laws forbade, but could not prevent, the mixing of Indian and Negro blood and the result was a combination of the vices of each. The preservation of the Indian and his general fusion with the Spaniard created a type of society distinguished by the position of social and economic inferiority held by the "castes," the name applied to all persons below the creoles. Such a social system bred incompetency and lack of initiative in the group which grew fastest in numbers. The evil effect of the land system, which was in turn the result of climate, topography and social organization, completed the vicious circle. It was a natural, tragic dénouement. Publicists of constructive vision saw the impending disaster and Charles III battled with it valiantly; but like all the other powers, Spain lacked the imagination to foresee the trend of the Revolutionary epoch. In the new colonial era that dawned with the passing of the desire of the European white man to hold in political and economic dependence his white nationals in the world of Ultramar, the ideal of an empire of coöperating nations, as the British Commonwealth, was to rise. Beyond that still lies the empire of the man of other colors. Whether the world is to learn the lesson of the Spaniard or that of the Englishman in its solution of relations with this newer mass of humanity is the problem of today.

# CHAPTER VIII

## THE BUILDERS OF FRENCH EMPIRE

THE early French voyages, like those of the English, affected colonization only indirectly. If Jean Cousin, with Pinzón, made a western discovery in 1487, five years before Columbus, the French won nothing by it, the incident having received far less notice than the Norse voyages.[1] Verrazano gave impulse to Cartier and the fisherfolk who followed his seaways; but real French beginnings awaited a new century. When Cartier on his second voyage undertook the first Canadian colonial enterprise, Cortés was on his way to Lower California, New Spain had been made a viceroyalty, the foundations of Lima were being laid. While Roberval was trying ineffectually to plant a jailbird colony on the frigid Saguenay, Coronado was overrunning New Mexico and marching into eastern Kansas, and Orellano was floating down the Amazon. The fastnesses of two continents were penetrated by the lions of Castile while the English and the French were yet hovering in the coastal stages of empire. The colonial efforts of these two during the sixteenth century ran closely parallel in purpose, inadequacy for their task and similarity of failure. Their challenge was first to Spain; but with the establishment of Quebec in 1608, the second attempt to colonize on the

[1] Justin Winsor, *Narrative and Critical History of America* (Boston, 1884-1889), II, 34, *n.* 6. While most writers discredit the claim, Paul Gaffarel, *Découverte du Brésil par Jean Cousin* (Paris, 1847), advocated it.

St. Lawrence, began their mutual rivalry for the north-ward reaches.

Until 1667 Canada was a fur-trading area exploited by companies, and not primarily a colony of *peuplement* such as the English enterprises had soon come to be. French efforts, probably because Breton sailors knew the whole American shore line, were more widely distributed than was wise; the French plantations in the Caribbean were closer to Senegambia than to the north. On the other hand, the Spanish had a fairly compact empire; the English, while without contiguous territory, were not widely separated by distance and interests. The French weakness through territorial scattering was in-creased by English inroads. Canada was in English hands from 1628 to 1632; Acadia was English for a some-what longer time, from 1654 to 1667, and permanently after 1710, along with Newfoundland. The longest period of French possession of the coast (1667-1710) was barely forty-three years. Acadia was significant as an active smuggling center, as the scene of romantic episodes of international rivalry on a very small scale, and as the one French colony of the Old Régime where the popular town meeting became a vital agency of government.[1]

Canada was but a puny undertaking until Colbert assumed control of colonial policy in 1667. French im-perial cupidity was not enticed by the possibilities of this bleak northland in spite of the propaganda of the enthusiastic *Jesuit Relations* and the lure of fur. Under Colbert France was willing and able to assume direct control of overseas effort as England never tried to do

[1] This may well have come about because of New England influence. See J. B. Brebner, *New England's Outpost; Acadia before the Conquest of Canada* (Columbia Univ., *Studies*, no. 293).

save in Georgia, Halifax, Sydney and Port Elizabeth on Algoa Bay. By 1663 the hold on the St. Lawrence was doubled, the population reaching twenty-five hundred, of whom eight hundred were in Quebec.[1] The real period of empire building for France lay within the seventeenth century.

The French had been slow to migrate for many reasons. They loved to dwell in peace at home, as they do yet. They dreaded the dreary Canadian winters and the fierce Indians. For the most part they had no need of a haven from religious persecution and would not provide one under the national flag for the Huguenots. Nor were they enticed by the company system to undertake to win fortune in the wilderness. In the West Indies, where settlement began in 1625, success against English pressure and Spanish hostility was greater; for, though the various companies which operated there went successively bankrupt, the French islands, home of tropical products, grew in population to seven thousand by 1642, whereas Canada then had only two hundred and fifty. By 1665 France held fourteen Caribbean islands with a population of over fifteen thousand whites and almost as many Negro slaves. Prosperity continued, Guadeloupe being in the eighteenth century the most lucrative colonial holding in the world.

The occupation of the Great Lakes region and the later thrust down the Mississippi was, though tardy, the most brilliant strategical move in the fight for the continent. It was done with the small resources of Canada, the more opulent and populous Caribbean settlements having proved of economic significance but

[1] C. Le Clercq, *First Establishment of the Faith in New France* (N. Y., 1881), II, 11, and note.

not political. The French settlements on the Gulf of Mexico were made by *coureurs de bois,* whose hope of a river to the Pacific had first tempted them down the Mississippi. La Salle had been lured by tales of New Mexico, the exiled governor of which, Diego de Peñalosa, had held out to Frenchmen hope of conquest of the great silver country. The Spanish trade was also a continuing incentive.[1] After La Salle the rivalry between France and Spain ceased because Spain was the appanage of France for half a century. Frenchmen could not be kept out of the Spanish Gulf Coast or the Indian interior. When the two countries joined in an effort to defeat the English, France always profited at the expense of Spain; the latter, indeed, was the first rival to lose in the great triangular struggle for the middle reaches of North America.

Notwithstanding the poverty of her resources as compared with Louisiana, Quebec amid her dolorous winters of isolation—prey to hostile natives, isolated from Acadia and the West Indies—always held the dominant place in the scheme of French-American affairs. The lake and river fur trade, over which the rock of Quebec gave protection at a narrow passage, the supposed impregnability of the fortress and the pride of long possession determined the relative importance of Canada.[2] That

[1] La Salle, "Memoir on the Necessity of Fitting Out an Expedition to take Possession of Louisiana," B. F. French, *Hist. Colls. of La.* (N. Y., 1846), I, 25-34.

[2] R. G. Thwaites, *France in America* (A. B. Hart, ed., *The American Nation: a History,* N. Y., 1904-1918, VII), 41. See the brief summary of the geographical and climatic characteristics of the St. Lawrence Valley in Émile Salone, *La Colonisation de la Nouvelle-France* (Paris, 1907), 1-14. A remarkably fine reproduction of French-Canadian life, the struggle with winter, anxiety for crops, the part of the fur trade in existence, along with the pioneer spirit, is Louis Hémon, *Maria Chapdelaine* (N. Y., 1921).

great Latin citadel looked far away toward the other Latin stronghold, beautiful Mexico on the Plateau of Anáhuac, with as much jealousy and anxiety as toward New England. The Anglo-Saxons feared the union of the two hostile powers long before it happened, but proved too strong for them both when the Seven Years' War ended the rivalry.

There were odds to face other than those of scattered geographical distribution. The St. Lawrence was closed to navigation half the year, and the winter enforced idleness among the inhabitants for the same interval. Moreover, French command of the river was more apparent than real. With the English holding the coast the isolation of Quebec was a liability which increased as the disparity between the English and French fleets grew. Had the French chosen the Hudson instead of the St. Lawrence, or seized it when the intendant Talon made the proposal in 1665, the problem of access to the back country below the lakes, as well as that of coastal control, would have been simplified. The main motives of the French—desire for furs and yearning for Indian souls—were offset by the languid interest of the peasants in the breaking of the wilderness. Yet there was abundant enterprise among the individual soldiers, traders and priests; their rivalries as well as their common drive give the heroic dispersal over a third of the continent vivid flashes of dramatic coloring which challenge the imagination quite as sharply as do the tremendous spurts of energy of the sixteenth-century Spanish conquistadores.

Those rapierlike thrusts for empire owed their force to the religious impulse of the adventuresome Jesuits and to the race-amalgamation ideal exemplified in the

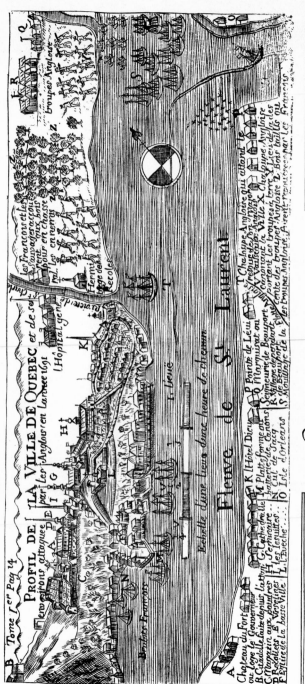

QUEBEC IN 1690

quickly risen class of coureurs de bois, men who sought the untrammeled and exhilarating life of the forest fur trade. The St. Lawrence, the Great Lakes and the affluent streams were under French influence long before effective occupation. A few years after Colbert's accession to power the upper lakes were occupied by missions controlling the Northwest. In the seventies the movement toward the Mississippi began, culminating in Spanish-French rivalry in the valley and the Gulf littoral; Hudson's Bay was the scene of French-English rivalry from 1670 to the Peace of Utrecht. It was the loss of this area and of the Acadian Coast which impelled the new activity to hold the Ohio and the Mississippi. This motive, combined with desire for the Spanish mines and trade and the need to check English aggression from the east, brought Louisiana into existence.[1]

In 1698 Spain fortified Pensacola while the French set up Biloxi, soon moving the establishment to St. Louis on Mobile Bay. Government administration proving too expensive, Antoine Crozat was made a company proprietor with monopoly privileges. Soon seven hundred settlers collected, escaping the feudal devices of Canada and bringing into being a colony with New Orleans as its center. John Law's boom brought five thousand more settlers. The Compagnie d'Occident in Louisiana worked nearly as did the companies of Canada, with much the same story of Indian wars, the erection and Indian destruction of Jesuit missions and the mutual jealousies of governors and intendants. After the

[1] C. W. Alvord, The Illinois Country (C. W. Alvord, ed., The Centennial History of Illinois, Springfield, Ill., 1918-1920, I), 127; "Memoire sur les Colonies Françaises sur le Golfe du Mexique [1736]," Collection de Manuscrits . . . Relatifs à la Nouvelle-France (Quebec, 1883-1885), III, 178-181.

desolating Natchez wars the crown resumed control in 1731; but Chickasaw raids incited by the English reduced the population after 1740. When England bested France in 1763 there were only some seven thousand people in the Gulf territory. Three thousand or so lived in the Illinois country, and there were several hundred near the mines of Missouri. More than half the population of this Mississippi region were slaves.

In the meantime Canadian traders from Illinois had almost reached New Mexico in 1703; traders and explorers on the Rio Grande, Osage and Arkansas rivers sought alliances with the Indians which opened the way to Santa Fé by the middle of the century, though the Spaniards, always alert, caught every band they could and sent the intruders to Mexico City. At the north La Vérendrye worked ten years in establishing posts beyond Lake Superior. In 1743 he saw the Rockies, and nine years later his successor built a fort on the Saskatchewan at their feet. The French farthest west had been attained.

The colonial mechanism through which French social ideals expressed themselves exhibits interesting variations from the form and spirit of rival organizations. The state policy demanded expansion of commerce, and Cartier and Roberval began their colonizing scheme with state funds.[1] When they failed, tacit permission sufficed to send the Huguenots to Brazil and Florida; but the quest for religious security, which might have made great French colonies, was neglected. Furthermore, the driving individual will, which in England's expansion sought adventure and wealth for personal gratification, was

[1] "Lettres Patentes . . . à François de la Roque," *Collection de Manuscrits Relatifs à la Nouvelle-France*, I, 30-36, and "Mons' Proposals," same vol., 40-43.

lacking. The expansionist organization, created by governmental initiative, was, then, more like the Spanish in spirit though it had the company form used by the English and the Dutch. The effect of this dependence upon royal favor determined the type of society that grew up in the French and Spanish areas, where feudalism and paternalism fixed the forms of landed proprietorship, the enjoyment of commerce and the practice of religion.

French trading companies, whatever their form, had no such impulse to activity as those of England and Holland. Their driving force was governmental, not the initiative of the merchant class. In 1603 the De Monts Company received the monopoly right to the fur trade between the fortieth and forty-sixth degrees of north latitude, coupled with the obligation to colonize the country and convert the savages of the coast. The Acadian colony at Port Royal and the post at Quebec were both given the same scheme of government as had been provided in the monopoly granted in 1540 to Roberval. De Monts and Samuel Champlain, Huguenot and Catholic, attempted at Port Royal a trading post and a haven for liberty of conscience. De Monts had to return to France to defend his viceroyal title, the navigator busied himself in explorations. Conversion of the Indians by Huguenot pastors and the care of settlers by Catholic priests brought the reverend leaders of the two faiths into frequent conflict, so that religious strife was concurrent with the quarrels of traders. Basque interlopers seized six thousand furs; the winters were terrible; the word of the government could not be relied upon. The monopoly was revoked in three years, and De Monts transferred his interest to the St. Lawrence Valley, Champlain founding Quebec for him in 1608; after this, Acadia and Canada were separate. The De Caens succeeded to the monopoly centered at Quebec, and retained control until 1627 when the period of dominant Huguenot influence in the fur trade was ended by the formation of Richelieu's famous but ill-fated Company of One Hundred Associates.[1]

This was the great cardinal's chief contribution to American colonization. The government was now willing, or rather obliged, to contribute to the enterprise because conditions prevented investment of enough private money. It was decreed that no noble would lose rank by trading or owning stock in the company; on the contrary, twelve plebeians were to be ennobled for so doing. The need of such a decree shows the rigidity of French society, the faintness of the colonial impulse, the lack of love of the sea except amid the west-coast towns. Emulation of Spain gave as great an impulse. Champlain, founder of Acadia and Canada, had been in active service on Spanish ships in the West Indies through the influence of his Spanish uncle.

Government patronage was doubly necessary: not only did France have little surplus capital but the risk in overseas investment was still great. The plan was to send three hundred colonists annually, and religion and agriculture were to have proper attention. But imperial policy was in advance of colonial desire. The first defect of Richelieu's reorganization was that it was too much like previous attempts; the only notable differences were the efforts to instill greater energy, to enlist greater

[1] French activity was plainly emulative of Dutch and English successes in East and West. See "Commerce des Hollandois-Compagnie des Indes, 1608," *Collection de Manuscrits . . . Relatifs à la Nouvelle-France*, I, 52-57, 62-85; H. P. Biggar, *The Early Trading Companies of New France* (Toronto, 1901), 38-68, 115-166.

capital and to exclude Huguenots.[1] The substitution of Jesuits for Recollects was in expectation of greater commercial activity than the friars had shown—since the Jesuits had no vow of poverty—as well as for reasons of international advantage.

But the capital was still too small, and much was lost in adjusting the claims of the old company. Then, too, just as the change was to be made Canada and Acadia fell before the Kirkes and remained English, as we have seen, until the Treaty of St. Germain in 1632. Richelieu, too busy with the Thirty Years' War and with "increasing the majesty of the King," gave little of his enthusiasm to colonization, while the company lost sight of such activities altogether. Perhaps the substitution of the Jesuits was the best stroke; their work for the Indians stands unchallenged for its heroism, and the priests aided exploration and served in diplomatic errands to the Indians and the New Englanders as more simple-minded men of the mendicant orders might not have done. But their notable *Relations* emphasized the creation of a new civilization through the priestly agency alone; they diverted attention and money from practical colonization when the great need was for solid agricultural settlement such as later developed in the Illinois country. The free hand given the Jesuits seems the more remarkable since they did not believe, as did Champlain and his successors, in gallicization, but hoped to develop a native culture on the lines of their Lower Californian and Paraguayan enterprises.

[1] Salone, *La Colonisation de la Nouvelle-France*, 43-46. Salone feels that the Kirkes, who chose not to recognize their French blood, but took Canada as Scotchmen, may have influenced Richelieu to exclude Huguenots, and adds that the failure of Protestants to colonize actively in the early period was their own fault and explains the exclusion.

With Colbert and his organization of the West India Company in 1664, the scattered colonies were first envisaged as an imperial whole, as was demonstrated when De Tracy was sent as lieutenant general over all the insular and continental governors. Now at last the game of occupation was to be creditably played for the glory of God and the king. The settlers were secured from the long Iroquois devastations by a good military force,[1] immigration was urged, industry was built up, expansion hurried forward. But in a short ten years the pseudo-monopoly was abandoned for frank government control; the crown took over company debts of three and a half-million livres and opened trade to all nationals. This was an abandonment of the company idea under which England had been able to induce active immigration and the Dutch to build up a prosperous trade, and a resort to the older type of government control direct, which Spain had found at first successful but which was now weak because of continuous competition against her pretensions to monopoly. And yet the colonies were still mere fields of exploitation in spite of a new solicitude for justice and liberty, increased freedom of commerce and the development of production. The exclusive system still served to enrich a few merchants. Colbert created a great colonial empire in appearance only; he could not make the French a colonizing people. After his passing, France turned again, under the influence of the minister Louvois, from expansion to the old complications of European politics.

If the differing organization and aims of the colonial societies were determined by home governmental policies,

[1] *Collection de Manuscrits . . . Relatifs à la Nouvelle-France,* I, 20; Léon Deschamps, *Histoire de la Question Coloniale en France* (Paris, 1891), 149, 229.

their contrasts in character were none the less clearly revealed in the various attitudes of the nations toward the natives. Parkman, epitomizing and contrasting these attitudes, says, "Spanish civilization crushed the Indian, England scorned and neglected him, while France embraced and cherished him." [1] This sweeping comparison overlooks the basic truth that each group of white men used the Indians for its own purposes as best it could, according to the character of the white men, the objects of their enterprise, the economic possibilities of their country, and the kind of Indians they found. It would be truer to say that the Protestant Teutonic nations felt indifferent to the uplift of the natives and thought marriage with them miscegenation, while the Catholic Latin nations tried to convert them to Christianity and their own type of society and, legally or illegally, intermarried widely with them. [2]

But in all cases European contact acted as a withering blast on the tender plant of weaker culture. Spanish civilization did oppress the Indian, but the mortality among the Huron and Algonquin was as severe as in any Spanish area; neither the Dutch nor the English wars with the red men were models of civilized practice. The Frenchman "cherished" the Indian with brandy for furs and fighting men, with a spirit of *camaraderie* natural to the French mind perhaps, but consciously intended to win its purpose; the Spanish land system used and preserved the red man at the lowest level of

[1] Francis Parkman, *The Jesuits in North America in the Seventeenth Century* (Centenary Edn., Boston, 1922), 131. Cf. T. J. Wertenbaker, *The First Americans* (*A History of American Life*, II), 232.

[2] An interesting account of proposed subsidies to Englishmen for marrying Indian women in Nova Scotia between 1719 and 1773 is in a contribution by J. B. Brebner to "Notes and Documents," *Canadian Hist. Rev.*, VI, 33-38.

subsistence and survival. It was everywhere too easy to kill off the Indians in Spanish territory, if need be, save on the fierce northern frontiers. The French had a trading system in which Indians were useful collaborators on a plane of practical equality—if they could not be bested in barter while drunk. The bond of union rested on the difference between the European and the American valuation of beaver skins. The imputation of vice or virtue to the attitude of any white nation merely overlooks the self-interest under which each worked, and seeks to impose secondary psychological reactions as prime factors. In the English labor system the Indian had no place, and so he was "scorned." But the French plan meant his extermination when the expansive life of the trapper should vanish, just as surely as did the English plan a little more promptly.[1]

The effect on colonial expansion was characteristic. The English, feeling no strong missionary impulse, still kept near the coast when the French had reached Georgian Bay. Canadian society developed the *métis*, cognate with the *mestizos* of Spanish America, but negligible elements in Dutch and English areas. The métis, though relatively few as compared with the mestizos, made worthy contributions to civilization. The half-breed type of the French and Spanish areas marked one of the chief differences between the kind of society evolved in the Latin areas and that of the Teutonic colonies.

The absolutist ideal of French government gave Canadian life an evolution and finally a certain fixity of form

[1] W. B. Munro, *Crusaders of New France* (Allen Johnson, ed., *The Chronicles of America Series*, New Haven, 1918-1921, IV), 64-66. Indian policy demanded the same prohibitions against sale of liquor and firearms as prevailed in other colonial areas. Cf. Montmagny, "Ordonnance, July 9, 1644," P. G. Roy, ed., *Ordonnances, Commissions*, etc. (Beauceville, 1924, in *Archives de la Province de Quebec*), I, 5.

strikingly comparable with that produced under administrative development in New Spain. While the colony was under company organization the direction of affairs by the governor was not highly developed, trading interests receiving chief stress in spite of the nearer and clearer vision of the chiefs on the spot who urged greater colonizing activity. The superior council of Canada, dating from 1647, was a counterpart of the audiencia of Spanish America. The governor (later the intendant) presided over it as did the viceroy or captain general over the audiencia. Both bodies were criminal and civil courts of last resort in ordinary cases, with appeal to the home government in extraordinary ones. Both were also administrative advisory bodies, directing general police regulations and supervising trade and finance. The Canadian councilors were appointed annually by the governor and the bishop, hence were more completely under control than the long-term royal appointees to judgeships in the audiencias. The superior council gave to the bishop (at first the Jesuit superior) a seat and a disproportionate influence, since he shared equally with the governor the civil and judicial power; whereas Spanish American archbishops, though they often became viceroys, were never officially coördinate with the king's representative.

The office of intendant, distinctively of French origin chiefly under Richelieu and Colbert, was gradually introduced by Spain into America beginning in 1764, after French power had disappeared from the continent.[1] Be-

---

[1] Thomas Chapais, *The Great Intendant* (Toronto, 1914), 15-21; W. B. Munro, "The Office of Intendant in New France," *Am. Hist. Rev.*, XII, 15 ff.; Gabriel Hanotaux, *Origines de l'Institution des Intendants des Provinces d'après les Documents Inédits* (Paris, 1884), 17-99; Charles Godard, *Les Pouvoirs des Intendants sous Louis XIV* (Paris, 1901), *passim.* See also, P. G. Roy, ed., *Ordonnances, Commissions*, I,

ginning with Jean Talon in 1665, the Canadian intendants as the confidential agents of the colonial ministry
served to check the governor and bishop, making a three-
sided division of the superior power. The intendant was
chief justice in civil matters, and had charge of police
and finance. In New Spain the *super intendente,* the
superior of twelve provincial intendants, was intended
to serve much the same purpose of checking the viceroy:
but, as we have seen, the office dimmed the viceroyal
luster so much that it endured only two years; in the
other Spanish areas, however, the clash between the two
executives was as frequent and as bitter as in the French
colonies. Both colonial establishments suffered greatly
from the continuous attention which French and Spanish officials gave to small matters, such as precedence in
religious processions, the order of seats at council tables,
in church or at other public functions. Yet quarrels
between coördinate executives and between officers of
church and state were part of the process through which
our modern differentiations of administrative functions
were worked out, partly by separation of church and
state, and partly by the overthrow of autocracy.

The chief social characteristics of both colonies were
evolved from their land systems, which gave distinctive
tone and color to the Latin occupation of America.
French and Spanish alike held that the king possessed
both the sovereignty and the direct dominion over the
land. The French applied the basic principles of their
land system at home to Canada, in part to the West
Indies and even to Louisiana, whereas the trend of Spanish land administration was a continuous effort to get

and same ed., *Inventaire des Ordonnances des Intendants* (Beauceville,
1919, in *Archives de la Province de Quebec*).

away from the vestiges of feudal form under which colonization began. The warm-hued Old-Worldliness of the Old Régime in Canada is tied up with this surviving feudalism. The French monarch based his title upon discovery and occupation, the kings of Spain upon these backed by the papal bulls. The French American area was granted *en bloc* as a fief to the successive trading companies. De la Roche had the privilege of subinfeudation in fiefs, seigneuries, chatellenies, earldoms, viscounties and baronies; no grants save of three seigneuries were made by Champlain; the Company of One Hundred Associates held feudal rights much more limited. No high nobility was provided for, and in the grants the distinction of the *noblesse* was not consistently observed. The *habitant* was at the base of the social pyramid, but the *seigneur* was bitingly poor and worked also with his hands; so no caste system developed. Society was made compact by the absence of the high nobility, by the obligations of habitant to seigneur, seigneur to company and company to king, with the exaction of dues, rents and symbolic ceremonies.[1]

In the Spanish system the land was granted direct by the king or his agencies, the viceroys, audiencias and municipalities. The adelantados who conquered great areas were under oaths of fealty and homage and could bestow lands, and the encomenderos received the fealty of their followers; but there was no bond of allegiance based on land tenure, for the recipient could acquire land in fee simple upon royal confirmation of his occupation after five years of continuous possession; nor did

[1] W. B. Munro, *The Seigniorial System in Canada* (*Harvard Hist. Studies*, XIII), 21, 159-160; W. B. Munro, ed., *Documents Relating to the Seigniorial Tenure in Canada* [1598-1854] (Champlain Soc., *Publs.*, III), pp. xxii, 1-3.

adelantados or encomenderos have direct intervention in justice officially. It follows that there were no banal rights in New Spain, the only mark of inferiority being the Indian tribute, a tax which no white man ever paid.

The alienation of land *en droit encensive* in New France had only an apparent counterpart in land sales under the *censo* in New Spain. The Canadian *cens* was the annual payment of a few sous each year to the seigneur. With it were imposed the *rentes*, annual payments in grain or poultry, not onerous burdens. The Spanish censo was a revenue or rent rather than the price of land; it was derived from the lease of municipal lands to individuals or from the emphyteutic use of public lands, waters and other royal properties. It might be paid indefinitely by the same tenant, or there may have even been private transfers of such tenancies, but the practice did not give rise to a general form of possession, though such tenures survive. After 1630 land in New Spain was more often sold directly than bestowed by grants.

The patriarchal rather than the feudal tenure of land was strengthened in Spanish America by the law of primogeniture, so that there was always a constant increase in the size of holdings instead of the diminution which occurred in New France under the *droit d'ainesse* of the Custom of Paris.[1] The effect of primogeniture was to withdraw land from circulation, making it impracticable for younger sons or less favored subjects to get it. In New France, on the other hand, the divided inheritance created parcels too small for practical cultivation. The social influence of the two contrasted land systems was in certain respects identical. In both colonies

[1] Munro, *Seigniorial System,* 82-84.

it became the practice for large landholders to build and occupy residences in the capital where they could enjoy social advantages and contacts with officialdom. In each case the social pleasures indulged in were censured by the church, but in New France the austerity of such relations was greater, before the military became dominant, than in New Spain.

The absence of the landlord from his estate was a greater economic handicap in New Spain than in New France, for in the latter the seigneurs spent only their idle winters in Quebec, while, in the traditional life of the hacendado, years on end were spent in Mexico City. The habitant or *censitaire*, contrasted with the Indian laborer under a driving major-domo, was a happy and contented man despite his isolation, lack of intellectual interest and poverty. He should rather be compared with the *labrador*, or the ranchero type of landowner of New Spain. Yet the comparison reveals that these though not numerous, were in somewhat happier circumstances than the farmers of New France. They were in free possession of a small parcel of land, commanded some available labor, had their homes in the midst of arable, pasture and forest lands, and lived in communities of their peers. Like the French they had their hostile Indians, with occasional warfare, and the same lack of markets; but they dwelt upon their self-sufficient acres in tolerable security and comfort.[1]

The feudalism of New France, under which the seigneurs worked in the fields with their tenants and married their daughters, was a sort of economic democracy rare in Spanish America, for no hacendado enter-

[1] H. I. Priestley, *The Mexican Nation* (N. Y., 1923), 100; A. Herrera y Ogazón, *El Arte Musical en México* (Mexico, 1917), 20-21.

tained the slightest notion of dismounting from his horse to do a manual task. It is an interesting paradox that the social mold of Mexico, where feudalism was rejected by royal authority, should have become far more feudalistic in its pervasive paternalism than Canada, where feudalism was more prevalent than in France itself at the time the institution was transmitted. It is explained by the caste line of New Spain, which was created by race cleavage and by the growth of vast wealth from mining and agriculture.

Land in New France remained a more fluid commodity than in New Spain in spite of the Canadian *lods et ventes*, or mutation fines when farms changed hands otherwise than by inheritance, and notwithstanding the tendency of the seigneurs to hold their best areas for special bonuses. There was no mutation fine at all in New Spain such as prevailed in New France and in the transfer of manorial leases in New York. In New France the only *banalité* was that which obliged the habitants to bring their grain to the seigneur's gristmill for grinding, paying him one fourteenth for so doing. This was not a serious burden on agriculture; in fact it was the current commercial rate in the English provinces.[1] The corvée usually called for "personal service" of from three to six days a year, divided between plowing, seedtime and harvest. In Spanish and French America alike land proprietorship became unavailable to the small worker—in New France because the seigneurs monopolized it; in New Spain because irrigable land was limited and because the system of forced labor encouraged the patriarchal institution. So the "hardy-

[1] See, for example, D. R. Fox, *Caleb Heathcote, Gentleman Colonist* (N. Y., 1926), 56.

pioneer" type, characteristic of the English frontier, was less frequent in the two Latin areas because free land did not exist. The Spaniard bewailed the situation and tried in vain to correct it; the French law of 1711, obliging the seigneurs to commute the lods et ventes when a tenant wanted to acquire title in fee simple, provided means for a movement opposite in tendency to the direction taken by landed propriety in New Spain.

The land tenure evolved by the French, excluding as it did any form of freehold save in isolated instances, was ill-adapted for frontier needs and inimical to agricultural expansion and the growth of a prosperous society. The *franc alleu roturier* (something like the English free-and-common socage and the grants to Spanish encomenderos or military colonists of Lower California and Sonora after 1767)[1] was used sparingly in Canada, and then only in places exposed to Indian attacks which the seigneur grantee was expected to repel. Canadian lands were rich, and though clearing was arduous and idle winters long, it would have been a boon to agriculture if land had been given freely to every pioneer. The autocrats of the Old Régime were unmoved by the fact that their system added one more handicap to those imposed by nature and the Indian, because there were certain merits in it and it was traditional.

Contemporary opinion as well as later judgment is divided as to whether the French land system was suited to the character of the habitants. It may be safely asserted that, while it no doubt served to promote solidarity and contributed to the French tenacity of occupation,

[1] Munro, *Seigniorial System*, 53, 83; same author "Seigneurs of Old Canada," chap. viii of his *Crusaders of New France*; H. I. Priestley, *José de Gálvez* (Univ. of Calif., *Publs.*, V.), 259-260, n. 37.

it also tended to stir up litigation [1] and to drive the most venturesome Canadians into the forest and the fur trade and thus to retard substantial growth. And yet, even with a more generous land policy, the problem of markets would have proved as serious as it often did for tobacco planters in Virginia or for stockbreeders and corn growers in New Spain. A more general agricultural opportunity was really dependent upon the development of American markets by the growth of population, for most farm products not tropical would have made unprofitable ocean freight.[2] Nearly all local communication was by water; the few roads built were quite inadequate to serve as incentive to agricultural expansion. In those goods which did admit of ocean transportation the trammels of mercantilism were effectively set aside by the wholesale smuggling activities of the European colonists of every nationality, activities which contributed to the final downfall of the exclusive system.

The agricultural production of Canada was thus restricted for the most part to supplying the wants of her population, though there was a limited export trade in wheat and flour. In 1716 this was made subject to the governor and the intendant if crops were light. The material aim of the colonists was primarily to support their own lives, and in this task they were often obliged to call upon the homeland for food. The characteristic condition of the inland as well as the coastal settlements was one of almost uniform poverty.

The land system was disliked by some of the habi-

---

[1] See J. B. Brebner, *New England's Outpost,* 140.
[2] Salone, *La Colonisation de la Nouvelle-France,* 371-373. In 1719 wheat production was 234,566 bushels, in 1734, 737,892 bushels; in the latter year there were 3462 bushels of barley, 5223 bushels of corn and 163,988 bushels of oats. Same vol., 374.

tants at least. Lord Durham reported that the people of Saguenay, when in dire circumstances, petitioned for land upon any terms except feudal tenure.[1] On the other hand, when the opportunity was given the farmers to end it by composition of their perpetual dues, they moved with exceeding slowness, and there still remain those who have never attempted to redeem their holdings. It was a social and economic advantage of the system that it tended to bind them to the soil, for they sometimes lost their land if it went uncleared. Yet this fact did not always deter them from deserting even cleared holdings for the more sprightly adventures of the fur trade.[2]

The relation of the church to the land presents in New France broad analogies with that in the older Latin establishments to the south. In each the ecclesiastical bodies, notably the Jesuits, gained control of superior holdings. Usually the type of agriculture maintained by the clerical bodies was of a better grade than that common among lay farmers. The possession of an undue amount of land by the church was characteristic of New France and of New Spain; in some of the English colonies the same economic phenomenon came into existence by action of large landholders of nonclerical status. But the church of New France, for obvious reasons, did not function as banker and mortgagee to the extent that it did in New Spain.[3]

[1] Lord Durham, *Report on the Affairs of British North America* (Oxford, 1912), II, 25.

[2] Munro, *Seigniorial System*, 36, 38, 42-44; H. I. Priestley, "Land Legislation in Mexico," R. G. Cleland, ed., *Mexican Year Book for 1922-1924*, 221; Roy, *Ordonnances, Commissions*, II, 168-170 [1687].

[3] Francis Parkman, *The Old Régime* (Boston, 1910), 393-395, summarizes the evidence of Jesuit fur trading, and praises their example in industry.

The continuous process in New France was toward the absorption of power over the public domain by the king. The change in the status of the granting power after the time of De la Roche has been mentioned. The repeated attempts of the crown to reabsorb the uncleared lands of the seigneuries; the requirement after 1676 that grants receive the concurrence of the government and the intendant, beside the royal approval, within one year; the expressed intention (1680) to take back annually one twentieth of the uncleared lands; individual commands to speed clearing, like those of Champigny; and the important Arrèts of Marly on July 8, 1711, which protected the habitants from seigneurial speculation and encroachment and made the seigneurs virtual trustees of the king's rights in lands for the sake of the small developer—all these are conspicuous evidences of the tendency. The forfeiture of some twenty seigneuries in 1741 for nonclearance had its counterpart in Mexican land history in the royal order of 1576 requiring that land taken by squatters be relinquished to the crown. Spanish *entrepreneurs* had a genuine land hunger, and the reversion of the lands caused such widespread discontent that squatters' claims were thereafter habitually legalized by composition upon proof of ten years' prescriptive right.

In both French and Spanish areas, perhaps on account of the cheapness of land, grants and purchases were vaguely defined. The French transferred land without any measurements at all or upon mere description by a petitioner, or with metes and bounds based on previous ill-defined contiguous properties. Inevitably litigation over land became as acrimonious as it did in New Spain, or occasionally in English America. The French system enjoyed one very marked superiority in that the title deeds were registered in a public *cadastre* to which recourse could be had in difficulties, whereas no general *catastro* was attempted in Mexico until the days of Porfirio Díaz. The Canadians had also, in the *aveu et dénombrement,* or report of the seigneuries, especially in those required every twenty years, a means of preserving agricultural history paralleled most successfully in Spanish America only by church organizations.[1]

Yet we know that New Spain supported its four or five million inhabitants, in spite of recurrent crop failures, with little food importation, while New France, with less than eighty thousand inhabitants, was never entirely free from such aid. The Spaniards regularly exported the tropical agricultural products, cacao, indigo and sugar, and even at times wheat and flour, as did the Canadians occasionally. Up to 1661, after fifty years, Canada was not self-supporting, even though the rural population around Quebec was three times that of the five hundred and forty-seven inhabitants of the city itself.

In stock raising New France should be compared with New Netherland, where animal husbandry was also on the domestic rather than the ranch scale from the beginning. In 1647, when there was but one horse in New France, there were hundreds of thousands of cattle and horses in the valleys of New Spain; Champlain himself had remarked upon their number at an earlier date.[2]

[1] Munro, *Documents Relating to Seigniorial Tenure,* 167-168.
[2] Samuel de Champlain, "Brief Discourse," H. P. Biggar, ed., *The Works of Samuel de Champlain* (Champlain Soc., *Publs.,* new ser.), I, 40. The inroads upon Canadian commerce by Frenchmen who had not borne the brunt of colonization injured the settlers, leading the council to limit the season for "marchands forains." Roy, *Ordonnances, Commissions,* II, 12-16 [1683]; *Collection de Manuscrits . . . Relatifs à la Nouvelle-France,* I, 309; Salone, *La Colonisation de la Nouvelle-France,* 381.

Before the seventeenth century was well ushered in the Indians were driving off the ranches of northern Mexico more animals than the whole of New France ever possessed. In 1683 Canada, with ten thousand settlers, had 7025 horned cattle, fifty-six horses, six hundred and twenty-five sheep and 2320 hogs. New France was spared the Indian use of the horse in warfare because there were forests instead of plains, bitter winters instead of perpetual summer, and because the French had not been brought up in the tradition of grazing which made the cattle industry a great Spanish institution. Yet animal husbandry had moderate success. In 1719 cattle had grown to 18,241, and 33,179 in 1734; hogs in 1720 numbered 13,823 and 19,815 in 1734; sheep rose from 1820 in 1706 to 13,823 in 1720 and 19,815 in 1734. Horses numbered about 5000, causing the authorities much disquietude, for beef would have utilized forage to better advantage.

Uniform poverty, due largely to the land system, did not, in general, mean lack of actual food, clothing, warmth and shelter—discomforts often bitterly experienced in New Spain—save in the early days when there was too little preparation for the cold Canadian winter. Canada was much like New Netherland in that there was a liberal supply of wild food, and in great diversity, from both forest and stream. Agricultural methods were extremely wasteful, as in other American frontier communities; this was the more surprising since crop rotation and fertilization were skillfully practised in France. Gédéon de Catalogne, the inspector of ninety-two seigneuries in 1710-1712, said that if the methods of the Canadians were to be employed in the home country three fourths of the people would starve.

The Canadians felt little distinction between American- and European-born, perhaps because there was not time for society to crystallize in this way, and because fur trading as well as seigniorial life had its elements of equality. Not a conspicuously large number of Canadian-born seemed inclined to seek administrative positions, the famous sons of Le Moyne serving to illustrate the exception which emphasizes the rule. Little racial strife entered church circles. In spite of the all-pervasive control over their lives, the habitants developed surprisingly little rancor toward their rulers. The preliminary protests, which led to the organization of the Company of New France for habitant control of the fur trade in 1645, are strikingly mild in tone compared with the *Representation of New Netherland* in 1650. In the rural communities the seigneur and the curé—the estate and the parish being practically coterminous—were the arbiters of life among the habitants, just as corregidor and *cura* managed the people of New Spain. But the latter rarely showed mutual helpfulness such as prevailed in New France, because their interests were opposite, each seeking control of the Indians for his own ends.

# CHAPTER IX

## FRENCH HOMES IN THE NORTHERN WILDERNESS

IT is often pointed out that their absolutist rule, holding all the American settlers under a rigidly centralized control, permitted the French to withstand for years the aggressions of the numerically superior English, who were divided in counsel among many colonial governments not coördinated for statecraft or strategy. Emphasis is merely transferred to another essential phase of the situation if we say that during the time of Colbert, when the French empire in America was first looked upon as a great military enterprise, a real continental strategy was undertaken. At that time the competitors of France had not been aroused to united action. Until fortune favored the English in the Seven Years' War, none of them put into the conquest of the continent a military effort at all comparable with that of France. It is true that Cromwell had dreamed of snatching empire from England's rivals, but his plans had come to little.

Thus it was due not merely to the direct need of fighting the Iroquois but to imperial policy that the French system imposed a much more formal and continual military service upon the habitant than was demanded of the Spanish American vecino or the English head of a family. The Spaniards depended more upon professional soldiers or, in default of these, upon mission establishments to hold the frontiers. Each of the European settlements had its frontier fringe; those of the French and Spanish being wide and sparsely settled, and each in turn was menaced not only by the Indians but by its European rivals. Continuously on the defensive against the others, each was convinced of the malevolent aggressiveness of all competitors. Everywhere the normal condition of society was that of Indian warfare interrupted by short truces; in all areas the loss of life and property was greater from hostile Indians than from European enemies.

To meet this situation the French policy responded with an exceptionally strong militaristic spirit and organization. The government counted upon war service even from nonlandholders, and it was rendered with unquestioned willingness as a normal social duty, perhaps even as a welcome variation from the dull routine of colonial life. The Spaniards used presidios, or forts, in strategic positions, manned by professional soldiers who might expect, after thirty years with the colors, to become agricultural settlers with their fort as the nucleus of a town—a sort of survival of the Roman fashion of colonization that was interestingly illustrated in the case of San Francisco in Spanish California[1] and which was also perpetuated in New France and Louisiana. This sort of settlement, however, never proved very successful. The reason was that the military forces, militia or professional, were rarely adequate, and demands for added troops were often pitilessly ignored; nor did the detachments usually consist of the kind of men who would make admirable settlers, what with their army back-

[1] Bernard Moses, *The Establishment of Municipal Government in San Francisco* (Johns Hopkins Univ., *Studies*, VII, nos. 2-3), 6-7.

ground and agricultural inexperience.[1] Moreover, the French and Spanish habit of interspersing whites among the Indians proved less effective for permanent organization than did English exclusion and extermination. Everywhere the Frenchman had to be armed; the gun and powderhorn hung over each habitant's fireplace, whence it could be quickly grasped at the order of the village captain of militia to repel sudden attack or share in a brief campaign. The guerdon of this unpaid service was simply continued existence.[2]

The Carignan-Salières regiment, which came in 1665 with twelve hundred valuable soldiers, brought not only respite from devastating Iroquois raids, but most of the soldiers and officers were, after it was disbanded, induced to settle on lands along the Richelieu and St. Lawrence rivers to inspire savage respect. A large part of the four thousand soldiers who later came were also so used.[3] They were expected to serve until they were forty or fifty years old or until their enlistment expired. Men hitherto consigned to the galleys for smuggling were granted expiation by the alternative of colonial service.

As most of the peasants who immigrated were single,

[1] The policy of westward expansion of the military power by forts protecting the fur trade reached its height under Frontenac. With the English military pressure the expansion had to be stopped; and in the interest of retrenchment the western Canadian country beyond Fort Frontenac (near modern Kingston) was abandoned by the military force in 1698 upon the promulgation of a decree of 1696 recalling the fur traders from the west.

[2] Talon and Tracy argued eloquently for the encouragement of military colonists. P. G. Roy, ed., *Ordonnances, Commissions*, etc. (Beauceville, 1924, in *Archives de la Province de Quebec*), I, 55-64. De la Barre repeated in 1682 the order that all habitants capable of bearing arms should buy them. Same work, II, 11-12.

[3] Colbert to Talon, Paris, February 20, 1668—extract in Francis Parkman, *The Old Régime* (Boston, 1910), 493. See also, same vol., 276-279; C. W. Alvord, *The Illinois Country* (C. W. Alvord, ed., *The Centennial History of Illinois*, Springfield, Ill., 1918-1920, I), 108-109.

and the soldiers invariably so, wives were provided by recruiting from the villages and slums and foundling asylums of northwestern France. The intendant Talon in 1670 asked for from one hundred and fifty to two hundred "not at all deformed or repulsive in appearance," with three or four young ladies for officers' wives. But the response to the latter order was unexpectedly eager; instead of three or four, there came fifteen, and a halt was called for the nonce. The peasant wives mothered large families from the first. In 1671 Canadian births numbered between six hundred and eight hundred. Not all the pioneer mothers were angelic in figure or temper; Mother Marie de l'Incarnation, of the order of Ursulines, admitted that there was *beaucoup de canaille* among them as well as among the men. Baron Lahontan, no doubt a trifle maliciously, depicted the disposal of a shipload of prospective wives for the soldiers as follows:

> . . . several ships were sent hither from France with a cargo of women of an ordinary reputation, under the direction of some stale old nuns, who ranged them in three classes. The vestal virgins were heaped up (if I may so speak) one above another in three different compartments, where the bridegrooms singled out their brides. . . . There was such variety . . . as could satisfy the most whimsical; some were big, some little, some fair, some brown, some fat, and some meager; in fine, there was such accommodation that everyone might be fitted to his mind; and indeed the market had such a run that in fifteen days' time they were all disposed of. . . . The sparks that wanted to be married made their addresses to the above-mentioned governesses, to whom they were obliged to give an account of their goods and estates before they were allowed to make their choice. . . . After this the marriage was concluded upon the

spot, in the presence of a priest and a public notary; and the next day the governor-general bestowed upon the married couple an ox, a cow, a hog, a sow, a cock, a hen, two barrels of salt meat, and eleven crowns.[1]

It ought to be added that the bachelors had as little choice as the damsels, for if they were not married within a fortnight after the arrival of the young women, their hunting licenses would be revoked.

Even with such official encouragement the population grew but slowly. Indeed, many returned to France rather than brave the wilderness in quest of an independence that was a mere dream, life being hedged in with so many disadvantages. But the growth of the colony received impetus from bounties upon children. Parents of living families of ten received pensions of three hundred livres a year, and of four hundred for twelve. Girls who married before the age of sixteen, and boys before twenty, received twenty livres as a dowry. There were marriages where the bride was but twelve years of age. Families of from six to ten children were common, and there were much larger ones; but the rate of infant mortality was necessarily high because of improper feeding.[2]

[1] Baron Lahontan, *New Voyages to North America* (R. G. Thwaites, ed., Chicago, 1905), I, letter ii, 36-37; W. B. Munro, *Seigneurs of Old Canada* (G. M. Wrong and H. H. Langton, eds., *Chronicles of Canada*, Toronto, 1914-1916, V), 36-37; *Collection de Manuscrits . . . Relatifs à la Nouvelle-France* (Quebec, 1883-1885), I, 206; Roy, *Ordonnances, Commissions*, I, 104-105.

[2] Parkman, *Old Régime*, 289-290; John Davidson, "Growth of the French Canadian Race," Am. Acad. of Polit. and Social Sci., *Annals*, VIII, 213-235. The census of Canada shows the following seventeenth-century figures: 1608, Quebec founded (28 wintered there); 1620, population of Quebec, 60 persons; 1628, population of New France, 76, including 20 French and the missionary returning from the Hurons; 1629, 117 wintered, including 90 English of Kirke's expedition; 1641, sedentary population, 240; 1653, about 2000; 1663, 2500, of whom 800 were in Quebec; 1665, official census, 3215; 1667, 3918; 1668, 6282; 1673, 6705; 1675, 7382; 1676, 8415; 1679, 9400; 1680, 9719;

The *gentilhomme*—a discharged army officer, habitant or merchant whose influence or worth had commended him to the intendant for a seigneury—was sometimes but not always an addition to society. Said the intendant Jean Bochart de Champigny, "It is pitiful to see their children, of which they have great numbers, passing all summer with nothing on them but a shirt, and their wives and daughters working in the fields." And he continued, "Pride and sloth are the great faults of the people of Canada, and especially of the nobles and those who pretend to be such. I pray you grant no more letters of nobility, unless you want to multiply beggars." It would be easy to add numerous quotations showing the uncomplimentary notions of their compatriots treasured by the officials of New France. It is to be remembered, however, that the pessimistic note of colonial correspondence was usually intended to magnify the merit of the achievements attained in spite of all the handicaps imposed alike by nature and society.[1]

New France cannot be vividly recalled to the imagination without remembering that the establishment of religion concerned the state vitally, and that, formally at least, to proselyte the Indians and gallicize them was as much a part of public policy as though a contractual obligation to do so had been assumed as in the case of Spain. Though no papal bulls imposed the task, New France was as much a mission as a fur-trading concern or a military rampart of empire. Recollects, Jesuits and

1681, 9677; 1683, 10,251; 1685, 12,263, including 1538 Indians in villages; 1686, 12,373; 1688, 11,562; 1692, 12,431; 1695, 13,639; and 1698, 15,355.

[1] Parkman, *Old Régime*, 319-320, cites his letter of August 26, 1687, to the minister. On Champlain's use of the Recollects, see W. L. Grant, ed., *Voyages of Samuel de Champlain, 1604-1618* (N. Y., 1907), 270-274.

Sulpitians emulated each other in the conversion of the savages and set the moral tone among the colonists. No less important in the picture were the secular clergy, headed by their doughty bishop François de Laval de Montmorency (1659-1685), of the conspicuous French house which made so much European history. A proud and pious aristocrat, militant and uncompromising in matters of faith and government alike, he, though a secular, organized the Canadian church on lines as centralist and effective as those of the Jesuits, whom he admired profoundly. His organization lives after him, making his influence more lasting than that of any other French American colonial.

The secular church radiated its authority over the continental holdings, except lower Louisiana, from its seminary at Quebec. In this home all the priests were trained and inspired for service; to its kindly shelter they retired in sickness and old age. There they passed annual retreats, and from the field reported regularly to it for advice from their head. It flourished as it deserved, being still the center of the Catholic church in Canada. Before the end of the French dominion every village had a neat church of stone or wood, in many cases with shining tin spire. In it were gathered the visible tokens of the child-like reverence of the habitant:

> In the midst of the village [La Prairie] is a pretty church of stone, with a steeple at the west end of it furnished with bells. Before the door is a cross, together with ladder, tongs, hammer, nails, etc., which were to represent all the instruments made use of at the crucifixion of Our Saviour, and perhaps many more beside them.[1]

[1] Peter Kalm, "Travels into North America," John Pinkerton, ed., *Voyages and Travels* (London, 1808-1814), XIII, 620.

For the Habitant there were, and are,
two centers of life, the church and the home.

A glimpse of old Three Rivers.

On the Isle of Orleans.

At intervals along the roads stood frequent wayside crosses, with the image of the Virgin set behind a panel of glass, and at the top a figure of the cock that crowed when Peter denied his Lord. In this general atmosphere of faith that bordered upon simplicity, if not superstition, the mystic Jeanne de Ber could have herself immured behind the altar of the Montreal church, and so enjoy a reputation for piety which made her words oracular and endowed her garments with the virtue of relics. Weld, the English traveler in Canada in 1798, sat down one evening to dine in the home of a habitant by the glow of a lamp suspended from the ceiling, so dimly lighting the table that the host added a candle from the cupboard. The wife broke forth in a volley of execrations, reviling her spouse for his sacrilege in requisitioning *la chandelle bénite* in the name of hospitality. It had been consecrated at the neighboring church, to be kept burning only in case of tempest, to prevent injury to house, barn and all therein contained, or in sickness to bring instant recovery.

Parish priests, chosen from the best seminary students, often included men of but middling capacity who found the Latin of the mass and sacraments something of a trial, but who possessed ample quality for wilderness services. On snowshoes or in canoe, the curé traveled long miles to give extreme unction, baptize a new child, or marry a pair of his impatient wards.[1] Nor were his rewards of this world; thrifty parishioners were sparing with their tithes, over the size of which high officials might wrangle long without affecting the happy rela-

[1] Isaac Weld, *Travels through the States of North America and the Provinces of Upper and Lower Canada* (London, 1800), I, 339-341; Denonville au Ministre, Quebec, November 15, 1685—extract in Parkman, *Old Régime*, 520-523.

tions between the actual shepherds and the members of their flocks.

The pervasiveness of church control over the colony made the Canada of early days a perfect theocracy. The bishop sat in the supreme council; the church not only controlled all education but set the code of morals, and, by excluding foreigners and heretics and banning all objectionable books, restrained public opinion. As early as 1636 a wooden horse was set up before the Quebec church for the punishment of blasphemy, drunkenness and absence from mass; within a week the first victim was exposed upon it. Indians were not spared correction for delinquencies, and sometimes had influence enough to compel the French to mete out punishment to their own kind as severe as had been dealt to them. In 1669 the cabarets and taverns were denied opportunity to serve meals and drinks on Sundays and feast days. In 1671, for selling liquor to the Indians, an offender was flogged at the church door, kneeling partly stripped with a crucifix in his hands.

Nor were those of high degree exempt from admonition. Bishop Saint Vallier in 1685 outlined to the new governor, Denonville, what were the proprieties for him and his family. He must avoid late dinners and frown upon any that were too sumptuous. He might attend no dances, but his daughter, being young, might indulge in a little "moderate and proper dancing, provided that it be solely with persons of her own sex." There must be no private theatricals; feminine dress, prescribed in great detail, must not hint the remotest suggestion of physical charm.[1] Such regulations as these suggest that

[1] James Douglas, *Old France in the New World* (Cleveland, 1905), 252, 318, 400, 401; *Mémoire de Dumesnil* [1671], cited by Parkman,

what is today called Puritanism was perhaps more a matter of the *Zeitgeist* than of sectarian conviction. The early moral codes of New France, Virginia and New England had much in common.[1]

Frontenac found the supervision of the clergy a bit trying. He even declared that the Sulpitians at Montreal, notable for bleak holiness, had a number who wanted to control the people with greater severity than shown by the Spanish Inquisition.[2] Lahontan, perhaps smarting from the mutilation of his beloved copy of Petronius by the meddlesome curé of Montreal, averred that the curés visited the habitants too often and pried into their minutest family affairs with irritating impertinence. Perhaps one of the local reasons why Huguenot heresy was rigidly kept out was derived from Champlain's experience at Sainte Croix in 1605:

> I have seen the [Huguenot] minister and our curé engage in fisticuffs over the differences in our religion. I cannot say which was the more valiant, or which struck the best blows, but . . . the minister complained . . . several times that he had been beaten. . . . I leave it to you if this was a pretty sight to see! The savages were sometimes on one side and sometimes on the other; and the French, locking horns each according to his belief, sent each other's religion to the devil.[3]

Huguenots who strayed in were converted or deported. Denonville was advised by the king in 1686 to quarter

*Old Régime*, 389; "Ordonnance . . . aux cabaretiers de Montreal, 2 avril 1669," Roy, *Ordonnances, Commissions*, I, 86-89.

[1] Cf. T. J. Wertenbaker, *The First Americans* (*A History of American Life*, II), chap. viii.

[2] Talon the intendant fined Jacques Bigeon, habitant, six livres "pour avoir juré et blasphemé le sainct nom de Dieu." Roy, *Ordonnances, Commissions*, I, 26, 77.

[3] Benjamin Sulte, *Histoire des Canadiens Français* (Montreal, 1882-1884), I, 58; Lahontan, "Mémoirs," *New Voyages*, I, 391.

troops on opinionated Protestants who refused conversion or put them in prison, but at the same time to work with the bishop to obtain their conversion.

As was natural, the soldier-settlers, after a training of licentious camp life in Europe or savage contacts in America, found clerical tutelage unbearable, for toil was irksome, drink was cheap, and life after the savage model had its attractions. Monsieur de la Barre had to suppress a certain order of knighthood which sprang up among the scions of gentilshommes who thought it "a good joke to go about naked and tricked out like Indians" on feast days. The Indian life was too appealing, consisting in "doing nothing, caring for nothing, following every inclination, and getting out of the way of all correction." Not all the liquor in Canada was traded for fur. There was an "infinite number" of drinking shops—half the houses on some seigneuries purveyed the cheering cup; at Three Rivers eighteen out of twenty-five houses did so, and Villemarie (Montreal) and Quebec were proportionately supplied.

Amid white and red men alike the church sought to raise the level of civilization by educational ministrations. The Jesuit missions among the Indians in French America employed much the same methods as those pursued in Lower California and Paraguay, save that the exclusion of white men from Indian areas, being impractical, was not insisted upon.[1] Unlike Champlain and Colbert, the Society disbelieved in gallicization, but nevertheless attempted to give their wards fixed domiciles where they might gain an appreciation of the amenities of civil life such as the Recollects had earlier at-

[1] The Jesuits insisted upon exercising guardianship over the Indians in the control of their properties. "Ordonnance de De Lanzon, May 12, 1656," Roy, *Ordonnances, Commissions*, I, 12.

tempted to instill at Quebec. When this method proved ineffective, the Black Robes carried religion over forest and plain in the wake of their nomad converts. But not even Jesuit adaptability could make the Indian over in a few short generations, nor do much to conserve his numbers, for his close identification with wilderness life meant his disappearance as the more intensive white occupation progressed. Gallicization produced the coureur de bois and lapse into savagery, not the elevation of the redskin. Peter Kalm noted the same social devolution among his Swedish compatriots on the Delaware, while the Spanish suffered from it more than any save perhaps the Portuguese in the Orient. Even among the Dutch and English illicit unions produced a half-breed type whose influence was leveling.

When the Recollects left Canada with the departure of the Kirkes, the Jesuits conducted the religious and educational work alone for twenty-seven years. In 1642 the Sulpitians began parish work from their seat at Montreal, where they had just set up their pious institution; seculars began at Quebec with Laval in 1659; the Recollects reëntered French America in 1670, serving as parish priests in Acadia. The number of churchmen was never disproportionate; and though the Jesuit missions diverted much capital from the exploitation of natural resources and colonization, the church was no such serious economic burden as in New Spain, where by the middle of the seventeenth century were to be found four hundred convents, with a thousand regulars in Mexico City alone, and probably eight hundred friars throughout the viceroyalty. The Canadian church held vast tracts of the best land; but its influence upon agriculture was constructive rather than otherwise, as shown by its superior cultivation at the model farm at the Quebec Seminary, while little influence was exerted by the religious orders of New Spain upon the white man's methods of farming.[1]

As in the other colonies, New France was permeated with the idea that education under the ægis of religion was the effective means of perfecting human nature and of perpetuating the church. This was as true of "heretical" as of orthodox societies. Even the English sometimes admitted Indians to their colleges—a single seventeenth-century bachelor's degree was granted by one of them in 1675. The French were much more active; the colleges founded by the seculars were widespread, and the brief domination of the country perhaps accounts for the lack of intellectual achievement otherwise. Neither the French nor the English devloped a native literature comparable with that of the creole Jesuits of Mexico. Intellectual independence was not one of the fruits of colonialism—there was only one Franklin in the English colonies—everywhere in America the scientific spirit was kept alive by European visitors rather than by native Americans, though examples of ability to follow the best European thought were conspicuous in all the colonies.[2] But French America was especially laggard in independent thought and public opinion. No newspaper or book was printed in it until the middle of the eighteenth century. All Canadian government orders were penned, and even paper money was manuscript.

The prevalence of illiteracy hardly means as much for

[1] C. B. Reed, *Masters of the Wilderness* (Chicago, 1914), 28-30; Lewis Drummond, S. J., "The Church and the Colony," Adam Shortt and A. G. Doughty, eds., *Canada and its Provinces* (Edinburgh, 1914-1917), II, 379-442.

[2] *Cf.* J. T. Adams, *Provincial Society* (*A History of American Life*, III), 113-114, 130-131.

the seventeenth century as it does for today. The Frenchmen in Canada were as well adapted for their task as were any of the European colonists, save perhaps the New England Puritans. In such a state of society as that of seventeenth-century Canada the Jesuit and the official contributions to intellectuality were as much as the colony could well support. It was a time of conflict with forces more primitive than those the intellect could master.

The Jesuits have been conceded on every hand full recognition for their high-minded bravery, abnegation and devotion to their work. They served in the most dangerous places, often seeking and attaining the crown of martyrdom. Their influence over the colonists was always marked. Imperialists and expansionists, they rendered conspicuous diplomatic services among the Indians and among the English colonists. The Sulpitians, between whom and the Jesuits there existed a "thinly disguised jealousy," deserve as much commendation as they for their contribution to social stability, though their service was not so widespread.[1] The Jesuits were gradually eliminated under British rule, whereas the Sulpitians still remain and have become the wealthiest Canadian religious community.

The secular church, through the influence of Laval, was kept on the ultramontanist side of the national church controversy. Gallicanism, though thriving in

[1] Louise P. Kellogg, *The French Régime in Wisconsin and the Northwest* (Madison, 1915), thinks that the service of the Jesuits in exploration has been overestimated, but gives them great credit for their advance work in the civilization of the Northwest. See in particular chap. viii, "The Missions." On June 21, 1925, eight Canadian Jesuits were beatified: six priests and two *frères donnés*, Isaac Jogues, John de Brebeuf, Gabriel Lalemant, Noel Chabanel, Anthony Daniel, Charles Gernier, René Goupil and John de Lalande. For further details see V. J. Dowling, "Heroes of America's Origins," *Ill. Catholic Hist. Rev.*, IX, 39-55.

France, achieved little influence in Canada where the idea prevailed that the church was immortal, a perfectly organized society superior to the state, and that the latter must yield if interests clashed.[1] The Quebec Seminary has already been spoken of as a training house for priests; beside it was a sort of trade and agricultural school for humbler pupils not of the stuff fit for the cloth. Some knowledge of handicraft was taught, a great deal of doctrine and discipline, and some pupils even studied Latin. But at no time was the mechanical education of Canadian youth adequate; and architecture, cabinet making and turning were far behind that of New England. Nor did discharged soldier-colonists have many of these practical accomplishments. There was one Canadian clockmaker of sorts, and the father of Joliet was a wagon builder; but the implements of agriculture, though widely needed, were marked by their crudity. Harrows were entirely of wood and triangular in form; plows went on wooden wheels as thick as cart wheels, and were so clumsily made as to require a horse to move one upon a smooth field. The failure to develop mechanical skill was due to overemphasis on religious education and to the call of the wild, for Canadians had some natural aptitude for mechanics.[2]

Farm life in the Quebec area was subject to serious climatic limitations. As the spring was always late but a single crop of hay could be cut. No winter wheat could be planted because of the extremely cold winters. No

[1] A concise account of the struggle of the Church with Gallicanism in Canada and Louisiana is Sister M. Theodosia O'Callaghan, "Echoes of Gallicanism in New France," *Catholic Hist. Rev.*, new ser., VI, 16-58, with ample bibliography.

[2] Kalm, "Travels," Pinkerton, *Voyages and Travels*, XIII, 609, 619, 622. The Canadian tools were not at the beginning conspicuously worse than those in use in the English colonies, but they improved more slowly.

fertilizer was used, fallowing being the method used for restoring the land, but during the fallow season the weeds were allowed to choke the land. The cornfields were only insufficiently drained. But farther up the river not even the crudity of methods could entirely discourage nature:

> About four French miles from Fort St. John, the country makes quite another appearance . . . with excellent wheat, pease and oats, presented to our view; but we saw no other kinds of corn. The farms stood scattered, and each of them was surrounded by its cornfields, and meadows. . . . The forests are pretty much cleared, and it is to be feared, that there will be a time, when wood will become scarce. . . . This country was in my opinion the finest of North America.[1]

Corn was planted in May and harvested about mid-September. The ears were carried into the barns on the stalks, where they were shucked in the cold months at the *corvées recreatives* with which the habitants varied winter isolation. Peas were as much a favorite crop as in New Netherland, but all sorts of grains were cheap for food, as were meat and fowl. Indeed the habitant, though poor, lived in physical comfort; only in famine years did he lack actual food, or when war carried the men away at sowing or reaping time.[2] As fodder was often scarce for the long winter the fall butchering disposed of surplus livestock. Meat was dried and hung on the kitchen rafters or stored underground with the winter vegetables to keep as well as unseasonable thaws would

[1] Kalm, "Travels," 619.

[2] Lahontan, "Memoirs," *New Voyages*, I, 353-356; W. B. Munro, *Crusaders of New France* (Allen Johnson, ed., *The Chronicles of America Series*, New Haven, 1918-1921, IV), 181-183. Note Montmagny's order of June 8, 1639, Roy, *Ordonnances, Commissions*, I, 1-2, for an instance of food conservation in the face of need.

permit. No observer failed to mention the eels from the river which were smoked and hung with the meat and formed a large share of the winter provender.

Agriculture might have flourished better and spread wider had it not been for the bugbear of forest clearing. Cold winters, church holidays and the fur trade kept it back. When the British took the colony in 1759 there were three hundred thousand *arpents* (some two hundred and fifty thousand acres) under cultivation, and seventy-five per cent of the sixty thousand population were engaged in it. That is to say, it had taken one hundred years of active colonization to put under the plow an area less than one third that of Rhode Island. About five arpents per capita were then tilled.

The share of women in building New France has often been remarked. With the growth of a French American population girls were taught obedience to authority and instructed in the household arts, in which they became adept. The homespun made by the women and girls clad the men; in winter they plaited straw hats and made the fur caps and bright toques which individualized Canadian headdress. Their own handicraft supplied the small fineries of feminine apparel which were too costly for import. Immigrant Frenchwomen possessed all the politeness characteristic of their nation, the American-born of Quebec being not at all inferior in this. But those of Montreal had not as much contact with European life, since ships seldom ascended the river so far, and they were accused of developing an Indian-like pride and of being somewhat lacking in good breeding. Like most Canadian women, they paid too much attention to dressing their heads, and when making social visits decked themselves as though "their parents possessed the greatest dignities in the state." As in every age and clime, the men complained of their improvident attention to the newest fashions—already old or discarded in France; and they had still other traits of Mother Eve:

> One of the first questions they propose to a stranger is, whether he is married. The next, how he likes the ladies in the country, and whether he thinks them handsomer than those of his own country; and the third, whether he will take one of them home with him.[1]

Kalm preferred those of Montreal as the better looking and more modest. Those of Quebec he thought not very industrious. "A girl of eighteen is reckoned very poorly off if she cannot enumerate at least twenty lovers." Women of rank rose at seven, dressed until nine, then did needlework by a window whence they could watch the street. "When a young fellow comes in, whether they are acquainted with him or not, they immediately lay aside their work, sit down by him and begin to chat, laugh, joke and invent *double-entendres,* and this is reckoned being very witty." Meantime the mothers attended to all the tasks of the home. Montreal maids, more industrious, plied their needles actively. They were busy, cheerful and contented, at the same time lacking not for wit or charm. Girls of all ranks went to market and carried home what they bought. Yet these daughters of Montreal thought well of themselves and were much displeased that those of Quebec got husbands sooner than they, as they had the first choice of the young men from France.

But femininity contributed more than frivolity. We must not forget the patient mothers at household tasks

[1] Kalm, "Travels," 691-692.

caring for swarms of children or helping in the rougher labors of garden and field. Nor can we pass by the often praised nuns and sisters of the church whose influence was so marked in teaching and nursing. The Hospitalières of Dieppe began their ministrations at Quebec in 1639 under the patronage of the Duchesse d'Aiguillon. At the same time began the work of the Ursulines, whose patroness was Mme. de la Peltrie, and whose mother superior was Mère Marie de l'Incarnation, an educator of great piety and administrative skill; her influence on the young French girls and Indian children is the traditional pride of the present inhabitants. The novices of this order were as a matter of policy chosen from among Canadians. Jeanne Mance and Marguerite Bourgeoys made lasting names for themselves by their work at Montreal for religion and charity. And no less influence for the refinement of society was exercised by many a nameless heroine who endured the hazards of farm life and Indian hostilities for the unrecorded glory of proving a good mother and housewife.[1]

Geographical setting and pioneer inclination determined the distribution of the population. The St. Lawrence led past the settlements to the ever receding fur country. Still important today, it was then even more the indispensable thoroughfare since roads were poor or absent, and all required access to it. So the seigneuries had small frontages on it, extending indefinitely back from each bank. Sub-allotments to the habitants took the same shape.

The only consideration was to get as far away from each other as possible, so as to be able to spread out

[1] C. W. Colby, *Canadian Types of the Old Régime* (N. Y., 1910), 322-357.

more, without thinking that in that fashion they were placing themselves beyond the possibility of helping each other, and that by embracing an immense territory . . . no one could be safe from the insults of the enemy. But the court has given orders in vain to remedy this great evil and reduce the parishes to villages; it was never possible to have them executed. . . . The course that was taken was to build forts in each seigneury in which the people and cattle were to take refuge; even so, the tillable lands are so far apart, and so surrounded by woods that in every field a body of troops must be kept to protect the workers.[1]

Ocean-going vessels, aided by the tides, could reach Quebec, some leagues below which the water was too salty to drink. Above the fortress the river led toward the wilderness with an urgency that made many a habitant learn the knack of canoeing to follow where it beckoned; it was not surprising that most of them preferred to voyage on the St. Lawrence or its tributaries rather than suffer the ennui of the eventless farm. But the river was frozen from November to May, which gave to winter a monotony broken only by anxiety over keeping the cattle alive on scant fodder and by social amusements. One colonial luxury for New France was the horse, introduced, as we have seen, in 1647. It flourished amazingly, shifting for itself in winter until the snow became too deep and bearing the lowest temperatures well. Tails were docked, and the animals driven tandem over the narrow roads as they still are in old France. The habitants were so fond of horses that forage was often short in winter for the more essential kine, and proposals were officially made to limit their

[1] Sulte, *Histoire des Canadiens Français*, V, 128; P. F. X. de Charlevoix, S. J., *History . . . of New France* (J. G. Shea, tr., N. Y., 1900), IV, 46-47.

number at the ratio of one to five cattle; but they were not acted upon.

At Quebec the houses were built compactly of logs or stone, and plastered or whitewashed outside. Lime was plentiful but bricks were scarce. A fireplace graced each living room, and, much later, stoves, cast at Three Rivers from local iron, helped conquer the winter's cold. Further upstream houses were

> generally built of stone, but sometimes of timber, and have three or four rooms. The windows are seldom of glass, but most frequently of paper. They have iron stoves in one of the rooms and chimneys in the rest. The roofs are covered with boards. The crevices and chinks are filled with clay. The other buildings are covered with straw.[1]

Weld said the houses were better built at the end of the eighteenth century than those in the United States; the logs fitted together better and were planed before being whitewashed. The inside walls were usually covered with deal boards, whereas those of the Americans were left "as rough within as they are without." One circumstance, however, made the Canadian interiors very disagreeable, "the inattention of the inhabitants to air them occasionally by opening the windows." [2] Kalm, perturbed by the ubiquitous dirt and bedbugs, said that

> sometimes the floors, both in town and country, were hardly cleaned once in six months, which is a disagreeable sight to one who comes from among the Dutch and English, where the constant scouring and scrubbing of floors is reckoned as important as the exercise of religion itself. . . . Upon the whole, however, they are

[1] Kalm, "Travels," 628.
[2] Kalm, "Travels," 653, 658; Weld, *Travels*, I, 337-338.

not averse to taking part in all the business of house-keeping, and I have with pleasure seen the daughters of the better sort of people and of the governor himself, not too finely dressed, going into kitchens and cellars to look that everything be done as it ought.[1]

In winter, when the daily chores were done, the whole family, bundled in furs, might get into a sleigh and visit relatives fifty miles away, for their sturdy horses could cover great distances; "The sound of these bells and horns appears to be very conducive to cheerfulness, for you seldom see a dull face in a cariole." In the bitterest weather the poorer women sometimes had to stay close to the home fire for want of sufficient clothing but generally they could flit across the snow to a neighbor's house for an hour's gossip. For the dignitaries and their families there were formal dinners where there were observed all the little punctilios they had learned at the governor's little court at Quebec.

When one entered the home of a Canadian farmer, the latter rose, doffing his hat, offered the visitor a seat, and then replaced his hat as he sat down again. Acquaintances of either sex, meeting after an interval, saluted each other with kisses. The poorest peasants as well as ladies and gentlemen were called monsieur and madame. The peasant wore shoes hollowed from wood. Boys and girls wore their hair in cues behind, generally with woolen toques, red near Quebec and blue about Montreal; some of the gentlemen wore wigs. In winter, oiled moccasins, laced nearly to the knees, were universally worn, two or more pairs of woolen socks inside completing the foot dress. In summer women and children ran barefoot, but the men usually preferred to wear cowhide clogs.

[1] Kalm, "Travels," 621, 646; Weld, *Travels*, I, 390-396.

"Best clothes" came out on Sundays and feasts; then the men surmounted their dignity with tall beaver hats, and the women in bodices and petticoats decked themselves with ribbons and laces from France. Town dwellers often wore scarlet cloaks and perukes, buckled slippers and silk stockings.[1]

Altogether it was a happy little society that the eighteenth-century traveler encountered along the St. Lawrence, however "unprogressive" he might judge it. The home life of the French peasant had been transferred to an entirely different environment. Savage neighbors, slowly conquered by the cross and the trader's trinkets rather than by the royal standard, became allies and companions. The French character coöperated with the circumstances of the fur trade to bring about this contrast with the state of faltering diplomacy and recurrent warfare between colonist and native along the Atlantic Coast and on the southwest plains, and with that of the semislavery in the Mexican mines. Few men of Quebec or Montreal accumulated fortunes that could be compared with those of the colonists of New Spain or even those of the seaports and plantations of the English colonies. Little that was memorable in art or letters came from New France and no political institution that has influenced the world. The cultural level that contented the habitants would never have satisfied men of enterprise like the Huguenots who were excluded. Yet meager in numbers and achievement though it was, it would be hard to dismiss New France as a failure; in fact, under another flag, it still persists.

[1] Munro, *Crusaders of New France*, 211, 213.

*Montreal, solid and somber, long remained French under the British flag.*

# CHAPTER X

## THE MEN OF THE MIDDLE BORDER

THE French occupation of the lower reaches of the Mississippi, brought within the imperial purview by La Salle, took place only after the Peace of Ryswick and under an impulse from New France. The Canadian-born sons of Charles Le Moyne, Pierre Le Moyne d'Iberville and Jean Baptiste Le Moyne de Bienville, took up the task of anticipating the possible Spanish and the English seizure of the Gulf region. The English movement was narrowly averted; that of Spain to Pensacola in 1698 was met by the prompt founding of Biloxi, which was moved to Mobile Bay in 1702 and named St. Louis. Eight years later a further removal was made to the site of the present city of Mobile.

The tiny population was more than doubled in 1704 when seventy-five new soldiers arrived with supplies, some artisans, a priest, and twenty-three girls—in charge of two Grey Sisters—for wives. Unlike some of the later shipments to the matrimonial market, these young women were industrious and respectable.[1] By 1706 the land inclosed within Mobile measured one hundred and ninety arpents and held nearly ninety settlers; the presence of some two hundred soldiers emphasized the character of what was always a military occupation, and the slavery of Indians had begun. In 1712 the Crozat Com-

[1] André Pénicaut. "Relation," Pierre Margry, ed., *Découvertes et Établissements des Français* (Paris, 1879-1888), V, 581, describes the coming of eighty-eight women; in 1719, 1720 and 1721 shiploads of profligate women arrived; the last load of marriageable females was sent in 1751.

pany, that year superseding crown administration, raised the population to four hundred. Under Lamothe-Cadillac, who had charge, active efforts were made to establish trade with the Spaniards, Natchitoches being established for this purpose in 1713. Fort Toulouse on the Alabama among the Creek became a fur post the next year, and served later to ward off the English from Georgia, whose Fort Okfuskee on the Talapoosa stood only forty miles away. Fort Rosalie, at the Natchez site, was established in 1716 in a vain attempt to subdue the tribe of that name. Fort de Chartres, built by Boisbriant, a cousin of Bienville—later to become the Quebec of the middle border—was founded in 1718-1720 in the Illinois country.[1]

When John Law began in 1717 to make Louisiana the bright flower of his great design of French colonial empire and finance, the peopling of the valley received decided impetus. In that year New Orleans was begun, to become the capital five years later. The "Law People" were brought out to be settlers on Law's two concessions, one on the Arkansas, and the other some twenty-one miles below New Orleans on the Mississippi. They were Rhinelanders and German Swiss, who came out under the influence of "boom" literature portraying the prospective wealth awaiting them after their sufferings in a land that had not yet recovered from the Thirty Years' War. Of the ten thousand who, it has been asserted, were intended for the venture, some two thousand arrived; the others deserted the enterprise or perished in ports of

[1] For the strategic value of Chartres and Detroit, see Margry, *Découvertes*, VI, p. xvii, and T. H. Holdich, *Political Frontiers* (London, 1916), 38. *Cf.* E. G. Mason, *Chapters from Illinois History* (Chicago, 1901), 212-249, "Old Fort Chartres"; and Philip Pittman, *The Present State of the European Settlements on the Mississippi* (Cleveland, 1906), 88-90.

embarkation, in pest ships on the ocean, or on the miasmatic coast after landing. These people were Catholics. In the time of Bienville the Huguenots were denied entrance, though there were four hundred of them in the Carolinas who had left France after the revocation of the Edict of Nantes and now sought a welcome in Louisiana. By this rebuff to Protestant nationals an industrious element of population was rejected, but it may be that the English conquest was delayed by the same act, for the Huguenots planned close relations with the English pioneers among the Cherokee.

A large installment of settlers numbering eight hundred, arriving in 1718, doubled the French population of the province, but was apparently more impressive in size than in quality. In these times such immigrants were rounded up in France by a regiment of archers at a hundred livres per head. Then, too, prisoners were set free if they would marry prostitutes; otherwise, chained together, they were cast aboard ship and hurried off to certain misfortune or death in the wilderness. This kind of recruiting lasted for only two or three years, and the slum element is declared to have proved remarkably sterile, scarcely a score of families of that origin surviving until the Independence epoch.[1] After the bursting of Law's "Bubble" some of his colonists stayed on the Arkansas, while others came down to the settled region near the Gulf. The soldiers who garrisoned the district were released by two's from their companies each year, so that they formed a small but steady accretion to the agricultural element.

There were also Jews among the early arrivals, though they were forbidden in 1724. But the most valuable ele-

[1] Pierre le Moyne d'Iberville, "Journal," Margry, *Découvertes*, IV, 395.

ment was furnished by the Germans, who settled on the "Côte des Allemands," which came to mean both sides of the river for a distance of from twenty-five to forty miles above New Orleans, in what are now St. Charles and St. John the Baptist parishes. This German Coast was described fifty years after its beginning as the best worked and most thickly settled part of the province; with the Acadians who came later, its cultivators formed the backbone of Louisiana colonization.[1] More Germans came in 1754 from Lorraine, and others in 1774 from Frederick County, Maryland. "Dutch Highlands," near Hackett's point, commemorates their advent.

Local conditions made for somewhat the same kind of disposal of arable holdings as existed in Canada.[2] The tillable land ran back some three miles from the alluvial rise at the river bank to cypress swamps. Single holdings measured an arpent in width (one hundred and eighty-two feet) on the river and about forty arpents in depth. Levee building and clearing had to be done without animals. The levees, finally some twenty or thirty feet high, grew annually with the danger from floods; but they furnished precarious security from the waters which might break through a crevasse and sweep miles of farm away. The settlers faced danger from spring floods and hurricanes, performed their daily toil on monotonous diet, and cleared forest and jungle in which lurked stealthy Indians and wild animals.[3] Another disadvantage of the colony was the yellow fever which appeared in

[1] Jean de Champigny, État Présent de la Louisiane, quoted in J. H. Deiler, The Settlement of the German Coast of Louisiana (M. D. Learned, ed., Americana Germanica, new ser., VIII), 17-18.

[2] Cf. H. E. Chambers, Mississippi Valley Beginnings (N. Y., 1922), 60-68.

[3] Pénicaut, "Relation," 576-578; Deiler, Settlement of the German Coast, 58-59.

1701 and again in 1704, possibly from Santo Domingo; in the latter year Tonty of the Iron Hand was one of the victims at Mobile.

Indian troubles, such as the Natchez massacre of 1729, and expeditions like those against the Chickasaws in 1726 and 1740 were recurrent for the greater part of the period of French domination. The Natchez were dispersed in 1742, but hostile tribes frequently cut off communications with the Illinois country northward, and raids on the lower settlers occurred in 1747 and 1748. In early times the farmers tilled their fields while their wives watched from treetops with flintlock in hand to anticipate attacks. During later years the stirring up of the eastern tribes by the English formed an unremitting peril of colonial life.[1]

Negro slavery gave impetus to agriculture, as did also free trade with France and her colonies. The main crops were rice, tobacco, cotton and indigo; sugar cultivation began as early as 1751, but was not of prime importance until nearly a half century later when a way was found to accommodate it perfectly to the climate. Cattle were never numerous and horses were brought in from the Spaniards in the west; they were dear, and even the thrifty Germans could obtain them, as well as slaves, only by mortgaging their properties. As land was soon scarce, the governors were denied agricultural grants for themselves; but Bienville evaded the regulation by taking large "vegetable gardens" and fixing his "habitation" upon one of them. He also undertook a system of feudal

[1] Margry, *Découvertes*, VI, p. xv; Alexander Franz, *Kolonisation des Mississippitales* (Leipzig, 1906), 127-128. The most ample summaries of economic and social conditions are in the notes to Paul Alliot, "Historical and Political Reflections on Louisiana," J. A. Robertson, ed., *Louisiana under the Rule of Spain, France and the United States* (Cleveland, 1911), I, 145-232.

tenure, the exaction of ground rents, products and services; but as all large concessions below Manchac were canceled by royal edict of August 10, 1728, for the purpose of redistribution, feudal organization did not become characteristic. As they prospered, the country folk would send their farm produce to New Orleans by rowboat to be sold on Sundays in front of the cathedral. Closer neighbors sent such stuffs on the heads of slaves who vended them from door to door.

Ten years after the British dispersed the Acadian "neutrals" from the shores of the Basin of Minas, these exiles began to appear in Louisiana from Halifax as well as from their temporary homes in New England, Santo Domingo and France. Though skillful farmers, they came empty-handed, in ill health, and sadly lacking many of those gentle graces attributed to the principals of Longfellow's poem. About one thousand of them were located in various parts, notably at Opelousas in the country of the Attakapas, and at Cahabanoce or "Attakaban nosse." They were scantily provided with subsistence, in some cases by the king of France while en route; later when Spain ruled the province that court took an interest in their needs and aided them to find homes along the lakes and bayous of the region. Known colloquially in later days as "Cajuns," they did not generally enter the upper ranks of society, though some of them intermarried with the French creole element and a few attained to political and economic importance. They spread gradually and widely from their original location in what is now St. James Parish.[1] Their coming severely tried the patience of the officials, who resented

[1] Deiler, *Settlement of the German Coast*, 68-69 (citing *Concessions*, 18, 448), 106-107.

the expense and trouble they entailed, their complaints about the raids of hostile Indians, and their demands for frequent assistance for their agriculture.[1]

The composite social character of Louisiana under the French was further increased by the large Negro population. When the Spaniards took over the trans-Mississippi territory in 1769, the population numbered probably between 8250 and 11,500. Between Pointe Coupé and New Orleans there were more than seven thousand people, but two thirds of them were Negroes, who increased much faster than the whites. Negro slaves were used in both field and home, where they absorbed many of the characteristics of the whites. In turn, they had a varied influence upon the white society: they fostered the Frenchman's disinclination for work; their presence led to miscegenation; and their outlandish tongues modified the spoken language. The simplicity of the Negro mind developed a peculiar *patois* in which the slaves perpetuated many of their old African animal stories of the Brer Rabbit type, fairy tales mysteriously borrowed from India, and songs, often accompanied by grotesque dances. It was known, through some confusion, as the "creole dialect." In like manner did they affect the white population during the later Spanish and American periods.

---

[1] Bernardo Gálvez reported on July 19, 1781, that five new towns had been formed from three hundred Acadian families at a cost of 40,000 pesos. (Bernardo to José de Gálvez.) Antonio Ulloa expected to bring into Louisiana one thousand Catholic families from Maryland on the strength of the Acadian movement. (Ulloa to Grimaldi, New Orleans, Feb. 11, 1768.) See Archivo General de Indias, Papeles de Cuba, no. 608; nos. 109, 119, 137, 181 187, 573, 576, 608 and 626, estante 86, cajón 6, legajo 6. In 1785 and 1786 three hundred families of Acadians were brought out from France and Spain, where they had taken refuge and had been supported after their dispersal along the Atlantic colonies of England; their way was paid, tools, seeds and lands were given them, and they were maintained until their crops ripened. MSS. cited, Bancroft Library.

In spite of the obvious danger in the practice and the prohibition against their bearing arms, it soon became a necessity to use Negroes in fighting the Indians. Many of them helped defend Louisiana for the French king; still others became renegades among the savages, where life was easier, and turned their strength against their old masters. The Spaniards from Catalonia mingled on familiar terms with the Negroes, causing the French much uneasiness because of the danger to white rule. Fear of insurrections, indeed, led Bienville in 1724 to promulgate the *Code Noir*. This legislation imposed heavy fines for marriage between blacks and whites and punished illicit relations between masters and Negro women. Children of mixed unions, with their mothers, were to become the property of the New Orleans hospital.[1]

In the presence of a dominant number of blacks the Negro strain soon became a social taint. The institution of marriage among the whites was fortified by the legal requirement of four birth certificates from each high contracting party; yet this did not prevent admixture, though even the remotest tinge continued to place the bearer among the tabooed race. It has often been said that the Code Noir was a cruel system of laws, but it should be remembered that it was for the control, not only of Negroes but of their white superiors. It provided for the humane treatment of slaves according to the quality of mercy of the times, including a system of manumission; for the exclusion of Jews and Protestants; and for the observance of religion.

The creole society bred in Louisiana claims fairly un-

---

[1] The edition printed in Paris in 1767 contains, in addition to the Code, French colonial administrative legislation between 1671 and 1762. Alcée Fortier, *Louisiana Folk Tales* (Am. Folk-Lore Soc., *Memoirs*, II), pp. ix-x; same author, *Louisiana Studies* (New Orleans, 1894), 149-197.

mixed descent from the officials who were first in the province. The Canadians did not use the word creole; *criollo* was an habitual designation among the Spaniards for those of full Iberian blood born in America. In this sense it was used by the Louisianians, perhaps as a result of contiguity with the Spanish. By extension the designation creole was applied to children of European parents born in the colonies; so there came to be in Louisiana French, Spanish, German, Scotch and Irish creoles. It seems to be agreed that creole origins belong only to the French and Spanish periods; those who entered Louisiana after 1803 did not assimilate with the creole stock and have never claimed the designation. Possession of Negro blood precludes a claim upon it. There is no good linguistic reason why all Americans of pure European descent should not be known as creoles; in this sense, we are largely a nation of creoles.[1]

At the close of the Latin domination Perrin du Lac, visiting the "Two Louisianas," had this characterization to make of Louisiana society:

The creoles of Louisiana have not lost, under a foreign government, either their love for the mother country or the tastes which characterize its inhabitants. More than in Europe, they devote themselves with excess to pleasure. Women, the table, and gaming occupy all their time. Addiction to the latter seems to be, however, the most generally dominant. They often spend the entire night at it, dissipating the rich proceeds of their estates. As in all the colonies, their taste in women leans especially toward those of color, whom they prefer to white ones because they exact fewer of the troublesome consid-

[1] See the discussion of creoles in Deiler, *Settlement of the German Coast*, 111-116; an unsympathetic account of them, by Berquin-Duvallon, *Vue de la Colonie Espagnole*, 201-247, is translated in J. A. Robertson, *Louisiana under Spain, France and the United States*, I, 186-204.

erations which oppose their desire for independence. Thus a great number prefer to live in concubinage rather than to marry. For in it they enjoy the double advantage of being served with the most scrupulous exactness, and, in case of discontent or inconstancy, of replacing their housekeeper (that is the sincere name they give to this sort of woman). . . . The creole women have for the most part good blood; the freshness of their complexions contrasts extraordinarily with the insalubrity of the country they inhabit. They are generally sedentary, living in indolence, without society or much diversion. Yet they like to dance to excess, and give themselves up to it without restraint whenever occasion offers.

The traveler was not more favorably impressed with the young men. He describes their air of ennui, their ignorance, their addiction to gambling; but he recognized them as brave, hardy and enterprising, qualities which showed well in their pastime of hunting. Vanity they had, too, and nothing pleased a youngster more than to wear an officer's uniform which he might don even at thirteen or fourteen years of age. "Thus in this country as well as elsewhere, man sets his ambitions to commanding others at an age when he is incapable of ruling himself." [1]

New Orleans, once made the capital, never lost its ascendancy over the other Gulf settlements. When Charlevoix saw it in 1722, it was a "wild, lovely place," with about one hundred huts among trees and underbrush. There were only two or three good houses and a

[1] Perrin du Lac, *Voyage dans les Deux Louisianes* (Lyóns, 1805), 393-396; P. F. X. de Charlevoix, S. J., *Journal*, 481, cited in P. F. X. de Charlevoix, *History of New France* (J. G. Shea, tr., N. Y., 1900), VI, 67. Cf. Amos Stoddard, *Sketches of Louisiana* (Phila., 1812), 319-330. The survival and social status of the Louisiana Isleños, or Canary Islanders, who were brought in 1778, establishing Galveston and other settlements, are noted in Fortier, *Louisiana Studies*, 197-210.

*magasin,* one half of which was used for church services. Forty years later, when it passed into the possession of Spain, the capital had a population of about thirty-two hundred of whom nineteen hundred were free, including thirty-one blacks. There were sixty-eight persons of mixed breed; slaves numbered twelve hundred and twenty-five, sixty of them Indians. The streets, set at right angles, made blocks around which ditches for drainage were dug, each block being called an "islet." Every block originally provided for four lots and as many residences, but these came to number twelve. The houses, four hundred and sixty-eight in all, were low, built of cypress logs, with steep, bark-covered roofs sheltering from four to eight rooms. They were set about eight feet above the ground level, with galleries all around them; the doors and windows were of solid cypress.

Some of these old houses stood for a hundred and fifty years; but most of Bienville's old city was wiped out by the destructive fires of 1787 and 1794. The rebuilding was confined by law to brick, in which material the town then assumed much of its present appearance. The yards were surrounded by high sharp-pointed picket fences; sour-orange trees lined the streets, loading the moist hot air with languorous perfume. Toward the quay was the Place d'Armes, the long low church of St. Louis facing one side, with the cemetery behind. On the other side of this "civic center" stood a prison, a convent, the government buildings with a pillory facing them on the Place, and quarters for the troops. Palisades inclosed the whole, with a ditch to serve as protection against uprisings of plantation blacks or forest redskins.

The tradespeople and artisans lived mostly on Royal and Bourbon streets; the Jesuit Convent was on Chartres, while Bienville Street was the aristocratic section, with the house of the governor among its attractions. The city boasted three surgeons, two of them in private practice. Life for the upper classes was not uncomfortable. Linen, furniture and glassware were brought from France, while imported laces, jewelry, silk and satin were among the delights of feminine souls.[1] Some of the men of the upper class wore perukes and queues, silk stockings and silver-buckled shoes. Servants were plentiful and well-trained, and the markets, or the slaves who vended wares from near-by plantations, purveyed game, vegetables and fruits. Imports from Illinois were usually on hand unless Indian hostilities interrupted communications. The practice of depending upon importations was well-nigh constant.[2]

The forced colonization from France tended to create a discontented element in society which refused to look upon the Valley as a real home and taught its children to assume the attitude of exiles. Even officials as a rule looked upon the mother country as home, and exerted themselves to acquire a competency and depart in hope of a promotion. Many of the immigrants, disillusioned of their dreams of easily acquired wealth, as described in Law's propaganda, went home in disgust. On the other hand many of the best families date back to the earliest settlements at Biloxi, Dauphin Island and Mobile. They formed the nucleus of the early aristoc-

---

[1] Pittman, *Present State of the European Settlements*, 41-44, describes the city. See also Grace King, *Creole Families of Louisiana* (N. Y., 1921), 4.

[2] King, *Creole Families*, 7, 81, 85. Perrin du Lac in 1803 found the streets unpaved and filthy, with conditions at the quay responsible for the almost annual recurrence of yellow fever. The city stood about eight feet below the level of the river, and fear of inundation was seasonal. See Perrin du Lac, *Voyage*, 393.

racy of New Orleans, and their members have left enviable records of service during every period of subsequent history.

During the Spanish domination there was an influx of Spaniards of the official class and also of Mexican troops. Despite the early antipathy created by the policies of Ulloa and O'Reilly, the Spaniards and the French rapidly came to live upon amicable terms, and soon began to intermarry. Governor Gálvez later took as his wife a daughter of the Maxent family. German young women also married freely into the French families; the gallicization of family names served to conceal German identity and to blend these two elements.

Not much can be said for the opportunities for education in the Gulf territory. It began, if we may stretch the meaning of the word a little and ignore for the moment the work of the church, with the efforts of the literary carpenter André Pénicaut, whose *Relation* is one of the earliest, if somewhat romantic, sources of the history of the region. Voyaging to the Natchez in 1706, he spent the winter among them, whiling away its tedium by teaching the chieftain's daughters to dance minuets and speak French. "They nearly made me die with laughter," he says, "with their savage pronunciation, which comes only from the throat." [1] In later days the spread of culture was much in the hands of the Capuchin friars, who managed to hold their own against the bishop of Canada and the Jesuits, and received the

---

[1] King, *Creole Families*, pp. vii, ix, 3. Thirty families are noted, much intermarried, with notable public records. See also Deiler, *Settlement of the German Coast, passim*, for the contributions of the German creoles. Pénicaut, "Relation," Margry, *Découvertes*, V, 470; *cf.* Alcée Fortier, *History of Louisiana* (N. Y., 1904), I, 56; [F. P. Watrin, S. J.], "Banishment of the Jesuits from Louisiana," Edna Kenton, ed., *The Jesuit Relations* (Toronto, 1925), 475-484.

clerical effects of the latter when they were expelled in 1764. The Mobile region was under the ministration of the Carmelites; the Ursuline nuns had a school in New Orleans.

Such education as was given by the church was quite elementary. Masters of slaves were supposed to attend to their educational needs, which cannot be imagined as urgent. The official and aristocratic elements possessed such enlightenment as was essential to the performance of duty or the management of plantations worked by slaves. There were two elementary church schools in New Orleans in Spanish days and several insignificant private ones. As in Canada, there was no early newspaper, the *Moniteur de la Louisiane* not being established until 1794 and finding even then but few readers.[1]

After the two terms as governor held by Bienville, perhaps the most notable administrator was the Marquis de Vaudreuil who ruled for many years and was reputed a calm and judicious official. In 1783 Kerlerec began, proving a violent contrast to the marquis, and a characteristic feud was waged between himself and the commissary or intendant over some point of official prerogative. This sort of controversy was the bane of the duplex system of administration sustained by France in her colonies. In this case the wives of the two officers divided the capital into two warring factions who took ladylike slaps at each other by posting lampoons on the street corners, exchanging anonymously their mutual sarcastic disrespects—a form of social exhilaration common

[1] Fortier, *History of Louisiana*, II, 155. Slavery in Louisiana in colonial days is discussed in Stoddard, *Sketches of Louisiana*, 331-343. The first press entered New Mexico in 1834, that at Monterey, California, dating from 1835.

enough in Mexico City among the colonial-born, but not usually indulged in by the ladies.

It was during the term of Baron Carondelet that the province came again into world notice, this time because of the demand in the United States for navigation of the Mississippi to the Gulf and the right of deposit at New Orleans. A scion of one of the old creole families, Joseph Delfau de Pontalba, wrote during that year a series of letters to his young wife then absent in Europe. No better picture could be formed than they give of Louisiana life shortly before the transfer to France and the United States. Young Pontalba, who lived on a plantation near the city, spent his leisure hours in his garden, raising strawberries to give to his friends and magnificent cabbages, fringed-headed lettuce, broccoli and spinach for the market. His vegetables were always ready earliest of all and he preserved the secret of his success for a long time; it was that he brought his seeds from the north instead of using those locally grown.

His evenings he spent at the home of Madame Carondelet, where the amusement was cards, the games of *bourre* and *coq* being the favorites. A popular social diversion, also, was found in the bathing parties in the canal which supplied water for the mill; Madame Macarty gave them often, inviting the best ladies and gentlemen of the city; two or three hours were thus enjoyed in the water. There was also an opera house, maintained by subscription or the purchase of boxes by the best families; loges cost from one to two hundred dollars. "The Honest Criminal," with rather indifferent presentation, was heard during the year; in November "Eugenie" was given, followed by a compliment to the king and the baron. The latter, wrote Pontalba, "was flattered in the most servile manner and in the most tasteless way for a full hour. Two hands were made to appear clasping each other, representing the king of Spain and the French Republic, with the epigraph: 'Let us ever be united! ' "

A young member of the well-known Marigny family, who had just returned from attending a school in the United States, was making an unhappy impression upon his old friends by his newly acquired tastes.

> He holds himself bent over, he chews tobacco continually, swears at everything, and looks bored by everything he sees as well as by everything he hears. He speaks English very well. . . . On his arrival he came up to his father very slowly and told him good day as if he had not been absent.

Fear of Negro uprisings was never quite absent, especially after the bloody events in which the blacks of Santo Domingo had expressed their appreciation of *liberté, fraternité* and *egalité* by the massacres of 1791. It was well known in Louisiana that the Negroes were in complete control of the island and were savagely mistreating the survivors of the former planter population; they wanted independence of everything white, even of the French Republic. Le Baron Carondelet was much upset over the prospect of a spread of the same spirit to his territory. Many of the planters in March brought their families into New Orleans for safety, which alarmed everyone and was not lost on the slaves. Two or three Negroes had been discovered talking about possibilities, but no plot could be unearthed—the mere fact of the superior numbers of blacks made the planters panicky. By May Carondelet, becoming convinced of this, began to relax the unusual precautions he had been taking.[1]

A more real danger was the epidemic of yellow fever. The people, especially the women, were in abject fear; they took precaution "to wear garlic on their bodies and carry hartshorn; everywhere tar is being burned." The strong, young and wealthy were succumbing; a captain of the Mexican regiment was seized with the malady. Corpses were found unburied in the Protestant corner of the cemetery, hastily concealed by branches and leaves; no one knew who was guilty, all were afraid to touch the bodies. Though the authorities made efforts to conceal the deaths of from fifteen to seventeen daily victims, those who had country places to go to fled the city. "We are all agreed that it is the yellow fever, which rages nearly every year in Philadelphia, and that the Americans brought it in." The governor would not leave, lest his departure increase the panic. He, Pontalba and their set made an earnest pretense of enjoying themselves in all sorts of frolics and extravagances, but they were constantly chewing quinine nevertheless. By mid-November, with sharp winds and cold weather, the plague departed.

When news of the treaty of 1795 came down by way of Kentucky, with its promise of free navigation of the river and the right of deposit, there was a stir of new life:

This country is going to become one of the most prosperous in the world. The population will increase in an incredible manner; property will double in value; stores and houses will be rented at exorbitant prices and our city will soon resemble Philadelphia in the diversity of nations that will live here. One of the articles of the

[1] *Cf.* J. J. D. de Pontalba, *Mémoire,* quoted in Charles Gayarré, *History of Louisiana* (N. Y., 1903), III, 333; pp. 354-356 present this rising in a more serious aspect.

Treaty permits liberty of worship, and the Americans will be permitted to bring their own lawyers to settle their differences. . . . I think from all this that I shall be able to sell advantageously all my built-up lots. . . . The city is building up all with terraced roofs and framework covered with brick or plaster. . . . I judge that this great rush of building will make rents fall, and for this reason I feel like not putting the ceilings in the houses of your aunt and leaving the woodwork very simple . . . for fear she might not receive the rent I flattered myself she would. I am following the same course with mine. . . .[1]

The costs of building are shown by the fact that two little houses, thirty-four by twenty-eight feet in dimension, were to cost a total of $8000, each to have one little story and a kitchen. A house which Pontalba built on the levee would bring a rent of one hundred and seventy-eight dollars a month, and one facing the Place d'Armes one hundred and eighteen. He had finished building eleven stores, though only five were rented.[2] Then came news by sea that Spain had declared war upon England, and there was an ugly rumor that the king expected within three or four months to free all the slaves within his dominions; "If that should happen in so short a time we should all find ourselves ruined."[3]

[1] Pontalba to his wife, excerpts in King, *Creole Families*, 89-91.

[2] One could buy land more cheaply just outside the city, he further said, and live economically on a capital of forty thousand dollars. A lot with one hundred and twenty feet frontage by two hundred and twenty deep could be had for eight hundred dollars on long time; the property was supplied with Negroes, animals and implements, with all the resources needed for the table, a garden, a dairy, and so forth. It was within easy reach of the city, and the purchaser could have his daughters where they could cultivate good society.

[3] For the whole account, see King, *Creole Families*, 85-114. Slaves were valuable chattels. Annette, the cook of Madame Pontalba, sold for nine hundred dollars, and she knew how to "make good gombos and calas." Baptiste, a domestic, sold for four hundred. Other prices mentioned were lower.

After the fire of 1788 the Cathedral of St. Louis was rebuilt; flanked by the Calaboose and the Cabildo, it still dominates the old Place d'Armes, since called Jackson Square.

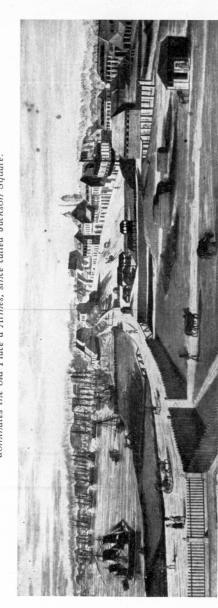

New Orleans, the Crescent City, soon after it became a part of the United States.

In the Illinois country the French pioneers, who linked Canada with Lower Louisiana, led a simpler, harder life. These frontiersmen were in theory subject to all the whims of far-away imperial control, but their remoteness actually gave them relief from too close supervision. Their rather indeterminate territory was a strip extending from the Alleghanies to beyond the Mississippi and from the Ohio northward. There was also the larger area of the commandery, which included a small post and settlement on the Arkansas, another on the Missouri and Vincennes on the Wabash. This great area was subordinate to Louisiana after 1731.[1] Its governing head, the major commandant, not only had charge of the military establishment, but also promoted agriculture, watched the fur trade, protected religion and supervised the annual census, all for a stipend of twelve hundred livres. His chief post was Fort de Chartres, some sixteen miles above Kaskaskia on the left bank of the Mississippi. The garrison was never over three hundred men, and usually about one hundred. In 1734 the head of the district, La Loëre Flancourt, was the representative of the home department of marine and of the *commissaire ordonnateur* or intendant of Louisiana; as such he had charge of justice, police and finance, serving also as civil and criminal judge.

Like the Spaniards and the Canadians, these Frenchmen loved lawsuits, preferring them to the satisfaction obtained from the fist-fighting methods by which American frontiersmen maintained the externals of self-respect.

[1] Pittman, *Present State of the European Settlements*, 82-86. The following pages on the Illinois country are drawn from C. W. Alvord, *The Illinois Country* (C. W. Alvord, ed., *The Centennial History of Illinois*, Springfield, Ill., 1918-1920, I), chiefly chap. x. Cf. Mason, *Chapters from Illinois History*, 217-218, and notes.

Lawyers were excluded as dangerous to the public peace, so litigants appeared in person before the court pleading their own cases; of course there were no juries. Here prevailed that *Coûtume de Paris* which France spread everywhere throughout her colonial world and which survived in France itself, among two hundred and eighty-five similar local codes of justice, until the outburst of the Revolution. It was supplemented by royal edicts and orders legally registered by the provincial council of Louisiana. An influential officer was the *garde-magasin*, who had custody of the royal supplies and received the exports pending shipment, giving receipts which served as local legal tender; he also sold surplus government supplies to the people. The royal notary, another important factotum, was present at every civil and social function. Wearing a black suit appropriate alike for wedding or funeral, he drew up and attested all legal papers and served as clerk of court. There was also a government physician, of somewhat dubious medical skill, an interpreter and even at one time an official midwife.

Religion was in charge of the bishop of Quebec; the workers in the field were Jesuits—their pioneer having been Père Marquette—and priests of the Quebec Seminary of Foreign Missions. Parishes were informally organized after 1720 for the settlements at Chartres, Kaskaskia and Cahokia.[1] The first church, at Kaskaskia, was a sym-

[1] Perrin du Lac, *Voyage*, 167-170, describes Ste. Geneviève and tells how the commandant served the medical needs of his post, visiting the sick at all hours of day and night. W. B. Munro, *The Seigniorial System in Canada* (*Harvard Hist. Studies*, XIII), 182. Chevalier, who was garde-magasin in the Illinois, died leaving an estate of 600,000 livres, though he brought but 40,000 into the country and had 1000 livres annual salary. See Alvord, *Illinois Country*, 230. The best survey of Canadian fiscal and financial conditions is the interesting introduction of Adam Shortt, ed., *Documents Relatifs à la Monnaie, au Change, et aux Finances du Canada sous le Régime Français* (Ottawa, 1925), pp. xxxii-lxxxix.

bol of sacrifice rather than a work of beauty, as it was built through the application of the parish fees by several successive priests. Its ugly walls were of hewn timbers set perpendicular in the manner in which the houses were built; inside, it was lime-plastered and adorned with indifferent paintings, while the floor was of loose boards. The Society also served at Ste. Geneviève, the lead-mining settlement on the west side of the river,[1] and at Vincennes on the Wabash. They had also Indian churches at Kaskaskia and Cahokia and one for a short time at Michigamea.

Education, in the hands of the assiduous Jesuits, afforded the French children religious rather than intellectual nourishment. The Quebec priests, or Seminarists, had a white and an Indian church at Cahokia, the most notable servant among them being Père Mercier, who ministered here for forty-five years. Sometimes they sent missions to the Missouri Indians and they maintained mission chapels at Prairie du Rocher. They quarreled with the Jesuits for ten years over the church of Ste. Anne at Fort de Chartres, until the Jesuits yielded. The Compagnie des Indes and later the royal government promised the priests six hundred livres annually, and two hundred as gratuity for five years for each mission founded; but the stipends were often in arrears and frequently were defaulted altogether, so that the church was largely sustained by its own faith and the love of its people.

The population was always small. In 1723 there were

[1] Nicknamed "Misère" because of the unfortunate site, which was subject to flood and had to be changed. Victor Collot, *Voyage dans l'Amérique Septentrionale* (Paris, 1826), I, 345. Louis Houck, *A History of Missouri* (Chicago, 1908), I, 274-286, gives a brief description of the mineral region.

one hundred and ninety-six whites in Kaskaskia, one hundred and twenty-six in Chartres village and twelve in Cahokia, a total of three hundred and thirty-four men, women and children; in 1732 the population numbered perhaps six hundred. After the English had taken the country and many French had gone over for the time being to the newly founded St. Louis on what was supposedly French soil, there were six hundred people in Kaskaskia, twenty-five families at Prairie du Rocher, three each at Chartres village and St. Philippe and six at Cahokia. The total free population at the height of prosperity was not over fifteen hundred or two thousand, including soldiers. At the time of the French exodus the remaining settlers were estimated at twelve hundred adults, six hundred children and some nine hundred blacks.

No real seigniorial system existed though La Salle had contemplated a great feudal tenure centering at his Fort St. Louis; Crozat's company gave full title to lands. In 1723 and 1726 the official ban against seigniorial grants in Louisiana north of Manchac was withdrawn, but it would seem that in 1728 it was restored; at any event none was made in the Illinois. Cessions were made *en franc alleu,* probably noble rather than *roturier;* they were often large, and officials received them in spite of legal prohibitions. The church participated in this distribution; the Jesuit plantation at Kaskaskia, dating from 1716, was large; the Seminarists had four leagues square after 1722, upon which plot Cahokia grew up. The land of "the American Bottom" along the lower Illinois and the flats beside the Mississippi, not granted by cession or held by Indians, was parceled out by company, king or large concessionaires to small tenants; but the habitants who received lands *en censive* or *en roture* paid none of the customary feudal dues save perhaps the corvée.[1] Fishing and hunting were by royal decree open to all the inhabitants of Louisiana. Probably not even the banal right of having their corn ground at the seigneur's mill was exacted, as gristmills were common. At Cahokia several purchases were made from the Indians direct, but the authorities granted lands freely, probably en franc alleu roturier, from the royal domains of Kaskaskia and Chartres. All lands paid a "tithe" of one twenty-sixth for the support of the church, though probably most of the church expenses were met by the products of their farms.

Lands were laid out on much the same plan as was used in Canada. The houses clustered in the village, with the cultivated fields running in long strips with a few rods' frontage and sides many times as long. At Kaskaskia they stretched from the village to the Mississippi. Separate possessions were marked by furrows and contained from forty to one hundred and eighty-three acres, the latter being the size of the Jesuit farm. Along the front of the fields nearest the village a common fence was kept up by the owners of the strips to keep the cattle out of the crops; but the livestock grazed at will in the commons, each animal bearing its owner's brand. As these pioneers were not expert farmers, the returns were always disappointing; where large estates depended upon

[1] Perrin du Lac, *Voyage*, 186-191, describes the new fur post built by Laclede and Choutoux and extols its importance. About 1780 it had a stockade and stone fortifications. See Mason, *Chapters from Illinois History*, 294. He found Kaskaskia in ruins. Justin Winsor, *The Mississippi Basin* (Boston, 1898), 432; Alvord, *The Illinois Country*, 205, citing Archives Nationales C13A, etc. For vital statistics of the various parts of Louisiana, see Robertson, *Louisiana under Spain, France and the United States*, I, 149-150, *n.* 3.

Indian or Negro slave labor, it was least satisfactory. Fertilization was little used and, as in the English colonies along the Atlantic, the tools were crude. The wooden plow, with iron point tied in place with a leather thong, scratched the virgin soil as it did in Canada, New Spain and New England.[1] Two-wheeled carts, drawn by oxen with a bar fastened across their horns instead of a yoke, as in present-day Mexico, or horses driven tandem by voice and whip but no reins, animated the rural picture.

The common-fields system limited initiative; everyone must plow, plant, cultivate and harvest at the same time and in the same way. All this was determined by the village assembly whose voice, expressed in churchyard meetings presided over either by syndics or *marguilliers,* was decisive. Spring wheat, introduced by the Jesuits, was the chief crop, the surplus being exported to New Orleans. Two thousand hundredweight went in 1732 and six thousand in 1740; in 1745 Louisiana was saved from threatened famine after a hurricane by Illinois wheat. Oats, hemp, hops and some tobacco were raised. The French used little corn and that only for their livestock. Melons, potatoes and squashes grew in their gardens, and their fruits were apples, pears and peaches; European grapes could not be acclimated though wine was made from the wild ones. Small sturdy cattle, driven down from Canada, mingled on the common with horses often wild, brought in from the Spanish to the southwest. A little butter was made by shaking cream in bottles. Bear meat and grease, venison, hides and buffalo

[1] Collot, *Voyage,* I, 316-369. *Cf.* T. J. Wertenbaker, *The First Americans* (*A History of American Life,* II), 38, 58; J. T. Adams, *Provincial Society* (same series, III), 26.

wool were obtained in sufficient surplus to export regularly to New Orleans.[1]

Lead mining began about 1719. Though open to all the inhabitants and soldiers, it was under control of a council of ten. In 1720 Philippe François Renault brought out miners and slaves for work in lead mines west of the Mississippi on the Meramec River; he prospected for copper and silver on the Illinois and operated until 1744 when he sold out to the government. Mines were opened in the Galena district, and St. Geneviève, on the right bank, continued to thrive; but mining never rose to large-scale importance under the French flag as it did under the Spanish.

The fur trade rivaled agriculture. The attempt of Talon by ordinance of 1672 to forbid it to the inhabitants of Canada, and the order of 1680 prohibiting the issue of trade permits by the governor, served only to spread the coureurs de bois over the west and divert their peltries to the British at Albany. In 1681 issue of *congés*, or permits, twenty-five in number, had like effects. The order of 1696, recalling all these proscribed forest traders under pain of sentence to the galleys, was equally inefficacious. In 1700 the king took in charge the entire beaver trade and the service was leased at various posts. This method rendered collection easy from the French point of view, but worked hardship upon the Indians, who had become accustomed to receive in their villages such European artifacts as they required. After the failure of Crozat the usual method was to leave the trade of the southern province free though prices were fixed. Inasmuch as furs shipped to New Orleans spoiled in the heat, the trade went regularly north by way of Detroit

[1] Alvord, *Illinois Country,* 205-209.

or Mackinac, but most of the imports into Illinois came from the south at a price of perhaps one hundred per cent above their cost in France.[1] The circulating medium consisted of beaver skins, Spanish coins smuggled through in large quantities, and paper tokens of various kinds carefully marked in a vain attempt to prevent forgery.

Communication was largely by canoe, pirogue or bateau over the rivers and portages to the north and down the Mississippi to New Orleans. Pirogues, or hollowed tree trunks, had no keels and were guided by oars fastened at the stern, or even plank rudders; they were used as convoys, but like canoes were easily capsized or captured. *Cajens,* or sets of canoes fastened together, were used in the lower country. In 1732 began the use of large bateaux of from sixteen to twenty tons' burden, propelled by sails and oars; and numerous other craft with sails came into use in time. The royal convoy usually left New Orleans in late winter or early spring, a second one setting out in August. The upstream voyage consumed from seventy days to three months, but in the spring fast bateaux went downstream to the capital in twelve or thirteen days. Private boats were constantly plying up and down, merchants often combining forces for sociable coöperation in landing for the nights on the

[1] Perrin du Lac. *Voyage,* 167-173, found Ste. Geneviève in 1802 a town of thirteen hundred inhabitants, one third slaves; most of them had come from the left bank at the time of the English and American cessions. Fur export from Canada under the French averaged £135,000 annually as estimated by H. T. Cramahe, 1761, in *Mich. Pioneer and Hist. Colls.,* XIX, 14. For an excellent and easily available discussion of the coureurs de bois, see W. B. Munro, *Crusaders of New France* (Allen Johnson, ed., *The Chronicles of America Series,* New Haven, 1918-1921, IV), chap. ix. For hostile legislation by Talon and Frontenac, see P. G. Roy, ed., *Ordonnances, Commissions,* etc. (Beauceville, 1924, in *Archives de la Province de Quebec*), I, 107-108, 111-112; *cf.* same works, II, 7-9, 26-27, and III, 284-286.

high bluffs, for protection from accidents of travel, such as snags and shoals, and Indian hostility. Voyages to Canada consumed several weeks. A wagon road connecting Kaskaskia with Cahokia was built at an early date and other roads in many directions followed old Indian and buffalo trails; one of these ran from Cahokia to Peoria and Galena, another to the mouth of the Tennessee, and there was a well-worn road between Peoria and Detroit.[1]

Kaskaskia was typical in many ways of other French villages. At its center was a large grass-covered square with narrow streets leading at right angles from it; facing it stood the church and the picketed fort. The blocks were some three hundred feet square and each contained four lots. Because of its many stone houses, this peaceful village had an air of permanence unusual for the frontier. The wooden houses were of upright timbers hewn with concave sides, the spaces between filled with clay, straw and stone, no iron being used in their construction. The pointed roofs, covered with thatch or bark, extended over the front, making a porch or gallery such as may still be seen in parts of the South. Most of the houses were of one story and a half, though some boasted two; chimneys stood at one end, sometimes at both. Set in friendly fashion close to the street, the homes were surrounded by whitewashed picket fences inclosing the flower garden, fruit trees, vegetables, the slaves' cabins and barns.

In a home of comparative wealth one would find a

[1] An interesting picture, by an American, of the condition of the French settlements in and around Detroit is B. W. Bond, jr., ed., "The Captivity of Charles Stuart, 1755-1757," *Miss. Valley Hist. Rev.*, XIII, 58-81. See also Mrs. N. M. Surrey, *The Commerce of Louisiana during the French Régime* (Columbia Univ., *Studies*, LXXI), 62-63, 82-92.

hall running from the front gallery to the back, flanked by the various rooms—not an unusual feature of Southern houses today. The important furniture was good; there was even some silver plate; usually religious pictures hung beside French mirrors in gilt frames; and sometimes there was a billiard table. The homes of the habitants possessed little decoration and had only home-made furniture. One of the finest establishments was that of the Jesuits. The house was one hundred and twenty feet long; another building was divided into many low apartments; there were also Negro cabins, cowsheds, a barn, a stable, a weaving room, a horse-mill and a dovecote. Sixty-eight Negro slaves served as farmers, blacksmiths, carpenters, brewers and masons. Several private farms were developed on a similar scale.[1]

The highest social caste was represented by the military officers, who belonged to the gentry at home or even to noble families. Their bright uniforms of long coats, embroidered vests and knee breeches set them in sharp contrast to the enlisted men, whose ragged poverty and underfed condition made them caricatures of soldiers. The latter came from the slums of France and often cheerfully deserted to the Spanish or English settlements, knowing their lot could be no worse. Fur traders, following Paris styles tardily through New Orleans, wore lavish costumes with richly trimmed hats, embroidered waistcoats with "diamond" buttons, silk hose and silver buckles. The habitants wore *capots* of Mackinaw blankets, a blue hood for winter, deerskin trousers and moccasins. A short clay pipe blackened with much communion, a shirt of colored cotton, and trousers held up

[1] On the work of the Jesuits among the Illinois, see Kenton, *Jesuit Relations*, 333-387, 392-395; H. S. Spaulding, S. J., "The Life of James Marquette," *Ill. Catholic Hist. Rev.*, IX, nos. 1-2.

by a broad beaded sash tied outside the coat, often figured in the costume; over the head was the invariable colored handkerchief. The vivacious and turbulent *voyageurs* affected leather-ruffled shirts and bright caps with tassels hanging on one side. As the women did not spin or weave, their clothing included imported fabrics. Those of the lower class were clad in short skirts reaching to the knees, underneath them long petticoats; their heads they covered with straw hats or, in winter, with fur hats or bonnets. On their feet they wore the habitual moccasin.

Illiteracy was general among the habitants, while education among the gentry was comparable with that of France. In 1796 two thirds of the population of Vincennes could not read or write. A certain social charm these western Frenchmen retained, it is true, but they slowly lost all traces of the mental alertness of their race.[1] As to their morals, these were, if court records mean much, as good as those of the traditional frontier, in spite of the accusations of priests and officers who confessed their lack of influence by blaming the people with low habits. Certainly they were thrifty, even niggardly, and as crafty as one need be to fight the battle of the wilderness. Light-hearted and easy-going, they all danced on Sunday evenings; even the priest dropped in for a chat at the home of the well-to-do farmer where the party was held. Mixture with the native race was chiefly at the lowest level; the coureurs de bois married squaws freely, celebrating the ceremony when the priests could compel them. Kaskaskia was for two decades mostly of such origin. In 1735 the commandant's consent was re-

[1] See R. L. Rusk, *The Literature of the Middle Western Frontier* (N. Y., 1925), I, 6-13, for an interesting treatment.

quired for mixed unions, the Jesuits submitting with forced grace. The number of illegitimate children was always high.

Church festivals were frequent enough to hurt agriculture; Mardi Gras, which still survives in New Orleans, was everywhere a popular feast. It was celebrated at one or other of the large homes, where a favorite sport was competition in flopping pancakes; then came the dancing. New Year's calling was brightened by the hostesses' custom of presenting their cheeks for farewell kisses from departing guests. Playing cards, a universal pastime, was in good weather enjoyed on the wide front galleries. Undue hilarity, such as broke out at the return of the voyageurs, was held in check by priests and officials, whose staid influence preserved Old World conventions and lent an air of conservatism.

The Illinois country had a democratic institution, the village meeting, not used in Canada. The people elected syndics to represent them in lawsuits, and the church congregations elected marguilliers, or wardens, at Kaskaskia, Cahokia and perhaps at Chartres. These local officers functioned with some regularity, reporting to their constituents after mass at the church doors, where auctions and other public meetings were held; the priest presided in case of church affairs, but the syndics at civil convocations. Here the people, including boys over fourteen and perhaps widows, elected officers, chose the times for farm operations, church repairing and road building, and decided other community interests.

After about 1723 everyone rendered militia service. The village captain, like his Canadian counterpart, was an important individual representing the commandant and hearing the arguments in disputes, which might be

appealed to the judge. Troubles with the Indians usually resulted from the proximity of their villages to those
of the French. When on a peace footing, whites and redskins quarreled about the Indians' dogs and brought
charges and countercharges about cattle which strayed
into the fields. These Indian villagers came to be degen-
erate reminders of former native stoicism, too lazy to
work and afraid to take the warpath—this was their
gift from the white man. They especially resented the
preëmption of their lands without payment. The French
soon learned that *Pani* slavery was unprofitable and too
humiliating for a race which they sought to dwell among
in fraternity and safety.[1] The religious development of
the red men was no more successful than in Canada,
though the Illinois wore out their missionaries by addiction to instruction and confession. They liked vesper
services and masses, chanting couplets in their own tongue
in response to the Latin of the French. Before they
passed from the page of history they had learned some
of the arts of peace in agriculture and some lessening of
the cruelties of warfare.[2]

Farther to the north and more within the area of
Canadian than Louisiana influence, the French trappers
and woodsmen left their impress upon Wisconsin society in remnants of imperial design now surviving
in vestiges of the fur trade at occasional posts,
where memories linger on the path of enterprise now
trod by more vigorous feet. The wide middle border of
French-American empire was to become in time the real
heart of the continent, where the races of men were to

[1] Pani came to mean an Indian slave because the Pawnees were those
most frequently reduced to slavery.
[2] Alvord, *Illinois Country*, 224.

mingle in an actual conquest dreamed of by Versailles
and Quebec, but unrealized until American colonization
of the Middle West supplanted the overseas efforts of
men of mixed minds and interests.[1]

[1] Fourteen of seventy-one Wisconsin counties, four lakes, numerous
rivers and six cities as well as seven towns bear French names. Louise P.
Kellogg, *The French Régime in Wisconsin and the Northwest* (State Hist.
Soc. of Wis., *Publs.*, I), 441. A multitude of similar survivals in many
regions is recalled in J. H. Finley, *The French in the Heart of America*
(N. Y., 1915), 394. Americans of French extraction, Huguenot or
French-Canadian, will regret no more than the author of this book the
lack of opportunity to allude to the wide influence of the French dispersal
throughout the United States, which, however, may be traced in other
volumes of this series.

# CHAPTER XI

## LIFE AMONG THE DUTCH AND SWEDES

"AMONG all the people in the world industrious in seeking out foreign lands, navigable waters, and trade, those who bear the name of Netherlanders will very easily hold their place with the first, as is sufficiently known to all who have in any wise saluted the threshold of history and as will be confirmed by the following relation." [1] Thus confidently and justly a seventeenth-century historian described the essential contribution which Holland and the neighboring Low Countries had been making to the European occupation of the world beyond the seas. Those who, confused by Washington Irving's playful satire in the *Knickerbocker History*, recall the Dutchman of that day as a fat, slow, dull-witted fellow, will be shaken out of this delusion by a glance here and there at the letters home from English, French and Spanish colonial governors, especially in the West Indies. It was the Dutchman, the shrewd and energetic business man, the conqueror of markets, that was always the menace to their peace. The map itself attests his tireless enterprise on the sea. Dutch names appear, from Spitzbergen near the northern pole around to Cape Horn in the south; many, like New Zealand, are still marked on British territory and some, like New Holland and Van Diemen's Land, the historian may re-

[1] Adriaen van der Donck and ten others. "The Representation of New Netherland, 1650," J. F. Jameson, ed., *Narratives of New Netherland* (same ed., *Original Narratives of Early American History*, N. Y., 1906-   ), 293.

member as having been superseded by the modern designations, Australia and Tasmania.

No one who has read the stirring story of the long Dutch war of independence could disparage the national character on grounds of zeal or ability; no one who knows the art of Rembrandt and his great contemporaries or the beneficent reasoning of Grotius or the close scientific work of Leeuwenhoek and Huygens, could fail to appreciate the intellectual force of that small people or their influence on the European mind. They so nicely reconciled the claims of individual liberty with those of public order that their success in government has been a favorite instance among writers upon politics. Their prosperity, beginning with the order which closed Lisbon against the Dutch, surpassed that of any other country, bringing a glory as brilliant and brief as the Golden Age of Portugal under King Manuel.

In face of this impressive record the small achievement of the Dutch in the New World strikes the curious reader at first as unexpected if not unaccountable. But there was, in fact, no Dutch claim to, or conscious effort at, the building of a great empire or the transmission of national culture or institutions. The rôle of the Netherlands during the colonial epoch was peculiarly that of a commercial carrier.

Yet there is deep meaning in the history of the Dutch effort in the Western Hemisphere. Disregarding the revolt of the Low Countries as a phase of European politics, and considering all transatlantic thrusts in their relation to one another, we can see that it was the unrequited task of the Dutch to strike telling blows at the monopolies of Spain and Portugal, to open the way for states unfavored by papal sanction and, finally, to yield to

England their hard-earned commercial eminence. Without their aggressive naval warfare Spain would not have become so weak, nor England so strong. How bitter, then, that when the old colonial world was reorganized following the destruction of Napoleon's dream of empire, Holland was almost as great a loser as Spain herself!

Thus he who would properly estimate Dutch colonial history will see more than a story of conflicting interests on the Hudson. Irving, Joseph Jefferson and the genealogists have contrived among them to distort the popular conception of the historical meaning of New Netherland. Most significant for the student of American civilization is the fact that the Dutch adventure made possible the survival of English control. Whether that was best or not will have varying answers throughout the centuries. For immediate values, however, the important thing is that the Dutch wars for independence helped to break the colonial power of Spain and so gave the Teutonic strain preponderance in North America; conversely, by sending their fleets east and west to the Indies, the Dutch obliged the Spaniards to strengthen their overseas defenses, thus reducing their chances of success in the Low Countries.[1]

Dutch voyages outside of Europe, beginning in 1589, were undertaken because of the war decree of Philip II in 1585 which closed to the Lowlanders, a commercial people since 1500, the distributing trade out of Lisbon to northern Europe. Soon thereafter began the great series of Dutch efforts to reach the Orient by way of Good Hope, around the Horn, and from Nova Zembla. Henry Hudson came to what is now New York Harbor

[1] Charles de Lannoy, *Histoire de l'Expansion des Peuples Européens: Néerlande et Danemark* (Brussels, 1911), 332.

during a voyage which had actually begun as a search
by the last-named route. Until 1602, when the East
India Company was chartered, the navigation of Holland had been free to all her citizens, and it continued
virtually so for voyages to America until the New
Netherland Company was chartered. Prior to 1614,
when this was done, annual voyages to the Hudson
River region had brought fur traders who several times
spent winters on Manhattan Island and at the head of
navigation near the site of modern Albany. Practically
until 1623, however, the efforts were unorganized and
desultory, the East India trade being amply lucrative.

As the twelve-year truce with Spain (1609-1621)
drew to a close, William Usselinx achieved the purpose
of his years of struggle and the long-dreamed-of West
India Company was organized with a form similar to
the English and Dutch East India companies. It was not
a complete triumph, for the chief founder cared little for
simple trading posts and mere barter with Indians, but
would have created enduring agricultural colonies. He
had lived in Seville and seen the Spanish plate fleets
arrive, and in the Azores he had observed the advantages
of the colonial ideal in operation. The tacit but thoroughly understood object of the new organization was
to prey upon the Spanish fleets and harry Spanish
American coastwise towns for booty as the war reopened.

> West India can bring Netherland great gain,
> Lessen the might, divert the wealth, of Spain.[1]

Thus the upper bourgeoisie began to share the overseas struggle for trade in direct competition with the aristocratic and peace-loving East India Company. The

[1] Jameson, *Narratives of New Netherland*, p. vii.

ulterior purpose was strategically justified, for the war in western waters was highly successful. As a trading venture, however, the undertaking did not prove so wise, for the fur trade of New Netherland was not long a prosperous business. The attempt to colonize Brazil, which absorbed Dutch energy in the west for over a quarter of a century, was almost the sole example of failure to oust the Portuguese; and the policy pursued in New Netherland was marked by such wavering of aim and such commercial selfishness that success would have been doubtful, even without the steady aggressions of the near-by English.

The war upon the Spaniards could be carried on without land holdings, but not without commerce or the fur trade. Nor could the company's agents firmly hold their territory without self-support by agriculture. Step by step, prodded by necessity and the demand of the colonists, the directors were led into greater expansive effort in New Netherland than had been intended. A nation of only two million members spread its energies over four continents without winning success in any. This diffusion of aim was due to emulation of England, France and Spain, all apparently successful in the same wide fields. The hard logic of unsuccessful wars against the Portuguese and the English at last convinced Holland that the best results could be attained by concentrating on the Oriental spice trade. The result is the great modern Oriental empire of Insulinde with its fifty million subjects.

The inevitable conflict with near-by competitors in the Guianas, Brazil, the West Indies and North America might easily have been foreseen. The Netherlands counted overmuch upon the friendship of England dur-

ing their invasion of the carrying trade—the logical outcome of the struggle with Spain—but the English merchants would not share this amicably with any nation,
not even a closely related Protestant neighbor. The end
of the strife was hastened by the imprudent and irres-
olute methods of the West India Company. Its *dorp* or
village of Manhattan was admirably located for the en-
trepôt desired; but the very location of the settlement,
with the coastal and insular trade developed from it, was
the surest kind of a bid for destruction by the English,
who could not endure a Dutch enclave with commercial
possibilities to separate New England from their other
colonies.

The Provisional Conditions of March, 1624, under
which an early shipload of emigrants came to New
Netherland, repeatedly called them "colonists" and not
merely company servants; they provided for allotment
of lands, for supplies to be furnished on installment
payments and for free trading privileges. The only restrictions were that they must contract to stay six years,
during which time they must not sell land to any but
the company; they might then freely sell to any remaining colonist. The intent to create permanent colonies was
shown again in 1625 by the importation of livestock,
tools and seeds. But in after years the company was continually criticized for its reluctance to enlarge the colony
or make permanent improvements. The company contemplated the colony as a private commercial venture,
not as a national enterprise. Every contemporary account
of the country speaks of its obvious value for agriculture
and of the need of laborers. The Dutch did not lack the
instinct to colonize; but desire for quick returns in the
first place, and bankruptcy in the second, prevented im-

provement of the North American opportunity before they were outdistanced by the English.]

To make a colony practicable there must be an adequate supply of colonists. In certain times and places governments have solved this problem by sending to the colonies, as if to the galleys, those who forfeited their liberty to the state, such as criminals, vagrants and paupers; but generally colonies must be peopled with volunteers whose migration seems to them a private venture involving better living for themselves and their families. Besides these economically ambitious migrants there are oftentimes many who regard themselves oppressed on account of their differences—racial, religious or political—from the national standard set up by the government. [The failure of New Netherland was due in part to the lack of a driving discontent at home. It was really a testimony to the success of the Dutch Republic as a community.] The Dutch had been engrossed in the struggle for independence; with that won the national spirit was suffused with great contentment, there being no persecution of any class for religion's sake and no policy of economic oppression.

[All these conditions and influences brought about a delay that was fatal.] The projects at the Cape of Good Hope and in Brazil were inadequately pursued; and New Netherland sprang up and disappeared in a short space of forty years.[1] Its basis in the fur trade was inadequate, for, conservation being then undreamed of, activity drove steadily toward exhaustion. The company monopoly in this trade, granted at the start, was a deterrent to immigration. We have just observed the lack of fac-

[1] A. J. F. van Laer, ed., *Documents Relating to New Netherland, 1624-1626, in the Henry E. Huntington Library* (Henry E. Huntington Library, *Publs. Americana*, no. 1), 2-18.

tors pushing from behind; here is revealed a factor mode-
rating the normal pull of the colony itself. Always it
must be borne in mind, too, that the government of the
Netherlands had little to do with this enterprise, so that
the colony was directed in the interest of commercial
speculation rather than in the light of farseeing statecraft. It was not until the last third of the seventeenth
century, indeed, that European governments fully realized the meaning of the battle for the continent and tried
to fill their areas with settlers interested in permanent
occupation. By 1664 the French were barely ready to
colonize after dallying more than a century. The Dutch,
after fifty years of vacillation, had then a handful of
ten thousand dissatisfied colonists, whom they lost without a blow.

Yet it was the lack of individual incentive that counted
most. The colonial empires, as devised in European
capitals, almost uniformly failed, whereas the transplanted social groups perpetuated themselves under new
political organizations. The essential characteristic of
New Netherland as a cultural entity was its closely restricted supervision by a commercial company in Europe.
This Dutch society along the Hudson was affected much
more nearly and directly by this regulation proceeding
from Amsterdam than is its successor by political control from Albany and Washington. Outside direction
figured much more prominently here than in any English colony. If, then, we seek to understand the genius
of the Dutch expansion and its transitory success in
North America, we shall find a large part of the explanation in the character of the framework of colonial administration.

The States General at home never exerted anything

save indirect influence upon colonization. Before the
monopolistic companies were organized, overseas affairs
concerned either the States General, Holland, Zealand
or the *stadholder,* as the case might be; no law determined under whose name territories should be acquired or treaties concluded. Acquisitions were really
private, the government limiting its interest to encouragement only. When the companies were chartered, they
became public institutions invested with most of the
rights of sovereignty in the direction of colonial affairs
for specified areas. The States General reappeared only
when petitioned by the colonists or, in case of foreign
conflict, when forced to acknowledge responsibility. The
companies, greedy for profits, were manipulated by
mutually jealous municipal and provincial chambers;
hence the system was without moral or ethical influence,
and the hesitant territorial policy observed is easy to
understand.[1]

The West India Company had an organization much
like that of the earlier company dealing with the East.
It chanced that for many years after 1629 the Amsterdam chamber, which dominated the company, was alter-
nately every two years in the hands of the friends and
then of the enemies of a constructive agricultural program for the colony. This crippled expansion. Matters
were made worse by the formation of independent groups
within the chambers of several of the member cities;
committees of surveillance hampered the directors by
inspecting the books and interfering with loans. Thus
the College of XIX Directors lacked the force needed for
effective administration. To lessen work it delegated New
Netherland to the Amsterdam chamber, the South

[1] De Lannoy, *Histoire de l'Expansion,* 185-187.

American colonies to Zealand, and other enterprises to single members. As a result New Netherland had a company for its proprietor, working through a committee. The consequence was that the colonists, when dissatisfied, had to resort first to their local director, then to their chamber, next to the college and, finally, to the States General for redress.[1] Immediate control of the colony was in the hands of a governor or director-general, usually chosen by the chamber in charge of the particular colony.

Under such circumstances much depended on the personal force and principles of the seven successive governors. The first three are shadowy figures, though they gave practical value to the company's land claims by purchases from the Indians and guided settlements to various sections of the broad domain. Cape May, named after the first incumbent, reminds us that New Netherland extended to the southern tip of the peninsula of New Jersey as well as to the "Fresh River," the Connecticut. Sebastiaen Jansen Crol, the *ad interim* fourth executive, who had come originally in the ecclesiastical office of comforter of the sick, is now best remembered, not for his piety or his mastery of the Indian tongues, but as the alleged adapter of the homeland *olykoek*, ancestor of the doughnut, into the toothsome cruller, by which his name is perpetuated.

Wouter van Twiller, his successor, curiously misrepresented by Irving, may stand for the gay and bibulous sort of young Dutchman, who nevertheless could lay up

[1] A. J. F. van Laer, "The Patroon System and the Colony of Rensselaerswyck," N. Y. State Hist. Assoc., *Proceeds.*, VIII, 222-233. Frequent cases of intervention by the States General upon petition by the colonists are given in H. L. Osgood, *The American Colonies in the Seventeenth Century* (N. Y., 1904-1907), II, 96-98.

a private fortune in the rising value of land. In William Kieft, who presided for a decade beginning in 1638, the ideal of paternalism found its first vigorous expression. He ruled with an erratic hand, and had a previous record of bankruptcy and personal "thrift" in handling trust funds. Domine Bogardus called him "a child of the devil" and threatened to expose all his shortcomings from the pulpit. Kieft retaliated by calling the minister a drunkard and had a drum beaten during the sermon in a last desperate effort to silence this troublesome censor.[1] On the one hand he curbed illicit trade with foreigners and stopped the sale of guns and liquors to the Indians, while on the other he snatched away the flowing bowl from the thirsty Dutchmen by renewing the former strict regulation of the taverns. He prescribed the hours for rising and retiring, for beginning and for quitting work, and tried to banish all immoralities by proclamation. Certainly his high-handed treatment of the Indians had its tragic issue. Recalling Kieft because of his arbitrary methods the company sent a governor not less determined but more competent as an administrator —"a man of character, brave, honest, capable and energetic; but . . . proud, headstrong and tyrannical, [with] high notions of a governor's prerogative"— Peter Stuyvesant.[2]

To realize the social habits of the New Netherlanders

[1] F. J. Zwierlein, *Religion in New Netherland* (Rochester, 1910), 68-70, 78-81; Ruth Putnam, "Annetje Jans' Farm," M. W. Goodwin and others, eds., *Half Moon Series* (N. Y., 1897-1898), I, 80.

[2] Jameson, *Narratives of New Netherland*, 287; *Documents Relating to the History and Settlements of the Towns along the Hudson and Mohawk Rivers* (E. B. O'Callaghan and Berthold Fernow, eds., *Documents Relative to the Colonial History of the State of New York*, Albany, 1853-1887, XIII), 6-22. The *Representation of New Netherland* charged him with incompetence as well; but these petitioners for representative government in the colony were doubtless oversevere.

one must imagine a little society controlled, more or less acceptably, from above. The governor issued his ukases with benevolent purpose; the magistrates in general were even-handed in adjusting difficulty. But it is impossible to resist the feeling that on the whole the people of the province were less well governed than were the French in Canada, the Spaniards in New Spain or the English colonists near by. Stuyvesant was the only governor of New Netherland who seemed to catch a faint glimmer of the possibilities of imperialism; the others were in spirit mere factors of a trading post.

The voluminous correspondence of the governors with the Amsterdam chamber suggests in its minuteness and extent the same autocratic attention to detail as marks the memorials of the officers of New France to Colbert, or the unending letters of the Spanish viceroys to the council, or to the minister, of the Indies. In fact, the government of New Netherland is replete with suggestions of the autocratic spirit of the Latin nations, far more than of the democratic institutions gradually to be absorbed from the English. The governor held wide powers in what are today the three branches of government; his provincial council was more like a Spanish American audiencia than an English council. The autocratic spirit shown by Stuyvesant would have won the warm commendation of any of the rulers of old Mexico. It was perhaps because the Dutch officials worked under their own adaptation of Roman law that their practices were so close to those of the French and the Spanish and involved such wide and intimate regulatory power.[1]

[1] E. B. O'Callaghan, *History of New Netherland* (N. Y., 1846), 244-245. The advantages and present survivals of Roman-Dutch law as practised in New Netherland are noticed by Mrs. Schuyler van Rensselaer, *History of the City of New York in the Seventeenth Century* (N. Y.,

Official control was made more pervasive by the judicial powers of the council, which possessed both civil and criminal jurisdiction and sat as surrogate court and court of admiralty.

The patroon system, used to a minor extent in New Netherland, was a vestige of that feudalism which lingered in the minds of all the Europeans who crossed the ocean. The French seigniories, the Spanish encomiendas and the English manors, were all derived from a common source. The more general use of the feudal device by the Spanish, French and Dutch shows the basic homogeneity of their colonial and social ideals; its relative infrequency in the English colonies manifests their greater removal from the medieval mental state.[1]

The Dutch used the patroonship to encourage private enterprise beyond areas controlled by organized companies. Patroons were thus analogous to the old-time counts of the marches or the Spanish American adelantados. The patroonships, established first in Guiana on the Oyapock River, were mandatories of the company: the scheme provided transportation, food and clothing in return for a part of the profit—a sort of wholesale farming on shares. In 1629 the device was introduced into New Netherland with some modification, perhaps due to the influence of the English colonial charters. The patroons were made feudal lords, almost completely independent of the governors. They were to receive grants on navigable streams four Dutch (or about sixteen Eng-

1909), I, 42, 426; II, 153-154, and by E. T. Corwin and others, *A History of the Reformed Church, Dutch* (Philip Schaff and others, eds., *The American Church History Series*, N. Y., 1893-1897, VIII), 58-59.

[1] *Cf.* Lynn Thorndike, "Survival of Mediaeval Intellectual Interests into Early Modern Times," *Speculum*, II, 147-159. The fact that the colonists of the Hudson Valley had been accustomed to this spirit may help to explain why nine English manors were successfully set up there later.

lish) miles long on one side or two on both; the depth
was to be left to future development. It was a condition
that fifty people over fifteen years old must be colonized
within four years. Perpetual title to the land and its
usufruct was conceded, with the reservation of the fur
trade by the company. In compensation the patroons
might fish, make salt, and trade along the Atlantic and
with neutrals. They had high, middle and low jurisdiction over their settlers, and paid small recognitions in
feudal homage to the company, to whose authority,
however, in actual practice they yielded little respect.

It was land hunger and desire for the status of overlord that impelled several directors of the company to
seek grants, but the few attempts to colonize under them
were failures save that of Kiliaen van Rensselaer. His
patroonship, built out by purchases, was twenty-eight
by forty-four miles in extent, lying on both sides of the
Hudson surrounding the company's Fort Orange; it
outlasted the Dutch period, becoming an English manor
in 1685.[1] An absentee landlord, he conducted the estate
as if he were a sovereign, even assessing dues on company
vessels and demanding that they salute his flag. His concern was for himself and his tenants, not for the colony
as a whole. Writing to his factor in 1636, he explained
that the expenses of marketing in America added nearly
fifty per cent to the original cost of goods, which, therefore, must be sold at a substantially higher margin than
that. "But I do not wish my own people to be charged
more than sixty per cent, since they must gain it by

[1] The Schuylers, Cuylers and others leased very extensive parts of Van
Rensselaer's patroonship, under provision that the lease should hold "while
water runs and grass grows," and the landlord received the tenth sheaf
of every kind of grain the ground produced. See Mrs. Anne Grant,
*Memoirs of an American Lady* (N. Y., 1909), 49; O'Callaghan, *History
of New Netherland*, 177-179.

their hard labor. But from others, for whom I need not care, you may take as much as the market rate and you can get." [1]

The failure of the other patroons was partly due to bickerings with the governor; in view of the liberties allowed to the grantees conflicts as to jurisdiction were inevitable. But another reason was the wavering policy of the company regarding agriculture. The early ideal was an active trading post with employees piling up the company's profits—a factory in the older sense. The grants of 1629 had been a definite step in the direction of real colonization, but after it was taken the company, as we have seen, seemed uncertain whether it should encourage these farming settlements. During Kieft's term, however, there came a salutary change in company policy in the abolition of the monopoly in trade and agriculture, activities to which even foreigners were admitted. The fur trade was thrown open and allodial land tenure was instituted. From this moment New Netherland became a colony of *peuplement*.[2]

[1] A. J. F. van Laer. *Van Rensselaer Bouwier MSS.* (Albany, 1908), 74.

[2] Feudal tenures were abolished in New York in 1787, and the law was construed as voiding a provision in a lease in fee made in 1785 in which the grantor reserved a preëmptive right of purchase and provided for a commutation fine of one fourth upon sale to a third party. The law made no provision for compensating lords of manors for losses of personal services. Although the old feudal holdings were thus done away with, Stephen van Rensselaer, advised by his brother-in-law Alexander Hamilton, estranged certain properties reserving dues and services feudal in character, the preëmptive purchase right, and the commutation fine in case the latter were ignored. Upon his death in 1839 attempts were made to collect dues then in arrears, and riots occurred. The New York Constitution of 1846 reasserted the abolition of feudal tenures, but reserved all rents and services created prior to the constitution, and all lands were declared to be allodial, leases over twelve years in duration being declared void, as were all fines, quarter-sales or other restraints reserved in any subsequent grant. Interesting cases at law occupied the courts of New York for many years without bringing final solution to some of the issues raised indirectly through the establishment of these feudal estates. In 1907 a number of cases were still

The New Netherland struggle for participation in general administration is the usual one of concessions wrung from the executives under financial duress. The governor's council was dependent upon his will, in no wise representing the colonists. Its inconsequence was humiliating when in 1638 Kieft reduced its membership from five to three, really himself and one councilor, he exercising two votes and the other but one. His need of help to punish Indian atrocities led him in 1641 to summon the heads of families, who chose a board of Twelve Men. In return for help they demanded that the emasculated council contain at least five men, four to be popularly elected, and that the governor give up his intimacy with men of lower sorts.[1] Such democratic effrontery was answered by curt denial of their right to ask such things; then the governor gave in with bad grace.

Desperate Indian fighting compelled him again in 1643 to appeal to the commonalty. This time a committee of Eight Men was chosen, a cosmopolitan group, containing one German and two Englishmen. When the Eight found themselves persistently ignored, they petitioned the States General for a new governor whose powers should be limited by the representatives of the towns. The answer, as we have seen, was Stuyvesant. He was to be assisted by a vice-director and a fiscal, the three forming a supreme council, but his personal force nullified even this intended check on his prerogative.

in dormant litigation. See Simon W. Rosendale, "Closing Phases of the Manorial System in Albany," N. Y. State Hist. Assoc., *Proceeds*, VIII, 234-245; C. Z. Lincoln, *The Constitutional History of the State of New York* (Rochester, 1906), I, 229; De Peyster *v.* Michael, 6 New York 467; J. R. Brodhead, *History of the State of New York* (N. Y., 1871-1872), I, 400-401; D. R. Fox, *Caleb Heathcote* (N. Y., 1926), 119.

[1] O'Callaghan, *History of New Netherland*, 245-246.

Yet by 1647 financial troubles caused him also to appeal to the people, who gave him a committee of Nine Men.[1] Like his predecessor, "de groot Direktor" tried to thwart the aims of the representatives of popular discontent. The tide of resentment rose. In 1650 his enemies, in the *Representation of New Netherland,* made complaints so bitter that they may be largely discounted, but the complainants thought them true, which is really what matters. The vehement remonstrance draws the best picture extant of public affairs in the rapidly growing colony.

Even under the influence of the neighboring English the Dutch were slow in creating local government. Village organizations had been provided in the revised Freedoms and Exemptions of 1640. Leaders of five adult colonists might establish a settlement which by growth could become entitled to town government with magistrates and officers of justice. Sixteen such municipalities were established between 1644 and 1664.[2] Their officers were annually chosen by the director and council from lists of nominees made by the freemen. Town officers passed ordinances concerning lands, highways, schools and churches, and administered local justice. Their acts were subject to superior review, but the colonial authority was tolerant or indifferent, and left them a good deal

---

[1] This body of Nine Men, originated by popular election, was analogous to old village organization in Holland. It was to be convoked only at the director's will, the membership was to be renewed annually by retirement of six; these were to nominate twelve candidates, from whom the director should choose six successors. This would make the Nine Men progressively more amenable to executive suggestion.

[2] Osgood, *American Colonies,* II, 107; Lincoln, *Constitutional History,* I, 3-16, 410-421. By 1660 Stuyvesant was ordering isolated farmers to move together and form villages for protection against the Indians. See I. N. P. Stokes, *Inconography of Manhattan Island* (N. Y., 1915-1928), I, 79; L. D. Scisco, "The Plantation Type of Colony," *Am. Hist. Rev.,* VIII, 260-270.

of independence. English towns under New Netherland control were treated rather gingerly, desire for colonists outweighing the hope of building up strong central supervision.

It was as a result of the work of the Nine Men that New Amsterdam was first so named and was given city government in 1653. Even then Stuyvesant could appoint the *schout,* burgomasters and *schepens* and, like a Spanish viceroy, make ordinances and publish interdicts for the control of the capital. New Amsterdam was administratively the counterpart of Quebec or Mexico City. No British-American capital during the seventeenth century so dominated its environment. For the Dutch areas on the South River (the Delaware), a commissary of the company was a veritable lord of the marches—he held off Swedish and English intruders, fostered the Indian trade, prevented the sale of firearms to the natives, granted land and meted out justice. After 1657 the creation of New Amstel at the head of Delaware Bay greatly reduced his importance, for this settlement (later renamed New Castle by the English) was dependent upon Amsterdam—the only instance of a city-colony in North America. Here the trammels upon local control were severe enough, to say nothing of poor crops or threatened absorption by Maryland, to discourage growth.

On the North River Rensselaerswyck completely surrounded the company's Fort Orange. This virtual principality tried to exclude the company's officers and monopolized the fur trade and the import business. Practical independence was preserved throughout Dutch times. In Van Slechtenhorst the director, Stuyvesant, encountered a man of his mettle who had to be put in

# NEW AMSTERDAM

*Left and right: Costumes in New Netherland.*

Below: "New Amsterdam lately called New York, and now retaken by the Netherlanders on August 24, 1673," showing the sky-line (a little idealized) in the times of Peter Stuyvesant.

*Nieuw Amsterdam onlangs Nieuw Jorck genaemt en de herwonnen by de Nederlanders op den 24 Aug 1673*

jail for resisting the establishment of a provincial court in his territory. Thus to the south and to the north there was lack of genius for the expansion of political control, just as there was restriction of territorial growth because of the near neighborhood of the French, the English and the Iroquois.

But the hope of widened boundaries was not absent. From Christiaensen's trading post at Fort Orange one Kleynties and a companion set out in 1614 or 1615 from the Mohawk to Otsego Lake, going then down the Susquehanna into the territory of modern Pennsylvania. The *bosch-loper* of the Dutch was the rival of the Canadian coureur de bois; his quest of peltries led him up the Mohawk through Lake Oneida to Oswego, along the shores of Lakes Ontario and Erie to Detroit, then by those of Lake Huron and across Saginaw Bay to Mackinac, always carrying with him a burden of merchandise for barter. The recurring voyages of the Dutch to this region might readily have led to such conquests as those of the French adventurers. There was no episode of the Dutch occupation that showed greater hardihood or intelligence than the effort to gain control of the Iroquois fur trade described by Van den Bogaert.[1]

But even this bit of courageous midwinter pioneering merely reached the area of the already widening influence of the French fur traders. The increasing importance of the Five Nations, giving them the balance of power between the rival European peoples competing

---

[1] F. W. Halsey, *The Old New York Frontier* (N. Y., 1901), 32; "Narrative of a Journey into the Mohawk and Oneida Country, 1634-1635," Jameson, *Narratives of New Netherland*, 137-162. The directors in 1653 sounded Stuyvesant on the advisability of establishing a post twenty Dutch miles north of Albany to attract furs from Canada. See *Documents Relating to the History and Settlement of the Towns along the Hudson and Mohawk Rivers*, 35.

for the northern region, set the limit to Dutch trade and expansion. In 1634 a trader setting out from Fort Orange could gather four hundred beaver pelts in four or five weeks.[1] Soon, however, the easy supply had diminished; even the Iroquois shortly had no furs and must depend on the inland trade for them. Brokers who went into the woods to attract savages with beavers, that is, who slyly carried on forbidden individual trade under excuses alleged with childish simplicity, were common until late in the Dutch occupation. It was exceedingly difficult for the government to stamp out these irregularities; men of substance and standing like Philip P. Schuyler were involved in them, and public opinion around Fort Orange was generally complaisant. In 1657 the authorities virtually admitted defeat by legalizing this trade for at least one year.[2]

The only other significant expansion was Stuyvesant's "conquest" of New Sweden in 1655; but that act was a mere defense measure with no policy of widening influence behind. Life in New Sweden was typical of the farming, fur-trading, forest-clearing American frontier. The population was a mixture of Swedes, Finns and Dutchmen; the first Negro slave came in 1639. Of the first Swedish comers it was said, somewhat ill-naturedly, that it was "impossible to find more stupid people in all Sweden." But skilled workmen were soon brought in and the woodsmen quickly gained renown with their flashing axes, the Finns clearing the forests by "svedging" or burning seasonally. The people indulged in

[1] Van Laer, *Van Rensselaer Bouwier MSS.*, 302-304.
[2] A. J. F. van Laer, *Minutes of the Court of Fort Orange and Beverwyck, 1652-1660* (Albany, 1920-1923), II, 39-40, 191, 192, 279, 280. The Indians had brokers too. Cf. J. T. Adams, *Provincial Society* (*A History of American Life*, III), 35-36.

mixed farming, and when the hunting season came, pursued their game with "long French guns" and similar fowling pieces. Cattle "of a middling sort" and horses were imported with much effort from various parts of the world, including the English and Spanish colonies.

The settlers wore buckskin coats and elk-skin trousers, sometimes varying the coarser materials with cloth. The women made cloth caps with tassels for the men, a style which the Indians admired and often imitated, just as the whites adopted Indian forest and river lore and learned to eat corn bread. Their simple log cabins often grew into two-story dwellings with shingle roofs, the second story, above log walls, being clapboarded; a stoop porch gave entry through a single door. Glass windows were early used and some furniture came from the old country. The early house form is still seen now and then in Eastern Pennsylvania. In these colonial homes the customs of northern Europe were observed as the seasons passed, such as the eating of Christmas porridge and drinking the *Jule-skoal,* though no Christmas tree had yet found place among Swedish customs.

The plantations on the Delaware exhibited far greater understanding of the practical methods of colonization than did those of the Dutch.[1] With a little earlier application to the task, the Swedes might have made a much wider and more lasting impression upon the settle-

[1] Amandus Johnson, *The Swedish Settlements on the Delaware* (N. Y., 1911), *passim;* Israel Acrelius, *A History of New Sweden* (Hist. Soc. of Pa., *Memoirs,* XI), 146-151; reports of Governor Johan Printz, 1647, 1654, of Governor Johan Rising, 1655, and letter of Thomas Paschall, 1683, in A. C. Myers, ed., *Narratives of Early Pennsylvania, West Jersey, and Delaware, 1630-1707* (*Original Narratives of Early American History*) ; *Documents Relating to the History of the Dutch and Swedish Settlements on the Delaware River* (*Documents Relative to the History of New York,* XII), *passim;* Kahn, *Travels* (Pinkerton), 400.

ment of the continent. As it was, probably not more than six or seven hundred Swedes and Finns in the colony had gathered in these settlements before they were taken over by the English. The international origins and history of the territory were marked by the fact that in 1683 most of the people spoke English, Swedish, Finnish and Dutch.

Life in New Netherland was colored not only by company control, but also by the existence of the monopoly enjoyed by the established Dutch Reformed Church. This was a Calvinistic body, practically Presbyterian in faith and organization after the first national synod, that of Dordrecht in 1618-1619. The West India Company assumed control of religion in New Netherland by virtue of the analogous authority exercised by the States General in the United Provinces, including the right of patronage or appointment of church officers; but actual administration was soon turned over to the Classis of Amsterdam which joined with the chamber of that city in this responsibility, the small salaries paid the ministers becoming obligations shared by the company and the congregations. Until 1624 there were no religious institutions of any kind; then followed a period of unchallenged monoply by the Reformed Church until 1654, after which, as we shall see, ensued a decade of organized dissent, in which Lutherans and others attempted to ignore or evade the religious prohibitions of the Exemptions and Privileges of 1640. Save for the toleration allowed, virtually of necessity, to the English Presbyterians and Congregationalists located on the eastern parts of Long Island or in Westchester, "dissenters" were restricted to family observance of their faiths.[1] Public offices were generally denied to all but members of the established church, though none but Quakers were denied citizenship, and Jews had various civic rights withheld. In each community the ideal organization included a minister, a comforter of the sick, wardens, sexton, a schoolmaster and a chorister. Oftentimes these functions, especially the last two named, were combined in one person.[2]

The head of the church was the director-general. He performed an ecclesiastical function when he undertook to uplift public morals. Kieft, and particularly Stuyvesant, were unceasingly industrious in this task of Sisyphus. Since it was against the law in 1641 and after to tap beer during "church," a regulation held "in disregard, nay, contempt," Stuyvesant stiffened the rules, allowing Sunday drinking only after two in the afternoon except for travelers and home consumers. To keep the Sabbath properly in other respects in 1656 required abstaining from

> any ordinary work such as ploughing, mowing, building, woodcutting, working in iron or tin, hunting, fishing, or . . . any other business permitted on other days . . . much less any lower or unlawful exercises or games, drunkenness, frequenting taverns or grog shops, dancing, card-playing, backgammon, tennis, ballplaying, bowling, rolling ninepins, racing with boats, cars or wagons before, during, or between divine service.

[1] E. T. Corwin, ed., *Ecclesiastical Records of the State of New York* (Albany, 1901-1916), I, 131-132; Zwierlein, *Religion in New Netherland*, 3; "Letters of the Dutch Ministers to the Classis of Amsterdam," Jameson, *Narratives of New Netherland*, 389-415.

[2] The comforter of the sick, the first ecclesiastical officer to arrive, read prayers and sermons aloud. He could not at first perform any of the sacraments, but later obtained authority to baptize and marry. See "Letter of Reverend Jonas Michaëlius," Jameson, *Narratives of New Netherland*, 124-125.

There should be no drinking or selling or giving of liquor on any night after the watch was set or the bell rung (at about nine o'clock), though there were certain minor exceptions from this prohibition. The fines imposed were increased for repeated offenses, and likewise were levied upon those who refused to inform; they were divided by thirds among the informant, the church and the public treasury.

In 1648, apparently, about one fourth of New Amsterdam consisted of places for the sale of brandy, tobacco and beer. Ordinances to rectify this permitted taverns already established to continue four years, but meantime "the owners shall be obliged to engage in some other honest business." [1] In 1661 and 1663 similar rules show by their repetition rather clearly what the normal Dutchman thought Sunday was for in spite of his opportunity to hear two long sermons morning and afternoon. Among the Sabbath diversions tabooed in 1663 were

> all unusual exercises ... fishing, fowling, running, sailing, nutting or picking strawberries, trafficking with Indians ... and ... all dissolute and licentious plays, riots, calling children out into the streets and highways.

This ordinance was not published, however, as the council thought it "too severe and too much opposed to Dutch liberties."

From the frequent issue of such sumptuary laws and the records of concubinage as well as of the irregular publication of marriage bans, it is clear that nonofficial Dutchmen did not take religion overseriously. Of the

[1] Berthold Fernow, ed., *The Records of New Amsterdam from 1653 to 1674* (N. Y., 1897), I, 6-8; II, 205-208.

society of Albany in the eighteenth century a reminiscent writer said: "Their religion . . . had in it little of fervor or enthusiasm. . . . If their piety, however, was without enthusiasm, it was also without bigotry; they wished others to think as they did, without showing rancor or contempt toward those who did not." [1]

Provision for the spiritual needs of New Netherland was much less adequate than that in New Spain, New France or New England. Dissuaded, perhaps, by the faltering colonial policy there was but slight propaganda from home to compare with that from the Catholic countries to their colonies. The casual character of the inhabitants afforded no such basis for self-sustained zeal for religion as distinguished New England.[2] There was no ordained minister until 1628 and no second until 1642 when the religious services of Rensselaerswyck, previously conducted by the schout or bailiff, were taken over by the Reverend John Megapolensis. His first audience of about a hundred persons showed "hardly any semblance of godliness or righteousness"; on the contrary he reported that there was soon evident much dishonesty, licentiousness and drunkenness.

Making due allowance in this and other clerical testimony for a certain censoriousness not unknown in the pulpit, one must conclude that religious leadership and inspiration could have been applied here to excellent purpose. But the clergy sent over, doubtless good as a whole, were not all able to give it. Domine Bogardus's fond-

[1] Grant, *Memoirs*, I, 70; E. B. O'Callaghan, *The Documentary History of the State of New York* (Albany, 1850-1851), III, 27; Albert Eekhof, *Jonas Michaëlius, Founder of the Church in New Netherland: His Life and Work* (Leyden, 1926), *passim*.

[2] The situation was more like that in the southern English colonies. See T. J. Wertenbaker, *The First Americans* (*A History of American Life*, II), chap. v.

ness for strong drink injured his influence, as we have seen; a pastor who came to Rensselaerswyck in 1650 under what were alleged to be falsified certificates of good character had to be sent back to clear his reputation; one of his successors, boisterous old Gideon Schaats, added to Governor Stuyvesant's cares.[1] The church was not lavishly supported. The Dutch towns on Long Island had no ministry till 1660; then Domine John T. Polhemus lived for a time in Midwout in biting poverty and Henricus Selyns was ordained in Breukelen, where he preached in a barn. Other preachers served for a period in one village along the river and then in another, while some communities like Harlem tried to maintain one all the time. None of the incumbents were allowed large salaries and several had difficulty in collecting the stipends that had been voted. The whole picture was in sharp contrast to that in New England where the minister was a figure of the highest dignity and authority.

The capture of New Netherland by the English in 1664 did not affect the polity of the Dutch church, which continued under the Classis of Amsterdam. As the Dutch population grew in numbers the church grew with it until in 1737 there were nineteen ministers serving nearly sixty churches. Only a few of these clergy or their predecessors had been of American birth and those who were had been obliged to go to Holland for ordination. An element now was demanding more self-government, and, after considerable controversy, succeeded ten years later in obtaining consent to set up an association

[1] Van Laer, *Van Rensselaer Bouwier MSS.*, 647, 652, 686-688; Corwin, *Ecclesiastical Records*, I, 256-257; Jasper Dankers [or Danckaerts] and Peter Sluyter, *Journal of a Voyage to New York, and a Tour in Several of the American Colonies, 1679-1680* (H. C. Murphy, ed., L. I. Hist. Soc., *Memoirs*, I), 44-45; O'Callaghan, *Documentary History*, III, 530-531; Van Laer, *Minutes of the Court of Fort Orange*, II, 24.

called a *Coetus,* which undertook church government except in matters of doctrine and ordination. It was now only a matter of time when the full status of a classis, including the right of ordination, should be reached; and in 1755 it was assumed. This American classis was now a sister member of the Reformed Church, Dutch; when the Revolution came it would not be difficult to change this status to one of complete independence.[1]

In New Sweden where Lutheran ministers served after 1639, Dutch settlers were free to practise the Reformed faith. Mass was said in the "good old Swedish tongue" as an aid in fortifying the people against inroads of English and Dutch neighbors, but there were never more than three pastors in the colony at a time. Johan Campanius was a faithful shepherd who served five years until he wearied of life "in a heathenish country." The notable exploit of the Reverend Lars Carlson Lock, who performed his own wedding ceremony, suggests traits which led the Dutch to call him a drunken unmannerly clown. The Dutch in the colony had no minister, a layman reading the sermons. The Lutherans on the Delaware were allowed to continue public worship after the conquest by Stuyvesant. New Amstel had a preacher for a brief space of time in 1659. The Mennonite settlers frugally dispensed with preachers, and Quakers were not permitted to enter.[2]

New Netherland itself harbored several dissenting groups. Presbyterians and Congregationalists were in 1678 the "most numerous and substantial." There were even a few Roman Catholics and members of the

---

[1] Corwin, *History of the Reformed Church, Dutch,* 133-157.
[2] Zwierlein, *Religion in New Netherland,* chap. iii; Johnson, *Swedish Settlements,* chaps. xxxiv, xxxvii, xli.

Church of England, numerous Quakers of many branches and some Jews. In 1686 there were to be found followers of almost every sort of religious opinion, but most of the inhabitants had none at all.[1] The English immigrants, mostly Presbyterians who had differed with the Congregationalists over the question of infant baptism, had several ministers who had led their congregations to New York to escape religious quarrels and persecutions. The Dutch Lutherans long worshipped with the Reformed Church in New Amsterdam; but in 1653 they began to demand the right of public worship according to the Augsburg Confession since they objected to the established doctrines with regard to baptism. Meeting opposition from the authorities, they began to organize private conventicles in anticipation of getting their own minister; but the government, with the situation in New Sweden in view, feared schisms and forbade such meetings as cutting down attendance upon the real Word of God and "paving the way for other sects." [2] When the Lutherans learned that the company thought Stuyvesant too zealous, and had even asked him to modify the baptismal rites, their hopes were renewed; but the influence of Megapolensis and Drisius prevented the realization of so much tolerance.

The Quakers fared much worse. They began proselyting in the second half of the fifties. When "two strong young women" of that faith appeared in 1657 and began a violent exhortation in the streets, the fiscal and an assistant, doubtless also strong, seized them and clapped them into jail. The domines were glad to see that this

[1] Zwierlein, *Religion in New Netherland*, 142, and chap. v; Fernow, *Records of New Amsterdam*, I, 20-21.
[2] Corwin, *Ecclesiastical Records*, I, 317, 320, 323.

sort of reception induced others to repair to Rhode Island, "the receptacle of all sorts of riff-raff people, and . . . nothing else than the sewer of New England." [1] But not all were so easily disposed of. Robert Hodgson who gathered crowds at Hempstead, an English settlement, was arrested for his preaching and dragged to New Amsterdam at the tail of a cart and thrust into a vermin-infested dungeon. Later, chained to a wheelbarrow and ordered to work, he was beaten by a Negro with a pitch-soaked rope when he refused. On two other occasions his obduracy caused him to be cruelly scourged while hung from a ceiling by his hands with a heavy log fastened to his feet. He was finally liberated and sent away. The sect also invaded several other English towns; severe persecutions were inflicted upon Thomas Bowne, for example, who was fined, imprisoned and banished.

Quite apart from their religion the Jews were disliked because they took business away from the Dutchmen, were unavailable for military service, and were alleged to be untrustworthy and penurious. Stuyvesant suspected them because of his experiences with them in Curaçao, where he had formerly been governor. They began to come to New Netherland in 1654, where the first ones made trouble through failure to pay for their meals and freight on shipboard. The director tried to get rid of them, but as Jews were important among the shareholders of the company, that body prevented official opposition. As time went on, the Jews were gradually freed from restrictions on their activities, such as exclusion from the retail trade; they gained the right to hold some property and finally, in 1657, received

[1] Corwin, *Ecclesiastical Records*, I, 399-400.

small-burgher rights or those of citizenship. The allotment of land about the same time for a burying ground may indicate that the Jews were recognized as a permanent factor on Manhattan Island.[1]

[1] Zwierlein, *Religion in New Netherland*, chap. viii; Fernow, *Records of New Amsterdam*, VII, 154. "Church and Sunday in Old New York" forms chap. xiii of Alice M. Earle, *Colonial Days in Old New York* (N. Y., 1899), 261-292. The fortunes of the Dutch Reformed Church after the cession are recorded in Corwin, *History of the Reformed Church, Dutch.*

# CHAPTER XII

## OUR DUTCH HERITAGE

NEW NETHERLAND, partly because of defects in policy, failed to establish itself as a strong well-based community. But ineptitude in politics was not the only shortcoming. It must be confessed that the Dutch, like the French, made no notable contribution to the transmission of the higher forms of European culture to America during their period of colonization. At a time when Amsterdam surpassed London in wealth and commercial importance, and the University of Leyden enjoyed better repute than Oxford, the Dutch colony on the Hudson produced little to compare even with the cultural achievements on Massachusetts Bay.[1]

There were good reasons why Dutch intellectuality and prosperity found feeble echo in early New Netherland. It was a small colony of less than ten thousand even at the end. Few if any of the immigrants were superior to those who were the original settlers of New France, New Spain or New England. As has been observed, life was sufficiently attractive in the old country to prevent a rush of talent to the new. Most of those who came could neither read nor write. Among the peasants who settled Rensselaerswyck hardly one pos-

[1] J. F. Jameson, ed., *Narratives of New Netherland* (same ed., *Original Narratives of Early American History*, N. Y., 1906-     ), 3; A. H. van Buren, "Wiltwyck under the Dutch," N. Y. State Hist. Assoc., *Proceeds.*, XI, 133; Ruth Putnam, "Annetje Jans' Farm," M. W. Goodwin and others, eds., *Half Moon Series* (N. Y., 1897-1898), I, 64; A. J. F. van Laer, *Van Rensselaer Bouwier MSS.* (Albany, 1908), 687-688; F. J. Zwierlein, *Religion in New Netherland* (Rochester, 1910), 78.

sessed a patronymic. Van Rensselaer said in 1642 that they were extravagant, licentious and wanton. During Kieft's war the colonists committed horrible murders and other excesses on the Indians. "They were a rough lot," writes a descendant, ". . . they cheated the savages . . . and most cruelly oppressed them. Also on occasion they cheated one another; out of which habit, as is shown by the verbose records of their little courts, arose much petty litigation of a snarling sort among themselves. . . . They consistently cheated the revenue laws . . . and . . . any other laws which happened to get in their way. . . . But also they had certain virtues. . . . With all their shortcomings they were tough and they were sturdy and they were as plucky as men could be." [1]

The fact is that the European character in the wilderness environment worked much the same in New Netherland as elsewhere in American colonization. The settlers there were unusually happy in their choice of a habitat, for the country was favorable both in climate and natural resources. Domestic cattle alone were lacking, but these were more plentifully imported than in New France, though never lavishly. The sowing of European seeds amply rewarded effort, so that there was little reason why a good agricultural colony should not have developed. The natives, though thieving and treacherous, were fearful and timid and were amenable

[1] T. A. Janvier, *The Dutch Founding of New York* (N. Y., 1903), 2-4. Janvier's point of view is aptly illustrated by A. J. F. van Laer, ed., *Minutes of the Court of Fort Orange and Beverwyck, 1652-1660* (Albany, 1920-1923). Some of the controversies seem naïve to us, as that over misnaming houses which set Fort Orange by the ears for a considerable time. A citizen amused himself by naming his neighbors' homes "The House of Discord," "The Cuckoo's Nest," "The House of Ill Manners," etc. A large amount of testimony was taken. See Van Laer, *Minutes*, I, 199, 201, 210, 213.

to kind treatment. It was said that they were willing to work for pay, especially for carrying burdens on long journeys. It did not help the relations of the races, however, that the white employers sometimes dismissed their Indians without paying them their wages.[1] If the Dutch patroons and farmers could have succeeded in developing a system of forced labor, milder and more domestic than the Spanish one, they might have created a temperate-zone plantation colony and preserved the native race. But they found that the Indians would not endure the exaction of tributes, and hence achieved no greater success than the French and English in the way of developing the human resources of the continent.

They did attempt the slavery of both Indians and Negroes, but the institution did not flourish. Indian slavery was almost casual in New Netherland; the colonists did not object, but the authorities feared that it would give the French a text upon which to urge the Iroquois to treat the Dutch as enemies. In 1679 the Indian slaves were declared free. The first blacks were brought over in 1625 or 1626, several years after the familiar Virginia episode. Their numbers were few until 1646 when a cargo from a slave ship was purchased with pork and peas. From them much was expected, "but they just dripped through the fingers." Inasmuch as agriculture suffered from lack of markets, the colonists were in 1648 allowed to export fish, flour and other produce to Brazil, for which they might accept in payment slaves among other things. Since this expansion of trade did not encourage agriculture as had been expected,

[1] I. N. P. Stokes, *Iconography of Manhattan Island* (N. Y., 1915-1928), I, 28.

the demand for Negroes remained slight. However, the burghers of the capital petitioned in 1660 to be allowed to enter the West African slave trade, and on the eve of the surrender to the English in 1664 a delayed shipload of three hundred Negroes arrived.

That slavery was fostered for its effect on trade rather than on industrial development is shown by the fact that the Negroes were brought over by merchants licensed by the company, largely in the hope that they could be sold to the neighboring English. Most of the blacks were used in domestic service, and when employed as farm hands were in a true domestic relation, often working side by side with their masters in the fields. The happy relations existing between masters and slaves near Albany during the eighteenth century were probably characteristic of other localities as well. Negro children were attached to young members of their own sex in their master's family and grew up with them in intimate friendship.[1]

The most terrible punishment for occasional malefactors among the blacks, short of death, was to be sold to the island of Jamaica. As late as 1703 there were but thirteen hundred Negroes to 7767 whites in five counties about New York city. Indians, mulattoes and *mustees* (mestizos) might also be found among the slave population as a result of voluntary sale, sentence for crime, or natural increase; children of slave mothers inherited the status.[2] Evidently the number of half-breeds was

[1] Mrs. Anne Grant, *Memoirs of an American Lady* (N. Y., 1901), I, 80-87; G. E. Hill and G. E. Waring, jr., "Old Wells and Water Courses," *Half Moon Series*, I, 315-316.

[2] E. B. O'Callaghan and Berthold Fernow, eds., *Documents Relative to the Colonial History of the State of New York* (Albany, 1853-1887), II, 222, 430, and *General Index* (XI) at the word *Slavery*; E. V. Morgan, "Slavery in New York," *Half Moon Series*, II, 3-6. The com-

fairly large, for they received legislative attention; but references to them are relatively few in the documents on New Netherland. Slaves might be beaten or sent to the house of correction, but masters might not kill them. They could testify in court against each other, though not against a freeman. When on trial they were denied benefit of counsel; nor could they hold property or engage in trade.

Fear of servile insurrections led to repressive laws. Not more than four slaves, after 1702 three, might congregate anywhere off their master's estate. On Sunday, their day of rest, they were closely watched. The corporation of New York forbade them to ride horseback on the streets or common; they might not go over to Brooklyn without permission. Negro plots in 1712 proved that the fear had some basis in fact though no such trouble had arisen under the Dutch régime. In this case the Negroes killed nine men and wounded six before they were dispersed by the troops. Twenty who were captured were hung, burned or broken on the wheel; six who escaped found refuge in committing suicide. In the second or Great Plot of 1741 newcomers from Africa probably incited incendiarism and thievery. There were then two thousand Negro slaves, representing about one fifth of the total population of the city of New York. A servant woman, Mary Barton, accused certain blacks who had met on the estate of her master. Upon these the whites fell, the victims of their own terror. They cast one hundred and fifty-four slaves into jail, burned fourteen, hanged eighteen, and arrested

pany itself held slaves, keeping them in a little colony by the East River at what is now Seventy-fifth Street. See Stokes, *Iconography*, I, 21, 104. On Indian slavery see A. M. Lauber, *Indian Slavery in Colonial Times* (Columbia Univ., *Studies*, LIV, no. 3), 253-571.

twenty-four whites, of whom four were executed. When Mary became so pleased at her success that she began to accuse people of the upper classes, society came to its senses.[1] But by this time the colony was losing its Dutch character.

In agriculture the settlers in New Netherland had much to learn from the Indians.[2] In the fields about the Fresh Water Pond, or Collect, the Manhatoes cultivated peas, beans, corn and pumpkins. To these simple farmers the whites were debtors for the delights of succotash. No dykes were required for tillage as in the fatherland; post and rail fences sufficed for inclosures, such materials being usually made available in clearing the land. Land grubbed and plowed twice was ready for winter grain; for summer grain one plowing was enough. The summer stubble was plowed in, but for the first nine years of Van der Donck's observation no fertilizer was used. Though peas were often sown to soften the soil, it was too rich to yield good ones, and probably the farmers did not know the nitrogenous effect of this crop; but two harvests of it could be taken in a year. Indian corn, then often called Turkish wheat, grew well in almost any soil; it was followed by winter grain. Rye grew taller than a man's head, as did barley, and both produced lavishly. Wheat could be sown as many as eleven years in the same soil without alternation, and thus became the agricultural staple of the province. Father Isaac Jogues visiting New Amsterdam in 1643 found that three hundred ships had been there to load wheat for the West India trade.[3] But much of the wheat

[1] Morgan, "Slavery in New York," 16-18.
[2] Cf. T. J. Wertenbaker, The First Americans (A History of American Life, II), 309-311.
[3] Jameson, Narratives of New Netherland, 260.

was kept at home and ground into flour in the various mills driven by wind, water or horses.[1]

The cultivation of tobacco was engaged in by most of the farmers, the leaf being considered second in value only to that of Virginia. The wealth of the latter colony from this source had been one of the incentives to Dutch emulation of English colonization, and by the middle of the thirties tobacco was being exported to Holland in substantial quantities. Nevertheless it was not allowed to supersede the food crops; when a famine seemed imminent in 1653 tobacco planters were ordered to plant as many hills of maize, peas or grain as they did of their commercial crop.[2] Flax and hemp would do well, but as the Dutch women did not spin much during the first two decades, and since the Indians used their own wild hemp for making ropes and nets, little attention was given these crops. All things considered it was hardly to be expected that the colony would sustain itself, yet shortly after 1630 that became the ideal. "If agriculture were promoted a little," wrote Governor Van Twiller, "we could arrange to have enough of everything with the exception of salt, oil and vinegar." [3]

In one of its bursts of generosity the company offered free sea passage for farmers and their families and, on their arrival, a grant of land partly cleared, a house, barn, tools and animals. The grantee was to have the usufruct of these advantages for six years, then return the

[1] Stokes, *Iconography*, I, 11, 27; III, 65. Bakers were closely supervised by law as to the price, quality and quantity of their bread. Berthold Fernow, ed., *The Records of New Amsterdam from 1653 to 1674* (N. Y., 1897), III, 285; IV, 218; VI, 30-31; VII, 219, etc.

[2] Stokes, *Iconography*, I, 45, 83, 88. To insure good quality all tobacco had to be shipped through New Amsterdam.

[3] A. J. F. van Laer, "Letters of Van Twiller," N. Y. State Hist. Assoc., *Quar. Journ.*, I, 44-50. Wassenaer (Jameson's *Narratives*) observes that some salt was manufactured by evaporation.

number of cattle originally placed at his disposal after retaining the increase. Under this plan six *bouweries* were laid out between Wall Street and Fourteenth Street early in the time of Kieft. Each was a little farmstead; the record shows one to have consisted of a dwelling house thirty by eighteen feet in area with two transom windows and two round windows, a tobacco barn sixty feet long and a separate kitchen building twenty feet by sixteen.[1] By 1635 there were eight of them above the town, reached by Bouwerie Lane; but despite their log palisades and their short distance from the main defenses, these farms were hazardous places of abode during Indian troubles. Emanuel de Groot, a freed Negro, took ten heads of colored families and founded an agricultural settlement at Werpoes. It became known later as the Bowery and was the first extensive clearing outside the original settlement. Peter Stuyvesant's pear orchard, planted about 1664, had in later years one sole surviving tree which long stood as a city landmark.[2]

In spite of the ideals of Usselinx and the efforts of men like Van Rensselaer and De Vries, agriculture remained of less importance than fur trading until about 1660. Van Rensselaer had begun farm operations thirty years before; his superintendent received from one hundred and fifty to one hundred and eighty guilders a year, and his laborers from forty to ninety, pledging themselves to four years' service. Mechanics earned as much as the superintendent, but were obliged to turn in half of all

[1] Stokes, *Iconography*, III, 94. Isolated farmsteads were surrounded by palisades of logs.

[2] Adriaen van der Donck, "Description of the New Netherlands," *Old South Leaflets*, no. lxix (Boston, 1896), 16, 18; Cornelius van Tienhoven, "Information Relative to taking up Land in New Netherland," E. B. O'Callaghan, *The Documentary History of the State of New York* (Albany, 1850-1851), IV, 21-26.

they received for outside work. Though the first harvests would not feed the people and provide seed, and though the cattle and hogs could not be eaten, the game hunted or bought from the Indians sufficed. Roelof Jans of Janssen, the superintendent at Rensselaerswyck, moved to Manhattan when he had finished his service, and began the farm known later by his wife's name, Annetje, and also as the Domine's Bouwerie. This piece of property, which brought no revenue for five years, was about sixty-two acres in size and of irregular shape. It finally became the property of Trinity Church.

Field husbandry was generally the task of the men with their Negroes and bound servants. But everyone in town or country in the Albany region of the eighteenth century had in addition a house garden whose plants received the skillful and loving attention of the women. There kidney beans, asparagus, celery and many sweet herbs now known no longer to average gardens grew in the closely planted rows and helped to vary the diet of the family. Red and white roses, eglantine, violets, marigolds and many other flowers were also found in the gardens. By Van der Donck's time many homes had fruit trees—peaches, apricots, cherries, figs, almonds, persimmons, plums, gooseberries and quinces from England.[1]

The relations of the Dutch with the Indians varied little from the experiences of the other European nations. Oft-repeated legislation proves that liquor and firearms were shamelessly sold to the natives for furs. The use of *seawant* (wampun) and beaver skins as media of ex-

[1] E. R. Hewitt and Mary A. Hewitt, "The Bowery," *Half Moon Series,* I, 371 ff.; Jasper Dankers [or Danckaerts] and Peter Sluyter, *Journal of a Voyage to New York, and a Tour in Several of the American Colonies, 1679-1680* (H. C. Murphy, ed., L. I. Hist. Soc., *Memoirs,* I), 44, 47.

change indicates the degree of dependence of the whites upon the redskins.[1] But there was little that was unique in these mutual manifestations of dependence; the Indian wars of New Netherland merely ring the changes on the continent-wide experience of Europeans. With but few exceptions, like that of Crol, they would not try to learn Indian languages, but developed a rude jargon suitable for the elementary needs of trading.

Contact with the Indians had the same demoralizing effect upon Dutchmen as it did upon the Spaniards, Swedes and French. They did not adopt the practice common among the French and Spanish of taking Indian women, with or without marriage ties, as heads of their households. Nevertheless there was a continuous illicit intercourse which affected the formation of society as it did on the English frontiers. The price of a Mohawk squaw's virtue, wrote Domine Megapolensis, was from one to three shillings, "and our Dutchmen run after them very much." [2] It is thus evident that the moral reaction of the Dutch pioneers to New World influences was like that of the English, and less idealistic than that of the French or the Spanish who professed the principle of race amalgamation and the universal acceptance of Christianity.

There were indeed several attempts to Christianize the Indians. Megapolensis tried to learn the Mohawk language for that purpose, but found its construction mystifying. One must smile at the solemn perplexity of

[1] The council of New Amsterdam decried the use of seawant and petitioned the directors in Holland, without much effect, to send them silver. For trading purposes they equated a beaver skin with six guilders and a pound of tobacco with four and a half stivers. See Fernow, *Records of New Amsterdam*, III, 383.

[2] Reverend Johannes Megapolensis, jr., "A Short Account of the Mohawk Indians," Jameson, *Narratives of New Netherland*, 174.

the reverend domine when he asked his dusky teachers by what names things were called. "One tells me the word in the infinitive mood, another in the indicative; one in the first, another in the second person; one in the present, another in the preterite. So I stand oftentimes and look, but do not know how to put it down." He reports of one savage who had been considered redeemed, having learned Dutch prayers, catechism and scripture; but "he took to drinking brandy, he pawned the Bible, and turned into a regular beast, doing more harm than good among the Indians." [1]

At all events the Indians took little stock in the Dutch exemplification of religion. "When we pray they laugh at us. . . . Some, when we tell them what we do when we pray, stand astonished." So, too, they found it hard to reconcile Dutch actions with their spiritual admonitions and decided after prolonged experience that the French "were better Christians than the men of New Netherland." Doubtless the dramatic features of Roman Catholic worship had something, though not everything, to do with this appreciation.

Public education began in New Amsterdam in 1638, shortly after its inception in New England. The first teacher, Adam Roelantsen, was a sorry scapegrace; Jan Cornelissen, who taught ten years, was a seasoned tippler. Six other schoolmasters, of general good repute, taught during the Dutch period, but the profession was apparently not always thought a high one. Everyone was ordered, when Evert Pietersen taught in the governor's bouwerie, not to molest or ridicule him, but "deliver him from every painful sensation." Teachers

[1] E. T. Corwin, ed., *Ecclesiastical Records of the State of New York* (Albany, 1901-1916), I, 398-399.

were licensed by the Classis of Amsterdam and engaged by the company, being considered servants of the church.

Generally in the city and throughout the ten or eleven villages which by the middle of the century were supporting schools, the public teacher was also the reader, the chorister and sexton of the church. The domine and wardens of the parish along with the magistrate supervised his work in the classroom. The latter was in most cases the schoolmaster's own house or at least a house built by the village for his lodging as well as for the school. Here from eight in the morning, except on Sundays and the five general holidays, he taught boys and girls reading and writing, the elements of arithmetic if local commerce had advanced enough to make it in request, and perhaps now and then even a little modern history; provision was made for girls to learn needlework at school as well as at home.

"The knowledge and fear of the Lord" was always stressed as a subject of teaching. Domine John Backerus, writing to Holland for a teacher in 1647, asked particularly for piety. "We must begin with the children," he said, "for many of the older people are so far depraved, that they are now ashamed to learn anything good." For his services the teacher collected a small salary, eked out by tuition fees paid in beaver or bearskins or the like, save from pupils who were poor and needy enough to ask free tuition "for God's sake."[1]

The course ranged from the dame schools, of which there were a few, like that in Flushing where, we read, the mistress in 1683 received "for teaching Martha Johanna, a scarlet petticoat," up to the Latin school.

---

[1] Stokes, *Iconography*, I, 29. There were also evening schools. See Van Laer, *Minutes of the Court of Fort Orange*, I, 238.

The latter was established apparently to keep Dutch boys from having to resort to New England to complete their education. One was set up in 1652, but it lasted only two years. In 1658 the agitation was renewed and the city fathers petitioned the directors in Amsterdam for a competent master to teach their children "the most useful languages, the chief of which is the Latin tongue." A Dr. Alexander Carolus Curtius, who had been a professor in Lithuania, was sent. He got five hundred florins from the directors, two hundred and fifty from the city, overcharged his seventeen or eighteen pupils for supplementary tuition and enlarged his income still further by practising medicine on the side. Under him and his successors the Latin school stood through the rest of the Dutch period and long afterward. The Dutch schools as a whole, indeed, continued like the church to serve their people long after the English had taken control of the colony. Their survival was an indication of that national feeling which found voice in the long retention of the Dutch language. The school of 1638 still continues, being one of the oldest of American elementary schools. And it is probable that the colonial school tradition is in some part responsible for the high rank of New York state in popular education today.[1]

The clergyman, as everywhere in early America, had been the first professional man, the schoolmaster developing as an inferior functionary under his control; the specialized medical doctor and the lawyer were more

[1] W. H. Kilpatrick, *The Dutch Schools of New Netherland and Colonial New York* (U. S. Bur. of Educ., *Bull.*, no. 483), 39-50, 67, 140-141, 188; Van Laer, "Letters of Van Twiller," N. Y. State Hist. Assoc., *Quar. Journ.*, I, 44-50. Cf. Alice M. Earle, *Colonial Days in Old New York* (N. Y., 1899), chap. ii, "Education and Child Life," 14-44; Stokes, *Iconography*, I, 75.

slowly needed. Amateur prescription for the soul, apparently, seemed less adequate than amateur prescription for the body. Yet certain professionals emerged in this department before the first two decades had passed. In 1638 a small house was built at public expense in New Amsterdam for the town midwife,[1] and a university-bred physician was to be found as well. Several other practitioners came, though generally they combined their healing function with other duties as in the case of Dr. Curtius. By the middle of the century, certainly, they could sue in the courts for their fees, as is revealed in an interesting case at Fort Orange. Master Jacob de Hince, the chirurgeon, sued for compensation for treating a wound of Mrs. Thomas Pouwelsen, claiming that his yearly contract with the defendant covered only accidents, whereas this injury, he alleges mysteriously, had been deliberately inflicted.[2]

Litigants in court—and they seem to have been astonishingly numerous—usually handled their own cases, and though some citizens sometimes acted for others as attorneys, there could hardly be said to have been professional lawyers. The one contribution which the Dutch courts and their immediate successors seem to have made was in the use of arbitration as a means of finding justice.[3] Singularly enough, New Netherland, which in most matters displayed a humane policy, seems to have been the only American colony consistently to employ the barbarous device of judicial torture. In 1662 when Reyer Cornelissen denied certain charges of theft,

---

[1] Stokes, *Iconography*, III, 78.
[2] Van Laer, *Minutes of the Court of Fort Orange*, II, 21.
[3] See, for example, van Laer, *Minutes of the Court of Fort Orange*, II, 140, and D. R. Fox, ed., *Minutes of the Court of Sessions, Westchester County* (White Plains, 1924), *passim*.

the court ordered that he should be heard further "after having been subjected to torture." The year before Mesaack Martenzen was "examined by torture as to how many cabbages, fowls, turkeys and how much butter he has stolen, and who his abettors and coöperators have been." What form this torture took we are not informed, but as Martenzen persisted in denying his guilt, it was probably not very severe.[1]

In spite of its autocratic organization and the arbitrary spirit of its governors, New Netherland provided an unfavorable soil for social and economic inequality. By the composition of the company the colony was in fact a bourgeois enterprise; and while the colonists improved in quality and worldly substance as time went on, particularly as agriculture superseded the fur interest, it was not a rich or aristocratic Dutch dependency. An attempt was made in 1657 in New Amsterdam to create a privileged class of "great" burghers: first, those who had been members of the supreme government; second, municipal officers past and present; third, ministers of the gospel; fourth, military officers. "Small" burghers were to be those who were bona fide residents, citizens in fact. When the ordinance was proclaimed only twenty persons presented claims for, or purchased, great-burgher rights, while two hundred became small burghers, the list later increasing. But these distinctions soon broke down, perhaps because the ranks were purchasable. In 1668 any householder might receive all the burgher privileges for fifty guilders. The right persisted in New York until 1815.

Under the English social gradations were really more marked than among the Dutch. During the eigh-

[1] Fernow, *Records of New Amsterdam*, III, 409; IV, 68.

teenth century the official group and the large landholders dominated politics and society. The country
dwellers, many of whom had developed estates of considerable importance, formed a rural gentry of sturdy
integrity, esteemed for their hospitality and public
spirit. Besides abundant food and little intellectual
stimulus, there must have been among the Dutch country folk some of that quaint phlegmatism, naïve philosophy, or apparent inability to see the humor in their
own odd quirks of indecision, which is suggested in more
than one writing on the period—in J. K. Paulding's
*Dutchman's Fireside*, for example. The homely virtues
of the provincials contrasted sharply with the sophisti-
cation of the city dwellers, who admired the airs of
English officialdom and aped imported social practices.[1]

New Netherland architecture went through the same
phases of development as did the modifications of society, and had a lasting influence. Though the house
in the fort on Manhattan built by Peter Minuit was
of stone, it was thatched with reeds, as was the near-by
treasury building. The original thirty bark huts of the
first settlers along the eastern river bank were the work
of quick necessity; indeed, some of the first comers were
obliged to live in pits in the ground or in caves. The
"mean barn" built within the fort for the first church,
with a dwelling and stable for the use of Domine Bogardus, marked more deliberate attention. In 1642 the
contract for the first schoolmaster's house showed further advance. This dwelling was to be thirty feet long
by eighteen wide and eight in height, with the beams

---

[1] Mrs. Schuyler van Rensselaer, *History of the City of New York in the
Seventeenth Century* (N. Y., 1909), I, 422-423, 425; J. K. Paulding,
*The Dutchman's Fireside* (N. Y., 1868), II, 243-246.

square-hewed, the sides tightly clapboarded, the roof reed-thatched and the floor boarded. Two doors, an entry, a pantry, a bed and a stairway to the garret added to the refinements of this early home, which was to cost about one hundred and forty dollars.[1]

When the houses became more elaborate they had brick gable ends set facing the street, with sides of planks; sometimes the bricks were of divers colors, arranged checkerboard fashion. In Albany white-pine shingles or Holland tiles were often used on the roofs, the use of such tiles spreading to New England by the early eighteenth century. Roof gutters projected into the middle of the streets, dripping rain on passers-by. Single story houses had high roofs, making lofts used for storage of food, as in old Holland today, and for other traditional purposes. As they rarely had eaves, the metes and bounds in old conveyances often contained provisions for "free drip." Front doors had top and bottom halves, and opened with latches. They had benches beside them on which the people sat and visited in good weather, receiving the merry greetings of their neighbors. Windows were quite small, frequently being of one or two panes of glass only, or simple apertures protected at option by wood shutters. The stairways were often white-tiled, the material being cheap. Bedsteads were frequently built in, and the people slept between two feather beds; there seem to have been no fire-heated beds. Early chimneys were of wood, lined with a coat of plaster, but as the congestion increased and with it the fire risk, an ordinance was passed in 1653 ordering all such chimneys as well as thatched roofs

[1] J. H. Innes, *New Amsterdam and its People* (N. Y., 1902), 16, 61-67.

and hayricks to be removed from New Amsterdam, a regulation but indifferently enforced.[1]

The farmhouses built about early New Amsterdam had the pleasing concave roof curve which has so strongly influenced modern architecture. Its extension over the front has become the typical American front porch, supported by the columns which its wide overhang made necessary. The gambrel roof, which had such wide vogue in New England, was likewise adapted from the Dutch. The high stoops of New York, derived from the Netherlands idea of having the main entrance on the second floor, led into the best rooms, which were set high so as to be dry when the ground floor might be damp.[2] Venerable houses, such as the Van Cortlandt mansion at Croton, illustrate the old design today.

New Netherland was the first American scene of sleighing, skating and coasting. The burghers skated to market. "It is admirable," wrote a visiting English clergyman in 1678, "to see Men and Women, as it were, flying upon their Skates from place to place with Markets [market baskets] on their Heads and Backs."[3] The children of Albany had to be restrained by law from endangering elderly limbs with their sleds. Ice carnivals, once unique on the Collect Pond, find their

[1] Stokes, *Iconography*, I, 29, 67. At the same time the city purchased 150 leather buckets for fire fighting. See A. E. Peterson and G. W. Edwards, *New York as an Eighteenth Century Municipality* (Columbia Univ., *Studies*, LXXV), 169-181.

[2] Emma van Vechten, "Early Schools and Schoolmasters of New Amsterdam," *Half Moon Series*, II, 324; Peter Kalm, "Travels into North America," John Pinkerton, ed., *Voyages and Travels* (London, 1808-1814), XIII, 452, 456-457. See also Earle, *Colonial Days in Old New York*, 98-127; Helen E. Smith, *Colonial Days and Ways* (N. Y., 1900), 93-101.

[3] Quoted in Eunice F. Barnard, "New York Still Has Dutch Habits," *N. Y. Times*, July 4, 1926.

modern counterparts in many American municipal parks.
Hockey and skate racing were popular, players and
watchers fortifying themselves against the cold by heartening nips of liquors sold at booths on the ice. Sleighing gave opportunity for colonial speed-limit breakers,
who rode several miles out to the Bowery to feast at
the resorts there.

In early summer the Long Islanders of 1670 "rushed
violently into the fields" to gather the ripe strawberries
which dyed the ground red with their profusion. Pic-
nics and boating parties were common. Later, at Albany,
the young people, mostly Dutch, had organizations
known as "companies" which made hunting and fishing excursions into the country. These were rather exclusive cliques within which the young people found
their whole enjoyment and traditionally married. In
the eighteenth century New Yorkers went for fish dinners to an inn on Brooklyn Heights, or went to eat
turtle on East River, the gentlemen appropriately sa-
luting their partners on Kissing Bridge as they returned.
Lovers rowed over to Brooklyn for parties under a famous tulip tree near the ferry. Callers on friends were
often hospitably invited to "take a syllabub with them,"
the confection being a mixture of cream or milk beaten
to a froth with wine or cider.

Calvinism in the Netherlands, old or new, was never
an enemy to innocent amusement as it was sometimes
among the English Puritans. Certainly there was no
lack of fun in those communities along the Hudson
River and on the near-by islands. The maypole, of im-
memorial antiquity, came with the baggage of European
civilization nearly everywhere; here it was set up without encountering the suspicions which it met at Merry

Mount in Massachusetts Bay.[1] At Shrovetide, the old feast of Bacchus, the Dutch farm boys pulled the goose; this was "a pagan and a popish feast . . . looked at through the fingers" in the Netherlands, and, because of its accompanying dissipation, at last rigorously forbidden by Stuyvesant. The boys greased a live goose thoroughly and suspended it between two poles; the test was to catch and hold it while riding by at full tilt.[2] There were contests in marksmanship here as elsewhere, particularly the shooting at the popinjay, a bird hung by the feet to a pole. A keen shot that severed the head from the body was, it seems, rewarded with the first prize while one which merely splintered off a feather got the least.[3]

Other sports had no such element of cruelty. Golf, the name of which is said to have been derived from *kolf,* the Dutch word for club, was an importation from the old country. Clumsy the implements doubtless were, but the ball must have been driven with dangerous force, for the principal towns forbade the game within the closely settled areas.[4] Bowling, we are bound to believe, whiled away the time of Rip Van Winkle's elves, and the great popularity of the game extended later into the English period. There was not as much card playing as in the other American colonies excepting New

---

[1] Wertenbaker, *The First Americans,* 277-278.

[2] *Documents Relating to the History of the Early Colonial Settlements* (*Documents Relative to the History of New York,* XIV), 249. The "popish" variant of this sport in colonial California was to bury a live chicken in the sand leaving the head only protruding, the riders trying to seize the fowl by the neck while galloping past.

[3] Van Laer, *Minutes of the Court of Fort Orange,* I, 220, Hamlin Garland gives the primitive Wisconsin variation of this sport in his chapter, "The Turkey Shoot," in *Trail-makers of the Middle Border* (N. Y., 1926).

[4] Van Laer, *Minutes of the Court of Fort Orange,* II, 234.

England. A favorite evening game was a species of back-gammon called tick-tack; if one touched his man he must complete his game, hence the name, which meant touch and take. Trock, the name of which came from the Spanish *troco*, to exchange, was played at a table by driving an ivory ball under a wicket with a cue. It was also played upon the lawn, thus joining in the ancestry of the modern game of croquet.

Reading did not figure largely among the diversions as far as the record goes; we know little of the importation of books, and there was, of course, no printing in the little province. The writing of the citizens themselves was confined to a few political letters, some histories and descriptions of the province and a very few adventures into *belles-lettres*. Jacob Steendam, clerk of the company and sea-wanderer, lived some years in the colony, writing verses of rather middling merit, but fresh with the aspirations of New World life.

There were festival customs, too, which entered permanently into the round of American life. Our use of Easter eggs is as Dutch as our Santa Claus; indeed, St. Nicholas was the patron saint of New Amsterdam, and the children set out their shoes in true Latin fashion on December sixth to receive his gifts, gradually shifting the observance to Christmas Eve. New Year's calls, now fallen into disuse, began, as far as America is concerned, in these settlements of New Netherland. The celebration was as vivacious, noisy and alcoholic as our modern Saturnalia on the same occasion, though nowadays we frown on the firing of guns in the public street.[1]

[1] Fernow, *Records of New Amsterdam*, VII, 262. On feasts and fasts in New Netherland, see W. D. Love, *The Fast and Thanksgiving Days of New England* (Boston, 1895), chap. xii.

The slaves' own frolic was "Pinkster" (Pentecost) Day on Whitsunday. Its most famous celebrations were at Albany on Capitol (then called Pinkster) Hill where criminals were hung. The Negroes kept up the fun for a week, dancing, eating gingerbread and drinking in honor of their legendary "Old King Charley." They used cast-off finery to bedeck themselves and consumed so much liquor that the bacchanalia had finally to be suppressed. On Long Island the festival was observed by whites as well as blacks; in parts of Pennsylvania and Maryland, usually by the Negroes only. It was perhaps a corruption of some Dark Continent land-distribution ceremonial; from its description it seems to have analogies to certain American Indian festivals. Vestiges of the tradition subsisted among rural New Yorkers long after the name of the feast and the Negro custom had been forgotten.[1]

In 1659 the New Netherlanders began the celebration of the Low Countries *kermis,* an annual trade festival at which fat cattle and the produce of the farm were offered for sale along with the products of the handicraft of the housewives. It was held near the church and had religious associations as in the Netherlands, where it marked the observance of the day of the saint of the chief church in the town. In this respect the Dutch kermis was almost the exact counterpart of the annual fair observed for centuries since 1623 in Mexico by the Indians of San Juan de los Lagos and elsewhere. The Dutch made it a time of rejoicing, continuing the buying and selling for six weeks without interfering with the weekly market day. The first celebration was held on the parade ground, which came

[1] Earle, *Colonial Days in Old New York,* 184-209.

to be known as the Marck Velt; but the horseplay indulged in by country boors brought the event into such
disrepute that all the boisterous features of the institution were stopped and the event transferred to the town
common.[1] In many parts of the United States the word
kermis survives to designate a church bazaar or other
similar social function at which homemade articles are
sold for the support of popular charities.

The trading privileges conceded by the company
helped to spread Dutch influences along the Atlantic
Coast despite the official resistance of the English. This
influence, for instance, was shown by the distribution of
furniture and household effects. Card tables, Dutch fold-
ing tables, Spanish tables and leather-covered brass-
nailed chairs, called "Cromwell chairs," were imported
into Virginia, either directly or through England. The
Southern Atlantic colonies imported darnick or "silk
dornex," a coarse table damask, from their thrifty neighbors. Francis Daniel Pastorius, founder of Germantown,
Pennsylvania, had Dutch books worth £11, and Governor Gordon of that colony, fond of Dutch paintings,
prided himself on landskips of Low Country origin.[2]
Flanders bedticks and Ghentish sheeting were gifts of
Benjamin Franklin to his wife. Leyden and New

[1] Mrs. J. K. van Rensselaer, The Goede Vrouw of Mana-ha-ta (N. Y.,
1898), 78-80; Sociedad Mexicana de Geografía y Estadística, Boletín,
VI, 310-311. There were special fairs decreed, as under Kieft, the cattle
fair October 15 and the hog fair November 1. E. B. O'Callaghan, Laws
and Ordinances of New Netherland (Albany, 1868), 29. See also, T. F.
De Voe, The Market Book (N. Y., 1862), I, 38.

[2] The famous Rembrandt, "The Lesson in Anatomy," now in the
Mauritshuis at The Hague, has an interesting though indirect relation with
New Netherland history in that the central figure of the painting is that
Dr. Claes Petersz before whom the colonists who came in 1624 took their
oaths. A. J. F. van Laer, ed., Documents Relating to New Netherland,
1624-1626, in the Henry E. Huntington Library (Henry E. Huntington
Library, Publs. Americana, no. 1), 256.

Amsterdam provided New England with rush-bottomed green chairs such as the Pilgrims had brought from the place of their Dutch sojourn.

The period after 1656 showed the evolution of luxury among well-to-do merchants of New Amsterdam, their lists of household effects making evident the changes which society underwent. By 1674, when Fort Orange finally became English,[1] ninety-four citizens were worth over one thousand guilders, and twenty-two had between five and ten thousand guilders each. In 1686 Cornelis Steenwyck, opulent when New Netherland fell, died worth £15,930. Visitors like the famous Labadist voyagers, Danckaerts and Sluyter, could be received in a kermis bed built like a huge box, ceiling high, in the corner "alongside of a good fire." Warming pans of copper or brass, Spanish leather stools, Turkey-work and Oriental goods found their places with pictures and the inevitable *kas* or *kos,* a huge wardrobe of plain but substantial build, oftentimes decorated with brightly painted flowers.

The New Netherland *Doten-Kammer* was a room in some houses which was always closed until a funeral occasion caused it to be opened for ceremonial grief. Delftware, founded upon Japanese models, came among the earliest forms of imported pottery, replacing pewter; it was traded across the Connecticut border at an early date for farm produce. The coarser "blew and white" was not highly esteemed by the Dutch, though it became common by the latter part of the seventeenth century and many rare pieces survive in homes along the Hudson and on Long Island. Dutch silversmiths pro-

[1] It will be remembered that in 1673 New York was recaptured by the Dutch; the following year, by the Treaty of Westminster, it was restored to the English.

*Oloff Stevense van Cortlandt, a merchant of New Netherland.*

duced attractive pieces, but chiefly in the later period of
English rule. Looking-glasses and framed pictures were
objects of interest and envy by the middle of the century. After 1660 they were in common use, in small
olivewood frames, replaced by oak in the eighteenth
century. There were few paintings produced in the
little colony, quite naturally, though the creditable por-
trait of Peter Stuyvesant, now hanging in the rooms of
the New York Historical Society, is thought to have been
done in New Amsterdam by Hendrick Coutourier.

In 1695 New York contained three thousand families, half of whom were Dutch, with many English
and some French inhabitants. The Reverend John Miller
said that they were divided in religion, a few of them
intelligent and sincere, but the most part ignorant, con-
ceited and fickle. The Dutch were "rich and sparing,"
the English "neither very rich nor too great husbands,"
while the French were "poor, and therefore penurious."

New Netherland as a Dutch enterprise was out of the
reckoning before the real English battle with France
began. The Peace of Westphalia, concluding the Dutch
struggle against Spain, also closed the chief fields of
enterprise to the West India Company. It was even then
in turbulent financial waters and, after the adjustment
with Spain, was never able to recuperate its financial
status. Thus when the need of an effectual colonization
policy had finally been driven home by the New Netherland settlers it had no funds for expansion. A new
danger now appeared. With Spain reduced to impotence
on the sea there arose the vital matter of English trade
ambitions. While England was weak on the seas the
Dutch and the French had had their opportunity; but
when English merchants saw the long lines of Dutch

ships anchored on the Thames for the English carrying trade, it was time to pass navigation acts, measures which forgot old alliances and ties of blood, religion and politics. Only four short years after her success against Spain, Holland had to take up a struggle with England which ended in colonial disaster.

England's early and incessant protests against Dutch intrusion in the area of the plantations were prophetic of her yet unconscious aim. In the uncertain status of international right of those days the better claim to the territory belonged to the Netherlands; a constructive policy might have made the right secure. But the critical period was wasted in fruitless efforts in Brazil and, when that episode ended, the die was cast by the rapidly increasing population of the English settlements. Early protest was followed by armed action in 1635 when the Virginians took Fort Nassau on the Delaware, though Van Twiller retook it without difficulty. Previously, in 1633, the English ship *William* had flouted the authority of "Wouter the Doubter" by sailing up to Rensselaerswyck and asserting the English right to the territory.[1]

Military hostility was, in such trifling episodes, much less effective than the steady stream of settlers pouring in from the English colonies. It was inspired by authority. "Doe not forbeare to put forward their plantations," urged Sir William Boswell upon the governor of Connecticut in 1642, "and crowd on, crowding the Dutch out of those places where they have occupied, but without hostility or any act of violence." Such urging was needless as the policy was already established. Religious

---

[1] David de Vries, "From the 'Korte Historiael,' " Jameson, *Narratives of New Netherland*, 188, 195.

liberty and easy terms of land tenure were the direct attractions. Similarity of blood, previous contacts in Europe during the Puritan migration, practical identity of religious faith, were all influences which encouraged rather than checked English aggressions. The men of Connecticut were willing to "enter into an agreement and to make a yearly acknowledgment or an absolute purchase, which is indeed proof positive that our right was well known to them." The English would call upon the Dutch and use them in time of need, "but when that is past, they no longer regard them but play the fool with them." In 1640 the men of Hartford seized the company's farm at Fort Good Hope on the Connecticut, belabored the colonists with sticks and clubs and threw their tools into the river.

By 1650 thirty English villages lay between Cape Cod and Stamford, half of the area claimed by New Netherland then having been occupied. The same process had gone on elsewhere, on the Delaware and on Long Island. In September, 1663, Stuyvesant tried, as he had in 1650, to obtain a firm boundary agreement with the commissioners of the United Colonies of New England; his envoys tried again in October before the general assembly of Connecticut. Meantime discontent had been shaking the company's rule; possibly the fall of the colony in 1664 had Dutch support from within, though conclusive proof is not available.[1]

The two peoples had, indeed, preserved mutual amen-

[1] Intro. to "Description of the Towne of Mannadens," Jameson, *Narratives of New Netherland*, 419-420; *cf.* J. W. Redway, "Some Side-Lights on the Passing of New Netherland viewed from Westchester County," N. Y. State Hist. Assoc., *Proceeds.*, IX, 152-159; Adriaen van der Donck and ten others, "The Representation of New Netherland," Jameson, *Narratives of New Netherland*, 305 ff.; W. R. Shepherd, *The Story of New Amsterdam* (N. Y., 1917), 93-100.

ities during their close contacts. There were plenty of Dutch wives of Englishmen. Captain Underhill it was who brought to a decisive end Kieft's unrighteous Indian war. Stuyvesant favored admitting the English to responsible government positions, and the company welcomed them, so that the Dutch had not much complaint against the logic of events whatever they may have thought of the policies of the fatherland.

Finally, in reviewing the Dutch episode in America, we must ask ourselves what were its real and lasting values. Some forty years of effective occupation by not more than ten thousand people at the maximum would seem but a tiny eddy in the current of human endeavor sweeping on to the conquest of the continent. In the matter of territorial expansion and the subjugation of the forces of nature the Dutch performance was meager and progressively restricted. In the transmission of governmental institutions they were on the losing side as society swung from autocracy to democracy. In the art and literature of colonial times or the present day their contribution has not been significant; with a few notable exceptions even their history has been written by persons in whom other blood predominated. In disseminating the artifacts of European civilization they performed the carrier's part, initiating little and estab-

---

[1] The influence of New Netherland upon the life of American institutions is discussed by Douglas Campbell, *The Puritan in England, Holland and America* (N. Y., 1892), but most of his claims are refuted by H. T. Colenbrander, "The Dutch Element in American History," Am. Hist. Assoc., *Ann. Rep. for 1909*, 198 ff. "It is impossible to deny that the characteristics which have become typical of the political and social life of America have for the most part produced themselves at an earlier date and in a higher degree in the English colonies than in New Netherland." The people of New Amsterdam complained in 1649 to the States General, "asking for civil rights that were enjoyed by their neighbors in New England, where, as they expressed it, the word "patroon," "lord" or "Prince" is not heard, and the people "is all in all."

lishing no widely spread permanent adoptions. In education and religion they left a creditable tradition and an admirable, though conservative, institution.

In social customs they made their most profound impression because their practices elicited interest and sympathy as those of a closely related people. In our internal life their value lies in those traits which gave this country a stable, conservative element which, however much imbued with the "feeling of kind" almost to clannishness, was yet so tolerant of other men. Their city harbored, with eighteen languages spoken and many sects present, a most cosmopolitan society in an age when the bigotry of Old World religiosity was still the binding tie in most New World transplantations. That spirit of tolerance and world-mindedness has yielded rich results in welding the nation into unity. The genuine sons of New York are, in much the same spirit as Californians and Texans, prone to indulge themselves in what may be smiled at as egocentric interpretations of history. There are even other parts of the United States, where the present inhabitants share little in the blood, language or traditions of the first alien settlers, in which the people are obsessed with the old Hebraic idea that a perfect society is one in which the chosen few hold fast all that is good against a great outer darkness. That is the great American illusion, the sure mark of immanent provincialism. When we rid ourselves of the fatuous notion of a providence, divine or otherwise, which bestows special favors on any race or people, we attain a dignified, self-reliant realization that there is no guarantee or promise of grandeur or permanence for any

[1] Cf. J. R. Brodhead, *History of the State of New York* (N. Y., 1871-1872), I, 36.

nation or its institutions save in its own creative force.)

We think that man as a social being has existed for some half-million years; we know but partially his doings for six or seven thousand only. Within the last four hundred lie the most significant social developments. These have all been concomitants of the unification of the world which began with the coming of the white man to America. Then began that movement of populations and numerical increase which have seemingly brought us today to the end of an epoch. We have arrived at the sobering realization that movement from continent to continent, migration for economic or political betterment, has about reached its limits of safety. The white man, who without invitation seized and subjected the whole New World, now holds up in our land restraining hands to check the hitherward alien flow; our northern and southern neighbors show determination to assert like policies. We think of saturation points in colonization, in commerce, in populations; of checking the increasing demands upon the feeding power of the earth. We notice with apprehension the rising spirit of nationality among dependent and exploited peoples; we contemplate the possible end of white domination—or the substitution of a more self-contained development of mankind through modification of exploitative aims and the effort of society to take a hand in the conscious control of its destiny. We stand at a moment when America, with the new responsibility of economic ascendancy emerging from the struggle of the colonizing nations of Europe for a place in the sun, holds control of the directive force of civilization. With what seeds of destiny were freighted the tiny holds of the *Niña*, the *Pinta* and the *Santa Maria!*

# CHAPTER XIII

## CRITICAL ESSAY ON AUTHORITIES

### PHYSICAL SURVIVALS

NONDOCUMENTARY records recalling the settlement of North America by the Spaniards, the French and the Dutch are so abundant that only the more important remains can be mentioned here. This is especially true of the former Spanish areas. In old Mexico hundreds of houses are still in active use which were built in colonial times, many of them dating from the sixteenth century, as in certain sections of Mexico City. Many roads and bridges still survive, with little subsequent restoration. Several of the public buildings, notably the Cathedral of Mexico, are products of more than one century of construction. The same old mines and farms are frequently worked, often with the same primitive implements side by side with modern improvements. The costumes of many of the humbler classes are not far removed from those of colonial times, though there has been marked change since the passing of Porfirio Díaz. The former white suit of the peasant has unhappily given way to the cheaper and more durable denim of American manufacture. The old-time hat, in many variations, survives even in some urban centers. Assorted relics of former days are best preserved and seen in the Museo Nacional in the capital, and there are numerous paintings from the colonial epoch in the Academia de San Carlos. The former Mining School preserves some of the old implements. In the Biblioteca Nacional are thousands of ancient tomes in colonial vellum, while provincial libraries, as that at Guadalajara, preserve thousands more.

Within our borders architectural remains abound in the old Franciscan missions along the Camino Real in California. Elsewhere, as at Monterey, there are numerous old buildings plainly labeled for the ubiquitous tourist or the seeker for historical monuments. The Camino itself is marked with small bronze bells. In the California missions are preserved examples of Spanish and Indian painting, with occasional samples of the native handicrafts as taught by the mission fathers; the collection at Santa Barbara Mission is exceptionally good. The Glenwood Mission Inn at Riverside, California, is well known for its collection of mission bells and its Spanish and Mexican art objects, many of which are antique. The Southwest Museum at Los Angeles contains the San Gabriel Mission records and the C. F. Lummis collection from the Southwest, including many Spanish and Indian folk songs. There are more objects at the Henry E. Huntington Library at San Marino; in the Coliseum in Los Angeles is the Coronel Collection of costumes and artifacts. The Oakland Public Museum and the De Young Memorial Museum in Golden Gate Park contain many memorials of Spanish and Mexican days; Stanford Museum at Palo Alto contains others. Picture material for Spanish and Mexican California is included in O. C. Coy, comp., *Pictorial History of California* (Berkeley, 1925). The influence of California Spanish architecture is seen in Rexford Newcomb, *The Old Mission Churches and Historic Houses of California* (Phila., 1925). Mission records and old vellum choir books may be seen in several places, as at the Bancroft Library at the University of California, Berkeley, the principal storehouse of documentary material on Spanish and Mexican California.

The Spanish influence pervades Texas in much the same manner. The Álamo at San Antonio preserves the memory of pioneer heroism and the flavor of Spain in numerous objects of apparel and domestic use. The city itself is almost Latin in architecture. The Franciscan missions of the vicinity present a variant from the architecture used in California. Similar mementos of the past, dating from the former occupation, are found in El Paso and other Texan towns. The University of Arizona Museum at Tucson contains relics of the Spaniards and figures showing costumes of Mexicans. In Albuquerque and Santa Fé, New Mexico, the mementos of Spain and Mexico are seen and there, as elsewhere in the

Southwest, a large element of the population preserves the language and tradition of their predecessors.

In New Orleans, where the French influence and spirit are strong, one may still see a portion of the old Spanish *cabildo* or town hall, built in 1795, and, among other monuments, the church erected by Don Pedro Almonester. Spanish names of streets help to flavor the more dominant French influence as shown in language, family estates and family pride. One may see the colonial architecture portrayed in W. P. Spratling and N. Scott, *Old Plantation Houses in Louisiana* (N. Y., 1928). In Florida the remains are more scant. The modern so-called "Spanish architecture" is not colonial; it is an innovation from American influence. The Spanish silver coins, once widely used throughout all the white man's conquests on the continent, especially the Spanish peso, godmother of the American dollar, are so widely distributed that they have scarcely appreciated in value.

French survivals are most abundant in Canada. The Museum of the Natural History Association at Chatham, New Brunswick, has relics of the early French occupation. At St. John the museum contains a series of model dwellings illustrating Indian, French and colonial periods. The Numismatic and Antiquarian Society of Montreal, at the museum in Château de Ramesay, has historical specimens, including a room as occupied by a habitant with the furniture of the French time. As a guide to certain historic remains one should consult *Vieux Manoirs Vieilles Maisons: publié par la Commission des Monuments Historiques de la Province de Québec* (Quebec, 1927). A row of stone houses on Huguenot Street, New Paltz, New York, built by French immigrants early in the eighteenth century, is still standing.

The Dutch tradition is highly prized in New York. The State Museum has an historical department devoted to the various cultures. At Amsterdam the County Historical Society preserves rare colonial furniture in a baronial mansion built in 1742. In the Brooklyn Children's Museum pictures and dolls illustrate colonial costumes and there are reproductions of houses and furniture of the colonial era. There are documents and relics of similar character in the history department of the Staten Island Association of Arts and Sciences at New Brighton, while the College of the City of New York also has a collection of historical interest. There are paintings, furniture and other relics of Dutch influence in the buildings of the New York Historical Society and the Albany Institute. The Schuyler House at Albany has material of Dutch as well as English-colonial origin. The Van Cortlandt Manor, the Dyckman and the Ditmars houses, and others in various parts of the metropolis, though dating after the Dutch period, are representative of the older influence.

R. T. H. Halsey and C. O. Cornelius, *A Handbook of the American Wing* [Metropolitan Museum of Art] (N. Y., 1926), gives an account of the presence and influence of *k'ang-hsi* porcelains (used as models by colonial silver-smiths) and, among other items, of seventeenth-century painting. One may pursue these interests farther in a multitude of books, among which and not mentioned in the text of this volume are R. T. H. Halsey and E. Tower, *The Homes of our Ancestors* (Garden City, 1925), and C. Louise Avery, *American Silver of the Seventeenth and Eighteenth Centuries* (N. Y., 1920). A number of volumes issued from time to time by the New York City History Club should also be consulted. These began with M. W. Goodwin and others, eds., *Half Moon Series* (N. Y., 1897-1899); and the latest is A. E. Peterson, ed., *Landmarks of New York* (N. Y., 1923), in which the casual visitor may find his way rapidly amid the multiplied reminders of the colonial period. T. E. Tallmadge, *The Story of Architecture in America* (N. Y., 1927), is helpful toward an understanding of the remains in each of the four chief colonial areas.

The multiplicity of foreign influences which even in the colonial time helped to form the composite of American society is epitomized in the curious way in which we have adopted and use the words, porch, verandah, piazza, stoop, portico, patio, gallery and even rotunda, to indicate that part of the home which is dedicated to almost identical domestic uses in a variety of architectural designs. All the colonial influences may be seen pictorially preserved in R. H. Gabriel, ed., *The Pageant of America* (15 vols., twelve having been published, New Haven, 1926-    ). R. G. Adams, *The Gateway to American History* (N. Y., 1927), has reproductions of drawings representing sixteenth and seventeenth-century European conceptions of American scenes.

## NEW SPAIN

### BIBLIOGRAPHIES

Numerous bibliographies of Spanish-American historical literature list a wide range of items referring to social life. The interested reader will find the standard contemporary writers listed in F. Weber, *Beiträge zur Charakteristik der älteren Geschichtsschreiber über Spanisch-Amerika* (Leipzig, 1911), and in José Toribio Medina, *Biblioteca Hispano-Americana, 1493-1810* (7 vols., Santiago, 1898-1907), VI, "Prólogo," sección iii, pp. cxi-cxx. C. K. Jones of the Library of Congress translated Medina's "Advertencia sobre las Obras de Bibliografía Hispano-Americana" as "Critical Notes on Sources," and published them in the supplement of his "Hispanic American Bibliographies," *Hisp. Am. Hist. Rev.*, III, nos. 2 and 4, and IV, nos. 1-4 (reprinted, Baltimore, 1922). The section referring to Mexico includes 232 items which cover essential lists to his date of issue. An inclusive list of Spanish Americana is the recent A. Palau y Dulcet, *Manual del Librero Hispano-Americano* (7 vols., Barcelona, 1923-1927).

A useful survey of the literature of the viceroyalty of New Spain, 1539 to 1800, may be obtained from Joaquin Garcia Icazbalceta, *Bibliografía Mexicana del Siglo XVI . . . de 1539 a 1600* (Mexico, 1886), adding Vicente de Paula Andrade, *Ensayo Bibliográfico Mexicano del Siglo XVII* (2d edn., Mexico, 1889), and Nicolás León, *Bibliografía Mexicana del Siglo XVIII* (5 vols., Mexico, 1902-1908). There is a partial list in the United States War Department Library, *Index to Publications, Articles, and Maps Relating to Mexico* in its *Subject Catalogue*, no. 3 (Wash., 1896); another is by the New York Public Library, "List of Works . . . Relating to Mexico" in its *Bull.*, XIII, 622-662

737. See also the extensive lists in the first volumes of H. H. Bancroft, *History of Central America* (3 vols., San Francisco, 1882-1887); *History of Mexico* (6 vols., San Francisco, 1883-1887); and the following volumes of his *History of the Pacific States* (34 vols., San Francisco, 1882-1890): *California* (XIII-XIX); *North Mexican States and Texas* (X-XI); and *Arizona and New Mexico* (XII).

From the Biblioteca Nacional of Mexico comes José M. Vigil, *Catálogos de la Biblioteca Nacional* (9 vols., Mexico, 1889; supplements, 1893, 1895, 1897); its *Catálogo especial de las Obras Mexicanas o sobre México* (Mexico, 1911) lists also manuscripts in the collection. José Toribio Medina, *La Imprenta en México 1539-1821* (8 vols., Santiago, 1907-1912), is supplemented by his *La Imprenta en Guadalajara* (1904), . . . *Oaxaca* (1904), . . . *Vera Cruz* (1904), . . . *Mérida* (1904), and *Puebla* (1908). His *Guatemala* (1910) and *Habana* (1904) amplify the showing for North American presses.

John Carter Brown Library, *Catalogue of Books Relating to North and South America* (2 vols., Providence, 1875, 1882), with the later volumes, *Biblioteca Americana; Catalogue of the . . . Library* (4 vols., Providence, 1919-1921), including only books printed prior to 1800, lists valuable Mexicana. Justin Winsor, ed., *Narrative and Critical History of America* (8 vols., Boston, 1884-1889), presents Spanish-American items in vols. ii and viii down to 1886. J. N. Larned, ed., *Literature of American History, a Bibliographical Guide* (Boston, 1902), is supplemented by E. C. Richardson and A. E. Morse, *Writings on American History* (Princeton, 1904), and A. C. McLaughlin, same title (Wash., 1905). Since 1906 Grace G. Griffin continues this publication annually (Washington), indicating partially the vast Southern output. H. Keniston, *List of Works for the Study of Hispanic American History* (N. Y., 1920), has a good selection.

Current publication in the general fields of the history and geography of New Spain may be followed in A. H. Petermann, *Mitteilungen aus Justus Perthes' Geographischer Anstalt* (Gotha, 1855-    ), and H. Wagner, *Geographisches Jahrbuch* (Gotha, 1866-    ). Current reviews appear in

*Revista de Archivos, Bibliotecas, y Museos* (Madrid, 1871-
), the *Revue de l'Histoire des Colonies Françaises* (Paris,
1913-    ), and the *Boletín* of the Real Academia de la
Historia (Madrid, 1877-    ). One must also consult the
*American Historical Review* (N. Y., 1896-    ), the *New
Mexico Historical Review* (Santa Fé, 1926-    ), and the
*Hispanic American Historical Review* (Baltimore and Durham, 1918-    ). In Mexico City, *El Libro y el Pueblo*
(1922-    ), by the Secretariat of Education, and *Biblos,*
by the Biblioteca Nacional, contain notices of current items.

Topical surveys with applied bibliographical notes are
found in W. W. Pierson, *Hispanic American History, a
Syllabus* (Univ. of N. C., Chapel Hill, 1926), and J. L.
Mecham, *A Syllabus of Hispanic American History* (N. Y.,
1924). W. S. Robertson, *History of the Latin American
Nations* (N. Y., 1922), has topical references for his chapters; similar aids are in H. I. Priestley, *The Mexican Nation,
a History* (N. Y., 1923), and his *Modern Mexican History
Syllabus* (N. Y., 1920; *Supplement,* 1925).

## SOURCES IN PRINT

Among general collections of printed sources dealing with
social institutions should be mentioned M. F. Navarrete, ed.,
*Colección de los Viajes y Descubrimientos* (5 vols., Madrid,
1825-1837). The *Colección de Documentos Inéditos para la
Historia de España* (112 vols., Madrid, 1842-1895; index
by G. P. Winship in Boston Public Library, *Bull.* XIII, 250-
263) has some material. The so-called Pacheco y Cárdenas,
eds., *Colección de Documentos Inéditos relativos al Descubrimiento Conquista y Organización de las antiguas Posesiones
Españolas de América y Oceanía* (42 vols., Madrid, Real
Academia de Historia, 1864-1884), has a chronological table
of contents in vol. xxxiii. For its use B. M. Read, *Chronological Index* (Albuquerque, 1914), provides substantial assistance; material of great value to 1796 is included. The
continuation, *Colección de Documentos Inéditos . . . de
Ultramar* (ser. 2, 19 vols., Madrid, 1885-1926), has a
topical arrangement. The *Colección de Libros y Documentos*

*referentes a la Historia de América* (20 vols., Madrid, 1904-1925), the *Nueva Colección de Documentos Inéditos para la Historia de España y de sus Indias* (6 vols., Madrid, 1892-1896), and the *Colección de Libros Raros y Curiosos que tratan de América* (21 vols., Madrid, 1891-1912), present unexhausted sources. Cía. Gral. de Tabacos de Filipinas, eds., *Colección General de Documentos relativos a las Islas Filipinas.* (5 vols., Barcelona, 1918-        ), includes important New Spain materials. H. Terneaux-Compans, *Voyages, Relations, et Mémoires Originaux pour servir à l'Histoire de la Découverte de l'Amérique* (20 vols., Paris, 1837-1841), contains valuable materials badly translated; the same may be said of a number of collections of voyages, *e.g.*, those published by A. Churchill, W. Dampier, R. Kerr, J. Pinkerton and A. F. Prévost.

Sets of documents especially on New Spain include F. J. Hernáez, *Colección de Bulas, Breves, y otros documentos relativos a la Iglesia de América y Filipinas* (2 vols., Brussels, 1879). Further sources for church history are in F. H. Vera, ed., *Colección de Documentos Eclesiásticos de México, o sea Antigua y Moderna Legislación de la Iglesia Mexicana* (3 vols., Amecameca, 1887), and the *Colección Eclesiástica Mejicana* (4 vols., Mexico, 1834). See also L. Garcia Pimentel, ed., *Documentos Históricos de Méjico: I, Descripción del Arzobispado de México* (Mexico, 1887); II, *Relación de los Obispados de Tlaxcala, Michoacan, Oaxaca, y otros Lugares en el Siglo XVI* (1904). The *Archivo Mexicano: Documentos para la Historia de México* (2 vols., Mexico, 1852-1853) has *residencia* materials of prime value. The *Documentos para la Historia de México* (19 vols. in 17, Mexico, 1853-1857) pertains to the Northwestern provinces. It was indexed by G. García, "Índice Alfabético de los 'Documentos . . . ' publicados . . . por . . . Orozco y Berra," *Anales del Museo Nacional,* ser. 2, III (Mexico, 1906), 523-540. G. García and C. Pereyra, eds., *Documentos Inéditos o muy raros para la Historia de México* (35 vols., Mexico, 1905-        ), has in certain volumes rich colonial materials. J. García Icazbalceta, ed., *Colección de Documentos para la Historia de México* (2 vols., Mexico, 1858-1866), like his

*Nueva Colección de Documentos* (5 vols., Mexico, 1886-1892), deals largely with primitive Mexico, Indian society and the labors of the early Franciscans. J. E. Hernández y Dávalos, *Colección de Documentos para la Historia de la Guerra de Independencia* (6 vols., Mexico, 1877-1882), indexed by G. García in *Anales del Museo,* ser. 2, IV (1907), 225-305, is complemented by García's *Documentos Históricos Mexicanos, Obra Conmemorativa del Primer Centenario de la Independencia de México* (7 vols., Mexico, 1910-1912). A. Peñafiel, ed., *Colección de Documentos para la Historia Mexicana* (6 vols., Mexico, 1897-1903), is devoted to Mexican antiquities, on which the editor wrote profusely in other works.

## MANUSCRIPT SOURCES

The unpublished documentation for the social history of Mexico is only partially listed. A survey of the Mexican archives is H. E. Bolton, *Guide to Materials for the History of the United States in the Principal Archives of Mexico* (Wash., 1913). C. E. Chapman, *Catalogue of Materials in the Archivo General de Indias for the History of the Pacific Coast and the American Southwest* (Univ. of Calif., *Publs. in Hist.,* VIII, 1919), concerns chiefly the movement into California. R. R. Hill, *Descriptive Catalogue of the Documents Relating to the History of the United States in the Papeles Procedentes de Cuba* (Wash., 1916), and W. R. Shepherd, *Guide to the Materials for the History of the United States in the Spanish Archives* (Wash., 1907), combine with J. A. Robertson, *List of Documents in Spanish Archives Relating to the History of the United States which have been Printed or of which Transcripts are Preserved in American Libraries* (Wash., 1910), to present available materials on Mexican history. Thousands of new documents are continually being received in this country, and those printed are rapidly increasing in number. The Library of Congress has in hand the project of forming a list of them. The work of P. Torres Lanzas, *Independencia de América: Fuentes para su Estudio* (Madrid, 1912), is supplemented currently by *Catálogos* of archive contents in the

*Boletín* of the Centro de Estudios Americanistas (Seville, 1913-    ).

## LEGISLATIVE DOCUMENTS

The published laws offer bountiful material for the study of social life. The *Recopilación de Leyes de los Reinos de las Indias* (Madrid, 1681) went through numerous editions until 1841. Among Mexican collections are Vasco de Puga, *Provisiones, Cédulas, Instrucciones de su Magestad . . . desde el año 1525 hasta . . . 1563* (Mexico, 1563; reprinted 1878); and J. F. Montemayor y Córdova, *Sumarios de las Cédulas Órdenes, y Provisiones Reales, que se han despachado por su Magestad, para la Nueva España* (Mexico, 1678), which is complemented by E. Beleña, *Recopilación Sumaria de todos los Autos Acordados de la Real Audiencia y Sala del Crimen de esta Nueva España, y Providencias de su Superior Govierno* (Mexico, 1787). Three epochal legislative monuments of the Bourbon reforms are the *Real Ordenanza para el Establecimiento e Instrucción de Intendentes de Ejército y Provincia en el Reino de la Nueva España* (Madrid, 1786), the *Reales Ordenanzas para la Dirección, Régimen y Gobierno del Importante Cuerpo de la Minería de Nueva España, y de su Real Tribunal General* (Madrid, 1783), and the *Reglamento y Aranceles Reales para el Comercio Libre de España e Indias* (Madrid, 1778). The first of these collections has been edited and translated by Lillian E. Fisher (Berkeley, 1929).

F. Fonseca and C. de Urrutia, *Historia General de Real Hacienda, escrita por . . . orden del Virrey, Conde de Revillagigedo* (6 vols., Mexico, 1845-1853), is to be associated with the latter's *Instrucción Reservada* (Mexico, 1831) for the years 1789-1894 and the *Informe General* (Mexico, 1867), by José de Gálvez for the years of his visitation, 1765-1771, as of the highest importance for the period. The work of Fonseca and Urrutia was epitomized by J. Maniau y Torquemada in a *Compendio de la Historia de la Real Hacienda,* published in J. N. Rodríguez de San Miguel, *Pandectas Hispano-Megicanas* (3 vols., Mexico, 1852), and as a separate (Mexico, 1914) with commentaries by Alberto M.

Carreño. The *Pandectas* by Rodríguez set forth the Mexican survivals of the numerous previous Spanish codes. B. J. Arrillaga, *Recopilación de Leyes, Decretos, Bandos, Reglamentos, Circulares y Providencias* (Mexico, 1844-1849), dealing with the republic, and A. X. Pérez y López, *Teatro de la Legislación Universal de España e Indias* (28 vols., Madrid, 1791-1798), are alphabetical and comparative guides to important legislation.

## GENERAL HISTORIES

Among the general histories of Spanish America there are sections on New Spain in A. de Herrera, *Historia General de los Hechos de los Castellanos* (8 vols. in 4, Madrid, 1601-1615), G. F. Oviedo y Valdés, *Historia General y Natural de las Indias* (3 pts. in 4 vols., Madrid, 1851-1855), and J. de Torquemada, *Primera [segunda, tercera] parte de los Veinte i un Libros Rituales y Monarchía Indiana* (Seville, 1615; Madrid, 1723). For New Spain and Mexico, see I. Álvarez, *Estudios sobre la Historia General de México* (6 vols., Zacatecas, 1869-1877); Lúcas Alamán, *Disertaciones sobre la Historia de la República Mejicana . . . hasta la Independencia* (3 vols., Mexico, 1844-1849); same author, *Historia de Méjico, desde los Primeros Movimientos que Prepararon su Independencia* (5 vols., Mexico, 1849-1852); A. Cavo, *Los tres Siglos de México* (2 vols., Mexico, 1836-1838); F. Cervantes de Salazar, *Crónica de la Nueva España* (Madrid, 1914); J. Sierra, ed., *México, su Evolución Social* (Mexico, 1901; Engl. edn., 2 vols. in 3, Barcelona, 1900-1904); V. Riva Palacio, ed., *México a través de los Siglos* (5 vols., Barcelona, 1888-1889); M. Rivera Cambas, *Los Gobernantes de México* (2 vols., Mexico, 1872-1873); same author, *Historia Antigua y Moderna de Jalapa* (Mexico, 1869-1871); and N. de Zamacois, *Historia de Méjico desde sus Tiempos más Remotos* (18 vols., Mexico, 1877-1882). There are also many short compendiums, among them N. León, *Compendio de la Historia General de México* (Mexico, 1902); L. Pérez Verdía, *Compendio de la Historia de México* (Mexico, 1883) and many edns. to 1912; C. Pereyra,

# 362 THE COMING OF THE WHITE MAN

*Historia del Pueblo Mexicano* (2 vols., Mexico, 1909); and
R. García Granados, *Historia de México desde la Restauración
de la República . . . hasta la Caída de Porfirio Diaz* (4
vols., Mexico, n. d.). The student interested in social history
should also consult the reviews of sources mentioned in
Bancroft, *History of Mexico* (already cited), II, end of
volume, and III, chaps. xvii-xxiv.

## TRANSATLANTIC NAVIGATION

The struggle for the mastery of the sea by the early explorers, with illuminating social material, may be pursued
through the intriguing pages of C. Fernández Duro, *Disquisiciones Náuticas* (6 vols., Madrid, 1876-1881). The evolution of Spanish naval architecture appears in G. de Artíñano y Galdácano, *La Arquitectura Naval Española* (Madrid,
1920). The "Introducción" of the voyage of the *Sútil* and
*Mexicana* in search of the Northeast Passage is an epitome
of Spanish seamanship by M. Fernández de Navarrete, *Relación del Viage* (Madrid, 1802). Similar material, but largely
on naval warfare, is Fernández Duro, *La Armada Española
desde la Unión de los Reinos de Castilla y de Aragón* (9 vols.,
Madrid, 1895-1903); further interest may be fed in his
*De algunas Obras desconocidas de Cosmografía y de Nave-
gación y singularmente de la que escribió Alfonso de Chávez
a Principios del Siglo XVI* (Madrid, 1893). A summary of
Portuguese seafaring and its scientific contribution is in
Fidelino de Figueredo, "The Geographical Discoveries and
Conquests of the Portuguese," *Hisp. Am. Hist. Rev.*, VI, 47-
70. More ample treatment is in J. Bensaude, ed., *Histoire de
la Science Nautique Portugaise à l'Époque des grandes
Découvertes* (7 vols., Münich, 1914-1915). For the French
influence see Pierre Margry, *Les Navigations Françaises et la
Revolution Maritime du XIVᵉ au XVIᵉ Siècle* (Paris, 1867).
The legal side of maritime adventure is found in Sir Travers Twiss, ed., *Monumenta Juridica; The Black Book of
the Admiralty* (4 vols., London, 1871-1876), and his
works already cited; also in A. Capmany y Montpalaū,
*Código de las Costumbres Marítimas de Barcelona* (Madrid,

1791). Twiss and Capmany have written much on the subject.

José Toribio Medina, *El Descubrimiento del Océano Pacífico* (4 vols., Santiago, 1913-1920), is devoted to Balboa, Magellan and their companions. Emma H. Blair and J. A. Robertson, *The Philippine Islands* (55 vols., Cleveland, 1903-1909), is of prime value for navigation of the Pacific and the social history of New Spain. J. López de Velasco, *Geografía y Descripción Universal de las Indias* (Madrid, 1894), written in 1576 and even then belated in its survey, possesses value for its information on Spanish problems of the sea as well as on the transmission of physical forms of culture and economic conditions. H. de la Puente y Olea, *Los Trabajos Geográficos de la Casa de Contratación* (Seville, 1900), is a mine of information on early Spanish cartographical contributions. A brief but useful survey of later Spanish discovery is in E. Heawood, *A History of Geographical Discovery in the Seventeenth and Eighteenth Centuries* (Cambridge, 1912).

## INTERNATIONAL RELATIONS AND EXPANSION

National rivalries and diplomacy of European colonial powers may be studied to 1648 in Frances G. Davenport, *European Treaties bearing on the History of the United States* (Wash., 1917); suggestive cognate material is in A. Rein, *Der Kampf West Europas um Nord Amerika im 15 und 16 Jahrhundert* (Stuttgart, 1925), especially chap. iv on "Die Freiheit des Ozeans: Die Rechtsideen in Kampf um die Überseeische Ausdehnung." Further titles are indicated under the topic New France, below.

The spread of the borders of empire was chronicled by many writers of the regular religious orders, with emphasis on their own missions and the lives of their members. P. Beaumont, *Crónica de . . . Michoacan* (5 vols., Mexico, 1873-1874), has two volumes on the general Spanish conquest and three on the Franciscans; he is to be grouped with I. F. Espinosa, *Crónica Apostólica . . . de todos los Colegios de Propaganda Fide* (Mexico, 1746), J. C. Arricivita,

*Crónica seráfica . . . del Colegio de la Santa Cruz de Que-
rétaro* (Mexico, 1792), and J. Arlegui, *Crónica de la Provincia de San Francisco de Zacatecas* (Mexico, 1737). Among
Jesuit writings are F. X. Alegre, *Historia de la Compañía de
Jesús* (3 vols., Mexico, 1841-1842), A. Pérez de Ribas,
*Historia de los Triumphos de Nuestra Santa Fé* (Madrid,
1645), and F. X. Clavigero (on early Indian life), *Historia
Antigua de México y de su Conquista* (2 vols., Mexico,
1844). For Dominican records there is A. Dávila Padilla,
*Historia de la Fundación y Discurso de la Provincia de San-
tiago de México* (Madrid, 1596). For the Augustinians we
have J. de Grijalva, *Crónica de la Órden* (Mexico, 1624),
and its continuation by E. García, (Madrid, 1918). H. H.
Bancroft made analyses of practically all the church writers
and embodied his judgments, usually sound, in his works
noticed above.

Editing of documents by H. E. Bolton, *e.g.*, *Spanish Exploration in the Southwest* (N. Y., 1916), and others has
added detail to the expansion story. Pioneer work on the
Catholic missions was done by J. G. Shea, *History of the
Catholic Missions* (N. Y., 1855), and *The Catholic Church
in Colonial Days* (N. Y., 1886), and there is continual amplification in the periodical publications of Catholic historical
societies.

### GEOGRAPHIC INFLUENCES IN NEW SPAIN

The characteristic geographical conditions which confronted the Spaniards in their northward trek have never
been adequately treated. Few writers have noted their deter-
mining influence upon the extent, and fewer still upon the
quality, of Spanish civilization in North America. An introduction to the geography of Mexico may be gleaned from
the *Anales* de la Sociedad Científica "Antonio Alzate"
(Mexico, 1888-    ) and the *Boletín* de la Sociedad de
Geografía y Estadística (Mexico, 1852-    ). Some of the
influences of geography upon social and economic conditions
as a modern heritage appear in the multitudinous pamphlets
on the modern agrarian revolution, *e.g.*, F. González Roa,

*El Aspecto Agrario de la Revolución Mexicana* (Mexico, 1919). A serious study based on field work is G. M. McBride, *The Land Systems of Mexico* (N. Y., 1923); less detached though valuable is Helen Phipps, *Some Aspects of the Agrarian Question in Mexico* (Austin, 1925). Important but without historical setting for this topic are C. C. Colby, *Source Book for the Economic Geography of North America* (Chicago, 1922), chaps. xiii and xvi, and J. R. Smith, *North America* (N. Y., 1925), chaps. xlii-xlvi.

For the transmission of flora and fauna, De la Puente (cited above) is notable. Dr. N. Monardes, *Historia Medicinal de las Cosas que se traen de las Indias Occidentales* (Seville, 1574), tells the contributions of the American pharmacopœia, translated into English by J. Frampton as *Ioyfull Newes out of the New Founde Worlde* (London, 1577; reprinted, N. Y., 1925). Forty years residence and acquaintance with early settlers gave Bernabé Cobo, S. J., special opportunities to write on this subject in 1652; see his *Historia del Nuevo Mundo* (4 vols., Seville, 1890-1895), especially II, 340-435. For a good article on this general subject see J. A. Robertson, "Some Notes on the Transfer by Spain of Plants and Animals to its Colonies Overseas," *James Sprunt Hist. Studies* XIX, 7-21.

## SPECIAL AREAS OF NEW SPAIN

For the literature bearing on the general subject of the expansion of New Spain toward the north, see J. L. Mecham, "The Northern Expansion of New Spain, 1522-1822; a Selected Descriptive Bibliographical List," *Hisp. Am. Hist. Rev.*, VII, 237-276. A bibliography of the history of New Mexico can be developed from the lists in Bancroft, *New Mexico and Arizona* (mentioned above), and those in R. E. Twitchell, *The Leading Facts of New Mexican History* (6 vols., Cedar Rapids, 1911). The field is also covered by J. A. Munk, *Bibliography of Arizona* (Los Angeles, 1900), and same comp., *Arizona Bibliography* (Los Angeles, 1908). Much local as well as general material is in H. R. Wagner, *The Spanish Southwest, an Annotated Bibliography* (Berkeley,

1924). The archives cared for by the Southwest Society of the Archæological Society of America have not been listed. The Bandelier Papers, being edited by C. W. Hackett for the Carnegie Institution as *Historical Documents Relating to New Mexico* (Wash., 1923, 1926), with two volumes now done, will comprise four volumes of sources on New Mexico and Nueva Vizcaya under Spain. *The Publisher's Weekly*, CXI, 2247-2251, published a "Santa Fé Bookshelf" listing about one hundred popular yet useful titles, *e.g.*, G. W. James, *New Mexico, the Land of the Delight Makers* (Boston, 1920), by which the reader may be guided to readings on history, archæology, Indian legend and folk tale, the American frontier, poetry, music, etc., of the region. G. Pérez de Villagrá, *Historia de la Nueva México* (Alcalá, 1610; 2 vols., Mexico, 1910), is unique as a record in verse, authentic historically, of this northern conquest.

FLORIDA. The long struggle of Spain for a "window on the Atlantic" is beginning to be conceived in true continental perspective; much attention has been given to the early period because of its international interest. A bibliography of Florida history is being prepared for the State Historical Society by J. A. Robertson to supply the present lack. Original documents published by G. García, ed., *Dos Antiguas Relaciones de la Florida* (Mexico, 1902), give narratives of early French and Spanish missionary effort, and Pedro Menéndez documents are in E. Ruidíaz y Caravia, ed., *La Florida* (2 vols., Madrid, 1893). H. E. Bolton, ed., *Arredondo's Historical Proof of Spain's Title to Georgia* (Berkeley, 1925), recapitulates the struggle for possession down to 1742. The *Publications* of the Florida State Historical Society are valuable, notably the three works edited by Jeannette T. Connor: G. Solís de Merás, *Pedro Menéndez de Avilés* (III, 1923), *Colonial Records of Spanish Florida* (V, 1925), and *Jean Ribaut, the Whole and True Discouerye of Terra Florida* (VII, 1927); H. I. Priestley, ed., *The Luna Papers* (VIII, 2 vols., 1928); and C. M. Brevard, *A History of Florida* (IV, J. A. Robertson, ed., 2 vols., 1924-1925). The very rare Bernard Romans, *A Concise Natural History of East and West Florida* (N. Y., 1775), is distinctly useful for the early period. G. R. Fairbanks, *The History and Antiquities of the City of St. Augustine, Florida* (N. Y., 1858), is one of a small group of reminiscences.

TEXAS. The most satisfactory survey of Texan history is still Bancroft, *North Mexican States and Texas* (cited earlier). It surveys the approaches into Texas from the northern tier of states and has a wealth of bibliographical information on frontier conditions. W. E. Dunn, *Spanish and French Rivalry in the Gulf Region of the United States, 1678-1702* (Austin, 1917), has a good account of La Salle in Texas, and of the coast region during the lowest ebb of the Hapsburgs. H. E. Bolton, *Texas in the Middle Eighteenth Century* (Univ. of Calif., *Publs.*, III, 1915), covers the period 1731-1788 in a collection of special studies with an introductory survey. A. Bonilla, "Brief Compendium of the Events which have occurred in the Province of Texas, [1772]," *Texas State Hist. Quar.*, VIII, 9-22, Elizabeth H. West, tr., is essential for the official point of view. This *Quarterly* (Austin, 1897-1912), continued as the *Southwestern Historical Quarterly* (Austin, 1912-    ), has much source material and interpretation of value for the colonial period of society. M. Ramos de Arizpe, *Memorial on the Natural, Political, and Civil State of the Province of Coahuila* (Phila., 1814), is excellent for the condition of the northern frontier, reflecting the background of Texan conditions on the eve of the War of Independence. Surveys by American writers, such as G. P. Garrison, *Texas: a Contest of Civilizations* (Boston, 1903), complemented by R. C. Clark, *The Beginnings of Texas* (Austin, 1907), are concerned first with the detailed account of the French-Spanish conflict in Texas; but these works were written before the archives of Spain yielded materials used by Dunn (cited above) and others.

CALIFORNIA. Valuable guides are R. E. Cowan, *A Bibliography of the History of California and the Pacific West, 1510-1906* (San Francisco, 1914), and Wagner, *The Spanish Southwest* (mentioned above). Bancroft, *California*, I, still contains the most complete list, and his *California Pastoral, 1768-1848* (San Francisco, 1888) is useful, with bibliography in chap. xxiii. T. H. Hittell, *History of California* (4 vols., San Francisco, 1885), is sound. I. B. Richman, *California under Spain and Mexico* (Boston, 1911), is readable and has invaluable notes. *The History of California, the Spanish Period,* by C. E. Chapman (N. Y., 1921), and *the American Period,* by R. G. Cleland, cover a wide field of investigation. Alberta J. Denis, *The History of California* (N. Y., 1927), closely follows the published documentation. The numerous writings of Father Zephyrin Engelhardt, of which the chief is *The Missions and Missionaries of California* (4 vols., San Francisco, 1908), present political history as well as general and local mission history from the point of view of religion. The Academy of Pacific Coast History, *Publications* (Berkeley, 1909-1914), contain in three volumes much source material on the first occupation of Upper California. H. E. Bolton, ed., *Palóu's Historical Memoirs of New California* (4 vols., Berkeley, 1926), and *Fray Juan Crespi* (Berkeley, 1927), accent the religious phase. Pedro Fages, "An Historical, Political, and Natural Description of California," translated by H. I. Priestley in *Catholic Hist. Rev.,* IV, 486-509; V, 71-90, is useful for Indian California.

SOCIAL AND ECONOMIC CONDITIONS IN NEW SPAIN

Treatment in English of the fundamental qualities of Spanish American society has been little developed. E. G. Bourne, *Spain in America* (A. B. Hart, ed., *The American Nation: a History,* N. Y., 1904-1918, V), is based on J. López de Velasco (mentioned above), and barely touches the period after 1580. F. W. Blackmar, *Spanish Institutions of the Southwest* (Johns Hopkins Univ., *Studies,* extra vol. x, 1891), is basic, but requires emendation and amplification. Ernest Gruening, *Mexico and Its Heritage* (N. Y., 1928), is a brilliant study of interpenetration of Spanish and Indian customs with respect to religion, economics, law and manners. To materials mentioned in the notes to chap. v of the present work may be added Sir Arthur Helps, *The Spanish Conquest in America* (4 vols., London, 1855-1861; M. Oppenheim,

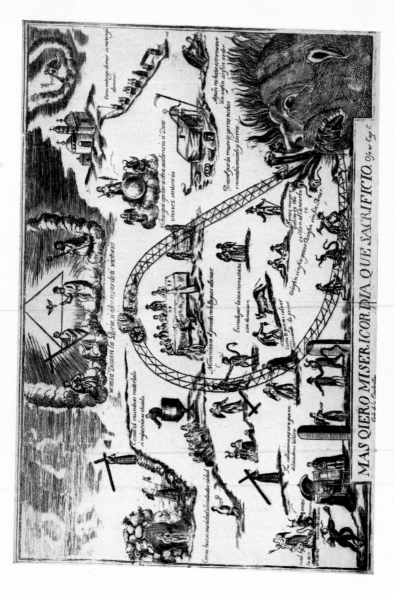

A graphic sermon for the faithful in Eighteenth-Century New Spain.

ed., 4 vols., London, 1900-1904), and his *Life of Las Casas* (London, 1868). Much is available in the popular and often erroneous F. A. McNutt, *Bartholomew de Las Casas* (N. Y., 1909), which is comparable with A. M. Fabié, *El P. Fr. Bartolomé de Las Casas* (Madrid, 1892). *Las Casas* has fascinated a number of writers more distinguished for romantic enthusiasm than for historical caution. There is a wide range of scholarly writing, however, on the treatment of the Indians, *e.g.*, J. J. Ramírez, *Noticias de la Vida y Escritos de Fray Toribio de Benavente o Motolinía* (Icazbalceta, ed., *Colección de Documentos para la Historia de México,* I). The early documentation bearing on this important theme has received a brilliant revaluation in L. B. Simpson, *The Encomienda in New Spain* (Berkeley, 1929).

For the condition of the Spanish artisans, see the reprint by G. Estrada of J. F. del Barrio Lorenzot, *El Trabajo en México durante la Época Colonial. Ordenanzas de Gremios de la Nueva España* (Mexico, 1920). Complementary to Hipólito Villaroel, *Enfermedades Políticas* (MS., 4 vols., 1785-1787), are the writings of Bishop Manuel Abad y Queipo as found in L. Mora, *Obras Sueltas* (2 vols., Paris, 1837), and the *Instrucciones que los Virreyes de la Nueva España dejaron a sus Sucesores. . . .* (2 vols., Mexico, 1873); these, with the writings of Revillagigedo, deserve translation and synthesis for better understanding of the policies of Spain in North America.

Conditions affecting trade and navigation and their influence on social life may be studied in R. Antúnez y Acevedo. *Memorias históricas sobre la Legislación y Gobierno del Comercio de los Españoles con sus Colonias.* (Madrid, 1797), and J. Veitia Linaje, *Norte de la Contratación de las Indias Occidentales* (Seville, 1672), the latter poorly translated by J. Stevens, *The Spanish Rule of Trade to the West Indies* (London, 1702). G. Artíñano y Galdácano, *Historia del Comercio con las Indias durante el Dominio de los Austrias* (Barcelona, 1917), is readable but diffuse; C. H. Haring, *Trade and Navigation between Spain and the Indies in the Time of the Hapsburgs* (*Harvard Econ. Studies,* XIX,

1918), is meaty; more readable is his *The Buccaneers in the West Indies in the XVII Century* (N. Y., 1910) on the long private warfare on Spanish trade. Haring's various articles on finance and taxation appear in the *Quarterly Journal of Economics,* XXIX, 433-479, the *American Historical Review,* XXIII, 779-796, etc.

## THE AMENITIES OF LIFE IN NEW SPAIN

Colonial life and letters have been treated but fragmentarily. Other than the works cited in chap. vi, we have L. González Obregón, *Méjico Viejo* (Mexico, 1900), and A. de Valle-Arizpe, *La muy Noble y Leal Ciudad de México según Relatos de Antaño y de Hogaño* (Mexico, 1924). Many interesting brochures are issued by the publishing house "Cultura" in Mexico City, *e.g.,* A. Cravioto, *El Alma Nueva de las Cosas Viejas* (1921), and G. Estrada, *Visionario de la Nueva España* (1921), which, while "mere" poetry and fiction, faithfully reflect colonial society. The early chapters of Estrada's novelesque *Pero Galín* (Mexico, 1926) are rich in antiquarian interest. For social and intellectual conditions in the northern provinces one may add to the materials already noted items from Eustaquio Buelna, *Apuntes para la Historia de Sinaloa* (G. Estrada, ed., Mexico, 1924), and V. A. Robles, *Bibliografía de Coahuila* (Mexico, 1927).

## THE FRENCH IN AMERICA

### GENERAL BIBLIOGRAPHIES

French activities in North America have been studied with more attention to their social significance than have those of the Spaniards. Interpretation has also escaped the unfortunate teleological atmosphere which beclouds the study of things Spanish American, perhaps because the power of France entirely disappeared during the colonial epoch. Yet it is not easy to segregate the social studies from those of a political nature. Initial bibliographical inquiry may begin with R. G. Thwaites, ed., *Jesuit Relations and Allied Documents* (73 vols., Cleveland, 1896-1901), LXI, 219-365, and his *France in America (The American Nation: a History,* VII), 296-305, where lists of authorities are presented. Further aid, though earlier, is in Winsor, *Narrative and Critical History* (mentioned above). For more recent material the student should consult G. M. Wrong and H. H. Langton, eds., *Review of Historical Publications Relating to Canada* (22 vols., Toronto, 1896-1919), which is followed by the *Canadian Historical Review* (Toronto, 1920-    ). There is help, too, in the *Writings on American History,* listed above under New Spain, compiled by Grace G. Griffin and her predecessors.

Especially devoted to Canada are G. B. Fairibault, *Catalogue d'Ouvrages sur l'Histoire de l'Amérique, et en particulier sur celle du Canadá, de la Louisiane, de l'Arcadie, et autres Lieux* (Quebec, 1837); W. Kingsford, *The Early Bibliography of the Province of Ontario* (Toronto, 1892); P. Gagnon, *Essai de Bibliographie Canadienne* (2 vols., Quebec, 1895); the *Catalogue of Pamphlets, Journals, and Reports in the Dominion Archives, 1611-1867, with Index* (Ottawa, 1911); the list by the Toronto Public Library entitled *Books and Pamphlets published in Canada up to the Year Eighteen Hundred and Thirty-Seven* (Toronto, 1916); and the *Canadian Catalogue of Books published in Canada . . . during 1921 and 1926* (5 vols. in one, Toronto, 1926). Adam Shortt and A. G. Doughty, eds., *Canada and its Provinces* (23 vols., Toronto, 1914-1917), has a well-selected list in vol. xxiii, 233-283. Topical outlines with ample readings are in R. G. Trotter, *Canadian History, a Syllabus and Guide* (Toronto, 1926). The *Revue Historique* is about to publish a bibliography of early Canadian history prepared by H. P. Biggar.

## COLLECTIONS OF SOURCES

The collections of sources dealing chiefly with the French (and not the later English) period include Pierre Margry, ed., *Mémoires et Documents . . . Découvertes et Établissements des Français* (6 vols., Paris, 1879-1888), which contains much social material that needs to be winnowed from more or less apochryphal narratives of exploration. By the same editor is the earlier *Relations et Mémoires Inédites pour servir a l'Histoire de France d'Outre-Mer* (Paris, 1867). E. B. O'Callaghan and Berthold Fernow, eds., *Documents Relative to the Colonial History of New York* (15 vols., N. Y., 1853-1887), esp. IX-X, shed valuable light on the intercolonial wars. There are also Douglas Brymner, *Reports on Canadian Archives* (24 vols., Ottawa, 1884-1906), P. G. Roy, *Index du Bulletin de Recherches Historiques* (4 vols., Beauceville, 1925-1926), and the *Proceedings and Transactions* (ser. 1, 12 vols., 1882-1893, ser. 2, 9 vols., 1895-    ) of the Royal Society of Canada, containing, *e.g.*, P. G. Roy, "Les Conseillers au Conseil Souverain de la Nouvelle-France," ser. 3, IX, 173-187. The *Archives de la Province de Québec* contain, by the same editor, an *Inventaire des Insinuations du Conseil Souverain de la Nouvelle-France* (2 vols., Beauceville, 1921), *Lettres de Noblesse, Généalogies, Erections de Comtes et Baronnies insinuées par le Conseil Souverain* (2 vols., 1920), and an *Inventaire des Ordonnances des Intendants de la Nouvelle-France conservées aux Archives Provinciales de Québec* (4 vols., 1919-    ). Some social history may be extracted from the *Édits et Ordonnances Royaux concernant le Canada* (3 vols., Quebec, 1854-1856) and the *Jugements et Délibérations du Conseil Souverain de la Nouvelle-France* (6 vols., Quebec, 1890). From the *Judicial Archives* is also the *Inventaire d'une Collection de Pièces Judiciaries de Québec* (2 vols., Beauceville, 1917). Early materials illuminating the organization of society are in the *Collection de Manuscrits contenant Lettres, Mémoires, et autres Documents Historiques* (4 vols., Quebec, 1883-1885), the *Publications of the Canadian Archives* by various editors (Ottawa, 1872-    ), and the *Publications* of the Champlain Society (16 vols., Toronto, 1907-1927), L. J. Burpee, *Index and Dictionary of Canadian History* (D. C. Scott and others, eds., *The Makers of Canada Series*, XXI; Toronto, 1911), is also useful. There is also the *Collection de Documents Inédites sur le Canadá et l'Amérique* (3 vols., Quebec, Laval Univ., 1888-1890). The publications of the Champlain Society (Toronto) dealing with Champlain,

Lescarbot, Denys, Le Clercq and La Vérendrye, and like-wise those of the Prince Society (Boston) on Radisson, present material of interest to the social historian.

## INSTITUTIONAL GROWTH IN NEW FRANCE

Many of the general Canadian histories dwell intensively upon social development. It is scarcely necessary to particularize upon the works of Francis Parkman, whose twelve volumes are found in several editions. They represent pioneer work in popular writing with suitable documentation; their special interest for social institutions, along with a literary style the product of Parkman's times as well as of his genius, makes them a perpetual commemoration of the land and the man. The sources are often obscurely cited. Thwaites, *France in America* (cited earlier), 297, lists the volumes in their proper chronological order.

The discussion of phases of the discovery period may be followed beyond the citations in the present work by reading the numerous writings of H. P. Biggar, *e.g.*, "Charles V and the Discovery of Canada," Royal Hist. Soc., *Trans.* ser. 3, XI, 143-164; *The Early Trading Companies of New France* (Toronto, 1901); *The Voyages of Jacques Cartier* (Ottawa, 1924); and *The Precursors of Jacques Cartier* (Ottawa, 1911). A study of French beginnings by a versatile French historian is C. B. La Roncière, "Nôtre, Première Tentative de Colonisation au Canadá," Bibliothèque de l'École des Chartres, *Revue D'Érudition*, LXXXIII, 283-300. Among early views of French activities is M. de Bocqueville de la Potherie, *Histoire de l'Amérique Septentrionale* (4 vols., Paris, 1753), largely devoted to relations with the Indians and to aboriginal social structure.

P. V. Cayet, *Chronologie Septénaire de l'Histoire de la Paix entre les Roys de France et d'Espagne* (Paris, 1605), and J. Michaud, ed., *Nouvelle Collection des Mémoirs*, (32 vols., Paris, 1836-1839), XII, contain contemporary materials for the diplomatic approaches, which are more fully portrayed in Davenport, *European Treaties*, mentioned above under New Spain. Background material for the French overseas policies is in J. M. Bridges, *France under Richelieu and Colbert* (Edinburgh, 1866); F. C. Palm, *The Economic Policies of Richelieu* (Univ. of Ill., *Studies*, IX, 1922); A. J. Sergent, *The Economic Policy of Colbert* (London, 1899); P. Clement, *Histoire de Colbert et de son Administration* (Paris, 1874); E. Rameau, *Une Colonie Féodale en Amérique* (Paris, 1877); and S. L. Mims, *Colbert's West India Policy (Yale Hist. Studies*, I, 1912). W. Kingsford, *The History of Canada* (10 vols., Toronto, 1887-1898), has the first four volumes on the French; H. H. Miles, *The History of Canada under the French Régime* (Montreal, 1872), is another general work still valuable. The conservative point of view is presented in Benjamin Sulte, *Histoire des Canadiens-Français, 1606-1880* (8 vols., Montreal, 1882-1884), and F. X. Garneau, *Histoire du Canada* (6th edn., Paris, 1920). Shortt and Doughty, *Canada and its Provinces* (mentioned already), is popular but authoritative. Those preferring to study history through biography can be abundantly satisfied in D. C. Scott and others, eds., *The Makers of Canada Series* (21 vols.). G. M. Wrong and H. H. Langton, eds., *Chronicles of Canada Series* (32 vols., Toronto, 1914-1916), is instructive and entertaining, with much attention to human interest. Among its authoritative volumes is one by W. B. Munro, *The Seigneurs of Old Canada* (V). In Allen Johnson, ed., *The Chronicles of America Series* (50 vols., New Haven, 1918-1921), is Munro's *Crusaders of New France* (IV). His *Seigniorial System in Canada (Harvard Hist. Studies,* XIII, 1907) is basic for the land régime, with his editing of *Documents Relating to the Seigniorial Tenure in Canada* (Toronto, 1908) in *Publications* of the Champlain Society, III. See also, for feudal conditions, his "The Droit de Banalité during the French Régime in Canada," Am. Hist. Assoc., *Ann. Rep. for 1899,* I, 205-228, and the earlier work by F. J. Cugnet, *Traité de la Loi des Fiefs, Qui a Toujours été suivié en Canadá depuis son Établissement, tirées de celle contenue en la Coûtume . . . de Paris* (Quebec, 1775). The same author's *Traité de la Police,* with same imprint, discusses official control of society in another setting than that of E. Rameau, *Une*

*Colonie Féodale* (cited above). On the administration of New
France may be added an item demonstrating the perplexity
of the British mind faced with French local administration:
R. Burns, *Le Juge à paix, et Officier de Paroisse, pour la
Province de Quebec* (Montreal, 1789). Modern study of the
governmental mechanism is available in G. M. Wrong, *A
Canadian Manor and its Seigneurs; the Story of a Hundred
Years* (Toronto, 1908). The most recent scholarship is
summarized in the same author's *The Rise and Fall of New
France* (2 vols., N. Y., 1928), in which much attention is
paid to the European background. A short popular summary
is found in J. E. Wetherell, *Three Centuries of Canadian
Story* (Toronto, 1928).

### CHURCH AND RELIGION IN NEW FRANCE

The development of Christianity in New France is recorded
in many writings. Those of Champlain, Le Clercq and Charlevoix present official and ecclesiastical points of view from
diverse angles. The Jesuit *Lettres Édifiantes et Curieuses* (new
edn., Paris, 1870-1873), with wider scope than the *Jesuit
Relations,* serves to demonstrate the uniformity of the propaganda of that order. Numerous accounts of French Canada
are in the *Nouvelles Annales des Voyages, de la Geographie,
de l'Histoire, et de l'Archéologie* (188 vols. in 96, Paris,
1819-1865). G. Sagard-Théodat, *Histoire du Canadá* (Paris,
1836; 4 vols., 1866), is a general account from the Recollect point of view. See also Mack Eastman, *Church and State
in Early Canada* (Edinburgh, 1915), chaps. iv-ix.

Conspicuous individual servants of the faith have been
remembered in T. J. Campbell, S. J., *Pioneer Laymen of
North America* (N. Y., 1915), most of whom were Canadians. The accepted biography for the great bishop is A.
Leblond de Brumath, *Bishop Laval* (*The Makers of Canada
Series;* Toronto, 1906). Pierre F. X. de Charlevoix, *La Vie
de la Mère Marie de l'Incarnation, Institutrice et première
Supérieure des Ursulines de la Nouvelle-France* (Paris, 1724),
records the influence of this remarkable woman and of her
order. See also the enthusiastic biography by Agnes Repplier,

*Père Marquette: Priest, Pioneer and Adventurer* (N. Y. 1928).

The womanhood of the colony has won recognition in C. W. Colby, *Canadian Types of the Old Régime* [1608-1698] (N. Y., 1908), and Isabel Skelton, *The Backwoodswoman* (Toronto, 1924), chaps. i-iii. Similar material exclusively concerning women is in Mary S. Pepper, *Maids and Matrons of New France* (Boston, 1901). See also in this connection the Women's Canadian Historical Society of Ottawa, *Transactions* (9 vols. in 2, Ottawa, 1901-1925).

## ECONOMIC CONDITIONS IN NEW FRANCE

Less interesting than the travel accounts, cited in the text, by Lahontan, Kalm and Weld, but well-balanced and useful, are the Canadian portions of Edmund Burke, *An Account of the European Settlements in America* (2 vols., London, 1757); Thomas Jefferys, *The Natural and Civil History of the French Dominions in North America* (London, 1760); and R. Rogers, *A Concise Account of North America* (London, 1765). É. Salone, *La Colonisation de la Nouvelle-France* (Paris, 1907), is a careful digest of source materials in thesis form, presenting the economic phases of the French occupation. Invaluable material much used by Salone is in the Department of Agriculture, *Census of Canada* (*Censuses of Canada, 1608 to 1876,* 5 vols., Ottawa, 1873-1878). V. Salone's discussion of the fur trade may be supplemented by L. J. Burpee, "Highways of the Fur Trade," Royal Soc. of Canada, *Trans.*, ser. 3, VIII, sec. 2, 183-192. See Adam Shortt, "The Colony in its Economic Relations," *Canada and its Provinces*, II, 458-489; A. D. De Celles, "The Habitant, His Origin and History," same work, XV, 17-117; and C. W. Colby, *Canadian Types of the Old Régime* (cited earlier), chaps. vii-x.

Information concerning early artifacts may be gleaned from works like Lurelle van Arsdale, *The Geography of American Antiques* (Garden City, 1926). Excellent editorial material and, in the body of the text, prime sources for economic conditions are in A. Shortt, *Documents Relatifs à la*

*Monnaie, au Change, et aux Finances du Canadá sous le Régime Français* (2 vols., Ottawa, 1925).

## GENERAL SOURCES FOR LOUISIANA AND ILLINOIS

Only a brief survey of the literature of this important section can be given. Useful bibliographies include A. N. de Ménil, *The Literature of the Louisiana Territory* (St. Louis, 1904), and T. P. Thompson, *Catalogue of Americana, consisting principally of Books Relating to Louisiana and the Mississippi Valley* (New Orleans, 1903). Earlier, but of value, is G. B. Fairibault, *Catalogue,* mentioned above under bibliographies for New France.

Of source collections, a large portion of Margry, *Découvertes* (cited earlier), pertains to this area; Pénicaut's "Journal," in vol. v, is essential for early social conditions. B. F. French, *Historical Collections of Louisiana and Florida* (ser. 1, 5 vols., N. Y., 1846-1853; ser. 2, 2 vols., N. Y., 1869-1875), contains much borderland material. From the Mississippi Department of Archives and History were edited in 1927 by Dunbar Rowland and A. C. Sanders, *A Symposium on the Place of the Discovery of the Mississippi River by Hernando de Soto* (Miss. Hist. Soc., *Special Bull.* no. 1), and the more valuable *Mississippi Provincial Archives, 1729-1740.* For the Northwest, the Michigan Pioneer and Hist. Soc., *Historical Collections* (39 vols., Lansing, 1880-1915), esp. X and XIX, the *Wisconsin Historical Collections* (28 vols., Madison, 1854-1920), esp. V, XVI and XVII, and *Minnesota History* (10 vols., 1919-    ).

Many volumes of voyages of the eighteenth and early nineteenth centuries give brilliant social and economic sketches with a fine contemporary flavor which no later writing can reproduce; *e.g.,* N. Bossu, *Nouveaux Voyages aux Indes Occidentales, contenant une Relation des differens Peuples que habitent les Environs du Grand Fleuve Saint-Louis* (2 vols., Paris, 1768); J. Champigny, *État Présent de la Louisiane, avec toutes les Particularités de cette Province d'Amérique* (The Hague, 1776); F. M. Perrin du Lac, *Voyage dans les deux Louisianes et chez les Nations Sauvages du Missouri*

. . . en *1801, 1802, et 1803* (Paris, 1805); and G. H. Victor Collot, *Voyage dans l'Amérique Septentrionale . . . 1796* (2 vols., Paris, 1826; Engl. edn., same). Early English and American interest in the area is reflected by numerous works, among which the following are outstanding: Andrew Ellicott, *The Journal of Andrew Ellicott, late Commissioner on Behalf of the United States* (Phila., 1803); S. S. Forman, *Narrative of a Journey down the Ohio and Mississippi in 1789-1790* (Cin., 1888); A. Haswell, *Memoirs and Adventures of Captain Matthew Phelps . . . in Two Voyages to the Mississippi . . . 1773 to . . . 1780* (Bennington, Vt., 1802); Henry Ker, *Travels through the Western Interior of the United States . . . 1808 . . . 1816* (Elizabethtown, N. J., 1816); Philip Pittman, *The Present State of the European Settlements on the Mississippi* (London, 1770; reprinted, F. H. Hodder, ed., Cleveland, 1906); and Amos Stoddard, *Sketches Historical and Descriptive of Louisiana* (Phila., 1812). The early voyages are studied in J. G. Shea, *Discovery and Exploration of the Mississippi Valley* (Albany, 1852, 1903), and in Justin Winsor, *The Westward Movement* (Boston, 1897), and same author, *The Mississippi Basin* (Boston, 1898). There is a wealth of documentation with copious annotation in J. A. Robertson, *Louisiana under the Rule of France, Spain and the United States* (2 vols., Cleveland, 1911). H. M. Brackenridge, *Views of Louisiana, together with a Journal of a Voyage up the Missouri River in 1811* (Pittsburgh, 1814), is of a kind with Pittman and Stoddard. H. E. Bolton, ed., *Athanase de Mézières* (2 vols., Cleveland, 1914), is valuable for the transition to Spanish control, the fur trade and Indian policy. Louis Houck, ed., *The Spanish Régime in Missouri; a Collection of Papers and Documents* (Chicago, 1909), contains informative materials.

## SOCIAL GROWTH IN THE MISSISSIPPI VALLEY

Social materials may be gleaned from such general histories as Le Page du Pratz, *Histoire de la Louisiane* (3 vols., Paris, 1758; Engl. edns., London, 1763 and 1774); Timothy

Flint, *A Condensed Geography and History of the Western States, or the Mississippi Valley* (2 vols., Cin., 1828-1832); François Barbé-Marbois, *Histoire de la Louisiane* (Paris, 1829; Engl. edn., Phila., 1830); C. E. A. Gayarré, *Histoire de la Louisiane* (2 vols., N. Orleans, 1846-1847; Engl. edn., N. Y., 1866); J. F. H. Claiborne, *Mississippi as a Province, Territory, and State* (Jackson, 1880); Alcée Fortier, *A History of Louisiana* (4 vols., N. Y., 1904), and, for the upper country, Louis Houck, *A History of Missouri* (3 vols., Chicago, 1908) and C. W. Alvord, *The Illinois Country* (Springfield, 1920).

Of the works particularly concerned with social and intellectual life, the following deserve special notice: A. Franz, *Die Kolonisation des Mississippithales* (Leipzig, 1906), a treatise comparable to Salone's on Canada; J. H. Deiler, *The Settlement of the German Coast of Louisiana* (Phila., 1909) —valuable, but faultily presented; P. J. Hamilton, *Colonial Mobile* (Boston, 1898)—interesting; Alcée Fortier, *Louisiana Studies* (N. Orleans, 1894), and *Louisiana Folk Tales* (Boston, 1895)—written with affection and discernment. M. Villiers du Terrage, . . . *Les Dernières Années de la Louisiane Française* (Paris, 1904), studied the eve of the transition period. On Creole society G. W. Cable, *The Creoles of Louisiana* (N. Y., 1884), portrayed conditions to the displeasure of many Southerners. P. F. de Gourney, "Creole Peculiarities," *Mag. of Am. History*, XVI, 542-549, and Grace E. King, *Creole Families of New Orleans* (N. Y., 1921), should also be consulted. The crisis of the Jesuit expulsion is recorded in Auguste Carayon, *Bannissement des Jésuits de la Louisiane; Relations et Lettres Inédites* [1763] (Paris, 1865). The beginnings of Negro influence in Southern life are reflected in the *Code Noir* [decrees of 1724] (Paris, 1728) and in E. Petit, *Traité sur le Gouvernment des Esclaves* (2 vols., Paris, 1777). A happy description of prosperous agriculture in the Illinois is in *Documents Relative to the Colonial History of New York* (cited earlier), IX. The movement of pioneers into and across the valley is voluminously illustrated in R. G. Thwaites, *Early Western Travels* (32 vols., Cleveland, 1904-1907).

Special works on the northern area are legion. Among them may be noticed Louise P. Kellogg, *The French Régime in Wisconsin and the Northwest* (State Hist. Soc. of Wis., *Publs.*, I, 1925), and S. S. Hebbard, *Wisconsin under French Dominion* (Madison, 1890). The array of literary materials on the Middle Border may be seen in R. L. Rusk, *The Literature of the Middle Western Frontier* (2 vols., N. Y., 1925), in Lucy Hazard, *The Frontier in American Literature* (2 vols., N. Y., 1927), and in Dorothy Dondore, *The Prairie and the Making of Middle America* (Cedar Rapids, 1926).

The French influence is depicted in J. H. Finley, *The French in the Heart of America* (N. Y., 1915), but the treatment is emotional and sympathetic rather than scientific. The Huguenot dispersion in North America is uncritically recorded in L. J. Fosdick, *The French Blood in America* (Boston, 1911); consult also the older Charles Weiss, *History of the French Protestant Refugees and their Settlements in America* (2 vols., N. Y., 1854). One gains clearer views from a study of the *Proceedings* of the Huguenot Society of America, 1883-1909, or the *Transactions* of the Huguenot Society of South Carolina (16 vols., 1889-    ), or from R. A. Brock, ed., *Documents Relating to the Huguenot Emigration* (Va. Hist. Soc., *Colls.*, new ser., V). Jacques Fontaine, *Memoirs of a Huguenot Family* (Ann Maury, tr., N. Y., 1872), is useful. See also H. M. Jones' scholarly *America and French Culture* (Chapel Hill, N. C., 1927).

## NEW NETHERLAND

### BIBLIOGRAPHIES AND GENERAL SOURCES

Assistance in the selection of reading may be found in G. M. Asher, *A Bibliographical and Historical Essay on Dutch Books* . . . *Relating to New Netherland and to the Dutch West India Company* (Amsterdam, 1854-1867), and in appropriate sections of *Repertorium op de Literatuur betreffende de Nederlandsche Kolonien, voor zoover zij verspreid is in Tijdschriften en Mengelwerken*, I, *Oost-Indie, 1866-1893;* II, *West-Indie*, 1840-1893 ('s Gravenhage,

1895-1912). There is great value in M. Nijhoff, *Biblioteca Historica Neerlandica. Histoire des Pays-Bas* (The Hague, 1899), a collection of second-hand book catalogues, to be augmented by the same dealer's more recent *The Hollanders in America* (The Hague, 1925).

Of special interest in the immediate field is J. T. Jennings, *Bibliography of New York Colonial History* (N. Y. State Library, *Bull.*, no. 56, Albany, 1901), and anon., *List of Books relating to the State of New York* (Albany, 1916). Berthold Fernow in his chapter on New Netherland in Winsor, *Narrative and Critical History of America*, IV, 395-442, comments upon many works. But probably the most useful bibliographical guide is V. H. Paltsits, "An Exhibition of the History of New Netherland," N. Y. Public Library, *Bull.*, XXX, 655-684, 759-792.

I. N. Phelps Stokes, *Iconography of Manhattan Island* (6 vols., N. Y., 1915-1928), contains a great number of valuable source extracts. J. F. Jameson, ed., *Narratives of New Netherland, 1609-1664* (same ed., *Original Narratives of Early American History*, N. Y., 1906-    ), contains outstanding documents, most of which had not hitherto been printed. Of similar use and value is A. C. Myers, *Narratives of Early Pennsylvania, West New Jersey, and Delaware, 1630-1707* (*Original Narratives of Early American History*). There is also Jasper Dankers [or Danckaerts] and Peter Sluyter, *Journal of a Voyage to New York, and a Tour in Several of the American Colonies, 1679-1680* (H. C. Murphy, ed., L. I. Hist. Soc., *Memoirs*, I). A. J. F. van Laer, ed., *Documents Relating to New Netherland, 1624-1626, in the Henry E. Huntington Library* (Henry E. Huntington Library, *Publs. Americana*, no. 1, 1924), contains reproductions in facsimile, chiefly useful because of the illuminating annotation. The study of the archives and sources for the history of the Dutch West India Company in H. J. E. Wätjen, *Das Holländische Kolonialreich in Brasilien* (The Hague, 1921), is well documented and valuable for an interpretation of Dutch policy. Charles de Lannoy, *Histoire de l'Expansion Coloniale des Peuples Européens; Néerlande et Danemark* (Brussels, 1911), like Wätjen, cites sources not widely available in America, and is free from provincialism.

E. B. O'Callaghan and Berthold Fernow, eds., *Documents Relative to the Colonial History of the State of New York* (15 vols., Albany, 1853-1887), is monumental; the special volumes are noticed in footnotes in the present work. Berthold Fernow, ed., *The Records of New Amsterdam from 1653 to 1674 Anno Domini* (7 vols., N. Y., 1897); E. B. O'Callaghan, *The Documentary History of the State of New York* (4 vols., Albany, 1850-1851), and the latter's interpretative *History of New Netherland* (2 vols., N. Y., 1846-1848), contain illuminating materials. A unique contemporary interpretation is David de Vries, *Korte Historiael* (H. T. Colenbrander, ed., 's Gravenhage, 1911); in the same group for the southern area is Israel Acrelius, *A History of New Sweden* (Hist. Soc. of Pa., *Memoirs*, XI, 1874). De Vries's description of New Netherland is translated in H. C. Murphy, *Voyages from Holland to America* (N. Y., 1853).

Records of the patroonship of Rensselaerswyck are preserved in A. J. F. van Laer, ed., *Van Rensselaer Bouwier MSS.* (Albany, 1908), with which may be associated the *Minutes of the Court of Fort Orange and Beverwyck, 1652-1660* (same ed., 2 vols., Albany, 1920-1923). There is also Samuel Oppenheim, tr., "The Dutch Records of Kingston, New York," N. Y. State Hist. Assoc., *Proceeds.*, XI, app. 1. The *Collections* of the New York Historical Society, ser. 1, I-V; ser. 2, I-IV; ser. 3, I-LV, contain many items of social significance. Joel Munsell, *The Annals of Albany* (10 vols., Albany, N. Y., 1850-1859), is a miscellaneous collection of great value.

## HISTORIES OF NEW NETHERLAND

Important background material is in P. J. Blok, *History of the People of the Netherlands* (5 vols., N. Y., 1898-1912); J. L. Motley, *History of the United Netherlands* (4 vols., N. Y., 1861-1880); and Ruth Putnam, *William the Silent, Prince of Orange* (N. Y., 1911). Ranking with

O'Callaghan (mentioned above) is J. R. Brodhead, *History of the State of New York* (2 vols., N. Y., 1871-1872), though recent scholarship has made the narrative in vol. i subject to revision. J. G. Wilson, ed., *The Memorial History of the City of New York* (4 vols., N. Y., 1892-1894), has many chapters by different authors on New Netherland. Good local histories are Marius Schoonmaker, *History of Kingston, N. Y.* (N. Y., 1888), and H. R. Stiles, *History of the City of Brooklyn* (3 vols., Brooklyn, 1869-1870). Amandus Johnson, *The Swedish Settlements on the Delaware* (N. Y., 1911), is the authoritative work on its subject. Among more recent writings, with materials within the field of this volume, are Mrs. Schuyler van Rensselaer, *History of the City of New York in the Seventeenth Century* (2 vols., N. Y., 1909); C. Z. Lincoln, *The Constitutional History of New York* (5 vols., Rochester, 1906, I being esp. pertinent); and H. L. Osgood, *The American Colonies in the Seventeenth Century* (3 vols., N. Y., 1904-1907). V. H. Paltsits's chapter in Stokes, *Iconography* (cited above), is an excellent sketch. W. E. Griffis, *The Story of New Netherland* (N. Y., 1909), presents a very enthusiastic account, not always critical.

## DUTCH RELIGIOUS LIFE

Beginnings of church and religion are to be found in E. T. Corwin, ed., *Ecclesiastical Records of the State of New York* (7 vols., Albany, 1901-1916). The institutional life is portrayed in E. T. Corwin and others, *A History of the Reformed Church, Dutch* (Philip Schaff and others, eds., *The American Church History Series*, N. Y., 1893-1897, VIII). Source materials are in O'Callaghan, "Papers Relating to the City of New York," in his *Documentary History*, I. The "Letters of the Dutch Ministers to the Classis of Amsterdam" are in Jameson, *Narratives of New Netherland* (already cited), 389-415. The letter of Jonas Michaëlius to Smoutius, August 11, 1628, is in N. Y. Hist. Soc., *Colls.*, VI, 365-387; his known three letters from Manhattan are printed, with generous interpretation of his personality, and, indeed, of that of "Elder" Minuit, in Albert Eekhof, *Jonas*

*Michaëlius, Founder of the Church in New Netherland, his Life and Work* (Leyden, 1926). The life of the nonconforming elements, especially of the Jews, is sympathetically set forth in F. J. Zwierlein, *Religion in New Netherland* (Rochester, 1910). See also Samuel Oppenheim, *The Early History of the Jews in New York, 1654-1664* (N. Y., 1909). Lighter portrayals of the social influence of religion are in Alice M. Earle, *Colonial Days in Old New York* (N. Y., 1899), chap. xi. See also Henry E. Dosker, *The Dutch Anabaptists* (Phila., 1921). This phase of life is included in Esther Singleton, *Dutch New York* (N. Y., 1909), among many other topics well handled.

Identity of religious and educational interest is seen in H. W. Dunshee, *History of the School of the Reformed Protestant Dutch Church* (N. Y., 1853), and in the more recent synopsis by W. H. Kilpatrick, *The Dutch Schools of New Netherland and Colonial New York* (U. S. Bur. of Educ., *Bull.*, no. 483, 1912). Human interest comes out in Earle, *Colonial Days* (above mentioned), chap. ii, and Emma van Vechten, "Early Schools and Schoolmasters of New Amsterdam," *Half Moon Series*, II, 319-344.

## DUTCH SOCIAL INSTITUTIONS AND INFLUENCE

The debate on Dutch influence in the United States has been long and warm, if academic. Claims of a prior democracy among the Dutch and its transmission to America were advanced by Douglas Campbell, *The Puritan in England, Holland, and America* (2 vols., N. Y., 1892), and warmly refuted by John Fiske, *The Dutch and Quaker Colonies in America* (2 vols., Boston, 1899). H. T. Colenbrander, "The Dutch Element in American History," Am. Hist. Assoc., *Ann. Rep. for 1909*, 193-201, also takes exception to the extravagant claim of Campbell. The same volume, 203-218, has Ruth Putnam, "The Dutch Element in the United States." The Dutch claim is restated with more vehemence than proof in W. E. Griffis, *The Influence of the Netherlands in the Making of the English Commonwealth and the American Republic* (Boston, 1891), and in the very patriotic H. A. van Coenen Torchiana, *Holland, the Birthplace of American Political, Civic, and Religious Liberty; an Historical Essay* (San Francisco, 1915). The actual status of political rights in New Netherland may be seen in the "Remonstrance of the Deputies from New Netherland," *Pa. Archives*, ser. 3, V (Harrisburg, 1877), 124-170, by Adriaen van der Donck and others; and in the "Representation of New Netherland" in Jameson, *Narratives of New Netherland* (cited above). A rational view of the issue is upheld by Tiemen de Vries, *Dutch History, Art and Literature for Americans; Lectures given in the University of Chicago* (Grand Rapids, 1912).

Albert Eekhof, *Te Hervornde Kerk in Noord-Americka, 1624-1664* (2 vols., The Hague, 1913), offers the best picture of Dutch society in the Hudson Valley. Mrs. Schuyler van Rensselaer in the chapter on "The City and its People" in her *History of the City of New York* (cited above), I, presents what is probably the best short account. J. H. Innes, *New Amsterdam and its People* (N. Y., 1902), gives a full cross section of social conditions in the Dutch period. Intimate contemporary views are perennially absorbing, whether in Peter Kalm, *Travels into North America* (J. R. Forster, tr., 3 vols., Warrington and London, 1770-1771), or in such works as J. K. Paulding's novels, which are social documents of a high order. There is vigor in the point of view of T. A. Janvier, *The Dutch Founding of New York* (N. Y., 1903). Among many popular books are Helen E. Smith, *Colonial Days and Ways* (N. Y., 1900); W. R. Shepherd, *The Story of Manhattan* (N. Y., 1917; reprinted, 1927); and Mrs. J. K. van Rensselaer, *The Goede Vrouw of Mana-ha-ta* (N. Y., 1898), a work to be used with caution. Mrs. Anne Grant, *Memoirs of an American Lady* (N. Y., 1909), and Esther Singleton, *Dutch New York* (cited before), present the manners of the upper stratum in a later period. There is intimate interest in R. R. Wilson, *New York Old and New; its Story, Streets, and Landmarks* (2 vols., Phila., 1909). Theodore Roosevelt, *New York* (N. Y., 1891), contains brief reference to the social atmosphere of New Amsterdam. The conduct of the turbulent is revealed in Berthold Fernow, ed., *Records of New Amsterdam,* and A. J. F. van Laer, ed., *Minutes of the Court of Fort Orange and Beverwyck* (both cited earlier). For the manorial scheme one should consult A. J. F. van Laer, "The Patroon System and the Colony of Rensselaerswyck," N. Y. State Hist. Assoc., *Proceeds,* VIII, 222-233. On poor relief we have Berthold Fernon, ed., *Minutes of the Orphan Masters of New Amsterdam,* published by the Colonial Dames of the State of New York (2 vols., N. Y., 1902). The yearbooks of the Holland Society of New York (1886-    ) record an immense amount of genial postprandial oratory on the achievements of the Dutch stock in America.

# INDEX

ABO, New Mexican village, 61.

Absentee landlords, Mexican and Canadian, 227; Van Rensselaer as, 304. *See also* Land.

Absolutism, in New Spain, 111; and the individual, 191; and municipal life, 192-193; and commerce, 199-200; in New France, 222; and tenure of America, 236; in New Netherland, 298; and Dutch governors, 301-302; and the patroons, 303; and the commonalty, 305-306.

Acadians, and England, 211, 262; and German settlers, 262, 264; from France and Spain, 265 *note*.

Acapulco, cotton region, 100; reforms, 188.

Acoma, New Mexican village, 53.

*Adelantado*, function and duties, 11, 38, 225-226.

Administration, by Columbus, 2, 9; of New Spain, 18, 67; of New Mexico, 54, 132-134, 168, 177; local, 181, 190-191, 195, 199; of Louisiana, 216, 259; of Canada, 220, 223, 224; of Dutch colonies, 298, 299, 300, 302, 306, 348. *See also* Absolutism, *and* Representative Government.

Adultery, 63, 66.

Adventure, 3, 9, 19; distaste for, 37, 115; in New France, 212, 214, 215; Dutch spirit of, 309, 310.

Adverse possession, 99, 225, 232. *See also* Land.

Agriculture, of New Spain, 23-27; spread of, 36, 39; on the frontier, 48, 54; in Zacatecas, 92, 96, 99; education for, 135, 199; of California missions, 204; Canadian, 214, 229; in

Illinois, 219, 228; of the church, 231; records of, 233, 234; implements, 252, 262; slavery and, 263; Jesuits in, 280-281; desired by Usselinx, 294; in New Netherland, 295-296, 299, 305, 308, 311, 322, 326, 335. *See also* Crops.

Aguayo estate, 99.

Aguilar, Nicolás, *alcalde mayor*, 59; and Inquisition, 69.

Alabama River, fort on, 260.

Alaska, Russians in, 176.

Alba, estate, 99.

Albany, British at, 283; site of, 294, 328; "companies," 339; "Pinkster" celebration, 342.

*Alcabala. See* Sales Tax.

*Alcaldes mayores*, character, 39; as frontier rulers, 43; privileges, 58, 59; abuse of powers, 101, 119, 121; and *repartimientos*, 134.

*Alcaldía mayor*, of Zacatecas, 86.

Alcíbar, José, painter, 160.

Alegre, Father F. X., as historian, 148.

Almaden, Spain, mines, 93.

Alta California, expedition, 201-203.

Altamaha River, 82.

Álvarez, Cabral, Pedro, Portuguese navigator, 13.

Alzate, José Antonia, scientist, 159.

Amalgam process, mining, 20, 93, 149. *See also* Patio process, *and* Quicksilver.

Amazon River, navigated. *See* Orellano.

"American Bottom," in the Illinois, 280.

Amsterdam, in control of New Netherland, 298, 299, 308; Chamber, 312, 321; wealth of, 333.

387

# INDEX

# INDEX

399

generation of, 289; their lands purchased, 300; Dutch methods with, 323, 329, 330; Kieft's war, 348.

Infant mortality, 36, 240.

Initiative, in Spanish colonies, 115; in New France, 216, 217-219; in New Netherland, 298.

Inquisition, in New Mexico, 54, 56, 62, 66, and Peñalosa, 68; in Florida, 77; in Zacatecas, 91, 114, 125; local influence, 134; Indian exemption from its discipline, 137; futility of, 141; and importation of books, 143, 145.

Intellectual life, 140-146; on frontier, 61; of Zacatecas, 91; stagnant in Indian towns, 130; depicted by Dr. Cárdenas, 151-156, 157, 159; literary interest on the frontier, 172 note; laggard in New France, 248, 272; poverty of in the Illinois country, 287; of New Netherland, 292, 336.

Intendant system, 117; introduced, 199; French and Spanish, 223, 224.

International influences, 21, 32, 71, 79; rivalries, of Spain and England, 82, 104, 174, 176, 177, 196-197, 201; of Spain and France, 213, 215, 218, 259.

Dutch-English, 295, 299, and bibliography, 363-364.

Irish creoles, 267.

Iroquois, fur trade, 310; enmity, 323.

Irrigation, 35, 36, 47, 228.

Irving, Washington, and *Knickerbocker*, 291, 293, 300-301.

Isabella, of Castile, 3; her Indian laws, 111, 118.

Italians, with Magellan, 8.

JACKSON, General Andrew, in Florida, 79.

Jalapa, 165; the fair, 185.

Jalisco, 92.

Jamaica, Island, 324.

Janos, presidio, 50.

Jans, Annetje and Roelof, 329.

Japanese, influence on Dutch, 344.

*Jesuit Relations,* 211; influence on colonization of Canada, 219, 371.

Jesuits, expulsion of, 45, 177-178, 180, 182-183; murdered, 75; in Zacatecas, 91; in Puebla, 124; as historians, 148; conflict with Palafox, 168; influence, 183, 214, 223; proposed expansion, 179; restoration, 183; wide services of, 219, 249; replace Recollects in Canada, 219; policies, 241, 247, 248; expelled from Louisiana, 271-272; in the Illinois, 278-279; methods, 286.

Jews, 8, 58; rites, 62, 66; forbidden to enter Louisiana, 261, under *Code Noir;* found in New York, 318, but disliked for business skill, 319.

Jogues, Father Isaac, as diplomat, 320.

Joint-stock companies, 114, 116, 217; *see also* Companies.

Joliet, Louis, explorer, 250.

*Junta de guerra,* administration by, 41.

Justice, as administered in New Spain, 173, 189, 199; in the Illinois, 277; French codes of, 278, 289; of the patroons, 304, 309; by arbitration, 334.

KALM, Peter, *Travels* quoted, 242-243; cited, 247, 253, 256-257.

Kaskaskia, 277; parish, 278; described, 281, 285.

*Kermis,* 342, 343.

Kieft, Governor William, 301, 305; on morals, 313; his War, 322; autocracy, 328.

"King's house," 164; "king's wagons," 58, 65, in New Spain's finance.

Kino, Father Eusebio, as astronomer, 32, and explorer, 154, 155.

Kirkes, French-Scotchmen, seize Canada 219, 247.

Kleynties, pioneer journey of, 309.

12